REAL-TIME IMAGING

REAL-TIME IMAGING

Theory, Techniques, and Applications

Edited by

Phillip A. Laplante
BCC/NJIT Technology and Engineering Center

Alexander D. Stoyenko
New Jersey Institute of Technology

IEEE
PRESS

The Institute of Electrical and Electronics Engineers, Inc., New York

©1996 by the Institute of Electrical and Electronics Engineers, Inc.
345 East 47th Street, New York, NY 10017-2394

Printed in the United States of America

10   9   8   7   6   5   4   3   2   1

ISBN 0-7803-1068-3
IEEE Order Number: PC4242

Library of Congress Cataloging-in-Publication Data

Real-time imaging : theory, techniques, and applications / edited by
Phillip A. Laplante, Alexander D. Stoyenko.
    p.   cm.
Includes bibliographical references and index.
ISBN 0-7803-1068-3
    1. Image processing — Digital techniques.   2. Real-time data
processing.   I. Laplante, Phil.   II. Stoyenko, Alexander D., (date).
TA1637.R44   1996
621.36 ' 7 ' 0285433 — dc20   96-2258
                                                                   CIP

CONTENTS

Part II.   TECHNIQUES

Part III.   APPLICATIONS

6 REAL-TIME IMAGE PROCESSING FOR AUTOMOTIVE
APPLICATIONS   161
G. Adorni, A. Broggio, G. Conte, and V. D'Andrea

7 BIOLOGICALLY MOTIVATED IMAGE CLASSIFICATION
SYSTEM   195
N. Petkov

8 TESTING THE ROBUSTNESS OF AN UNDERWATER
VISION SYSTEM   225
J. O. Hallset

9 THE ART AND SCIENCE OF MULTIMEDIA
M. Nadin

INTRODUCTION

There are numerous texts on real-time systems (including ones by each of the editors of this book) and countless texts on image processing. However, rarely does one see image processing addressed in the real-time books (and then only on a cursory level). And in those image processing books that contain some discussion of real-time considerations, the discussions tend to focus on specific vendor hardware or on vague notions of response times. Yet, as we will argue, there are a great number of technologies that are rightly classified as real-time image processing. These technologies face the problems of constructing real-time systems, the difficulties of performing image processing functions, and the unique challenges produced by the combination.

Until recently, no texts existed that explicitly covered real-time image processing as a distinct subdiscipline. The first text to do so, *Introduction to Real-Time Image Processing* by Ed Dougherty and Phil Laplante (SPIE Press/IEEE Press, 1995) was successful in providing a starting point for the study of real-time image processing systems. The present book is designed to build on that starting point by discussing deeper theory, by providing additional and more advanced techniques than those discussed in the introductory book, and by describing applications that incorporate much of the basic theory and novel solutions into their design.

The reader is expected at least to be familiar with real-time systems and image processing. Reading the aforementioned introductory text is helpful but not essential in reading this book. (A suggested preparatory reading list is provided in the reference list at the end of this section.) To help those without ready access to these texts, we now provide a little background on real-time systems and real-time image processing.

WHAT IS A REAL-TIME SYSTEM?

Consider a software system in which the inputs represent digital data from hardware such as imaging devices or other software systems and the outputs are digital data that control external hardware such as displays. The time between the presentation of a set of inputs and the appearance of all the associated outputs is called the *response time*. A *real-time system* is one that must satisfy explicit bounded response-time constraints to avoid failure. Equivalently, a real-time system is one whose logical correctness is based both on the correctness of the outputs and their timeliness. Note that response times of, for example, microseconds are not needed to characterize a real-time system—it simply must have response times that are constrained and thus predictable. In fact, the misconception that real-time systems must be "fast" is because, in most instances, the deadlines are on the order of milliseconds. But the timeliness constraints or deadlines are generally a reflection of the underlying physical process being controlled. For example, in image processing involving screen update for viewing continuous motion, the deadlines are on the order of 30 ms. In practical situations, the main difference between real-time and non-real-time systems is an emphasis on response-time prediction and its reduction.

Upon reflection, one realizes that every system can be made to conform to the real-time definition simply by setting deadlines (arbitrary or otherwise). For example, a one-time image filtration algorithm for medical imaging, which might not be regarded as real-time, really is real-time if the procedure is related to an illness in which diagnosis and treatment have some realistic deadline. Because all systems can be made to look as if they were real-time, we refine the definition somewhat in terms of the system's tolerance to missed deadlines. For example, *hard real-time systems* are those where failure to meet even one deadline results in total system failure. In *firm real-time systems*, some fixed small number of deadlines can be missed without total system failure. Finally, in *soft real-time systems*, missing deadlines leads to performance degradation but not failure. Unless otherwise noted, when we say "real-time" throughout this tutorial, we mean hard real-time.

WHAT IS REAL-TIME IMAGE PROCESSING?

Real-time image processing differs from "ordinary" image processing in that the logical correctness of the system requires not only correct but also timely outputs; that is, semantic validity entails not only functional correctness but also deadline satisfaction. Because of its nature, there are both supports for and obstacles to real-time image processing. On the positive side, many imaging applications are well suited for parallelization and hence faster, parallel architectures. Furthermore, many imaging applications can be constructed without using language constructs that destroy determinism. Moreover, special real-time imaging architectures are available or can theoretically be constructed.

On the down side, many imaging applications are time critical and are computationally intensive or data intensive. And there are no standard programming languages available for real-time image processing. Finally, the science of real-time processing itself is still struggling to produce usable results, especially for parallel processing machines.

We have often heard the criticism that image processing in real-time is no more than a minor variation on image processing without regard to time—faster machinery will make any speed problems eventually go away. But real-time imaging is not just about speedy hardware. Real-time image processing involves at least three fundamental trade-offs: performance versus image resolution, performance versus storage and input/output bandwidth, and the number of tasks versus synchronization. Of these problems, only the first and possibly the second could be solved by faster machines. Furthermore, the problem of expressing image algorithms (especially for multiprocessing architectures), of finding appropriate programming languages, of testing and reliability, and of practical software engineering techniques are not readily solved simply with faster hardware.

Real-time image processing covers a multidisciplinary range of research areas including (but not limited to):

- image compression,
- target acquisition and tracking,
- remote control and sensing,
- image enhancement and filtering,
- networking for real-time imaging,
- advanced computer architectures,
- computer vision,
- optical measurement and inspection, and
- simulation.

These research areas are critical in such applications as:

- robotics,
- virtual reality,
- multimedia,
- industrial inspection,
- high-definition television,
- advanced simulators,
- computer-integrated manufacturing, and
- intelligent vehicles.

This text contains relevant theory and practical application discussions for many of these areas. Readers interested in other areas not covered in this text should consult advanced texts or journals in those areas, or our own journal, *Real-Time Imaging*, published by Academic Press.

ABOUT THE CONTRIBUTIONS

This book includes a collection of chapter contributions that can be classified loosely into three categories, namely, theory, techniques, and applications.

The first chapter, by Dougherty and Laplante, provides a theoretical introduction to nonlinear real-time image processing; that is, real-time image processing employing nonlinear techniques and relying mostly on specialized hardware. This chapter has been extracted and modified from one that appeared in the book *Introduction to Real-Time Image Processing*, discussed in the beginning of this introduction.

The chapter by Nesi provides a theoretical framework for an important basic operation in real-time imaging—motion detection. Most of the algorithms for motion analysis are based on the estimation of a projection of the 3-D motion onto a two-dimensional image plane. Recently, the need for performing motion analysis in real-time for robot navigation, object tracking, and so on has evoked a high interest in real-time estimation of motion fields. In this chapter, a comparison of the most important and well-known solutions to the motion detection problem is given. This comparison is performed by considering their applicability in order to obtain estimations in real-time. To this end, computational complexities for both sequential and parallel architectures are analyzed.

In the next chapter, Guan focuses on the issue of real-time image regularization as the first step in image processing and analysis. Image regularization is homogeneous processing that is traditionally based on high-dimensional mathematical programming. Image regularization shapes the raw image data captured from various primary imaging devices so that they are in a format suitable for image analysis or visualization. The image regularization tasks include enhancement, filtering, and restoration.

In the first "Techniques" chapter, Allen complements and extends the more theoretical treatment by Nesi and provides additional applications. Motion detection is such an important component of most real-time imaging that it merits the additional treatment and is in fact addressed in other chapters (such as the chapter by Furht).

The chapter by Furht is an extensive discussion of an important subspecialty and application area for real-time imaging—multimedia compression techniques and standards. Furht discusses several techniques with particular attention to the JPEG and MPEG standards, which have tremendous commercial importance.

In the first of the "Application" chapters, Adorni et al. discuss an approach to image processing algorithms for a real-time vision system devoted to assist vehicle drivers. In order to obtain the speed and efficiency required by the application, a massively parallel approach is considered, based on a VLSI architecture performing iconic processing. The approach discussed will be implemented as a vision support system into an experimental van (MOB-LAB). This van will support the experimental setup developed by the Italian research groups in the framework of the PROMETHEUS project.

In the chapter by Petkov, computer simulations of natural vision systems, artificial neural networks, scientific visualization, and high-performance computing are applied to a vision and cognition grand challenge problem. A computational model of simple cells in the primary visual cortex of primates is combined with a self-organizing artificial neural network to build a system that can mimic perceptual and cognitive abilities of natural vision systems. This system is capable of memorizing visual patterns, building autonomously its own internal representations, and correctly classifying new patterns without using any model knowledge. The proposed approach is computationally very intensive and the developed system is currently being ported to the Connection Machine CM-5 to operate as a self-learning classification system with reasonable response times.

In the next chapter, a vision system for Hallset's PISCIS project is described, and testing of its robustness is reported. PISCIS is a proposed project for use in an untethered autonomous underwater vehicle (AUV) for pipeline inspection. The vision system termed PVS (the PISCIS vision system) will assist the AUV in finding and following pipelines. A salient feature of the PVS is that it is designed to find all pipelines within the field of view and, thus, the AUV can follow any of them. Robust image interpretation is important as humans cannot interact with the PVS and correct errors. Furthermore, the image quality is reduced by backscatter, light absorption, a nonuniform background (the seabed), and marine material on the pipelines. The PVS is fixed to a vehicle and must rely on a heading sensor and an altitude sonar to match image features with pipeline models. The models are retrieved from a map based on the vehicle's position.

The final chapter, by Nadin, provides a theoretical framework for the aesthetic, practical, and logical aspects of an important real-time imaging domain—multimedia. He links these apparently disjoint aspects through a "gnoseological platform." Cognitive psychologists have long recognized the need to address aesthetic considerations in the construction of high-quality simulations. This chapter is an important step in that direction.

We hope that you find this book to be as interesting and informative to read as it was for us to compile.

Finally, we would like to thank the many persons who made this book possible. Obviously, the contributing authors deserve high praise, for without them, this book would not exist. Equally important, however, are the contributions of the development team at IEEE Press: Review Coordinator Lisa Mizrahi, Production Editor Debbie Graffox, and Production Manager Denise Gannon. Their assistance has been invaluable in guiding us throughout this project. Finally, we want to thank our families who have suffered patiently as we worked many hours on this and other projects.

Bibliography

Real-Time Systems

[1] Burns, Alan and Andy Wellings, *Real-Time Systems and Their Programming Languages*, Addison Wesley, New York, 1990.

[2] Halang, W. A. and A. D. Stoyenko, *Constructing predictable real-time systems*, Kluwer Academic Publishers, Boston, 1991.

[3] Laplante, P., *Real-Time Systems Design and Analysis: An Engineer's Handbook*, IEEE Press, Piscataway, NJ, 1992.

[4] van Tilborg, A. and G.M. Koob, editors, *Foundations of Real-Time Computing*, vols. I, II, Kluwer Academic Publishers, Boston, 1991.

Image Processing

[5] Dougherty, E. R., and C. R. Giardina, *Image Processing—Continuous to Discrete*, Prentice-Hall, Englewood Cliffs, 1987.

[6] Gonzalez, R. C., and R. E. Woods, *Digital Image Processing*, Addison-Wesley, Boston, 1992.

[7] Haralick, R. and L. Shapiro, *Machine Vision*, Addison-Wesley, Boston, 1991.

[8] Jain, A. K., *Fundamentals of Digital Image Processing*, Prentice-Hall, Englewood Cliffs, 1989.

[9] Lim, J. S., *Two-Dimensional Signal and Image Processing*, Prentice-Hall, Englewood Cliffs, 1990.

[10] Pratt, W. K., *Digital Image Processing*, 2nd ed., John Wiley, New York, 1991.

[11] Rosenfeld, A., and A. C. Kak, *Digital Picture Processing*, Academic Press, New York, 1992.

I

THEORY

1

NONLINEAR REAL-TIME IMAGE PROCESSING ALGORITHMS[1]

Edward R. Dougherty   *Center for Imaging Science,*
Rochester Institute of Technology

Phillip A. Laplante   *BCC/NJIT, Technology and Engineering Center*

1.1 INTRODUCTION

A key motivation for the study of nonlinear digital processing is the logical structure of the computer. All algorithms must be reduced to data and instruction flows through logic circuits, and this requirement restricts the mathematical structures that are directly appropriate to digital processing. Linear filters involve addition and multiplication. Multiplications, when used in a linear convolution, also often involve real numbers (referred to as *floating-point* numbers in computer architecture parlance), not just integers. Both addition and multiplication of floating-point numbers take significantly longer than their integer counterparts because these operations must be implemented via a firmware subroutine involving multiple integer shifts, adds, and multiplies. Although some arithmetic logic units (ALUs) support floating-point operations directly in microcode, and coprocessors are sometimes added to facilitate floating-point operations, these operations are still slower than integer operations.

As opposed to linear operations, nonlinear filters do not require multiplications. Although they may involve subtractions (additions), they only require integer operations. Perhaps the most salient point is that, for the most part, they involve maximum and minimum operations and their genesis lies in binary AND and OR operations, which are generally among the fastest macroinstructions provided by an ALU. Hence, nonlinear imaging is ideal for many real-time applications. We begin our discussion with a study of binary nonlinear filters defined via window logic.

---

[1]Reprinted with changes from "Nonlinear Image Processing Algorithms," ch. 5 in *Introduction to Real-Time Imaging*, by E. R. Dougherty and P. A. Laplante (Bellingham, Wash.: SPIE Press, 1995) by permission of the authors and publisher.

1.2   BOOLEAN FUNCTIONS

A Boolean function is a binary function $h(x_1, x_2, \ldots, x_n)$ defined on n binary
variables. Because each variable can take on two values, 0 or 1, there are 2^n
possible arguments for h. In effect, h is defined by a truth table having 2^n rows:
for each vector consisting of n 0's and 1's, there is associated a value of h, either
0 or 1. In conjunction with a window W, the Boolean function h defines a binary
window operator Ψ on binary images via the one-to-one correspondence between
the variables and pixels in the window. The operator Ψ is defined at a pixel z
by translating the window to z and applying the Boolean function h to the binary
values in the translated window (see Figure 1.1). The binary image is considered
to be a set of pixels and the procedure is in accordance with the digitally stored
image representation: 1 if a pixel is in the image and 0 if it is not. Geometrically,
if A is the input image, then z is an element of A if and only if $A(z) = 1$, $A(z)$
denoting the value of A at z. Because the same Boolean function is applied for
each translation of the window, the resulting window operator Ψ is translation
(spatially) invariant.

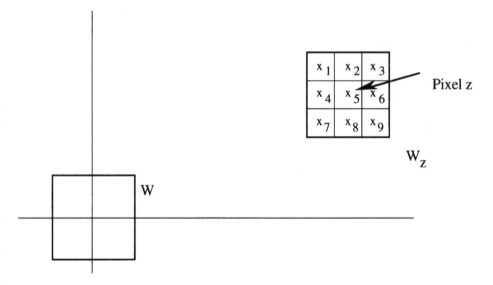

Figure 1.1 Translated logic mask.

From the standpoint of image processing, a binary window filter Ψ is defined
by specifying the filter output for each possible configuration in the window. Thus,
filter design involves the synthesis of Boolean functions via truth tables. Given
a truth table, construct an equivalent logical operator. Such a logical synthesis
can always be accomplished directly from the truth values by defining the Boolean

function in disjunctive normal form. Specifically, it can be represented by a logical sum of products (maximum of minima):

$$h(x_1, x_2, \ldots, x_n) = \sum_i x_1^{p(i,1)} x_2^{p(i,2)} \ldots x_n^{p(i,n)} \tag{1-1}$$

where $p(i, j)$ is null or "c," indicating presence of the uncomplemented variable x_j or the complemented variable x_j^c in the ith product (minterm), respectively. There are up to 2^n minterms forming the maximum, one for each row of the corresponding truth table for which h has value 1. For instance, if there are three variables and the row 011 has value 1, then $x_1^c x_2 x_3$ is a minterm.

Reduction of the disjunctive normal form can be accomplished in accordance with the laws of logic to yield a reduced expansion

$$h(x_1, x_2, \ldots, x_n) = \sum_i x_{i,1}^{p(i,1)} x_{i,2}^{p(i,2)} \ldots x_{i,n(i)}^{p[i,n(i)]} \tag{1-2}$$

where $x_{i,1}, x_{i,2}, \ldots, x_{i,n(i)}$ denote the $n(i)$ distinct variables in the ith product of the expansion and where there are at most 2^n distinct products in the expansion [1]. Reduction is important because, if a binary filter is synthesized in its disjunctive normal form, that expression at once implies an implementation in combinational logic; however, reduction can provide a less costly implementation. Reduction is similarly beneficial for efficient software implementation. There are numerous reduction algorithms such as Karnaugh-map reduction, the Quine-McCluskey method, and the McCalla minterm-ring algorithm.

1.3 INCREASING BOOLEAN FUNCTIONS

A Boolean function h is increasing if $(x_1, x_2, \ldots, x_n) \leq (y_1, y_2, \ldots, y_n)$ implies $h(x_1, x_2, \ldots, x_n) \leq h(y_1, y_2, \ldots, y_n)$, where $(x_1, x_2, \ldots, x_n) \leq (y_1, y_2, \ldots, y_n)$ if and only if $x_j \leq y_j$ for $j = 1, 2, \ldots, n$. Increasing Boolean functions are often called *positive Boolean functions*. A Boolean function h is positive if and only if it can be represented as a logical sum of products in which no variables are complemented:

$$h(x_1, x_2, \ldots, x_n) = \sum_i x_{i,1} x_{i,2} \ldots x_{i,n(i)} \tag{1-3}$$

If the set of variables in any product of the expansion contains as a subset the set of variables in a distinct product, then, whenever the former product has value 1, so too does the latter. Thus, inclusion of the former product in the maximum expansion is redundant and can be deleted from the expansion without changing the function defined by h. No product whose variable set does not contain the variable set of a distinct product can be deleted without changing the function h. Performing the permitted deletions produces a minimal representation of the positive Boolean function. The majority of commonly employed nonlinear filters involve positive Boolean functions. We shall now introduce some key filters defined via Boolean functions.

Consider a single-product positive Boolean function,

$$h_i(x_1, x_2, \ldots, x_n) = x_{i,1} x_{i,2} \ldots x_{i,n(i)} \qquad (1\text{-}4)$$

If the window operator Ψ is defined via h_i and A is the input image, then $z \in \Psi(A)$ if and only if $\Psi(A)(z) = 1$. In terms of window logic, this means that, when the window W is translated to z, the pixels in the translated window corresponding to the pixels $w_{i,1}, w_{i,2}, \ldots, w_{i,n(i)}$ in W must all have value 1, so that the product of Eq. (1-4) is 1; that is, so $x_{i,1} = x_{i,2} = \ldots = x_{i,n(i)} = 1$. Let B denote the set of pixels $w_{i,1}, w_{i,2}, \ldots, w_{i,n(i)}$ in W. The pixels in the translated window corresponding to $w_{i,1}, w_{i,2}, \ldots, w_{i,n(i)}$ are $w_{i,1} + z, w_{i,2} + z, \ldots, w_{i,n(i)} + z$, and the product of Eq. (1-4) is 1 if and only if all of these pixel translates lie in the set A. The set of translates by z of pixels in B is denoted by B_z. Thus, from a set perspective, $z \in \Psi(A)$ if and only if B_z is a subset of A.

In image processing, the operation defined by the single logical product of Eq. (1-4) is called *erosion*. Because the logical product defined by Eq. (1-4) is fully defined by the pixel set B, the erosion Ψ is defined once B is specified. Erosion of binary image A by B is denoted by $A \ominus B$. In this context, B is called a *structuring element*.

Figure 1.2 shows a set A and a structuring element B (with the origin marked). Part (a) shows a translate of B to a pixel z for which the translate B_z is a subset of A, so that z lies in the filtered image $A \ominus B$. Part (b) shows a translate of B to a pixel w for which the translate B_w is not a subset of A, so that w does not lie in the filtered image. Part (c) shows $A \ominus B$.

Because positive Boolean functions possess noncomplemented logical representations of the kind given in Eq. (1-3), erosions form the building blocks of increasing binary nonlinear filters. Regarding the representation of Eq. (1-3), we can take a number of viewpoints. Relative to logical variables, it is a logical sum of logical products. Architecturally, each erosion corresponds to an AND gate with an input for each logical variable in the product. The full representation is given by the various AND outputs feeding into an OR gate. Finally, we can view each erosion as providing a set—the set of pixels to which its structuring element can be translated and have the translate be a subset of the input image. The full filter, being defined by an OR function, then corresponds to the union of the resulting erosions. If there are m structuring elements (logical products), then the filter Ψ can be expressed by Eq. (1-3) or by

$$\Psi(A) = \bigcup_{i=1}^{m} A \ominus B_i \qquad (1\text{-}5)$$

where $B_1, B_2, \ldots, B_m$ are the m structuring elements [2].

Because each positive Boolean expression possesses a minimal form, so too does any union of erosions formed from structuring elements in a finite window. The structuring elements in the minimal expansion correspond to the minimal products. These structuring elements compose the basis, Bas $[\Psi]$, of the filter and the expansion of Eq. (1-5) need only be taken over the basis.

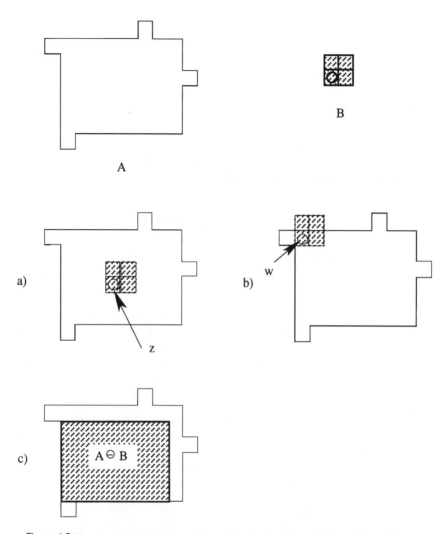

Figure I.2 Erosion: (a) pixel in eroded set; (b) pixel not in eroded set; (c) eroded set.

Positive Boolean functions are defined via logical variables and this makes them ideal for architectural analysis; nevertheless, it is useful to look at them in terms of fitting translates of structuring elements. This geometric approach lies at the root of morphological image processing.

Note that, if Eq. (1-5) were to be implemented directly in a high-level language, significant computation time would be required. For example, most programming languages that provide set types and the associated set operations of union, intersection, and complementation, do so at terrific execution time penalty—the data structures needed to provide the abstraction represent the bottleneck. Shortly, we show how, using Boolean functions, set operations can be implemented in an efficient manner. Moreover, direct specification of nonlinear operations using Boolean notation allows for the construction of gate-level logic and hence fast, dedicated architectures.

There exists a morphological operation that is dual to erosion: *dilation* of set A by structuring element B is defined by

$$A \oplus B = [A^c \ominus (-B)]^c \qquad (1\text{-}6)$$

where $-B = \{-b : b \in B\}$ is the reflection of B through the origin. Dilation also possesses an implementation without reference to complementation; however, we shall not pursue the matter here (see, for example [3, 4, 5]).

1.4 NONLINEAR NOISE SUPPRESSION USING INCREASING BINARY FILTERS

A key morphological filter is *opening*, which, for a set A and structuring element B, is defined by

$$A \circ B = \bigcup \{B_z : B_z \subset A\} \qquad (1\text{-}7)$$

$A \circ B$ is the union of all translates of B that are subsets of A: slide B around inside A and take as the filter output all pixels covered by the sliding structuring element. Whereas the position of the origin in the structuring element is crucial for erosion, it is irrelevant for opening. Opening can also be computed via erosion followed by dilation:

$$A \circ B = (A \ominus B) \oplus B \qquad (1\text{-}8)$$

If the observed image is an ideal image unioned with noise, then one way to employ opening is to choose a structuring element that fits inside the ideal image but not inside the noise. Opening will then remove the noise while keeping most of the signal. The method is depicted in Figure 1.3 for a square degraded by

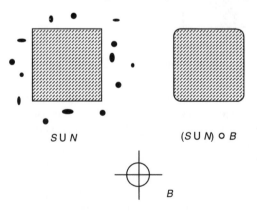

Figure 1.3 Suppression of clutter (union noise) by opening.

background clutter. Opening restoration of a text image degraded by pepper noise is demonstrated in Figure 1.4, which shows a text image, the text degraded by pepper, and the noisy image opened by a 3 × 3 square structuring element. It can be shown that opening is independent of structuring element location; thus, the position of the origin need not be specified.

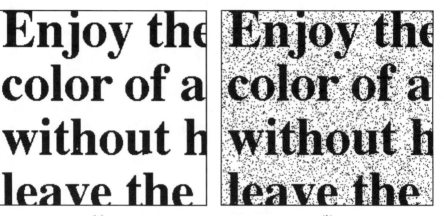

Figure 1.4 Restoration of text by opening: (a) original image; (b) image degraded by pepper noise; (c) filtered image.

The positive Boolean function corresponding to opening by a 2 × 2 square structuring element is

$$h(x_1, x_2, \ldots, x_9) = x_1 x_2 x_4 x_5 + x_2 x_3 x_5 x_6 + x_4 x_5 x_7 x_8 + x_5 x_6 x_8 x_9 \qquad (1\text{-}9)$$

where the nine variables correspond to the pixels in the 3 × 3 square window centered at the origin (Figure 1.1). The 2 × 2 opening can be found by moving the window and evaluating h at each location. The Boolean function can be implemented by the combinational logic circuit of Figure 1.5 in which there are four AND gates and one OR gate, each having four inputs [6]. An assembly program is implicit in Figure 1.5. Morphologically, the filter is defined by Eq. (1-5) with $m = 4$ and the basis is composed of the structuring elements B_1, B_2, B_3, and B_4 given by

$$B_1 = \begin{bmatrix} 0 & 0 & 0 \\ 0 & 1 & 1 \\ 0 & 1 & 1 \end{bmatrix} \quad B_2 = \begin{bmatrix} 0 & 1 & 1 \\ 0 & 1 & 1 \\ 0 & 0 & 0 \end{bmatrix}$$

$$B_3 = \begin{bmatrix} 0 & 0 & 0 \\ 1 & 1 & 0 \\ 1 & 1 & 0 \end{bmatrix} \quad B_4 = \begin{bmatrix} 1 & 1 & 0 \\ 1 & 1 & 0 \\ 0 & 0 & 0 \end{bmatrix}$$

(1-10)

The union expansion is graphically illustrated in Figure 1.6 for the set A of Figure 1.2.

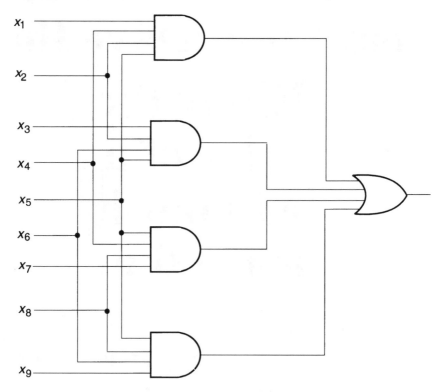

Figure 1.5 Combinational logic for 2×2 opening.

A commonly employed filter for restoring binary images is the median filter [7]. Given a window W containing an odd number of pixels, say n, the binary

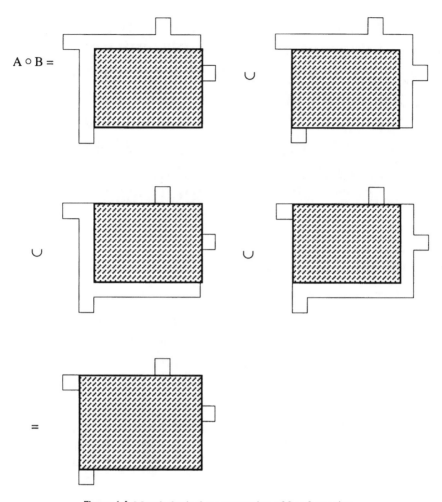

Figure 1.6 Morphological representation of 2×2 opening.

moving median is defined in the following manner: for each pixel z, W is translated to z and the filter outputs 1 if more than $n/2$ pixels in W_z are 1-valued; otherwise, the filter outputs 0. Medians are used to suppress salt-and-pepper noise and exhibit good edge preservation if the amount of noise is not excessive and the uncorrupted image does not possess much fine detail. Figures 1.7 through 1.10 show salt-and-pepper-degraded and median-restored text images. Note how the 5×5 median has yielded good restoration for the simple Helvetica font with only 5% noise in Figure 1.7, but poorer quality restoration for 20% noise and the finely detailed Monotype Corsiva font.

Because the median is based on pixel counts in windows, it is an increasing operator and must possess a basis expansion according to Eq. (1-5). Consider

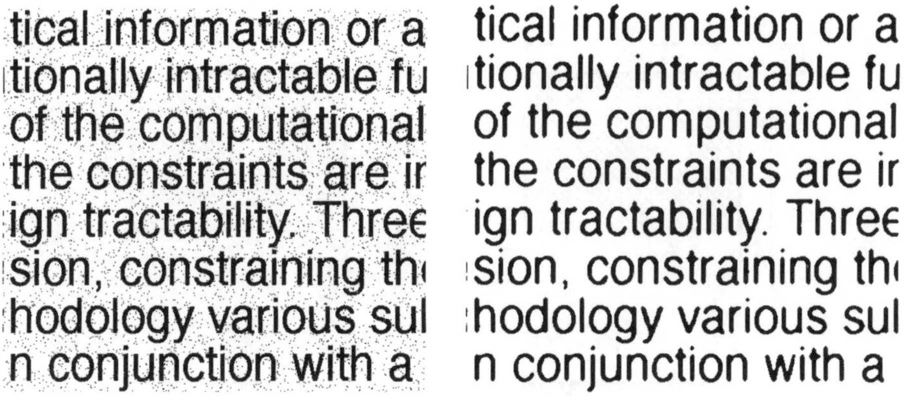

tical information or a	tical information or a
tionally intractable fu	tionally intractable fu
of the computational	of the computational
the constraints are ir	the constraints are ir
ign tractability. Three	ign tractability. Three
sion, constraining th	sion, constraining th
hodology various sul	hodology various sul
n conjunction with a	n conjunction with a

            (a)   (b)

Figure 1.7 Median restoration of Helvetica text degraded by 5% salt-and-pepper noise:
(a) degraded image; (b) restored image.

the median over the strong-neighbor mask (the origin and the pixels immediately
above, below, left, and right of it). A pixel lies in the filtered image if and only
if, among itself and its four strong neighbors, at least three pixels lie in the input
image. The following ten structuring elements compose a basis:

$$\begin{bmatrix} 0 & 1 & 0 \\ 1 & 1 & 0 \\ 0 & 0 & 0 \end{bmatrix} \begin{bmatrix} 0 & 1 & 0 \\ 1 & 0 & 1 \\ 0 & 0 & 0 \end{bmatrix} \begin{bmatrix} 0 & 1 & 0 \\ 0 & 1 & 1 \\ 0 & 0 & 0 \end{bmatrix} \begin{bmatrix} 0 & 1 & 0 \\ 1 & 0 & 0 \\ 0 & 1 & 0 \end{bmatrix}$$

$$\begin{bmatrix} 0 & 1 & 0 \\ 0 & 1 & 0 \\ 0 & 1 & 0 \end{bmatrix} \begin{bmatrix} 0 & 1 & 0 \\ 0 & 0 & 1 \\ 0 & 1 & 0 \end{bmatrix} \begin{bmatrix} 0 & 0 & 0 \\ 1 & 1 & 1 \\ 0 & 0 & 0 \end{bmatrix} \begin{bmatrix} 0 & 0 & 0 \\ 1 & 1 & 0 \\ 0 & 1 & 0 \end{bmatrix} \qquad (1\text{-}11)$$

$$\begin{bmatrix} 0 & 0 & 0 \\ 1 & 0 & 1 \\ 0 & 1 & 0 \end{bmatrix} \begin{bmatrix} 0 & 0 & 0 \\ 0 & 1 & 1 \\ 0 & 1 & 0 \end{bmatrix}$$

The strong-neighbor median can be evaluated by eroding by each of the ten structuring elements and then forming the union of Eq. (1-5).

To obtain a logical expression of the strong-neighbor median according to
Eq. (1-3), we assign five variables to the window pixels to obtain the logical mask
shown in Figure 1.11. The Boolean function corresponding to the union of erosions
with the ten structuring elements of Eq. (1-11) is

$$h = x_1x_2x_3 + x_1x_2x_4 + x_1x_3x_4 + x_1x_2x_5 + x_1x_3x_5 \qquad (1\text{-}12)$$
$$+x_1x_4x_5 + x_2x_3x_4 + x_2x_3x_5 + x_2x_4x_5 + x_3x_4x_5.$$

Both a hardware implementation and an assembly program are implicit in
Eq. (1-13).

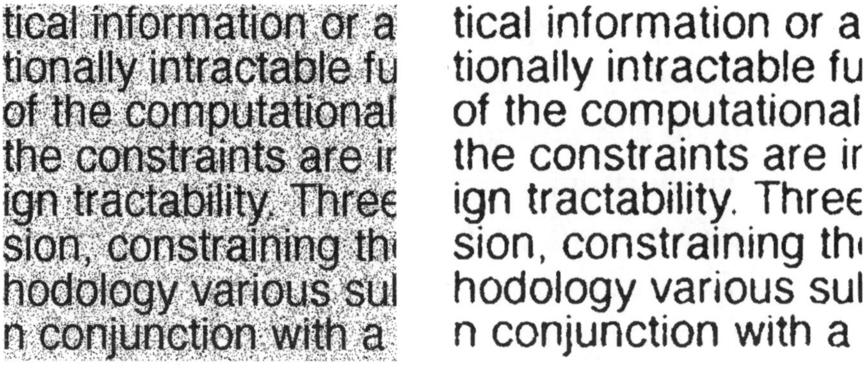

tical information or a
tionally intractable fu
of the computational
the constraints are ir
ign tractability. Three
sion, constraining th
hodology various sul
n conjunction with a

(a)

tical information or a
tionally intractable fu
of the computational
the constraints are ir
ign tractability. Three
sion, constraining th
hodology various sul
n conjunction with a

(b)

Figure 1.8 Median restoration of Helvetica text degraded by 20% salt-and-pepper noise: (a) degraded image; (b) restored image.

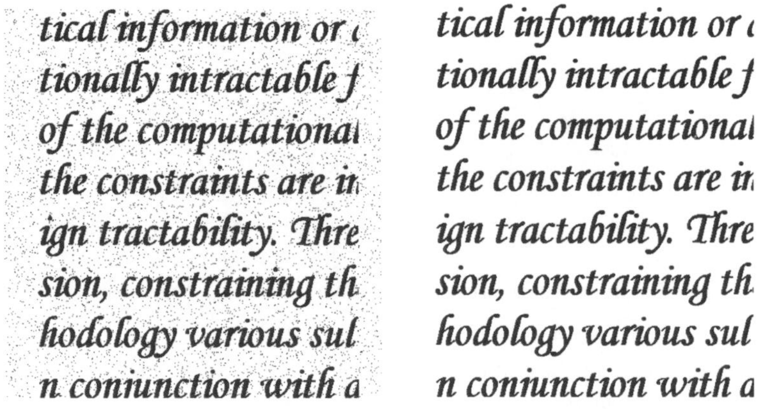

tical information or a
tionally intractable f
of the computational
the constraints are in
ign tractability. Thre
sion, constraining th
hodology various sul
n conjunction with a

(a)

tical information or a
tionally intractable f
of the computational
the constraints are in
ign tractability. Thre
sion, constraining th
hodology various sul
n conjunction with a

(b)

Figure 1.9 Median restoration of Monotype Corsiva text degraded by 5% salt-and-pepper noise: (a) degraded image; (b) restored image.

We next illustrate how nonincreasing binary filters can be used for restoration. First, we give the morphological interpretation of the general representations of Eqs. (1-1) and (1-2).

Consider a window W and two disjoint subsets E and F of W. A filter Ψ is defined in the following manner: if A is an input image and z is any pixel, then $z \in \Psi(A)$ if E_z is a subset of A and F_z is disjoint from A. Equivalently, E_z is a subset of A and F_z is a subset of A^c (complement of A). In morphological image processing, Ψ is called the *hit-or-miss transform*, E and F are known as the *hit* and *miss* structuring elements, respectively, and $\Psi(A)$ is written as $A \otimes (E, F)$,

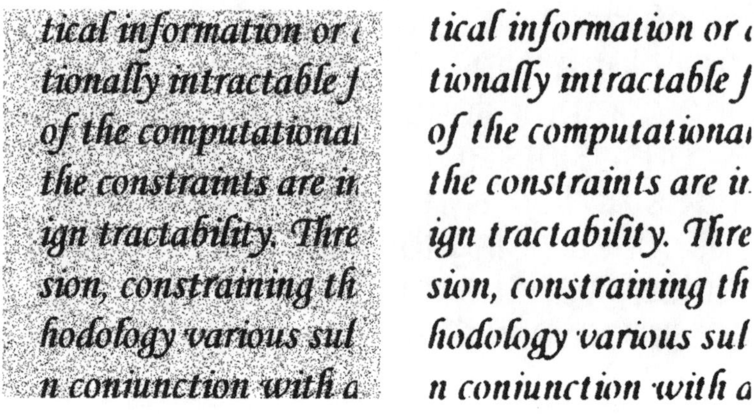

tical information or t *tionally intractable f* *of the computational* *the constraints are n* *ign tractability. Thre* *sion, constraining th* *hodology various sul* *n conjunction with a*	*tical information or t* *tionally intractable f* *of the computational* *the constraints are it* *ign tractability. Thre* *sion, constraining th* *hodology various sul* *n conjunction with a*
(*a*)	(*b*)

Figure 1.10 Median restoration of Monotype Corsiva text degraded by 20% salt-and-pepper noise: (a) degraded image; (b) restored image.

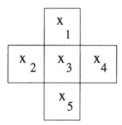

Figure 1.11 Logical mask for strong-neighbor median.

where (E, F) is treated as a structuring-element pair. In set notation,

$$A \otimes (E, F) = (A \ominus E) \cap (A^c \ominus F) \tag{1-13}$$

If E and F form a decomposition of W, meaning $E \cup F = W$, then the pair (E, F) is said to be *canonical*.

Canonical and noncanonical structuring pairs correspond to single product terms in Eqs. (1-1) and (1-2), respectively. In either case, E and F represent the sets of pixels in the window whose binary variables are uncomplemented and complemented, respectively. For instance, if W is 3×3 and centered at the origin and its variables are labeled according to Figure 1.1, then the product

$$h = x_1 x_2 x_3 x_5 x_7^c x_8^c x_9^c \tag{1-14}$$

corresponds to the hit-or-miss transform with the hit structuring element consisting of the upper row together with the origin and the miss structuring element corresponding to the lower row. This pair is depicted in Figure 1.12, where hit, miss, and "don't care" pixels are black, white, and gray, respectively.

The logic expansion of Eq. (1-1) provides the most general form of a binary windowed operator. Because each logical product defines a hit-or-miss operator,

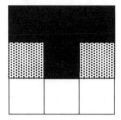

Figure 1.12 Hit-or-miss structuring pair.

the function expansion can be replaced by the equivalent morphological expansion

$$\Psi(A) = \bigcup_i A \otimes (E_i, F_i) \qquad (1\text{-}15)$$

where (E_i, F_i) is the structuring-element pair corresponding to the ith logical product.

1.5 NOISE SUPPRESSION USING NONINCREASING BINARY FILTERS

The hit-or-miss transform is employed in various ways to restore noise-degraded images. We illustrate only one approach, parallel thinning. Here, the original image has been degraded by adjoining noise pixels. Hit-or-miss transforms are used to identify pixels to be removed and then these are subtracted from the image. The resulting thinning filter takes the form

$$\Psi(A) = A - \bigcup_i A \otimes (E_i, F_i) \qquad (1\text{-}16)$$

where the pairs (E_i, F_i) are designed to locate noise pixels.

A standard approach to thinning is to employ the eight pruning structuring pairs shown in Figure 1.13 [8]. Examination of the pruners reveals them to be endpoint finders for the eight principal directions in the square grid. The assumption in using them for thinning is that most endpoints in an image degraded by spurious adjoined edge pixels are noise pixels. The pruners find endpoints and then, according to

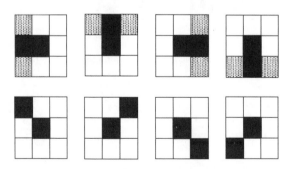

Figure 1.13 Classical pruners.

Eq. (1-16), the endpoints are removed to yield the filtered image. Figure 1.14 shows an original text image, an edge-degraded version of the text image, and the result of applying parallel thinning to the degraded image using the eight pruners.

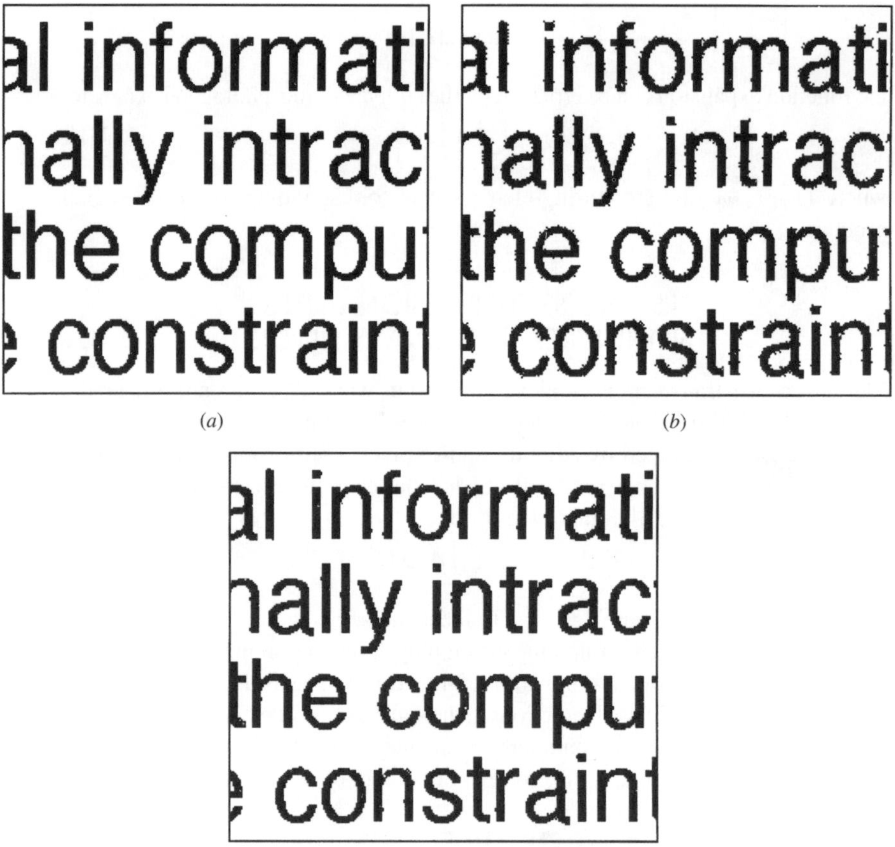

(a)
(b)

(c)

Figure 1.14 Text restoration using parallel thinning: (a) original text image; (b) edge-degraded text image; (c) restored text.

The classical pruners work well for noncomplex noise; however, for realistic noise models it is better to design the structuring pairs in a statistically optimal manner. A similar comment applies to application of increasing binary filters.

Direct implementation of Eq. (1-16) in a high-level language will usually result in very inefficient code, especially for large images.

1.6   MATCHED FILTERING USING NONINCREASING BINARY FILTERS

From its definition, the hit-or-miss transform is a matched filter—the hit structuring element fitting inside and the miss element fitting outside. The difficulty is that, for matched filtering, the window must be large: it must be sufficiently large to encompass whatever shapes are to be identified. Moreover, each element might contain a large number of pixels and therefore require a large amount of processing.

To illustrate the method, consider the letter "A" shown at the extreme left of the upper row in Figure 1.15 and its complement image shown at the extreme left of the second row. The second image in the top row is an inner boundary for "A," and succeeding images to the right show increasingly collapsed versions. The second image in the second row is an outer boundary for "A," and succeeding images show increasingly expanded versions. Let the inner boundary and its

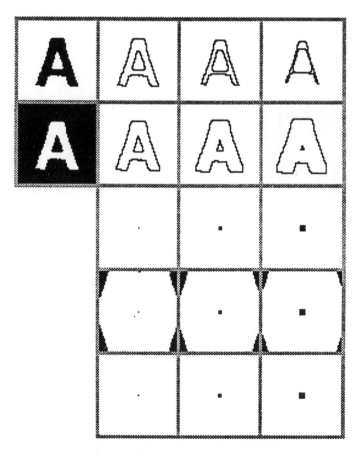

Figure 1.15 Hit-or-miss recognition.

shrunken versions be hit elements and the outer boundary and its enlarged versions be the corresponding miss elements. Let the window center be the origin for all structuring elements. The third row of the figure shows the pixel sets for which the corresponding hit elements fit in the letter and the fourth row shows the pixel sets for which the corresponding miss elements fit in the complement. Intersecting the corresponding hit and miss pixel sets provides the hit-or-miss outputs shown in the bottom row. Shrinking the hit element and enlarging the miss element makes for looser fitting. Loose fitting results in increased recognition regions; it also makes the matched filter less sensitive to shape irregularities.

To reduce processing and make the filter less noise sensitive, one can employ sparse structuring elements. The hit-or-miss application of Figure 1.15 is repeated in Figure 1.16 with sparse structuring elements. There is risk in using sparse structuring elements: too sparse elements can result in misrecognitions.

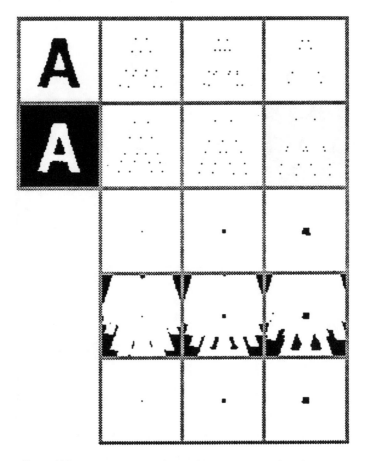

Figure 1.16 Hit-or-miss recognition with sparse structuring elements.

1.7 SUPPRESSION OF NOISE
BY GRAY-SCALE MEDIAN

In discussing nonlinear gray-scale filters we focus on a class of increasing filters known either as stack filters or flat morphological filters. This restriction is not great because most nonlinear-filter applications involve this class.

Perhaps the most widely used nonlinear gray-scale filter is the median filter. The gray-scale moving median filter is defined by choosing a window W containing an odd number of pixels, translating W to a pixel z, ordering the gray values from smallest to largest at the pixels in the translated window, and then defining the filter output at z to be the middle value in the ordering.

The median is good for suppressing impulsive noise and, as opposed to linear smoothing filters, does well at preserving edges. Impulse suppression is illustrated in Figure 1.17. There, an isolated impulse on a flat background signal is fully suppressed by the three-point median, whereas the unweighted three-point moving average lowers the impulse but also creates an artifact around it by raising some neighboring values. Edge preservation is illustrated in Figure 1.18. There, a signal step is invariant under the three-point median but is ramped by the unweighted three-point moving average. As with linear smoothing, the median does poorly on textured images. Whereas linear smoothers blur textures, median filters make them appear blotchy.

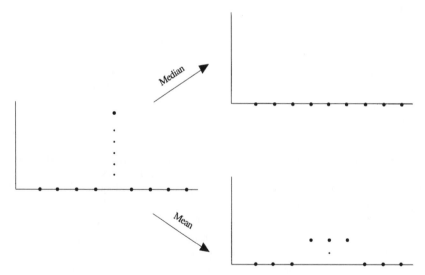

Figure 1.17 Impulse responses for three-point median and moving mean.

For linear filtering, if one wishes to give more weight to the center pixel or to pixels near the center, the convolution can be so weighted; a similar concept applies to medians. Suppose $x_1, x_2, \ldots, x_m$ are the observed values in the structuring set.

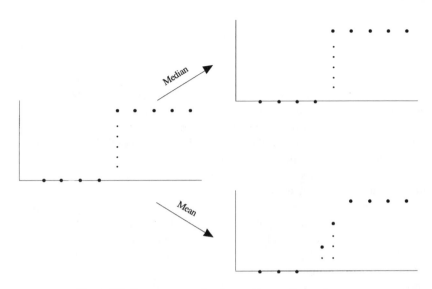

Figure I.18 Step responses for three-point median and mean.

The weighted median with integer weights $a_1, a_2, \ldots, a_m$ is found by repeating a_i times the observation x_i, ordering the new set of $a_1 + a_2 + \ldots + a_m$ values, and then choosing the middle value as the output. In particular, the center weighted median is found by repeating only the value at the window center.

I.8   THRESHOLD DECOMPOSITION

The median is a special case of a more general kind of increasing nonlinear gray-scale filter, these being defined via the method of threshold decomposition. Suppose the gray range has $M + 1$ values, $0, 1, \ldots, M - 1, M$. For each gray value k, define the threshold set of the image f by

$$A[k] = \{z : f(z) \geq k\} \qquad (1\text{-}17)$$

(Figure 1.19). If $k \leq j$, then $A[j]$ is a subset of $A[k]$. Thus, if an increasing binary filter Ψ_0 is applied to both $A[k]$ and $A[j]$, then $\Psi_0(A[j])$ is a subset of $\Psi_0(A[k])$. One can imagine the threshold sets of f as stacking on top of each other, with each being a subset of the one below it.

If an increasing binary filter Ψ_0 is applied to each set in the stack, then the stack sets are changed, but the order relations are preserved. A gray-scale filter Ψ is defined by taking $\Psi(f)(z)$, the value of the filtered signal at pixel z, to be the maximum gray value k for which z is an element of $\Psi_0(A[k])$. Equivalently,

$$\Psi(f)(z) = \sum_{k=1}^{M} \Psi_0(A[k])(z) \qquad (1\text{-}18)$$

The resulting filter Ψ is called a *stack filter*. Because Ψ_0 is an increasing binary filter, it is generated by a positive Boolean function, so that, in effect, at each level of

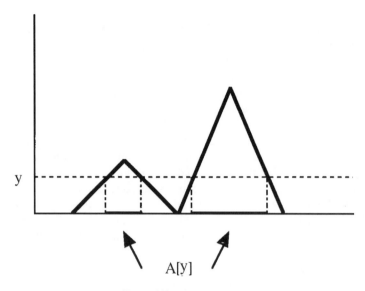

y

A[y]

Figure 1.19 Threshold set.

the stack the same logical operator [of the form given in Eq. (1-3)] is being applied to the variables in the defining window about each pixel. The method is illustrated for the three-point centered median in Figure 1.20. On the left are the threshold sets of the input signal and on the right are the threshold sets of the output signal, each output threshold set having been obtained by applying the binary median

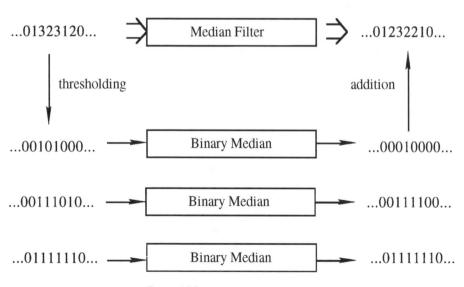

...01323120... ⟹ Median Filter ⟹ ...01232210...

thresholding   addition

...00101000... ⟶ Binary Median ⟶ ...00010000...

...00111010... ⟶ Binary Median ⟶ ...00111100...

...01111110... ⟶ Binary Median ⟶ ...01111110...

Figure 1.20 Median as a stack filter.

(the positive Boolean function for the binary median) to the corresponding input threshold set. Architecturally and programmatically, a gray-scale stack filter is built using only a single binary logical function.

Stack filters can be viewed morphologically. If f is an image and E is a set, then the moving minimum over E is found by translating E to a pixel z and then taking the minimum of all values in the translate E_z. The moving maximum is defined analogously. In the context of morphological image processing, the moving minimum is called a *flat erosion*, the moving maximum is called a *flat dilation*, and E is the structuring element. Flat erosion and flat dilation are denoted by $f \ominus E$ and $f \oplus E$, respectively. Both flat erosion and dilation are notoriously slow running if coded directly in a high-level language for a single instruction stream, single data stream (SISD) processor. We recommend always coding these operations using their Boolean analogs in both high-level languages and in assembly language.

Suppose h is a positive Boolean function defining stack filter Ψ, h has the logical sum-of-products representation given in Eq. (1-3), and h is applied over the variables in the window W. Each product in Eq. (1-3) corresponds to a subset E_i of W and Ψ has the maximum representation

$$\Psi(f) = \bigvee_i f \ominus E_i \qquad (1\text{-}19)$$

In short, a stack filter is a maximum of flat erosions.

Regarding the median, the structuring elements of Eq. (1-11), which served as a basis for the binary moving strong-neighbor median, also serve as the structuring elements for the gray-scale moving strong-neighbor median; that is, if ten erosions are employed in Eq. (1-19) using the structuring elements of Eq. (1-11), then the resulting filter Ψ is the strong-neighbor median.

1.9 NONLINEAR EDGE DETECTION VIA THE MORPHOLOGICAL GRADIENT

The nonlinear analog to linear gradient edge detection is edge detection via the morphological gradient. Given an image f and a structuring element E, the morphological gradient is defined by

$$\text{GRAD}[f] = [f \oplus E] - [f \ominus E] \qquad (1\text{-}20)$$

where "$-$" denotes the set difference. Because dilation and erosion by sets yield maximum and minimum filters, respectively, at each pixel the morphological gradient yields the difference between the maximum and minimum values over the set translated to the pixel. Its action is illustrated in Figure 1.21. Like linear gradients, once the morphological gradient has been found, an edge image can be created by thresholding. Rather than use gradient edge detection as a final edge result for image segmentation, it is better to use it as part of a more accurate morphological method known as *watershed segmentation*.

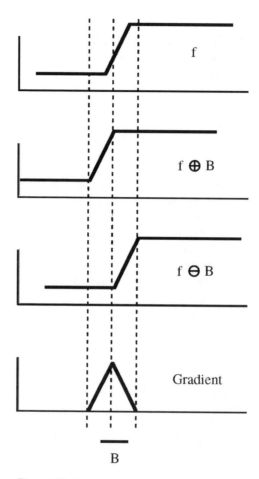

Figure I.21 Structure of morphological gradient.

1.10 FAST GRANULOMETRIC FILTERS

Fast matrix transforms reduce computation time by providing equivalent implementations involving sparse matrices containing mostly zeros and ones. More generally, one often attempts to find an equivalent algorithmic implementation that saves processing time on the available hardware. In the present section, we consider a nonlinear algorithm that lies at the base of a very powerful texture discrimination methodology and then discuss a fast implementation.

The opening filter introduced in Section 1.4 has a number of key properties, including that opening $A \circ B$ is always a subset of A. Moreover, for certain sequences of structuring elements that are increasing in size, say $B_0 \subset B_1 \subset B_2 \ldots$, the corresponding openings are decreasing in size, namely, $A \circ B_0 \supset A \circ B_1 \supset A \circ B_2 \supset \ldots$. The sequence of openings is called a *granulometry*. A granulometric size distribution $\Omega(k)$ corresponding to the binary image A is generated by counting the pixels in each succeeding filtered image $A \circ B_k$. The distribution $\Omega(k)$ is a decreasing function of k and, for sufficiently large k, $\Omega(k) = 0$. If we assume that B_0 consists of a single pixel, then $\Omega(0)$ gives the original pixel count in A and the normalization

$$\Phi(k) = 1 - \frac{\Omega(k)}{\Omega(0)} \tag{1-21}$$

is a digital function that increases from 0 to 1 over some finite k-interval. The term $\Phi(k)$ is called the *morphological pattern spectrum* of image A and is used in texture-classification schemes.

Two often-used suitable choices for the sequence $\{B_k\}$ are vertical and horizontal line segments of increasing length. The resulting opening sequences are called *linear granulometries*. Figure 1.22 shows two granular images, the one in part (a) exhibiting more horizontal length than the one in part (b). Figure 1.23 shows the corresponding pattern spectra derived from each image of Figure 1.22. Note how the greater horizontal length of the image in Figure 1.22a has resulted in a pattern spectrum whose main growth is to the right of the main growth region for the pattern spectrum corresponding to the image in Figure 1.22b.

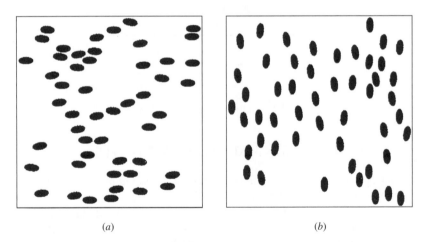

(a)   (b)

Figure I.22 Two granular images: (a) exhibiting more horizontal length; (b) exhibiting less horizontal length.

Ignoring initialization and letting $B[k]$ denote the horizontal pixel line of length k, a direct implementation of the definition leads to the following algorithm

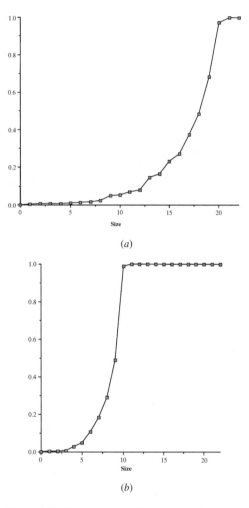

(a)

(b)

Figure 1.23 Pattern spectra for two granular images: (a) for Figure 1.22a; (b) for Figure 1.22b.

to compute a horizontal linear size distribution:

```
while omega[k] > 0
    begin
        A[k + 1] := open(A,B[k+1])
        omega[k+1] := count(A[k+1])
    end
```

where open is a procedure to perform morphological opening and count is a procedure to count the number of points. The while loop is bounded by the horizontal dimension of the image frame; nevertheless, whether each opening is computed via the fitting expression of Eq. (1-7) or as an erosion followed by dilation, the algorithm is computationally burdensome on standard SISD hardware.

Suppose the binary image A is in a run-length encoded form. Specifically, the image is stored as a sequence of triples $(x[i], y[i], r[i])$, $i = 1, 2, \ldots, n$, where $(x[i], y[i])$ specifies a pixel at which the image is black such that the pixel to the left is white, and $r[i]$ specifies the run length of the black pixels emanating at $(x[i], y[i])$. Such a compression scheme is lossless because the exact image can be reconstructed from the run-length encoding. The following algorithm can be employed to obtain the size distribution directly from the run-length encoding without recourse to actual image openings:

```
max := maximum(r[1],r[2],...,r[n])
for k = 1 to max
  for i = 1 to n
    if r[i] = k then
        temp[k] := temp[k] + k
    omega[k+1] := omega[k] - temp[k]
```

Here `maximum` is a procedure or macro to find the maximum of all the run-lengths. This improved code is significantly faster because of the aforementioned computational complexity of performing opening either using set operations or even the Boolean logic equivalent.

References

[1] E. R. Dougherty and J. Astola. *An Introduction to Nonlinear Image Processing.* Bellingham, WA: SPIE Press, 1994.

[2] J. Serra. *Image Analysis and Mathematical Morphology.* New York: Academic Press, 1982.

[3] J. Serra, ed. *Image Analysis and Mathematical Morphology*, Vol. 2, New York: Academic Press, 1988.

[4] C. R. Giardina and E. R. Dougherty. *Morphological Methods in Image and Signal Processing.* Englewood Cliffs, NJ: Prentice-Hall, 1988.

[5] E. R. Dougherty. *An Introduction to Morphological Image Processing.* Bellingham, WA: SPIE Press, 1992.

[6] J. Astola and E. R. Dougherty. "Nonlinear filters," in *Digital Image Processing Methods.* E. R. Dougherty, editor. New York: Marcel Dekker, 1994.

[7] E. R. Dougherty, ed. *Mathematical Morphology in Image Processing.* New York: Marcel Dekker, 1992.

[8] I. Pitas and A. Venetsanopoulos. *Nonlinear Digital Filters.* Boston: Kluwer Academic Publishers, 1990.

2

REAL-TIME MOTION ESTIMATION

P. Nesi   *Department of Systems and Informatics,*
              Faculty of Engineering,
              University of Florence

2.1 INTRODUCTION

The main issue of motion analysis is the estimation of the three-dimensional (3-D) motion components of the moving objects under observation. This is of relevance in many problems such as 3-D object reconstruction [1, 2], object tracking [3, 4], and robot navigation [5, 6]. The information available in a vision-based system focused on motion analysis is related to the projection of the 3-D real velocity on the image plane. For example, in Figure 2.1, the motion of an observer who walks toward the environment causes a divergent motion field in the projection of the environment on an image plane (placed between the observer and the scene, and joined with the observer). This apparent motion can be useful in understanding the 3-D motion. Therefore, motion analysis tries to estimate the apparent motion and then to evaluate the 3-D motion. This can be due to the motion of the observer in the environment as well as to the motion of the scene objects with respect to the observer. It should be noted that most of the techniques proposed in the literature for estimating the 3-D motion take for granted the estimation of a motion field—e.g., [7–9]. This assumption implies that the estimation of the two-dimensional (2-D) motion field is often considered as a simple and error-free process but, unfortunately, this is not true.

The problem of motion field estimation is intrinsically affected by three main difficulties. The first problem involves the discontinuities in the motion field that are originated by the presence of noise in the image brightness. This difficulty can generally be overcome (or only partially attenuated) by convolving the image with a 2-D or 3-D Gaussian smoothing operator [10]. The second problem is due to the presence of occlusions between different moving objects (which usually have different velocities) and between the moving objects and the stationary background.

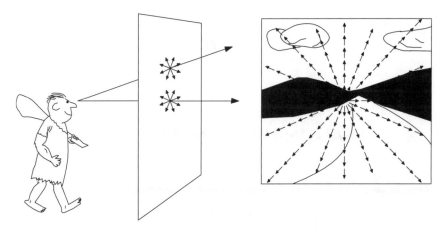

Figure 2.1 Apparent motion as the projection of the image plane.

This problem can lead to wrong estimations and can be corrected by means of a priori or a posteriori reasoning by considering the presence of the occlusion boundaries. The third difficulty is the so-called *problem of aperture*, which is also present in human vision. It is related to the impossibility of recovering univocally the direction of motion if the object is observed through an aperture that is smaller than the object size, and the references on the object under observation (such as textures—e.g., patterns) are not enough to perceive the transversal component of the object motion [11]. In this context, only the component of the real velocity that is normal to the object edge can be detected and estimated with some confidence (see Fig. 2.2).

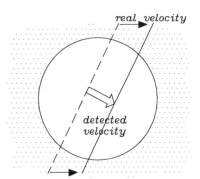

Figure 2.2 An instance of the problem of aperture.

Other very important errors are due to the computational methods adopted for estimating the motion field. In the rest of this chapter, some of the most important techniques for motion estimation are reviewed. For each of these, a discussion about the errors that are typical of the approach is reported.

Recently, the need for performing motion analysis in real-time for robot navigation, object tracking, and other applications has evoked a high interest in real-time estimation of motion fields ("real-time" in vision systems usually means at least 20 estimations per second). To this end, studies on computationally light estimation techniques and on parallel implementations have been performed. In many cases, the main goal of motion estimation is to estimate the so-called *motion field*, when the field is topologically dense or sparse. The motion field is called *dense* if the estimation process tries to yield the vectors of the motion field on a regular grid of the image plane. Due to this fact, certain mathematical solutions for motion estimation have been defined in terms of local operations, as have many other image processing elaborations [10], where *local* means that the estimation referred to an image point is obtained by using only the data that are located in the neighborhood of the reference point. In addition, the high complexity of the estimation techniques and the fact that the computational complexity for estimating a dense motion field depends on the square of the image resolution make the real-time motion field estimation by using a traditional sequential machine impossible. For these reasons, parallel architectures following the SIMD (single instruction and multiple data) paradigm are usually preferable for supporting parallel algorithms for motion field estimations (e.g., [12]). Presently, there are examples of parallel implementations for motion estimation in the literature, and several mathematical techniques for motion estimation are strongly parallelizable. The identification of computationally light estimation algorithms and the definition of parallel implementations open the way for the definition of specific hardware architectures for motion field estimation in real-time [13]. Actually, there are only a few examples of parallel hardware architectures for motion field estimation in real-time (e.g., [14]).

In the literature, two main approaches for real-time motion field estimation can be identified: *matching-based* (correspondence), and *gradient-based* approaches. In turn, gradient-based approaches can be classified in regularization- and multiconstraint-based techniques.

In the following sections of this chapter, a selection of the most important algorithms belonging to the above-mentioned approaches is reviewed. In Section 2.2, matching-based techniques are considered. The main issues of gradient-based approaches are reported in Section 2.3. Regularization-based and multiconstraint-based techniques are shown in Sections 2.4 and 2.5, respectively. Our review is focused on describing the attitude of these techniques in estimating motion fields in real-time. To this end, for many of the algorithms considered, the computational complexities in the case of sequential and parallel implementations have been estimated and reported. An analysis of the motion field quality for several of the methods reviewed is also reported by considering the main problems related to motion field estimation. Several examples are also included. Finally, comments and conclusions are reported in Section 2.6.

2.2   MATCHING-BASED APPROACHES

Matching-based approaches are based on the well-known techniques of correspondences [15–18], which, in turn, are based on the identification of a set of sparse and well-identifiable features of the moving object. By tracking these features, an interframe correspondence is searched to estimate the motion (displacement) of selected features on the image plane. The well-identifiable features can be classified in high-level (e.g., lines and shapes) and low-level features (e.g., corner points, image patterns, prominent color changes on the 3-D object, curvature). A field of feature displacements is equivalent to a sparse motion field. These techniques are very suitable for tracking moving objects in the 3-D space, because the features tracked can be relevant parts of the moving objects. For this purpose, better results are obtained by using high-level and well-identifiable features. On the other hand, the tracking of these features needs a preprocessing phase (e.g., filtering, edge extraction) on the images, with the corresponding computational costs. Moreover, the correspondence techniques should be independent of rotations and scale changes of the features under tracking. From this point of view, simpler solutions are obtained by using low-level features. Among these techniques, the most famous approach adopts as a feature the pattern of the image brightness itself; this is the so-called *block-matching* technique. With this technique, the estimation of motion field for long-term image sequences is affected by the accumulation error (mainly due to the image discretization) [19, 18].

Regarding parallel implementations, a matching-based approach has been utilized in [20] as a first step for defining an algorithm for motion estimation on a Connection Machine in close-to-real-time. In [21], the matching approach has been implemented on a pyramidal architecture. The process starts at the coarsest level, where the displacement components are shorter than one pixel, and then it passes to a finer level by using a matching-based algorithm.

2.2.1   The Block-Matching Technique

The block-matching technique is a matching-based technique where an image segment (i.e., with its pattern) is taken as the feature to be tracked [22, 18]. In this case, the motion field estimation consists in finding the coordinates (x', y') of the image segment center that minimize the correspondence between the image segments belonging to the image at time t and the reference image segment at time $(t - \Delta t)$ with coordinates x, y [22] (see Fig. 2.3). The estimation of the correspondence is obtained with:

$$C(x, y, x', y') = \sum_{m=-M/2}^{M/2} \sum_{l=-L/2}^{L/2} \left(E_{(x+m, y+l, t-\Delta t)} - E_{(x'+m, y'+l, t)} \right)^2$$

where $E_{(x,y,t)}$ is the image brightness value at time t with coordinates x, y (the time identifies the single image in the sequence); and M and L are the dimensions of the image segment along x- and y-axes, respectively (usually $M = L$). The

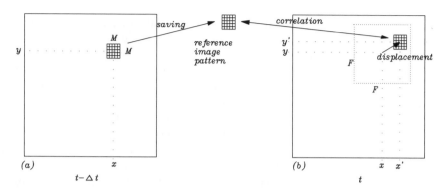

Figure 2.3 Block-matching technique for motion estimation with $M = L$: (a) image at time $t - \Delta t$, i.e., $E_{(x,y,t-\Delta t)}$; (b) image at time t, i.e., $E_{(x,y,t)}$.

minimization consists of searching the minima of function $C(x, y, x', y')$ around the image point x, y, for $x' = x - F/2, \ldots, x + F/2$ and $y' = y - F/2, \ldots, y + F/2$ (where F is the dimension of the image segment in which the minima is searched). Thus, the point of coordinates x', y', where $C(x, y, x', y')$ has its minima, identifies the position of the image segment tracked at time t. The differences $Sx = x' - x$, $Sy = y' - y$ are the components of the displacement of the image pattern under tracking—i.e., the velocity of the pixel placed in x, y at time $t - \Delta t$.

With the block-matching technique, the pattern of the image segment around the point under tracking at time $t - \Delta t$ is used as the reference pattern for searching the displacement at time t (see Fig. 2.3). With this mechanism, the pattern around the new position is considered as the new reference image segment for the next image. This mechanism of updating avoids the problems related to the progressive dismissal of the reference pattern with respect to what is projected on the image by the moving object (the dismissal can be due to object rotations, changes in illumination, etc.). As a result, the progressive dismissal can lead after a few instants to finding incorrect displacements. On the contrary, by updating the image pattern, the so-called *accumulation error* can be found [19, 18]. This is due to the accumulation of the error when measuring the displacement of the image pattern tracked. In fact, the error in estimating the displacement is propagated to the successive measurements because the reference pattern is updated by using an imprecise measurement. Furthermore, the components of displacement are measured by using integer numbers and, if the displacements are close to one pixel, the error can be very high. Therefore, the accumulation error tends to increase its value over time, leading to degenerative situations, so that the system can track in a few instants a pattern that is very far from the initial one. This problem can invalidate the motion tracking after a few images if the reference pattern is not strongly characterized. For this reason, corner points, edges, and so forth are usually preferred in order to reduce this problem [23–27]. Updating the image segment pattern at each time instant allows one to also estimate rotational movements. It should be noted that, if the accumulation error is in some way constrained to be very low, then long-term motion tracking is possible. To this end, active prediction/correction mechanisms have been defined in [19, 18].

The block-matching technique is also sensitive with respect to noise; but this problem can be mitigated by augmenting the dimensions of the reference segment (i.e., M and L). Other mechanisms to improve the robustness of the algorithm are 1) avoiding the tracking of not-enough characterized image patterns and 2) neglecting the displacements originated by the minimums of function $C()$ that are bigger than a predefined threshold. Regarding 1), it is better to neglect the points that are not characterized enough because there exists in these conditions a high probability that the pattern is mainly due to noise and, thus, the searching algorithm could find one or more minima that are seldom related to the reference pattern. This phenomenon can be considered an instance of the above-mentioned problem of aperture.

The block-matching technique can also be used for estimating dense motion fields by trying to measure the displacements of the image points that are located on a fixed regular grid on the image at each time instant, without considering the tracking of selected patterns associated with the moving objects. In these conditions, the problems related to the accumulation error are obviously missing.

In Figures 2.4 and 2.5, two test sequences of images are reported. The first is a synthetic scene for testing the algorithm behavior with respect to the presence of occlusions and discontinuities on moving object boundaries, while the second is a noisy real image for testing the algorithms in these conditions. In Figure 2.6, the behavior of a modified version of the block-matching algorithm

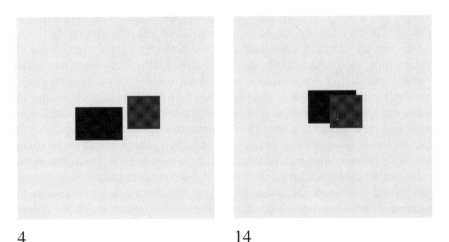

4   14

Figure 2.4 Sequence of images where two objects with a superimposed pattern move in opposite directions (180° and 45° with respect to the x-axis, respectively); (4th and 14th frame, $I = 128$).

1   9

Figure 2.5 Sequence of images where the camera is moving with respect to the scene with a translational motion parallel to the image plane (1st and 9th frame, $I = 128$).

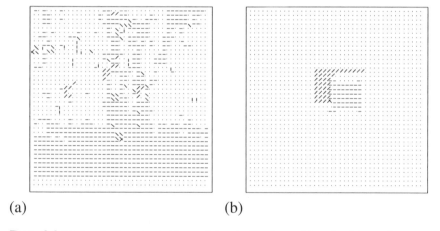

(a)   (b)

Figure 2.6 Motion fields estimated by applying the block-matching algorithm to the sequences: (a) Figure 2.5 (with $M = L = 5$, $F = 9$); (b) Figure 2.4 (with $M = L = 5$, $F = 9$).

with respect to these image sequences is reported. The classical block-matching algorithm has been modified according to 1) and 2) above. Thus, the estimations where 1) multiple minima of function $\mathcal{C}()$ are found and 2) a minima bigger than a predefined threshold is found have been neglected. As can be noted, by applying these simple rules quite good results have been obtained. In fact, only some discontinuities on the moving object boundaries and some wrong estimations for the presence of noise are obtained.

As for the computational complexity, if the image pattern is M^2, the cost of searching the minima of a pattern (in an $F \times F$ image area on a sequential machine) is $O(F^2M^2)$. Considering the case in which the matching is performed for each pixel of the image having dimensions $I \times I$, the asymptotical complexity of the whole process is $O(I^2F^2M^2)$. In the case of parallel implementation on an SIMD machine, where a processing element (PE) is assigned for each image pixel (e.g., a mesh of communicating PE, Figure 2.7a), the computational complexity is $O(F^2M^2)$. It should be noted that this architecture is not very suitable for the pattern-matching techniques, because the estimation of the correspondence function is not based on strictly local information; thus, several communications among the PEs are needed with their respective costs.

In general, with the block-matching approach, only displacements with components shorter than $F/2$ can be measured, which limits the maximum velocity of the observed objects. Multiresolution techniques have been repeatedly adopted in order to avoid this problem. One technique works at each time instant with a set of images having different resolutions which can be obtained by means of the application of a set of filters. The process of estimation begins at the lowest resolution, where the displacements must be less than one pixel. When the correspondence between two consecutive images is found, it is transferred from the current resolution to a finer one [28], an estimation process that is usually performed by relaxation. Multiresolution algorithms are highly suitable for implementation on pyramidal architectures where the current image can be directly stored in different meshes of PEs at different resolutions (see Figure 2.7b). These architectures are also integrated by specific mechanisms to reduce the cost of creating the sequence of images at different resolutions. In addition, the process of match propagation from one resolution to a finer one does not lead to the estimation of the correlation on the whole $F \times F$ image area,

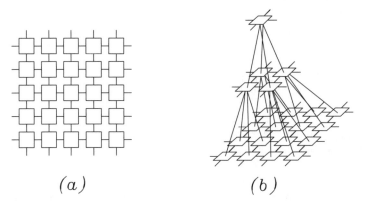

(a) (b)

Figure 2.7 (a) A portion of a processing-element mesh; (b) a portion of a pyramidal architecture of PEs.

because the most probable subarea is selected by means of the communications among the levels, such as those in Figure 2.7b. The computational complexity is then reduced.

2.3   GRADIENT-BASED APPROACHES

Gradient-based approaches provide a solution to motion estimation from the observation in time of changes in the image brightness. These changes are modeled by means of partial differential equations, which are usually called *constraint equations*. The field of velocity vectors obtained by solving such partial differential equations is normally called *optical flow* or *image flow*. Generally, the concept of optical flow field differs from that of motion field because the motion field is a pure geometric concept [29], while the optical flow concept is based on the observation of the changes in the image brightness. Physical conditions under which these two fields are equal have been discussed from different points of view in [30–33]. On the other hand, the estimation of an approximated motion field such as an optical flow can be very useful for 3-D motion estimation, object tracking, segmentation, and so on.

The most important partial differential equation for modeling optical flow fields is obtained by considering the changes in the image brightness $E_{(x(t),y(t),t)}$ as stationary with respect to t (i.e., $dE/dt = 0$) [34]:

$$\frac{dE}{dt} = \frac{\partial E}{\partial x}\frac{dx}{dt} + \frac{\partial E}{\partial y}\frac{dy}{dt} + \frac{\partial E}{\partial t} = 0 \qquad (2\text{-}1)$$

This equation can also be represented by using the abbreviations for the image brightness partial derivatives:

$$E_x u + E_y v + E_t = 0 \qquad (2\text{-}2)$$

where u, v correspond to dx/dt, dy/dt, representing the components of the local velocity vector $\mathbf{V}$ along the x and y directions, respectively: Equation (2-2) is usually called *optical flow constraint* (OFC). Moreover, the OFC in (2-2) can also be considered as the equation of a line in the (u, v) plane:

$$v = mu + c \qquad (2\text{-}3)$$

where $m = -(E_x/E_y)$ is the slope and $c = -(E_t/E_y)$ is the intercept. Any point along this line is a possible solution for the optical flow estimation problem [34, 35]. Therefore, Eq. (2-2) is not sufficient to provide a unique solution for the optical flow estimation; hence, the solution of the OFC equation is an ill-posed problem ([34, 11]) and boundary and smoothness constraints are needed to obtain a computational solution. The fact that the optical flow estimation by means of the OFC is an ill-posed problem does not mean that the problem of motion field estimation is an ill-posed problem too, as will be shown in the next sections. The already mentioned "problem of aperture" is also related to the ill-posed nature of the OFC. In fact, by considering the OFC equation, it can be observed that only the component of the apparent velocity, which is parallel to ∇E, can be perceived and estimated (see Fig. 2.2):

$$\mathbf{V}_\perp = -\frac{E_t}{\|\nabla E\|}\frac{\nabla E}{\|\nabla E\|} \tag{2-4}$$

where $dE/dt = 0$ and $\|\nabla E\| \neq 0$ have been assumed. It should be noted that, where it is possible to define at least two distinct constraint lines (equations) such as in the corner points, the problem of aperture is not present. The possibility of defining two different constraints in an infinitesimal neighborhood of the point under consideration mainly depends on the presence of a significant curvature in the image brightness.

An extended version of the OFC equation has been proposed in [36] and used in [37]:

$$E_x u + E_y v + E(u_x + v_y) + E_t = 0 \tag{2-5}$$

This extended constraint (extended optical flow constraint, EOFC) also presents a term including the divergence of velocity field $(u_x + v_y)$, and was proposed as a better model than the OFC for estimating the motion field by means of gradient-based approaches. In [33], an analysis on the validity and the applicability of these two constraints as a function of scene and optical system characteristics is presented. This analysis shows that, in the presence of calibration, the OFC is a better model than the EOFC in modeling the 3-D motion field in most of the motion conditions, while, in the absence of calibration, the EOFC is better than the OFC in the presence of 3-D rotations orthogonal to the axis of view and in some cases also of motions toward the camera [33]. By starting from the OFC and the EOFC, many other constraint equations have been defined in the literature, as will be shown later.

In estimating motion fields by means of the gradient-based techniques, there exist all the classical problems of motion estimation, such as noise, occlusion, and so forth; moreover, three other typical problems must be considered.

The first problem is due to the ill-posed nature of the defined constraint equations. This problem is related to the problem of aperture previously discussed [11]. Additional constraint equations are used in order to transform the ill-posed nature. Therefore, many different optical flows have been defined in the literature for different constraints and computational techniques. These optical flow fields also exhibit different behaviors in different conditions—e.g., [34, 38, 39, 11, 40].

The second source of approximation is related to the applicability of the constraint equations—i.e., to what extent the constraint actually models the motion field. Conditions under which the motion field is exactly modeled by the optical flow constraint equations were analyzed in [30, 32, 31, 33].

The third source of error is due to the differential model itself [41, 33], which is very sensitive to image-brightness discontinuities; these in turn are due to noise, too crisp patterns, occlusions, reflections, and so on. The sensitivity of differential models to the discontinuities is mainly due to the approximations adopted for estimating the partial derivatives of the image brightness that appear as coefficients in the constraint equations—i.e., $E_{x(i,j,t)}$, $E_{y(i,j,t)}$, and $E_{t(i,j,t)}$. These can be estimated by using forward or central differences; for example,

$$E_{x(i,j,t)} = (E_{(i+1,j,t)} - E_{(i-1,j,t)})/2$$
$$E_{y(i,j,t)} = (E_{(i,j+1,t)} - E_{(i,j-1,t)})/2 \qquad (2\text{-}6)$$
$$E_{t(i,j,t)} = (E_{(i,j,t+1)} - E_{(i,j,t-1)})/2$$

Regarding the object tracking, in gradient-based techniques, a stable correspondence is lacking between the vectors of motion field and 3-D points of the observed 3-D moving object, which generates changes in brightness on the image plane. This is due to the fact that the constraint equations are not related to the pattern of the image features; thus, the correspondence between motion vector and objects is not maintained between different time instants. For these reasons, unlike matching-based techniques, gradient-based approaches are unsuitable for tracking moving objects without the adoption of an ad hoc optical-flow-field understanding process.

Most of the gradient-based approaches are suitable for parallel implementation because they are based on partial differential equations, and it is well known that their solutions can be obtained by finite differences; thus, only the access to local image information is required.

Two main gradient-based approaches for optical flow estimation can be identified in the literature: *regularization-based* and *multiconstraint-based* algorithms. In the following two sections, these techniques are separately analyzed.

2.4   REGULARIZATION-BASED ALGORITHMS

Regularization-based approaches consider the optical flow estimation as an ill-posed problem according to Hadamard theory [42]. As in many other inverse problems in early-vision studies [43–48], classical regularization theory [49] is adopted. In these methods, a functional is defined where a smoothness constraint is used to regularize the solution of a partial differential equation and the influence of the smoothness constraint is weighted with a positive constant. The functional is minimized by using the calculus of variations or by stochastic relaxation (i.e., deterministic and stochastic regularization, respectively). Basically, these methods lead to iterative solutions—e.g., [34, 35, 50–52, 47, 11].

Among the many regularization-based solutions for optical flow estimation, the most famous has been proposed by Horn and Schunck in [34], which is based on the minimization of the functional:

$$\iint \left[(E_x u + E_v v + E_t)^2 + \alpha^2 (u_x^2 + u_y^2 + v_x^2 + v_y^2) \right] dx \, dy \qquad (2\text{-}7)$$

where the first term is the OFC (measure of the goodness of OFC approximation), the second is a measure of the optical-flow-field smoothness, and α is a weighting factor that controls the influence of the smoothness constraint. The functional is minimized by using the calculus of variations [53], which leads to a system of two coupled differential equations from the Euler-Lagrange equations:

$$\nabla^2 u = \frac{E_x}{\alpha^2}(E_x u + E_y v + E_t)$$

$$\nabla^2 v = \frac{E_y}{\alpha^2}(E_x u + E_y v + E_t)$$

(2-8)

These equations can be easily decoupled, and an iterative solution can be defined using the discrete approximation of the Laplacian operator with a finite difference method [12]. Therefore, the following couple of equations is used to estimate the optical flow components at each time instant:

$$u_{(i,j,t)}^{n+1} = \bar{u}_{(i,j,t)}^n - \frac{E_{x(i,j,t)}\left[E_{x(i,j,t)}\bar{u}_{(i,j,t)}^n + E_{y(i,j,t)}\bar{v}_{(i,j,t)}^n + E_{t(i,j,t)}\right]}{\left(\alpha^2 + E_{x(i,j,t)}^2 + E_{y(i,j,t)}^2\right)}$$

$$v_{(i,j,t)}^{n+1} = \bar{v}_{(i,j,t)}^n - \frac{E_{y(i,j,t)}\left[E_{x(i,j,t)}\bar{u}_{(i,j,t)}^n + E_{y(i,j,t)}\bar{v}_{(i,j,t)}^n + E_{t(i,j,t)}\right]}{\left(\alpha^2 + E_{x(i,j,t)}^2 + E_{y(i,j,t)}^2\right)}$$

(2-9)

where n is the iteration number. It should be noted that the estimations of $E_{x(i,j,t)}$, and $E_{y(i,j,t)}$ require the communication of the pixel data from the neighboring PEs as well as the estimation of:

$$\bar{u}_{(i,j,t)}^n = (u_{(i-1,j-1,t)} + u_{(i-1,j+1,t)} + u_{(i+1,j-1,t)} + u_{(i+1,j+1,t)})/12 + (u_{(i-1,j,t)}$$
$$+ u_{(i+1,j,t)} + u_{(i,j-1,t)} + u_{(i,j+1,t)})/6$$

$$\bar{v}_{(i,j,t)}^n = (v_{(i-1,j-1,t)} + v_{(i-1,j+1,t)} + v_{(i+1,j-1,t)} + v_{(i+1,j+1,t)})/12 + (v_{(i-1,j,t)}$$
$$+ v_{(i+1,j,t)} + v_{(i,j-1,t)} + v_{(i,j+1,t)})/6$$

As can be noted, the asymptotical complexity of the Horn and Schunck algorithm on a sequential machine is a function of the number of iterations, I_t, that are needed to obtain the final solution and of the image dimensions, which is $O(I_t^2 I^2)$. Therefore, the asymptotical complexity on an SIMD mesh-connected parallel architecture with a PE for each pixel is $O(I_t)$. It should be noted that, in the iterative solution presented, a guessed value for optical flow estimation at time t can be obtained from the previous time-step (i.e., $\bar{u}_{(i,j,t)}^0 = u_{(i,j,t-1)}^\omega$), where ω is the number of iterations executed at the previous time-step). This reduces the number of iterations needed to obtain the optical flow estimation, as well as the computational effort.

In Figure 2.8, two frames of an image sequence obtained by moving the camera toward the scene are reported. This sequence can be used for testing the algorithm's behavior in the presence of divergent motion such as that due to a relative zooming.

The Horn and Schunck algorithm, like many other regularization-based algorithms, tends to produce smooth optical flow fields for the propagation of velocity

1   20

Figure 2.8 Sequence of images where the camera is moving toward the image scene (1st and 20th frame, $I = 128$).

values from the estimation points (see Fig. 2.9). The depth of propagation depends on both the number of iterations and the weighting factor. The iterative process starts at the first iteration by estimating the optical flow vectors that are parallel to ∇E according to Eq. (2-4), and it continues by smoothing the field constrained by the OFC, as can be seen in Figure 2.9a. Even though the estimation process converges to a minima, it does not converge to an optimal solution, because the lowest error in estimating the optical flow does not correspond to the iteration in which the process obtains the minimum of the functional, as pointed out in [11]. In certain conditions, this is due to the fact that the propagation is also incorrectly performed by starting from wrong estimations due to noise and discontinuities in general.

Drawbacks in the regularization-based approaches also occur in the presence of object occlusions. In these cases, the optical flow exhibits discontinuities on the moving object boundaries, and there is the adverse effect that the optical flow field of one object propagates inside the overlapped objects with the increasing of the iteration number, when the velocity of propagation depends on the weighting factor (see Fig. 2.9a). Several approaches have been proposed in order to solve this problem by controlling the propagation effect—e.g., [54, 11].

After Horn and Schunck [34], many other regularization-based solutions for optical flow estimation have been proposed to improve the quality of the estimation and/or to solve the problem of the early solutions. For example, Nagel [51] derived a different functional and solutions were obtained in a closed form only at the corner points of an image. Konrad and Dubois [50] presented two solutions for motion estimation that use the regularization approach based on a Bayesian estimation. The first solution used a multigrid algorithm to handle large displacements for a maximum a posteriori (MAP) probability estimation of optical flow

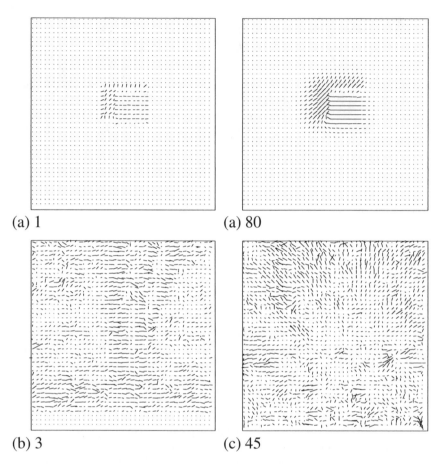

(a) 1   (a) 80

(b) 3   (c) 45

Figure 2.9 Optical flow estimation obtained by using the Horn and Schunck solution with $\alpha = 0.6$ on: (a) the 15th sequence frame in Figure 2.4 (iterations: 1, 80); (b) the 5th sequence frame in Figure 2.5 (iteration: 3); (c) the 6th sequence frame in Figure 2.8 (iteration: 45).

by simulated annealing. The second is an application of the minimum expected cost (MEC) estimation.

More recently, some solutions have been proposed in order to solve the problem of discontinuities and avoid the problem of propagation (typical of the regularization-based algorithms). These can be divided into two categories.

The solutions of the first category assume the "knowledge" of the moving object boundaries (which can be obtained by means of a stage of edge extraction or other techniques) before estimating the optical flow field by using a slightly modified Horn and Schunck solution—e.g., the solution proposed by Schnörr [55]. In [55], only contexts having a single moving object with quite uniform motion have been fully investigated. Moreover, the process complexity depends on the number of the moving objects in the scene.

The approaches of the second category define a specific functional where a bi-dimensional variable (control function) is added to control the effect of propagation as a function of discontinuities (the control function inhibits the smoothing action where there are discontinuities); that is, the solution based on the discontinuity-dependent penalty constraint proposed in [11]. The mechanism proposed maintains the profiles of the moving objects and improves the signal-to-noise ratio with respect to the solutions of Horn and Schunck [34]; thus, it avoids the problems of the loss of moving object boundaries in the presence of occlusions. In addition, the computational complexity is independent of the number of moving objects.

From the point of view of the computational complexity, most of the above methods are $O(I^2 I_t)$ [34, 12]. On the other hand, for the more complex solutions, such as [51] or [11], many mathematical operations are needed for each iteration; thus, the computational cost is higher with respect to the solution of Horn and Schunck [34]. A possibility for improving the performance of these iterative solutions is to adopt a multiresolution (pyramidal) architecture, such as that shown in Figure 2.7b. In this case, the performance enhancement depends only on the decrease of the number of iterations needed to reach the final result. For example, in [47], the multigrid approach (see [56] for solving Euler-Lagrange equations for some early-vision problems) has been discussed. It should be noted that the multigrid approach can be used for increasing the convergence velocity of low-frequency components (smooth modes) of the optical flow while, at the same time, the high-frequency components (such as discontinuities) are partially eliminated. In [57], a fully pyramidal implementation is presented, where a pyramid of images of different resolutions is obtained by using a Gaussian filter as a first step. Then, starting from the lowest resolution, the estimation algorithm moves to higher resolutions, thus improving the optical flow estimation at each step.

2.5 MULTICONSTRAINT-BASED ALGORITHMS

In order to transform the optical flow estimation based on the OFC equation from an ill-posed to a well-posed problem, several constraint equations have been defined by building determined and/or overdetermined systems of constraint equations. This technique is called the *multiconstraint-based approach*. These systems of equations are usually solved by using the least-squares technique or probabilistic reasoning (e.g., voting or clustering). The multiconstraint-based approaches can be classified on the basis of the method adopted for defining the system of equations and the mathematical technique chosen for its solution. By analyzing the literature, three different methods have been identified. In the rest of this chapter, these will be called **A**, **B**, and **C**.

For method **A**, the hypothesis about the stationarity (usually adopted on the image brightness, $dE/dt = 0$) is supposed to be valid for any motion-invariant function such as contrast, entropy, mean of the image brightness values, brightness variance, curvature, and so forth, instead of the image brightness. This allows us to define several partial differential equations structurally equal to the OFC for the same image point; thus, an overdetermined set of equations with u and v as unknowns is obtained. For example, Woodham [58] considered images grabbed with different light sources, and built an overdetermined system of equations by using one OFC equation for every illumination condition. Markandey and Flichbaugh [59] considered images grabbed at different spectra (visible and infrared), and used one OFC equation for each spectrum. Wohn, Davis, and Thirft [60] and Mitiche, Wang, and Aggarwal [61] used a set of motion-invariant image features.

For method **B**, new constraint equations are obtained by taking the derivative of fundamental constraint equations (i.e., OFC and EOFC) with respect to x, y, and t, or by evaluating the Taylor series of the constraint derivatives and assuming that these derivatives are equal to zero. In [38, 62, 39, 37, 40], a selection of the equations

$$E_{xx}u + E_{xy}v + E_{xt} = 0$$
$$E_{xy}u + E_{yy}v + E_{yt} = 0 \qquad\qquad (2\text{-}10)$$
$$E_{tx}u + E_{ty}v + E_{tt} = 0$$

has been used in different combinations for defining determined and/or overdetermined systems of equations. The first two equations can be obtained by taking the derivative of the OFC with respect to x and y and neglecting the terms with u_x, u_y, v_y, and v_x, or by estimating $d\nabla E/dt = 0$. In these cases, the second-order derivatives of the image brightness must be estimated, with the corresponding increase in the sensitivity to noise. For example, Haralick and Lee [38] proposed an overdetermined system of four equations—Eq. (2-10) plus the OFC—in two unknowns (u, v). Tretiak and Pastor [62] have used the first two equations of (2-10) together with the OFC for defining an overdetermined system of three equations. Tretiak and Pastor [62] have also used the first two equations of the system (2-10) for defining a determined system of equations. This approach was later improved by Verri, Girosi, and Torre [39]. For this class of solutions, the optical flow vectors are estimated in each point of the image by computing the inverse or the pseudo-inverse of the coefficient matrix of the system of equations.

For method **C**, it is supposed that the optical flow changes follow a law that is approximately linear; thus, a smoothed solution for optical flow estimation can be obtained from a linear approximation of the constraint used in the neighborhood of the point under consideration. This assumption is valid only if the optical flow field under observation is smooth. Then, the constraints evaluated in a set of neighboring pixels of a certain point represent the same velocity, as a first approximation. This assumption leads us to define a neighborhood of $N \times N$ constraint equations, obtaining in this way an overdetermined system of N^2 equations. A large N will smooth optical flow estimations and lead to a resolution loss. This approach is usually called *multipoint*. For example, Cafforio and Rocca [63], Campani and Verri [64], and Del Bimbo, Nesi, and Sanz [65] have proposed multipoint solutions based on the OFC, while Nesi, Del Bimbo, and Sanz [37] have used the EOFC.

For the definition of the system of equations, mixed approaches are obviously possible. For example, in [40], two solutions for optical flow estimation using both **B** and **C** techniques for defining the overdetermined system of equations have been presented.

The optical flow fields modeled by the constraint equations and defined as described above are conceptually and mathematically different from the optical flow fields modeled and estimated using the OFC or the EOFC. Therefore, several different optical flow fields have been defined on the basis of the constraints chosen and on the mathematical solution adopted.

It should be noted that the quality of the estimated optical flow fields strongly depends on the choice of the constraint equations. For example, the approaches based on second-order derivatives of image brightness are strongly sensitive to noise. In many cases, the optical flow fields estimated with multiconstraint-based methods have to be smoothed to be profitably used [38, 62]. For example, it is better to have smoother solutions in order to use the optical flow for segmentation of moving objects, for object tracking, and for the estimation of ego-motion. On the other hand, the optical flow or image filtering can destroy the important information for both 3-D object reconstruction and 3-D motion estimation.

In order to obtain smoother flow fields, most of the multiconstraint-based solutions adopt: 1) a prefiltering to regularize the initial data (sequence of images)— e.g., [39, 58]; and/or 2) a postfiltering[1] of the flow field components for regularization—e.g., [39, 60, 62]. The operations 1) and 2) also produce imprecisions in the measurement of the moving object boundaries, because a sort of diffusion is present as a side effect. This is also due to the size of the filter that is needed to obtain smooth fields (e.g., from 10×10 to 30×30). It should be noted that both these techniques attempt to transform the strongly ill-conditioned problem to a well-posed problem; therefore, these mechanisms can also be regarded as particular instances of regularization [48].

Most of the multiconstraint-based approaches are suitable for parallel implementation on an SIMD architecture because they require access only to local image information. Their performance obviously depends on the number of equations and on the technique adopted for solving the systems of equations. These mathematical techniques can be divided into two classes: *algebraic*—where the system of equations is solved with numerical methods for the pseudo-inversion of the coefficient matrix (e.g., least-squares technique, etc.) [38, 40, 61]; and *clustering*—where each possible solution (obtained by the equations of the overdetermined system)

---

[1]The postfiltering phase can be replaced by other techniques—in [11] and [35], regularization-based approaches for smoothing noisy optical flow fields have been proposed.

is considered as a point in a multidimensional domain. These points are clustered in order to select the most probable solution—[66, 35, 67].

2.5.1   Algebraic-Based Solutions

In general, the estimation process of algebraic solutions can be regarded as comprised of four phases: 1) the convolution of the images with a Gaussian filter (which is missing in most of the multipoint approaches); 2) the estimation of the image brightness derivatives (i.e., the estimation of equation coefficients, Q equations for each pixel); 3) (only for the approaches based on an overdetermined system of equations) the estimation of the determined "equivalent system of equations" (starting from the overdetermined system of equations) by means of the pseudo-inverse method; 4) the estimation of the velocity components by solving the determined system of equations (i.e., the equivalent system of equations for the approaches based on the overdetermined system of equations) using traditional methods, such as LUD [68].

In the following, the expression of the complexity for this class of solutions on a sequential machine is reported, where the four terms correspond to the complexities of the above-mentioned four phases, respectively. Therefore, the explicit complexity involved on a sequential machine is

$$C() = G^2 I^2 + Q n I^2 + Q N^2 \left[\frac{n}{2}(n-1) + n \right] I^2 + Q n^3 I^2$$

where I is the image dimension, G is the dimension of the Gaussian filtering pattern, Q is the number of constraint equations defined for each pixel, n is the number of unknowns of the system of equations, and N is the dimension of the area for the multipoint approaches ($N = 0$ for nonmultipoint approaches). For example, the asymptotical complexity on a sequential machine for a multipoint solution based on the OFC without image filtering is $O(N^2 I^2)$ ($G = 0$, $Q = 1$, $n = 2$), if $N^2 > 4$, while the asymptotical complexity on a sequential machine for a nonmultipoint solution based on Q constraint equations and with image filtering in two unknowns is $O(G^2 I^2 + 8 Q I^2)$. The asymptotical complexity on a parallel architecture such as a mesh of $I \times I$ PEs is, in the first case, $O(N^2)$ [12] while in the second case, it is $O(G^2 + 8Q)$, where the complexity is strongly dependent on the dimension G of the Gaussian pattern if $G^2 > Q n^3 > Q n$ (the filtering is dominant). It should be noted that the filtering is usually performed only on one image at each instant, even if the optical flow estimation needs three to five images; hence, by neglecting the initial phase, only one image is filtered each instant.

In order to perform a more accurate evaluation of the computational cost on a mesh-parallel architecture, it should be considered that the first three phases of the algorithm involve data communication among neighboring PEs.

The multiconstraint-based algorithms work locally on the immediate neighborhood of each pixel and, thus, this can be profitably mapped on a mesh architecture, where a PE is assigned to each pixel of the image. Corresponding pixels of consecutive images belonging to the same time window are stored in the same PE. Each PE can directly manage the time history of pixel values and, thus, it estimates the partial derivative of the image brightness with respect to t without involving any communication PE-to-PE [see Eq. (2-6c)].

An early parallel implementation on the Connection Machine-2 architecture of the algorithm presented by Tretiak and Pastor [62] has been proposed by Tistarelli [69], providing quasi-real-time estimations. An example of hardware implementation of the same algorithm can be found in Danielsson et al. [14], where an SIMD machine comprised of 512 processors is proposed to estimate (512×512) optical flow fields in real-time. Parallel implementations for a Connection Machine-2 of the algorithms proposed by Tretiak and Pastor [62] (improving the performance obtained in [69]), Del Bimbo, Nesi, and Sanz [65], and Horn and Schunck [34], have been presented in [12]; where, for the first two implementations, the real-time estimations have been obtained.

The parallel implementation of the solution of Tretiak and Pastor [62] proposed in [12] can be considered a good compromise between complexity and performance, without neglecting that such a solution is able to produce useful results only by working on filtered images or filtering the optical flow fields obtained. The parallel implementation of the multipoint OFC-based algorithm proposed in [65] is qualitatively better and is also faster but it is computationally more complex. From the computational point of view, the first solution adopts the first two equations of (2-10). The solution is obtained directly through the inversion of the Hessian matrix of coefficients. The system is able to produce results only for those points where the determinant ($g_c = E_{xx}E_{yy} - E_{xy}{}^2$) is bigger than a predefined threshold (g_c is directly related with the Gaussian curvature of the image brightness) according to the "problem of aperture" [11]. The components of the optical flow field are estimated in each pixel by using:

$$u_{(i,j,t)} = \frac{E_{xy(i,j,t)}E_{yt(i,j,t)} - E_{yy(i,j,t)}E_{tx(i,j,t)}}{g_{c(i,j,t)}}$$

$$v_{(i,j,t)} = \frac{E_{xy(i,j,t)}E_{tx(i,j,t)} - E_{xx(i,j,t)}E_{yt(i,j,t)}}{g_{c(i,j,t)}} \tag{2-11}$$

where the second-order partial derivatives of the image brightness are estimated by using the central difference on the first-order derivatives—e.g., $E_{xy(i,j,t)} = (E_{x(i,j+1,t)} - E_{x(i,j-1,t)})/2$. This solution is very sensitive to discontinuities, because it uses the second-order derivatives of the image brightness.

In Figure 2.10, some optical flow fields are reported. These have been obtained by using the parallel implementations of the solutions of Tretiak and Pastor [62], and that of Del Bimbo, Nesi, and Sanz [65] as in [12]. An image convolution with a Gaussian filter was adopted for the first solution in [62], and also in our experiments. As can be noted, the solution based on multipoint gives smoother results and is in general better ranked in the presence of discontinuities.

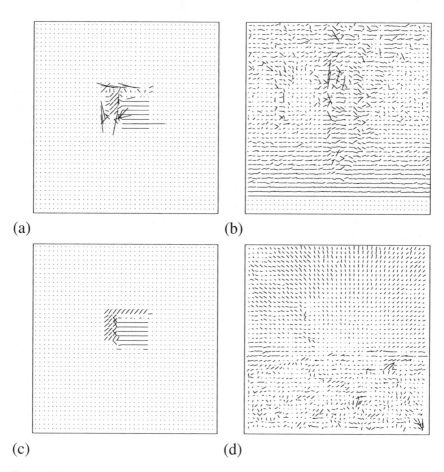

(a)   (b)

(c)   (d)

Figure 2.10 Optical flow fields obtained by using: (a) the solution of Tretiak and Pastor on the 15th sequence frame in Figure 2.4 with $G = 3$; (b) the OFC-based multipoint solution on the 5th sequence frame in Figure 2.5 with $N = 5$; (c) the OFC-based multipoint solution on the 15th sequence frame in Figure 2.4 with $N = 3$; (d) the OFC-based multipoint solution on the 6th sequence frame in Figure 2.8 with $N = 5$.

2.5.2 Clustering-Based Solutions

An overdetermined system of equations can also be profitably solved by using techniques that are very different from the traditional algebraic approaches, such as the least-squares technique with LUD [68]. The adoption of these techniques is easier if the number of unknowns is equal to two, such as in most of the constraint equations for optical flow estimation. In fact, in these cases, for each constraint equation a constraint line can be drawn in the (u, v) plane, as previously shown. Constraint lines representing the same optical flow should intersect at a common point.

The main goal of clustering techniques is to solve the typical problems of the least-squares solutions, in which the solution is located in the point placed at the minimum mean distance between the intersection points among the whole constraint lines. For example, note in Figure 2.11 two different conditions in which the least-squares technique failures are reported. Part (a) reports the typical distribution of constraint lines originated by a generic multiconstraint approach in the presence of noise, where these constraint lines are associated with the same pixel. As can be seen, the least-squares solution is obviously less representative than the solution based on clustering, because the first is located too far from the area in which a high concentration of line intersections is present. Part (b) reports the typical condition originated by a multipoint approach where the $N \times N$ area is placed on the occlusion of two objects having different velocities and, thus, N^2 constraint lines (belonging to two different objects) are present. In this case, it is better to choose one of the two solutions based on clustering and to correctly identify the velocity of a single object instead of accepting a mean value such as that produced by the least-squares approach.

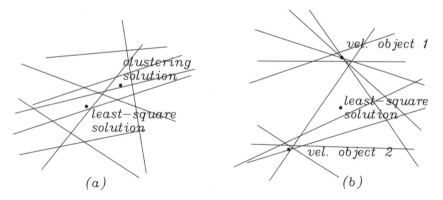

Figure 2.11 Representation of constraint lines on the u, v plane with the corresponding estimations based on least-squares and clustering techniques.

Therefore, a clustering-based technique must be able to identify the most probable solution, instead of the one that can be obtained by means of a least-squares technique, by also considering the constraint lines originated by wrong data.

One of the first clustering-based solutions has been proposed by Fennema and Thompson [66], where a solution based on the Hough transform and OFC has been suggested. This solution is based on the fact that the Hough transform of a line in the (u, v) corresponds to a point in the transformed domain. Lines having a common intersection in the u, v plane produce, in the transformed space, points that are distributed along well-defined curves. The verification of the presence of such curves is computationally heavy, and a large number of constraint lines must be analyzed in order to obtain robust estimations. In fact, in the experiments proposed in [66], the clustering has been performed by using the constraint equations produced by the whole-image pixels.

A different clustering approach for multipoint techniques based on OFC was proposed by Schunck in [35]. The solution is obtained by clustering the intersections of the various constraint lines with the constraint line of the central pixel of the neighborhood. The clustering is performed along the constraint line of the central pixel; hence, the more dominant group of intersections identifies the solution to the optical flow. However, this method relies heavily on the accuracy of the constraint line at the center pixel of each segment, and the resulting optical flow estimation is erroneous if the constraint line at the central pixel is affected by errors, as happens with noisy images.

Ben-Tzvi, Del Bimbo, and Nesi [67] have proposed a multipoint solution based on the OFC following the vote accumulation method. This approach was called *optical flow estimation* from *constraint line parametrization*. It identifies the most likely solution as the point (u, v) where most of the constraint lines in the vicinity of each pixel intersect (see Figure 2.12). By means of this approach, the characteristics of each constraint line are transformed from the (u, v) space in the slope-intercept space (c, m), where each constraint line is represented by a point according to Eq. (2-3). The requirement of a common intersection point in the (u, v) plane of a set of constraint lines is equivalent to the requirement of collinearity of their corresponding points in the parameter plane. The estimation of optical flow in each pixel is thus reduced to finding the best line that matches the pattern of points corresponding to the constraint lines (around each pixel) in the parameter plane (bidimensional clustering). The *best line* is the line on which the largest number of points reside and not the line that gives the minimum accumulative distance to the points. In the following, the best line is referred to as the *characteristic line*.

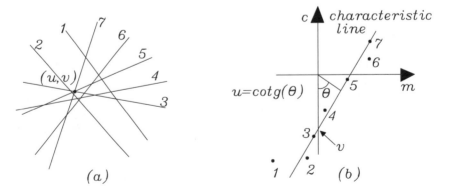

Figure 2.12 Constraint line parametrization: (a) constraint lines with the estimated optical flow vector components (u, v) in the u, v space; (b) corresponding characteristic line in the parameter plane.

Votes are cast using a Hough transform version, the Combinatorial Hough transform [70]. Each couple of points (m_1, c_1) and (m_2, c_2), in the slope-intercept plane, corresponding to a couple of constraint lines, adds a vote to a monodimensional accumulation histogram of the characteristic line θ (see Fig. 2.12):

$$\theta = \arctan\left(-\frac{m_2 - m_1}{c_2 - c_1}\right) \tag{2-12}$$

Therefore, according to the multipoint approach on an $N \times N$ area, there exist $(N^4 - N^2)/2$ couples of constraint equations, and thus solutions. This could lead to an asymptotical complexity equal to $O(I^2 N^4)$. This is simplified by considering only the combinations of the constraint lines associated with the pixels in the $N \times N$ area and the constraint line of the center of the multipoint area; thus, $(N^2 - 1)$ couples of equations and, hence, N^2 votes are obtained. The histogram in θ is inspected to find the most probable value, θ_{max} (the value corresponding to the peak of the histogram). By using that value, a second stage of N^2 votes is used to define another histogram for the other line parameter:

$$r_i = m_i \cos(\theta_{max}) + c_i \sin(\theta_{max}) \tag{2-13}$$

Hence, the best approximation of the characteristic line contains (θ_{max}, r_{max}). Therefore, the optical flow at each pixel is directly derivable from these line parameters:

$$u = \cotg(\theta_{max}); \qquad v = \frac{r_{max}}{\sin(\theta_{max})} \tag{2-14}$$

In Figure 2.13, the optical flow fields are reported, which were obtained by applying the algorithm proposed in [67] to some of the test image sequences previously presented. These fields show the high robustness of this algorithm with respect to noise even if the dimension of the neighborhood area is small.

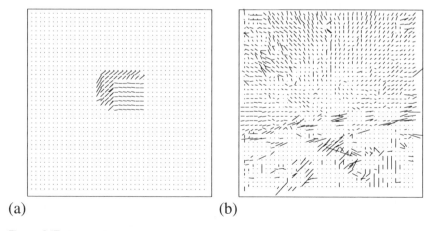

(a)   (b)

Figure 2.13 Optical flow fields obtained by using the solution of Ben-Tzvi, Del Bimbo and Nesi on: (a) the 15th sequence frame in Figure 2.4 with $N = 3$; (b) the 6th sequence frame in Figure 2.8 with $N = 5$.

The above algorithm has been implemented on the Connection Machine-2, with a PE for each image pixel where the algorithm complexity is $O(N^2)$. It should be noted that, though the complexity is similar to other multiconstraint-based algorithms, the real-time estimation has not been obtained, because the inspection of the histograms on the Connection Machine-2 is very expensive [67]. This is due to the fact that distinct PEs share a common memory to store data; therefore, they can access memory only sequentially, thus reducing the algorithm performance [71].

2.6 DISCUSSION AND CONCLUSIONS

Following are general comments on the main characteristics of the algorithms reviewed.

In Table 2.1, a comparison among gradient-based approaches is proposed. The comparison is focused on reporting the structural and the algorithmical characteristics of the algorithms reviewed. The table divides the approaches into

TABLE 2.1 Comparison Among the Gradient-Based Solutions

Algorithms	Iter.	Q	n	Const.	Ord.	PreF	PostF
Horn & Schunck [34]	Yes	2	2	OFC	1	No	No
Nagel [51]	Yes	2	2	OFC	2	No	No
Schnörr [55]	Yes	2	2	OFC	1	No	No
Nesi [11]	Yes	3	3	OFC	1	No	No
Hildreth [52]	Yes	2	1	OFC	1	No	No
Woodham [58]	No	3	2	OFC+A	1	Yes	No
Wohn et al. [60]	No	6	2	OFC+A	2	No	Yes
Markandey et al. [59]	No	2	2	OFC+A	2	Yes	Yes
Haralick & Lee [38]	No	4	2	OFC+B	2	Yes	No
Tretiak & Pastor 1^a [62]	No	2	2	OFC+B	2	Yes	Yes
Verri et al. [39]	No	2	2	OFC+B	2	Yes	Yes
Tretiak & Pastor 2^a [62]	No	3	2	OFC+B	2	Yes	Yes
Cafforio & Rocca [63]	No	N^2	2	OFC+C	1	No	No
Del Bimbo et al. [65]	No	N^2	2	OFC+C	1	No	No
Campani & Verri [64]	No	N^2	6	OFC+C	1	Yes	No
Nesi et al. 1^a [37]	No	N^2	4	EOFC+C	1	No	No
Del Bimbo et al. [40]	No	$3N^2$	2	OFC+B+C	2	No	No
Nesi et al. 2^a [37]	No	$3N^2$	6	EOFC+B+C	2	No	No
Fennema & Thompson [66]	No	I^2	2	OFC	1	Yes	No
Schunck [35]	No	N^2	2	OFC	1	Yes	Yes
Ben-Tzvi et al. [67]	No	N^2	2	OFC+C	1	No	No

N^2 = dimension of the multipoint area

I = the image resolution

regularization- and multiconstraint-based approaches. The first column, Iter., reports if the estimation process is iterative or not; Q is the number of equations; n is the number of unknowns of the system of equations define; the fourth column, Const., reports the approaches adopted to collect the constraint equations according to the classification given in Section 2.5; Ord. is the maximum order of the image brightness partial derivatives involved in the estimation; PreF indicates if the images have to be filtered or not; PostF indicates if the optical-flow-field components have to be filtered or not. Observing this table, it can be noted that most of the multiconstraint-based approaches need prefiltering (on the images) and postfiltering (on the optical flow components), while the multipoint- and regularization-based approaches are capable of producing smoother results directly from the estimation process by using unfiltered sequences of images.

The asymptotical complexities and the performance of several solutions previously compared are reported in Table 2.2. The following symbols are used for

TABLE 2.2 Complexity and Performance Comparisons

Algorithms	$O(\ )$	ETime
Block-matching (this paper)	$M^2 F^2 I^2$	9.1
Horn & Schunck [34]	$I_t I^2$	9.8*
Nesi [11]	$I_t I^2$	16.9*
Haralick & Lee [38]	$G^2 I^2$	37.2
Tretiak & Pastor 1[a] [62]	$G^2 I^2$	17.1
Verri et al. [39]	$G^2 I^2$	33.1
Tretiak & Pastor 2[a] [62]	$G^2 I^2$	35.2
Cafforio & Rocca [63]	$N^2 I^2$	21.6**
Del Bimbo et al. [65]	$N^2 I^2$	4.2
Campani & Verri [64]	$N^2 I^2$	15.3
Nesi et al. 1[a] [37]	$N^2 I^2$	7.1
Del Bimbo et al. [40]	$N^2 I^2$	27.1
Nesi et al. 2[a] [37]	$N^2 I^2$	56.0
Ben-Tzvi et al. [67]	$N^2 I^2$	5.2

$O(\ ) =$ asymptotical complexity

Etime $=$ elapsed CPU time expressed in seconds obtained on an i486 DX at 33 MHz

$M = 5$

$F = 9$

$G = 3$ (postfiltering on the optical flow field)

$N = 3$

$I = 128.$

* elapsed CPU time for each iteration;

** multipoint solution on an area of $N \times N$ (with $N = 3$) and a post-filtering, with $N > G$.

the parameters of interest: $I \times I$ is the size of the image; $M \times M$ is the dimension of the pattern in the block-matching approach; $F \times F$ is the dimension of the searching area in the block-matching approach; I_t is the number of iterations of the regularization-based approaches; $G \times G$ is the dimension of the Gaussian filter (pre- on image or post- on the optical-flow-field components); and $N \times N$ is the size of the neighborhood in multipoint approaches. The last column of Table 2.2 shows the elapsed CPU time measured on an i486 INTEL DX at 33 MHz. These measurements have been obtained in uniform conditions; therefore, they can be used as a measure of the relationship among the algorithms' performance. This means that, in general, for each algorithm an optimal implementation could be defined, thus improving the corresponding performance. The performance obtained on a parallel architecture, such as the Connection Machine-2, can be found in [12].

Tables 2.1 and 2.2 can be very useful to compare in detail the computational complexities of the different algorithms that have been proposed in this chapter.

During the last ten years, several solutions for optical flow estimation have been proposed by using more and more complex constraint equations (e.g., higher-order equations). This increment of complexity is due to the necessity of increasing the quality and precision of the estimations. In effect, in many cases, the increment of complexity is not always associated with an increment of quality in motion estimation. This fact is mainly due to the numerical approximations that must be applied for estimating the partial derivatives of the image brightness.

2.6.1 Conclusions

In the literature, two main approaches that are suitable for real-time motion field estimation can be identified: matching- and gradient-based approaches. Gradient-based approaches can be classified as regularization- and multiconstraint-based techniques. In this chapter, a comparison among the most important and well-known solutions belonging to the above-mentioned approaches was proposed. This comparison was performed by considering their applicability to obtaining estimations in real-time. To this end, their computational complexities and performance were analyzed.

From the qualitative point of view, several of the algorithms reviewed are capable of producing satisfactory optical flow fields if particular attention is given to reducing their drawbacks. As can be seen by observing the results reported in this chapter and in the literature, the multipoint algorithms are in many cases better ranked with respect to the multiconstraint solutions, which estimate the velocity vectors by using equations defined for each single pixel [62, 38]. Therefore, it is preferable to use multipoint solutions in applications where the robust and automatic motion field estimation are needed [13, 72]. On the other hand, the most frequently used algorithms are those derived from the solution of Tretiak and Pastor [62]. This is due to their simplicity of application, and to the fact that problems related to high noise sensitivity are avoided by using strong filtering. This is obviously obtained at the expense of boundary resolution.

On the contrary, the multipoint solutions do not need pre- or post-filtering because a reduction in high frequencies is inherent in the multipoint technique. Therefore, multipoint solutions based on clustering techniques are those that can potentially give the best results; unfortunately, they are computationally heavy and it is quite critical that they be tuned (e.g., resolutions and thresholds of histogram parameters). In our opinion, the multipoint approaches with algebraic solutions are those that achieve the best compromise among performance, complexity, and quality, as was also confirmed by the results reported in [12, 65].

References

[1] K. Prazdny, "On the information in optical flows," *Computer Vision, Graphics, and Image Processing*, vol. 23, pp. 239–259, 1983.

[2] G. Adiv, "Inherent ambiguities in recovering 3-D motion and structure from a noisy field," *IEEE Trans. Pattern Analysis and Machine Intelligence*, vol. 11, pp. 477–489, May 1989.

[3] P. J. Burt, J. R. Bergen, R. Hingorani, R. Kolczynski, W. A. Lee, A. Leung, J. Lubin, and H. Shvaytser, "Object tracking with a moving camera," in *Proc. IEEE Workshop on Visual Motion* (Irvine, CA), pp. 2–12, IEEE Computer Society, 20–22 March 1989.

[4] T. J. Broida and R. Chellappa, "Experiments and uniqueness results on object structure and kinematics from a sequence of monocular images," in *Proc. IEEE Workshop on Visual Motion* (Irvine, CA), pp. 21–30, IEEE Computer Society, 20–22 March 1989.

[5] R. C. Nelson and J. Y. Aloimonos, "Obstacle avoidance using field divergence," *IEEE Trans. Pattern Analysis and Machine Intelligence*, vol. 11, pp. 1102–1106, October 1989.

[6] M. Subbarao, "Bounds on time-to-collision and rotation component from first-order derivatives of image flow," *Computer Vision, Graphics, and Image Processing*, vol. 50, pp. 329–341, 1990.

[7] S. Ullman, *The Interpretation of Visual Motion*. Cambridge, MA and London, England: The MIT Press, 1979.

[8] R. Y. Tsai and T. S. Huang, "Uniqueness and estimation of three-dimensional motion parameters of a rigid object with curved surfaces," *IEEE Trans. Pattern Analysis and Machine Intelligence*, vol. 6, no. 3, 1984.

[9] H. Shariat and K. E. Price, "Motion estimation with more than two frames," *IEEE Trans. Pattern Analysis and Machine Intelligence*, vol. 12, pp. 417–434, May 1990.

[10] A. K. Jain. *Fundamentals of Digital Image Processing*. Englewood Cliffs, NJ: Prentice Hall, 1989.

[11] P. Nesi, "Variational approach for optical flow estimation managing discontinuities," *Image and Vision Computing*, vol. 11, no. 7, pp. 419–439, 1993.

[12] A. Del Bimbo and P. Nesi, "Real-time optical flow estimation," in *Proc. 1993 IEEE Systems, Man and Cybernetics Conf.*, (Le Touquet, France), 17–20 October 1993.

[13] A. Del Bimbo, P. Nesi, and J. L. C. Sanz, "Estimation and interpretation of optical flow fields for counting moving objects," in *Proc. MVA'92 IAPR Workshop on Machine Vision Applications* (NEC Super Tower, Minato-ku, Tokyo, Japan), 7–9 December 1992.

[14] P. Danielsson, P. Emanuelsson, K. Chen, P. Ingelhag, and C. Svensson, "Single-chip high-speed computation of optical flow," in *Proc. Int. Workshop on Machine Vision Applications, MVA'90 IAPR* (Tokyo), pp. 331–335, 28–30 November 1990.

[15] J. H. Duncan and T. Chou, "Temporal edges: the detection of motion and the computation of optical flow," in *Proc. 2nd IEEE Int. Conf. Computer Vision ICCV'88* (Tampa, FL), 1988.

[16] P. J. Burt, C. Yen, and X. Xu, "Multiresolution flow-through motion analysis," in *Proc. IEEE Conf. Computer Vision and Pattern Recognition, CVPR'83* (Washington D.C.), pp. 246–252, 19–23 June 1983.

[17] J. Wang, "A theory of image matching," in *Proc. 3rd IEEE Int. Conf. Computer, Vision ICCV'90* (Osaka, Japan), pp. 200–209, 4–7 December 1990.

[18] A. Borri, G. Bucci, and P. Nesi, "A robust tracking of 3D motion," in *Proc. European Conf. on Computer Vision, ECCV'94* (Stockholm, Sweden), pp. 181–188, 2-6 May 1994.

[19] H. Li, P. Roivainen, and R. Forchheimer, "3-D motion estimation in model-based facial image coding," *IEEE Trans. Pattern Analysis and Machine Intelligence*, vol. 15, pp. 545–555, June 1993.

[20] H. Bülthoff, J. J. Little, and T. Poggio, "A parallel algorithm for a real-time computation of optical-flow," *Nature*, vol. 337, pp. 549–553, 9 February 1989.

[21] F. Glazer, G. Reynolds, and P. Anandan, "Scene matching by hierarchical correlation," in *Proc. IEEE Conf. Computer Vision and Pattern Recognition, CVPR'83* (Washington D.C.), pp. 432–441, 19–23 June 1983.

[22] H. G. Musmann, P. Pirsh, and H.-J. Grallert, "Advances in picture coding," *Proc. IEEE*, vol. 73, pp. 523–548, April 1985.

[23] S. V. Fogel, "Implementation of a nonlinear approach to the motion correspondence problem," in *Proc. IEEE Workshop on Visual Motion* (Irvine, CA), pp. 87–98, IEEE Computer Society, 20–22 March 1989.

[24] W. E. Snyder, A. A. Rajala, and G. Hirzinger, "Image modeling the continuity assumption and tracking," in *Proc. 5th IEEE Int. Conf. Pattern Recognition, ICPR'80* (Florida), pp. 1111–1114, 1–4 December 1980.

[25] M. A. Snyder, "The precision of 3-D parameters in correspondence-based techniques: the case of uniform translational motion in a rigid environment," *IEEE Trans. Pattern Analysis and Machine Intelligence*, vol. 11, pp. 523–541, May 1989.

[26] J. Weng, T. S. Huang, and N. Ahuja, "Estimating motion and structure from line matches: performance obtained and beyond," in *Proc. 10th IEEE Int. Conf. Pattern Recognition, ICPR'90*, pp. 168–172, 16–21 June 1990.

[27] J. A. Noble, "Finding corners," *Image and Vision Computing*, vol. 6, pp. 121–128, May 1988.

[28] P. Anandan, "A computational framework and an algorithm for the measurement of visual motion," *Int. J. Computer Vision*, vol. 2, pp. 283–310, 1989.

[29] C. Longuet-Higgins and K. Prazdny, "The interpretation of a moving retinal image," *Proc. Roy. Soc. London B*, vol. 208, pp. 385–397, 1980.

[30] B. G. Schunck, "The image flow constraint equation," *Computer Vision, Graphics, and Image Processing*, vol. 35, pp. 20–46, 1986.

[31] H.-H. Nagel, "On a constraint equation for the estimation of displacement rates in image sequences," *IEEE Trans. Pattern Analysis and Machine Intelligence*, vol. 11, pp. 13–30, January 1989.

[32] A. Verri and T. Poggio, "Motion field and optical flow: qualitative properties," *IEEE Trans. Pattern Analysis and Machine Intelligence*, vol. 11, pp. 490–498, May 1989.

[33] A. Del Bimbo, P. Nesi, and J. L. C. Sanz, "Analysis of optical flow constraints," *IEEE Trans. Image Processing*, January 1995.

[34] B. K. P. Horn and B. G. Schunck, "Determining optical flow," *Artificial Intelligence*, vol. 17, pp. 185–203, 1981.

[35] B. G. Schunck, "Image flow segmentation and estimation by constraints line and clustering," *IEEE Trans. Pattern Analysis and Machine Intelligence*, vol. 11, pp. 1010–1027, October 1989.

[36] B. G. Schunck, "The motion constraint equation for optical flow," in *Proc. 7th IEEE Int. Conf. on Pattern Recognition*, pp. 20–22, 1984.

[37] P. Nesi, A. Del Bimbo, and J. L. C. Sanz, "Multiconstraints-based optical flow estimation and segmentation," in *Int. Workshop on Computer Architecture for Machine Perception* (Paris), pp. 419–426, DGA/ETCA, CNRS/IEF, and MEN/DRED, December 1991.

[38] R. M. Haralick and J. S. Lee, "The facet approach to optical flow," in *Proc. Image Understanding Workshop Science Applications* (Arlington, VA) (L. S. Baumann, ed.), 1983.

[39] A. Verri, F. Girosi, and V. Torre, "Differential techniques for optical flow," *J. Opt. Soc. Am. A*, vol. 7, pp. 912–922, May 1990.

[40] A. Del Bimbo, P. Nesi, and J. L. C. Sanz, "Optical flow estimation by using classical and extended constraints," in *Proc. 4th Int. Workshop on Time-Varying Image Processing and Moving Object Recognition*, 10–11 June 1993.

[41] J. K. Kearney, W. B. Thompson, and D. L. Boley, "Optical flow estimation: an error analysis of gradient-based methods with local optimization," *IEEE Trans. Pattern Analysis and Machine Intelligence*, vol. 9, pp. 229–244, March 1987.

[42] J. Hadamard, *Sur les problems aux derivees patielles et leur signification physique*, vol. 13. Princeton University Bulletin, 1902.

[43] T. Poggio, "Early vision: from computational structure to algorithms and parallel hardware," *Computer Graphics and Image Processing*, vol. 31, pp. 139–155, 1985.

[44] T. Poggio, V. Torre, and C. Koch, "Computational vision and regularization theory," *Nature*, vol. 317, pp. 314–319, 26 September 1985.

[45] V. Torre and T. Poggio, "On edge detection," *IEEE Trans. Pattern Analysis and Machine Intelligence*, vol. 8, pp. 147–163, March 1986.

[46] D. Terzopoulos, "Regularization of inverse visual problems involving discontinuities," *IEEE Trans. Pattern Analysis and Machine Intelligence*, vol. 8, pp. 413–424, July 1986.

[47] D. Terzopoulos, "Image analysis using multigrid relaxation methods," *IEEE Trans. Pattern Analysis and Machine Intelligence*, vol. 8, pp. 129–139, March 1986.

[48] M. Bertero, T. A. Poggio, and V. Torre, "Ill-posed problems in early vision," *Proc. IEEE*, vol. 76, pp. 869–889, August 1988.

[49] A. N. Tikhonov and V. Y. Arsenin. *Solution of Ill-Posed Problems*. Washington, D.C.: Winston & Sons, 1977.

[50] J. Konrad and E. Dubois, "Multigrid Bayesian estimation of the image motion fields using stochastic relaxation," in *Proc. 2nd IEEE Int. Conf. Computer Vision ICCV'88* (Tampa, FL), pp. 354–362, 1988.

[51] H.-H. Nagel, "Displacement vectors derived from second-order intensity variations in image sequences," *Computer Vision, Graphics, and Image Processing*, vol. 21, pp. 85–117, 1983.

[52] E. C. Hildreth, "Computing the velocity field along contours," in *Motion: Representation and Perception*, (N. I. Badler and J. K. Tsotsos, eds.), pp. 121–127, Elsevier Science Publishing, Co. Inc., by ACM, 1986.

[53] R. Courant and D. Hilbert. *Methods of Mathematical Physic*, vol. 1. New York, London: Interscience Publisher, Inc., 1955.

[54] M. Yachida, "Determining velocity maps by spatio-temporal neighborhoods from image sequences," *Computer Vision, Graphics, and Image Processing*, vol. 21, pp. 262–279, 1983.

[55] C. Schnörr, "Computation of discontinuous optical flow by domain decomposition and shape optimization," *Int. J. Computer Vision*, vol. 8, no. 2, pp. 153–165, 1992.

[56] W. L. Briggs. *A Multigrid Tutorial*. Philadelphia: SIAM, Society for Industrial and Applied Mathematics, 1987.

[57] W. Enkelmann, "Investigation of multigrid algorithms for the estimation of optical flow fields sequences," *Computer Vision, Graphics, and Image Processing*, vol. 43, pp. 150–177, 1988.

[58] R. J. Woodham, "Multiple light source optical flow," in *Proc. 3rd IEEE Int. Conf. Computer Vision ICCV'90* (Osaka, Japan), pp. 42–46, 4–7 December 1990.

[59] V. Markandey and B. E. Flichbaugh, "Multispectral constraints for optical flow computation," in *Proc. 3rd IEEE Int. Conf. Computer Vision ICCV'90* (Osaka, Japan), pp. 38–41, 4-7 December 1990.

[60] K. Wohn, L. S. Davis, and P. Thirft, "Motion estimation based on multiple local constraints and nonlinear smoothing," *Pattern Recognition*, vol. 16, no. 6, pp. 563–570, 1983.

[61] A. Mitiche, Y. F. Wang, and J. K. Aggarwal, "Experiments in computing optical flow with the gradient-based multiconstraint method," *Pattern Recognition*, vol. 20, no. 2, pp. 173–179, 1987.

[62] O. Tretiak and L. Pastor, "Velocity estimation from image sequences with second order differential operators," in *Proc. 7th IEEE Inter. Conf. Pattern Recognition*, pp. 16–19, 1984.

[63] C. Cafforio and F. Rocca, "Tracking moving objects in television images," *Signal Processing*, vol. 1, pp. 133–140, 1979.

[64] M. Campani and A. Verri, "Computing optical flow from an overconstrained system of linear algebraic equations," in *Proc. 3rd IEEE Int. Conf. Computer Vision ICCV'90* (Osaka, Japan), pp. 22–26, 4–7 December 1990.

[65] A. Del Bimbo, P. Nesi, and J. L. C. Sanz, "Optical flow computation using extended constraints," Tech. Rep., Dipartimento di Sistemi e Informatica, Facoltá di Ingegneria, Universitá di Firenze, DSI-RT 19/92, Florence, Italy, 1992.

[66] G. L. Fennema and W. B. Thompson, "Velocity determination in scene containing several moving objects," *Computer Graphics and Image Processing*, vol. 9, pp. 301–315, 1979.

[67] D. Ben-Tzvi, A. Del Bimbo, and P. Nesi, "Optical flow from constraint lines parametrization," *Pattern Recognition*, vol. 26, pp. 1549–1561, November 1993.

[68] W. H. Press, B. P. Flannery, S. A. Teukolsky, and W. T. Vettering. *Numerical Recipes in C*. Cambridge and New York: Cambridge University Press, 1988.

[69] M. Tistarelli, "Computing optical flow: a real time application of the connection machine system, TR V89-1," Tech. Rep., Thinking Machines Corporation, DIST Genova, Cambridge, MA, June 1989.

[70] D. Ben-Tzvi and M. Sandler, "A combinatorial Hough transform," *Pattern Recognition Letters*, vol. 11, no. 3, pp. 167–174, 1990.

[71] T. M. Co., "CM-2 Technical Summary," Tech. Rep., Thinking Machines Corporation, Cambridge, MA, 1989.

[72] A. Del Bimbo and P. Nesi, "Behavioral object recognition from multiple image frames," *Signal Processing*, vol. 27, no. 1, pp. 37–49, 1992.

3

REAL-TIME IMAGE REGULARIZATION
A Neural Computing Perspective
to Enhancement, Filtering, and Restoration

Ling Guan   *Department of Electrical Engineering,*
                 The University of Sydney

3.1 INTRODUCTION

This chapter focuses on the issue of real-time image regularization. As the first step in image processing and analysis, image regularization shapes the raw image data captured from various primary imaging devices so that they are in a format suitable for image analysis or visualization. The image regularization tasks include enhancement, filtering, and restoration.

Image regularization is homogeneous processing that is traditionally based, either on high-dimensional mathematical programming, or on ad hoc heuristic models. The former excludes the appropriate interpretation of the image formation model and drastically reduces the feasibility of real-time processing. The dominance of the global processing techniques in image restoration and statistical and model-based filterings are typical examples [1, 2]. On the other hand, the latter approach tends to oversimplify the scenarios dealt with, and the quality issue becomes of secondary importance. The convolutional enhancement and filtering techniques fall into this category [3, 2]. To some extent, both models ignore the regionally coordinated local structure embedded in the image formation model.

The return to popularity of neural computing gives new light to real-time image processing. Neural computing processes information in a local fashion with regional coordination that is well suited to the sparse nature of the image formation model [2]. Neural computing models have been proposed for restoration [4, 5], edge detection and enhancement [6, 7], image segmentation [8, 9], and surface reconstruction [10].

In this chapter, image regularization in real-time is addressed from a model-based neural computing perspective. First, the regionally coordinated local architecture embedded in image formation is explored. Then, a parallel processing framework is presented that is based on a neural network with hierarchical cluster architecture (NNHCA), utilizing human perception knowledge and the physical structure of the image formation model. Within this framework, real-time image processing algorithms are designed that have massively parallel architectures. Following this, the relationship between the image pixels and the neurons representing the pixels is studied. Based on the studies, discrete optimal neuron evaluation algorithms are presented that substantially reduce the processing time required. It is shown in the chapter that, by using continuous activation functions in the network, the effectiveness of the processing algorithms designed within the framework is further increased without losing efficiency. A scalar algorithm and a vector algorithm are presented.

The framework not only provides a genuine platform for parallelizing algorithms in the well-known space-invariant case, but also recommends feasible real-time solutions to a variety of processing techniques under conditions such as space variance and nonstationarity [1, 3, 2], as well as random uncertainties in the image formation procedure [11–13]. Most of the conditions are difficult, if not impossible, to deal with in real-time by conventional techniques.

3.2 IMAGE FORMATION AND REGULARIZATION

This section introduces the image formation model and the quadratic programming image processing structure. The sparse nature of the models facilitates real-time processing by neural computing.

3.2.1 The Image Formation Model

Let $\mathbf{F}$, $\mathbf{G}$, and $\mathbf{N}$ denote the original image, the observed image, and the random uncertain effect associated with the image formation model, respectively. The size of $\mathbf{F}$, $\mathbf{G}$, and $\mathbf{N}$ is $M \times M$. Then, in model-based image processing, the general image formation model is given by

$$\mathbf{g} = \mathbf{Tf} + \mathbf{n} \qquad (3\text{-}1)$$

where $\mathbf{f}$, $\mathbf{g}$, and $\mathbf{n}$ are the row-wise or column-wise lexicographically ordered vectors of $\mathbf{F}$, $\mathbf{G}$, and $\mathbf{N}$, respectively. The transformation matrix $\mathbf{T}$ is a general representation of the imaging effect. It could be the blurring function in restoration [1], or a piecewise linear/nonlinear model in model-based enhancement [14], or simply the identity matrix in statistical filtering [15]. Due to the local nature in image formation, $\mathbf{T}$ is extremely sparse, with the following structure:

$$\mathbf{T} = \begin{bmatrix} T_{11} & \cdots & T_{1N_1} & & & \phi \\ \vdots & \ddots & & \ddots & & \\ T_{N_1 1} & & \ddots & & \ddots & \\ & \ddots & & \ddots & & T_{M-N_1+1,M} \\ & & \ddots & & \ddots & \vdots \\ \phi & & & T_{M,M-N_1+1} & \cdots & T_{MM} \end{bmatrix} \qquad (3\text{-}2)$$

where $N_1 << M$. The nonzero submatrices T_{ij} are located around the main diagonal. Each of the nonzero submatrices in (3-3) has a structure similar to (3-2).

$$
T_{ij} = \begin{bmatrix}
t_{11}^{<ij>} & \cdots & t_{1N_2}^{<ij>} & & & \phi \\
\vdots & \ddots & & \ddots & & \\
t_{N_2 1}^{<ij>} & & \ddots & & & \ddots \\
& \ddots & & \ddots & & t_{M-N_2+1,M}^{<ij>} \\
& & \ddots & & \ddots & \vdots \\
\phi & & t_{M,M-N_2+1}^{<ij>} & \cdots & & t_{MM}^{<ij>}
\end{bmatrix}
\tag{3-3}
$$

where $N_2 << M$. The block diagonal structure of $\mathbf{T}$ comes from the lexicographic ordering of the images $\mathbf{f}$ and $\mathbf{g}$.

The sparse/localized nature of $\mathbf{T}$ in Eqs. (3-2) and (3-3) shows that the connections between pixels are local with limited regional influence. In many cases, the structure of $\mathbf{T}$ is symmetric. It is also block Toeplitz if $\mathbf{T}$ represents space-invariant imaging systems.

3.2.2 Processing by Quadratic Programming

In linear image formation models (including space invariance, space variance, non-stationarity, and random uncertainties in $\mathbf{T}$), the model-based processing resembles the minimization of a quadratic programming problem:

$$
\min(E) = \mathbf{x}^T \mathbf{A} \mathbf{x} + \mathbf{b}^T \mathbf{x} + c
\tag{3-4}
$$

In (3-4), $\mathbf{A}$, $\mathbf{b}$, and c are functions of $\mathbf{T}$, $\mathbf{n}$ plus other problem-related constraints. $\mathbf{A}$ is a very large sparse matrix, $\mathbf{b}$ is a vector, and c is a constant. The matrix $\mathbf{A}$ has a similar structure to $\mathbf{T}$:

$$
\mathbf{A} = \begin{bmatrix}
A_{11} & \cdots & A_{1P_1} & & & \phi \\
\vdots & \ddots & & \ddots & & \\
A_{P_1 1} & & \ddots & & & \ddots \\
& \ddots & & \ddots & & A_{M-P_1+1,M} \\
& & \ddots & & \ddots & \vdots \\
\phi & & A_{M,M-P_1+1} & \cdots & & A_{MM}
\end{bmatrix}
\tag{3-5}
$$

where

$$
A_{ij} = \begin{bmatrix}
a_{11}^{<ij>} & \cdots & a_{1P_2}^{<ij>} & & & \phi \\
\vdots & \ddots & & \ddots & & \\
a_{P_2 1}^{<ij>} & & \ddots & & & \ddots \\
& \ddots & & \ddots & & a_{M-P_2+1,M}^{<ij>} \\
& & \ddots & & \ddots & \vdots \\
\phi & & a_{M,M-P_2+1}^{<ij>} & \cdots & & a_{MM}^{<ij>}
\end{bmatrix}
\tag{3-6}
$$

The quadratic programming structure in (3-4) either comes directly from the optimization criteria utilized [2], or is converted from an equivalent statistical method [15]. From the viewpoint of mathematical programming, the solution to (3-3) is also the optimal solution to the underlying image regularization task. The conversion of three of the most popular regularization filters to the format shown in (3-4) is given below.

The Pseudo-Inverse Filter

The pseudo-inverse filter is given as

$$\mathbf{f} = \left[\mathbf{T}^T\mathbf{T} + \gamma\mathbf{I}\right]^{-1}\mathbf{T}^T\mathbf{g} \tag{3-7}$$

where γ is a very small positive constant and $\mathbf{I}$ is the identity matrix. The original optimization problem is in the format of (3-4) with $\mathbf{A} = \mathbf{T}^T\mathbf{T} + \gamma\mathbf{I}$, $\mathbf{b} = -\mathbf{T}^T\mathbf{g}$, and $\mathbf{f} = \mathbf{x}$.

The Constrained Least-Squares Filter

The original optimization problem of the constrained least-squares filter is in the format of (3-4)

$$E = \tfrac{1}{2}\|\mathbf{Cf}\|^2 + \tfrac{1}{2}\lambda\left[\|\mathbf{g} - \mathbf{Tf}\|^2 - \|\mathbf{n}\|^2\right] \tag{3-8}$$

Simple mathematical manipulation shows that $\mathbf{A} = \mathbf{C}^T\mathbf{C} + \lambda\mathbf{T}^T\mathbf{T}$, $\mathbf{b} = -\lambda\mathbf{g}^T\mathbf{T}$, $c = \tfrac{1}{2}\left[\|\mathbf{g}\|^2 - \|\mathbf{n}\|^2\right]$, and $\mathbf{f} = \mathbf{x}$.

The Wiener Filter

The Wiener filter is given as

$$\mathbf{f} = \mathbf{R}_f\mathbf{T}^T\left[\mathbf{TR}_f\mathbf{T}^T + \mathbf{R}_n\right]^{-1}\mathbf{g} \tag{3-9}$$

where $\mathbf{R}_f$ and $\mathbf{R}_n$ are the correlation matrices for $\mathbf{f}$ and $\mathbf{n}$, respectively. Although the filter is derived from a statistical criterion, the filter can be readily converted to the quadratic format of (3-4). The original problem in (3-7) can be reformulated by calculating $\mathbf{f}$ from a matrix-vector multiplication

$$\mathbf{f} = \mathbf{R}_f\mathbf{T}^T\mathbf{x} \tag{3-10}$$

after calculating $\mathbf{x}$ from the problem given in (3-4) with $\mathbf{A} = \mathbf{TR}_f\mathbf{T}^T + \mathbf{R}_n$ and $\mathbf{b} = \mathbf{g}$.

3.3   THE PARALLEL PROCESSING FRAMEWORK BY A NEURAL NETWORK WITH HIERARCHICAL CLUSTER ARCHITECTURE

In this section, neural computing is used to convert the quadratic programming structure in (3-4) into a parallel processing framework. It is first shown that the quadratic programming model in (3-4) is equivalent to the general energy function of a neural network. Then, the modeling scheme based on a neural network with hierarchical cluster architecture (NNHCA) is introduced. The framework processes images in a coordinated local processing fashion. It suggests a massive hierarchical real-time parallel processing architecture. Finally, by taking into account the sparse structure of the model, an efficient image partitioning method is presented.

The framework possesses some unique properties that are well suited for the parallelization of image regularization.

1. In digital image processing, the effect of the optical imaging system is local, as described in the previous section. However, the removal of the imaging effect must be coordinated in order to achieve global optimality; that is, to reach the minimum of the quadratic model in (3-4). The optimization procedure simulated by the parallel processing framework takes this fact into account and thus closely reflects the image formation model without losing generality.

2. Statistical processing techniques assume that the image to be processed is an ensemble from a stationary random process so that the algorithms can be designed to be computationally practical. This assumption is rarely true even for an image of medium size where nonstationary regions are easily identified. Because the parallel processing framework is based on the local information, the stationarity assumption is readily justified in most cases. Thus, the mechanism of the framework closely and adaptively simulates the underlying stochastic process.

3. Space-domain processing has always been a formidable task for model-based image processing techniques due to the size of the images being processed. However, the proposed framework easily resolves this problem because the computation involved is inherently local.

3.3.1 The General Neural Computing Model

The structure of the neural model could be any Hopfield-type networks [16]. One of the most popular networks [5] is utilized. The network topology consists of $M^2 \times L$ mutually interconnected neurons. Let $S = \{s_{ik}$ where $1 \leq i \leq M^2$, $1 \leq k \leq L\}$ be a set of binary states of the neural network with s_{iK} (1 for firing and 0 for resting) denoting the state of the (i, k)th neuron. Let $T_{ik,jl}$ denote the strength of the interconnection between neuron (i, k) and neuron (j, l). A symmetry condition is required such that:

$$T_{ik,jl} = T_{jl,ik} \qquad i \leq i, j \leq M^2, \qquad 1 \leq k, l \leq L$$

Neurons are also permitted to have self-feedback, i.e., $T_{ik,ik} \neq 0$. In this model, each neuron receives input from all neurons and a bias input term I_{ik}:

$$t_{ik} = \sum_{j}^{M^2} \sum_{l}^{L} T_{ik,jl} s_{jl} + I_{ik} \qquad (3\text{-}11)$$

Each t_{ik} is fed back to the corresponding neuron after thresholding:

$$s_{ik} = Z(t_{ik}) \tag{3-12}$$

where

$$Z(x) = \begin{cases} 1 & \text{if } x \geq 0 \\ 0 & \text{otherwise} \end{cases} \tag{3-13}$$

In a digital image, each image pixel is described by a finite set of gray-level functions $f_{(i-1)\times M+j}$ that denotes the gray-scale level of pixel (i, j). Assume row-wise order is used when converting $\mathbf{F}$ to $\mathbf{f}$, then the image gray-level function can be represented by a simple sum of the neuron state variables as

$$f_m = \sum_{k=1}^{L} s_{mk} \tag{3-14}$$

where $m = (i - 1) \times M + j$.

The stable state of the neural network model is reached by minimizing the energy function

$$E = -\frac{1}{2} \sum_{i=1}^{M^2} \sum_{j=1}^{M^2} \sum_{k=1}^{L} \sum_{l=1}^{L} T_{ik,jl} s_{ik} s_{jl} - \sum_{i=1}^{M^2} \sum_{k=1}^{L} I_{ik} s_{ik} \tag{3-15}$$

The determination of $T_{ik,jl}$ and I_{ik} can be obtained from Eq. (3-4), as will be shown in the following theorem.

THEOREM 1

The interconnection strengths $T_{ik,jl}$ and the bias inputs I_{ik} in (3-15) are determined from (3-16), and are given by

$$T_{ik,jl} = -a_{ij} \tag{3-16}$$

and

$$I_{ik} = -b_i \tag{3-17}$$

where a_{ij} is the (i, j)th element of the matrix $\mathbf{A}$, and b_i is the ith element of the vector $\mathbf{b}$.

Proof—First, rewrite (3-4) as

$$E = \frac{1}{2} \sum_{i=1}^{M^2} \sum_{j=1}^{M^2} a_{ij} f_i f_j + \sum_{i=1}^{M^2} b_i g_i + c \tag{3-18}$$

Substituting (3-16) into (3-18) yields

$$E = \frac{1}{2} \sum_{i=1}^{M^2} \sum_{j=1}^{M^2} a_{ij} \sum_{k=1}^{L} s_{ik} \sum_{l=1}^{L} s_{jl} + \sum_{i=1}^{M^2} b_i \sum_{k=1}^{L} s_{ik}$$

$$= -\frac{1}{2} \sum_{i=1}^{M^2} \sum_{j=1}^{M^2} \sum_{k=1}^{L} \sum_{l=1}^{L} (-a_{ij}) s_{ik} s_{jl} - \sum_{i=1}^{M^2} \sum_{k=1}^{L} (-b_i) s_{ik} + c \tag{3-19}$$

Comparing (3-19) with (3-15) and ignoring the constant term c, we obtain (3-16) and (3-17).

———

Hence, $T_{ik,jl}$ and I_{ik} are completely determined by known quantities. Therefore, they can be computed a priori.

3.3.2 Neural Networks with Hierarchical Cluster Architecture

NNHCA was first introduced by Sutton et al. [17, 18]. It is a multilevel neural network consisting of nested clusters of units capable of hierarchical memory and learning tasks. The architecture has a fractal-like structure in that each level of the organization consists of interconnected arrangements of neural clusters. Individual units in the model form the zeroth level of cluster organization. Local groupings among the units, via certain types of connections, produce the first-level clusters. Other connections link the first-level clusters to the second level, while the coalescence of the second-level clusters yields the third-level clusters, and so on. A typical three-level NNHCA is shown in Figure 3.1. There is considerable evidence suggesting that networks of this type are abundant in the cerebral cortex [17].

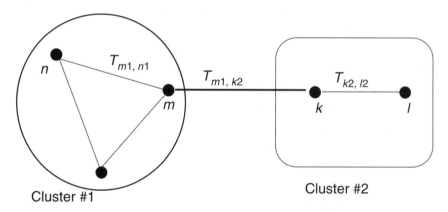

Figure 3.1 A three-level neural network with hierarchical cluster architecture; ● represents the level zero clusters (individual neurons), ——— represents the boundary for level one clusters, and ——— represents the boundary for level two cluster.

In general, the energy function of such a system is complicated. The equilibrium, or the optimal state of NNHCA, is reached by means of a mean field theory (MFT) learning approach proposed by Sutton [19].

3.3.3   The Processing Framework

The processing framework was first introduced to image restoration [20, 21], and later extended to general image regularization tasks [22, 15]. The processing framework consists of four levels of information processing. The zeroth level represents the individual information units, or the neurons, the first level simulates optimization that governs local processing, the second level acts as a link for information exchange between the local clusters in the first level, and the third level coordinates the complete process.

The number of second-level units is equal to the number of first-level clusters. The states of the neurons in the second level is binary (1 for TRUE and 0 for FALSE). Initially, each first-level cluster registers a FALSE status at its corresponding second-level unit, indicating that the cluster is in an unoptimized state.

The NNHCA model has a similar architecture of four levels of processing units; however, the NNHCA model must be modified as follows:

1. In Sutton's model [17, 18], each unit belongs to only one cluster; however, the image formation model may require that the units representing image pixels on the boundaries of clusters belong to two or more adjacent clusters [21].

2. Due to the boundary problem, the optimization procedure is broken into several stages. For the first level, a modified Hopfield learning scheme is applied. A simple but effective heuristic approach is used to execute the second-level information exchange.

The processing carried out at each level is described in detail in the following steps:

The Zeroth Level—Individual Neurons.   The zeroth level clusters are individual neurons. The states of the neurons are changed during regularization according to the processing carried out in the first level.

The First Level—Local Image Processing.   To utilize NNHCA, the recorded image **g** is partitioned into small regions or clusters to satisfy the requirement of locality. A few guidelines should be followed in the partitioning process:

1. From the viewpoint of NNHCA, the shape of a region is arbitrary. However, the image formation process suggests that squares or hexagons are preferred [2]. In this chapter, squares are used.

2. Let the size of a region be $M_* \times M_*$, $1 \leq M_* \leq M$ for **g**, and $(M_* + N_1 - 1) \times (M_* + N_2 - 1)$ for **f**. If $M_* = 1$, the most localized partition is achieved. On the other hand, if $M_* = M$, there is no locality in the partition. The value of M_* should be chosen such that it is large enough to avoid excessive overlap between adjacent regions but small enough to ensure significant parallelism. An appropriate choice for M_* is $8 \leq M_* \leq 32$. For homogeneous processing, it is convenient to choose M_* such that M/M_* is an integer.

3. The partition is overlapped with respect to **f** because the pixels in the boundary areas may belong to adjacent regions simultaneously. The size of the overlap regions contains $M_* \times (N_1 - 1)/2$ pixels for rows and $M_* \times (N_2 - 1)/2$ pixels for columns. An example of the partition is given in Figure 3.2, where the inner area represents a cluster in **g**, the shaded area represents the overlap, and the union of the two represents the corresponding cluster in **f**.

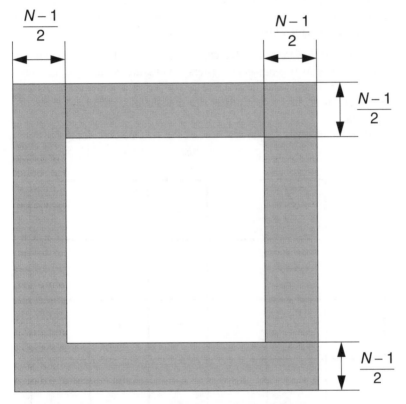

Figure 3.2 A cluster in the recorded and the original image. The inner white area represents a cluster in the recorded image, the shaded area represents overlap in the original image, and the union of the two represents the corresponding cluster in the original image.

The optimization criterion used in processing at the first level can be chosen from the criteria mentioned in Section 3.2. Based on the image formation model in (3-1), contribution to formation can be split into two parts. By rearranging the columns of **T**, Eq. (3-1) is rewritten as

$$\tilde{\mathbf{g}} = \tilde{\mathbf{T}}\tilde{\mathbf{f}} + \tilde{\mathbf{n}} = \begin{bmatrix} \mathbf{T}_1 & \mathbf{T}_2 \end{bmatrix} \begin{bmatrix} \mathbf{f}_1 \\ \mathbf{f}_2 \end{bmatrix} + \tilde{\mathbf{n}} = \mathbf{T}_1\mathbf{f}_1 + \mathbf{T}_2\mathbf{f}_2 + \tilde{\mathbf{n}} \qquad (3\text{-}20)$$

where $\mathbf{T}_1\mathbf{f}_1$ represents the contribution due to the pixels completely within the cluster, and $\mathbf{T}_2\mathbf{f}_2$ represents the contribution due to the boundary pixels in the shaded area in Figure 3.2. It may be seen that $\mathbf{T}_1$ is a square matrix of size $M_*^2 \times M_*^2$, and $\mathbf{T}_2$ is a matrix of size $M_*^2 \times (2M_* + N_1 - 1)(N_2 - 1)$.

Then the optimization criteria given in Section 3.2.2 and the neuron computing model given in Section 3.3.1 can be modified to accommodate the partitioning scheme. A complete description of the modification is given in [21]. Note that only elements in $\mathbf{f}_1$ are treated as variables during neuron evaluation carried out in this cluster because the elements of $\mathbf{f}_2$ are kept constant in the same time (due to the coordination scheme introduced in the next section).

The Second Level—Information Exchange.   As the boundary pixels (units) must be included in at least two adjacent clusters, conflicting boundary conditions are encountered if two adjacent clusters are processed simultaneously. A scheme is instrumented to avoid such conflicts. In the scheme, level one processing is split into phases. In each phase, only clusters without common boundaries are processed simultaneously. Figure 3.3 shows the scheme containing four phases. In Figure 3.3, each square represents a cluster. Clusters in the four phases are

1	2	1	2	1	2
3	4	3	4	3	4
1	2	1	2	1	2
3	4	3	4	3	4
1	2	1	2	1	2
3	4	3	4	3	4

Figure 3.3 The ordering scheme, with four phases in information exchange.

marked 1, 2, 3, and 4, respectively. Clearly, this strategy eliminates the contention. In the following description, a serial execution of the four phases is called a *sweep*.

A sweep is executed as follows:

1. In phase 1, neurons in clusters belonging to group 1 evolve. The initial states of the neurons correspond to initial image pixel values.

2. After equilibrium is reached for group 1, phase 2 begins. The neurons common to group 1 and group 2 take their initial states as the values reached at the end of phase 1.

3. After equilibrium is reached for group 2, phase 3 begins. The neurons common to at least two of the three groups take their initial states as the values reached at the end of phase 1 or phase 2, whichever is relevant.

4. After equilibrium is reached for group 3, phase 4 begins. The neurons common to at least two of the four groups take their initial states as the values reached at the end of phase 1, phase 2, or phase 3, whichever is relevant.

At the end of each phase, the status values of the clusters in the phase are changed to TRUE and the corresponding E_e's are recorded. Because the processing of the later phases might change the results of the earlier phases, the energy term E_e will be used to check if an optimal solution has been reached. After each sweep, the energy E for each cluster is calculated and compared with its respective E_e. For any cluster that has the difference $E - E_e$ greater than a predefined constant, it is said that the optimal status for that cluster is violated. The status value for that cluster is changed to FALSE. If the optimal status of one or more clusters is violated, another sweep will be executed for those clusters utilizing the current states as initial settings. So the function of level two is to check the local optimal condition. The procedure carries on until a globally stable state is reached.

The Third Level—Global Coordination. The third-level processing is straightforward as it contains only one neuron. The inputs to the neuron are the status values of level-one clusters stored at level two. After each level-one processing sweep is finished, the status values are summed at the third-level neuron. The sum S_c is compared with a predefined threshold $T = N_c$, the number of level-one clusters. If

$$T = S_c \qquad (3\text{-}21)$$

the restoration is complete. Otherwise, level-one processing continues.

It should be noted from the algorithm described above that the status values for all clusters will be TRUE immediately after the last phase is complete. The summation should be performed after the $E - E_e$ term is checked for each level-one cluster and the status values are adjusted.

When all the clusters eventually achieve equilibrium [Eq. (3-21) is satisfied], the level-three neuron emits a signal indicating that the optimization process is complete. The restored image is then constructed using (3-14).

When all the clusters achieve equilibrium, the processing is complete. Then the image is constructed.

3.3.4 A New Image Partitioning Scheme

More work has been done recently on the parallel processing framework [15]. One important part to the improved framework is the introduction of a new image partitioning scheme. By using this partitioning scheme, the problem of conflicting boundary conditions is effectively resolved. Using this scheme, all clusters may be processed simultaneously. This partitioning scheme takes into account the physical nature of the image formation model and is described below.

As long as the size of the partition M_* satisfies

$$M_* \geq \max\{2 * P_1 - 1, 2 * P_2 - 1\} \tag{3-22}$$

the conflicting boundary conditions can be avoided, provided that only neurons in different clusters that have the same row and column indices evolve simultaneously.

It is shown in [15] that to process a particular image pixel, only the information in a rectangular area surrounding the pixel is needed. The size of the area is $2 * P_1 - 1 \times 2 * P_2 - 1$. Due to the inequality in (3-22), no pixels are used by more than one cluster at the same time. Thus, the problem of conflicting boundary conditions is eliminated. A graphical interpretation of this partition scheme is shown in Figure 3.4.

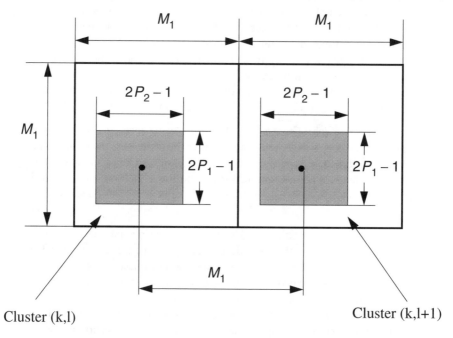

Figure 3.4 The new image partitioning scheme. The pixels being processed simultaneously in different clusters have the same within-cluster indices.

3.4 OPTIMAL NEURON EVALUATION

Information processing is carried out by neuron evaluation. Once the parameters $T_{ik,jl}$ and I_{ik} are computed, each neuron can randomly and asynchronously evaluate its state and adjust accordingly. The recorded image is taken as the initial state. When one minimum energy point (either global or local) is reached, the processing is complete. Therefore, neuron evaluation is an integral part of the real-time processing model. The neural computing framework provides a parallel processing structure. Neuron evaluation has a direct impact on the overall processing efficiency. This section shows that, within the framework, various optimal neuron evaluation algorithms can be designed independent of the particular processing tasks being considered.

3.4.1 Discrete Neuron Evaluation

The discrete neuron evaluation (DNE) algorithms are directly applicable to the framework presented in the previous section. Several DNE algorithms were reported in the literature [20, 23, 4, 5]. Here, only the most efficient one is presented. To utilize the algorithm, it is necessary to show that the system in (3-4) represents a symmetric positive definite quadratic programming (SPD-QP) problem. The SPD-QP structure of (3-4) can be verified by showing that $\mathbf{A}$ is symmetric positive definite (SPD). Because the matrix $\mathbf{A}$ can generally be decomposed into a matrix product $\mathbf{T}^T\mathbf{R}\mathbf{T}$, as shown in Section 3.2, it will be shown that the matrix product $\mathbf{T}^T\mathbf{R}\mathbf{T}$ is symmetric positive definite if the square matrix $\mathbf{T}$ has full column rank, and the matrix $\mathbf{R}$ is symmetric positive definite.

THEOREM 2
The matrix product $\mathbf{T}^T\mathbf{R}\mathbf{T}$ is SPD if the square matrix $\mathbf{T}$ has full column rank, and the matrix $\mathbf{R}$ is symmetric positive definite.

Proof—Proof of symmetry is straightforward because

$$\sum_{i,j} t_{ki} r_{ij} t_{kj} = \sum_{i,j} t_{kj} r_{ij} t_{ki}$$

where r_{ij} is the (i, j)th element of $\mathbf{R}$.

Now the positive definiteness is verified. Let $\mathbf{y} = \mathbf{T}\mathbf{x}$. Because $\mathbf{R}$ is SPD, the quadratic form $\mathbf{y}^T\mathbf{A}\mathbf{y}$ satisfies

$$\mathbf{y}^T\mathbf{R}\mathbf{y} \geq 0 \qquad (3\text{-}23)$$

Equality is reached when $\mathbf{y} = \mathbf{T}\mathbf{x} = \mathbf{0}$.

The property of full column rank for $\mathbf{T}$ implies that the system of homogeneous equations

$$\mathbf{T}\mathbf{x} = \mathbf{0} \qquad (3\text{-}24)$$

has only the trivial solution $\mathbf{x} = \mathbf{0}$. Therefore, equality in (3-23) is reached only when $\mathbf{x} = \mathbf{0}$. Thus, the matrix product of $\mathbf{T}^T\mathbf{R}\mathbf{T}$ is positive definite.

Because **R** is either a correlation matrix or the identity, it is generally SPD. The condition of full column rank for **T** can normally be satisfied in image regularization. In turn, matrix **A** is SPD and the solution to (3-4) is unique.

For the SPD-QP problem in (3-4), the uniqueness of the solution means that, whatever search direction is taken, the value of E can always be decreased unless the current point is within the vicinity of the minimum point for that direction. Because E is a function of f_i; $i = 1, \ldots, M^2$, the state transition of neuron s_{ik} is simply a one-step minimization of the energy function along a specific direction f_i when the values of f_j; $j = 1, 2, \ldots, i-1, i+1, \ldots, M^2$ are fixed.

Observation of (3-16) and (3-17) indicates that $T_{ik, jl}$ is a function of i, j, and I_{ik} is a function of i. The subscripts k and l can be dropped so that $T_{ik, jl} = T_{ij}$ and $I_{ik} = I_i$. Hence, if the state transition of neuron s_{ik} results in a decrease in E, the state transition of any neuron s_{in} with the same current state as s_{ik}, i.e.,

$$s_{ik} = s_{in} \tag{3-25}$$

will result in the same amount of decrease in E because

$$
\begin{aligned}
\Delta E_{in} &= -\left[\sum_{j}^{M^2} T_{ij} \sum_{l}^{L} s_{jl} + I_i\right] \Delta s_{in} - \frac{T_{ik;ik} \Delta s_{in}^2}{2} \\
&= -\left[\sum_{j}^{M^2} T_{ij} \sum_{l}^{L} s_{jl} + I_i\right] \Delta s_{ik} - \frac{T_{ik;ik} \Delta s_{ik}^2}{2} \\
&= \Delta E_{ik}
\end{aligned} \tag{3-26}
$$

However, the state transition of any neuron s_{im} with the opposite state as s_{ik},

$$s_{im} = 1 - s_{ik} \tag{3-27}$$

will result in an increase in E unless the current point is within the vicinity of the minimum along f_i due to the SPD-QP structure of (3-4). Again, by using the uniqueness of the solution to the SPD-QP problem of (3-4), the order of neuron evaluation should not affect the final outcome.

Considering the physical interpretation of gray-scale function, the algorithm can be further optimized. Let the gray-scale value for f_i in iteration m be N_i such that $0 \le N_i \le 255$. A physically meaningful value assignment for s_{ik} is that

$$s_{ik} = \begin{cases} 1 & \text{if } 0 \le k < N_i \\ 0 & \text{otherwise} \end{cases} \tag{3-28}$$

because the nonzero neurons should be consecutively numbered to form a physically realizable picture. Expression (3-28) suggests that only neurons with index k close to N_i may change their states in one iteration during neuron evaluation. The following is the optimal DNE algorithm.

Algorithm I: Optimal Discrete Neuron Evaluation.

1. Take the distorted image **g** as the initial estimate of **f**, and record N_i for each f_i.

2. In each iteration, for each image pixel f_i: visit the neurons s_{ik} sequentially, starting from $k = N_i$, and decreasing to $k = 0$ for index k (checking to see if the gray-scale value of f_i should be decreased).

3. Until for some k_1, the state transition of a neuron s_{ik_1} does not result in a decrease in E, i.e., $\Delta E_{ik_1} < 0$, set

$$s_{ik} \leftarrow s_{ik} + \Delta s_{ik} \tag{3-29}$$

where $\Delta s_{ik} = -1$. Figure 3.5a shows this case.

4. Once the aforementioned k_1 is encountered, k_1 is checked against N_i.

   • If $k_1 < N_i$, no more state transitions of s_{ik} are needed. The energy function E is at its minimum with respect to f_i. N_i is set to

   $$N_i \leftarrow k_1 \tag{3-30}$$

   • Else if $k_1 = N_i$, go to step 5.

5. Visit s_{ik}, in the increasing order of the index k, $N_i < k < L$ starts (checking to see if the gray-scale value of f_i should be increased),

6. Until for some k_2, the state transition of a neuron s_{ik_2} does not result in a decrease in E, i.e., $\Delta E_{ik} < 0$, set

$$s_{ik} \leftarrow s_{ik} + \Delta s_{ik} \tag{3-31}$$

where $\Delta s_{ik} = 1$. Figure 3.5b shows this case.

7. Once k_2 is identified, no more state transitions are needed. The energy function is at its minimum with respect to f_i. Then N_i is set to

$$N_i \leftarrow k_2 - 1 \tag{3-32}$$

3.4.2 Scalar Continuous Neuron Evaluation

The optimal DNE algorithm significantly increases the processing speed; however, the DNE algorithms are not optimal because, at best, a bidirectional search is required. Because the connection weights are identical to the neurons belonging to the same pixel, the neuron evaluation may start from (3-18). The neural network in (3-18) has M^2 neurons. The neuron states of the network take continuous values $0 \le f_i \le L; i = 1, 2, \ldots, M^2$. Neuron evaluation can be carried out in a continuous fashion. It was shown that the continuous neuron evaluation is equivalent to gradient optimization in a dimension by dimension sense [24]. Although the scalar continuous neuron evaluation (SCNE) algorithm is defined in the context of neural computing, it is more intuitive to consider it from a gradient optimization perspective.

Gradient optimization in image regularization problems involves the following procedures:

• Differentiate E with respect to $\mathbf{f}$:

$$\frac{\partial E}{\partial \mathbf{f}} = \mathbf{A}\mathbf{f} + \mathbf{b} \tag{3-33}$$

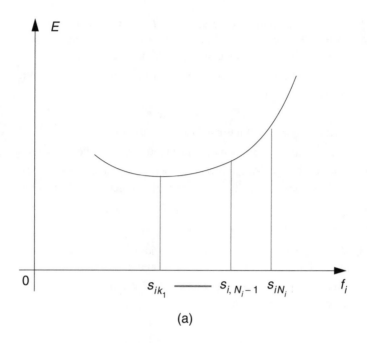

(a)

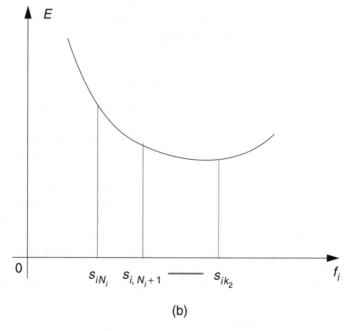

(b)

Figure 3.5 Search in Algorithm 1: (a) reduce the pixel value to reach the minimum along the current axis and (b) increase the pixel value to reach the minimum along the current axis.

- Set (3-33) equal to zero and solve for $\mathbf{f}$:

$$\mathbf{f} = \mathbf{A}^{-1}\mathbf{b} \tag{3-34}$$

The mathematics of (3-33) and (3-34) is straightforward, but the solution involves inverting a matrix $\mathbf{A}$ of size $M^2 \times M^2$, which is not practical in the space domain. However, because the structure of (3-33) is SPD, an iterative implementation of (3-34) can also reach the global minimum. Therefore, instead of inverting the matrix, an iterative algorithm is introduced. Like the DNE algorithm, this algorithm searches for the minimum along f_i. However, due to the SPD structure, the search is done in a single step. The following describes the SCNE algorithm.

Algorithm 2: Scalar Continuous Neuron Evaluation Algorithm.

1. Take the distorted image $\mathbf{g}$ as the initial estimate of $\mathbf{f}$.
2. In each iteration, for each image pixel f_i, keep the values of all f_k; $k = 1, \ldots, M^2$, $k \neq i$ unchanged.
3. Differentiate E with respect to f_i to obtain:

$$\frac{\partial E}{\partial f_i} = \sum_{k=1}^{M^2} a_{ik} f_k + b_i \tag{3-35}$$

4. Set (3-35) equal to zero and solve for f_i:

$$f_i^* = -\frac{1}{a_{ii}} \left\{ b_i + \sum_{k=1, k \neq i}^{M^2} a_{ik} f_k \right\} \tag{3-36}$$

f_i^* is the local optimum point along the current coordinate.

By comparing Algorithm 2 with Algorithm 1, it can be seen that Algorithm 2 is more efficient because the minimum with respect to each coordinate is guaranteed to be reached in one step. If sequential processing is restricted to intrapixel neurons, and interpixel processing is carried out in parallel, Algorithm 2 is a continuous implementation of the neural computing scheme. Here, each pixel is considered as a neuron, the state of which takes continuous values between 0 and L.

3.4.3 Vector Continuous Neuron Evaluation

The scalar neuron evaluation algorithms (discrete and continuous) achieve the maximum possible parallelism in image regularization. The nature of the algorithms, however, is heavily localized, which may affect the quality of processing. For example, if the optimal point lies in an elongated valley, scalar neuron evaluation algorithms may not be able to reach the ideal solution.

This problem is alleviated by a vector continuous neuron evaluation (VCNE) algorithm [15], which processes images row by row (or column by column). In other words, neurons representing pixels in the same row/column are processed simultaneously. It has a vector quadratic programming (VQP) structure evolved from the well-known Gauss-Seidel method [25].

To utilize the algorithm, Eq. (3-34) is rewritten as

$$\mathbf{Af} = \begin{bmatrix} A_{11} & \cdots & A_{1P_1} & & & & \phi \\ \vdots & \ddots & & \ddots & & & \\ A_{P_11} & & \ddots & & & \ddots & \\ & \ddots & & \ddots & & & A_{M-P_1+1,M} \\ & & \ddots & & \ddots & & \vdots \\ \phi & & & A_{M,M-P_1+1} & \cdots & & A_{MM} \end{bmatrix} \begin{bmatrix} \mathbf{f}_1 \\ \mathbf{f}_2 \\ \vdots \\ \mathbf{f}_M \end{bmatrix} = \begin{bmatrix} \mathbf{b}_1 \\ \mathbf{b}_2 \\ \vdots \\ \mathbf{b}_M \end{bmatrix}$$

$$(3\text{-}37)$$

where A_{ij} are matrices themselves, and $\mathbf{f}_i$ and $\mathbf{b}_i$ are columns of $\mathbf{f}$ and $\mathbf{b}$, respectively. The vector neuron evaluation algorithm evolves from the above expression immediately.

Algorithm 3: Vector Continuous Neuron Evaluation.

1. For $i = 1, 2, \ldots, M$, compute

$$\mathbf{f}_i^{\text{new}} = A_{ii}^{-1} \left[\mathbf{b}_i - \sum_{k \neq i} A_{ik} \mathbf{f}_k \right] \qquad (3\text{-}38)$$

2. If

$$\| \mathbf{f}^{\text{new}} - \mathbf{f}^{\text{old}} \| \leq \epsilon \qquad (3\text{-}39)$$

where ϵ is a predefined positive constant, stop iteration. Otherwise, go back to step 1.

The structure of matrix $\mathbf{A}$ ensures that many computational advantages can be utilized in the processing. Interested readers can refer to [15].

As the VQP method processes the image one column/row at a time, instead of a pixel at a time as the scalar optimal neuron evaluation algorithms do, it significantly increases the probability that the real solution is reached at the end of the process. The trade-off here is that, theoretically, parallelism is not utilized at the maximum possible level. However, if the algorithm is executed in parallel by a Jacobi-like algorithm [25] instead of a Gaussian-Seidel-like algorithm, reasonable real-time requirements can be achieved in many practical applications.

The relationship between the three algorithms presented in this section and the traditional global algorithm is graphically illustrated in Figure 3.6. When parallel processing hardware is used in computation, the efficiency–effectiveness trade-off shown in Figure 3.6 is valid as long as the following condition is satisfied

$$KM^2 > S \qquad (3\text{-}40)$$

where S is the number of processing elements, $K \geq 10$ is a positive integer, and M^2 is the image size. If condition (3-40) is violated, SCNE and DNE may swap their positions in the figure.

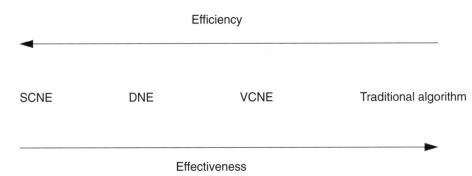

Figure 3.6 Efficiency versus effectiveness of the proposed neuron evaluation algorithms.

3.5 APPLICABILITY OF THE FRAMEWORK AND THE ALGORITHMS

From the above analysis, it can be seen that the establishment of the framework and the optimal neuron evaluation algorithms do not require any extra conditions as long as the problem can be cast into the quadratic programming model in (3-4). Therefore, space-variance, nonstationarity, uncertainties within $\mathbf{T}$, and other difficult conditions are accounted for. Processing speed under the difficult conditions is virtually the same as that of the well-known space-invariant case. This fact is very important to the efficiency issue because the traditional technique of frequency-domain processing only provides solutions to space-invariant and stationary conditions. However, space-invariance and stationarity imply that the structure of matrix $\mathbf{A}$ is block Toeplitz. The storage requirement for such a matrix is of order $O(P_1 P_2)$ instead of $O(4 P_1 P_2 M^2)$, as required by the general case.

3.6 EXAMPLES

In this section, image processing examples are used to demonstrate the performance of the processing framework and the neuron evaluation algorithms. Two application examples will be given: restoration and statistical filtering.

3.6.1 Image Restoration

It is universally accepted that the energy of the point spread function of an optical system is restricted in a finite spatial area [1, 2]. The fact is particularly true for digital systems due to truncation errors. The application of NNHCA to restoration is straightforward. In Eq. (3-1), $\mathbf{f}$ is the original image, and the transformation operator $\mathbf{T}$ becomes a Toeplitz matrix $\mathbf{H}$, underlying the effect of the point spread function. The support for $\mathbf{H}$ is $N \times N$; $N << M$. Hence, only N^2 pixels in $\mathbf{f}$

contribute to the formation of a particular pixel in **g**, and image formation is a local process. Only a finite number of pixels in the recorded image **g** contains relevant information to restore a particular pixel in the original image **f**. Hence, image restoration techniques with local structures should perform as well as, if not better than, those with global structures.

The optimization criterion used in the first level of the neural computing framework is the constrained least-squares filter as shown in (3-8). The result of the experiment is summarized in Figure 3.7.

Image "Lena" shown in Figure 3.7a is of size 256×256. The image was degraded by convolving with a 5×5 uniform point spread function. After convolution, 20 dB white Gaussian noise was added. Figure 3.7b shows the distorted image. The framework proposed in the previous sections was applied to this example. The size of a region was 32×32, so that each of the first-order clusters contains $32 \times 32 \times 256$ units for DNE (refer to Section 3.1), and 32×32 units for SCNE and VCNE. DNE and SCNE needed an average of three iterations for the first sweep. It was found that only 9 out of the 64 first-level clusters needed a second sweep. After the second sweep, the overall network entered a stable condition. The restored images were constructed and are shown in Figures 3.7c, and d, respectively. As expected, there is no visual difference in the two restored images. For VCNE, neurons in the same column in each cluster were processed simultaneously. Ten iterations were needed for the processing. The restored image is shown in Figure 3.7e.

3.6.2   Statistical Image Filtering

In filtering, the meanings of **g**, **f**, and **n** in (3-1) are kept unchanged. However, the transformation operator **T** is simply the identity matrix **I**. The minimum mean-square error (MMSE) criterion was used in the statistical filtering. The matrix **A** is given as

$$\mathbf{A} = \mathbf{R}_f + \mathbf{R}_n \tag{3-41}$$

Image "Lake" in Figure 3.8a was used in the experiment. The size of the image is 128×128. The original image was corrupted by 15 dB white Gaussian noise, which is shown in Figure 3.8b. The proposed framework was tailored to suit MMSE criterion. The size of a region was again 32×32, so that each of the first-order clusters contains $32 \times 32 \times 256$ units for DNE, and 32×32 units for SCNE and VCNE. DNE and SCNE needed an average of five iterations for the first sweep. Three out of the 16 first-level clusters needed a second sweep. After another two sweeps, the overall network entered a stable condition. The filtered images were constructed and are shown in Figures 3.8c and d, respectively. Again, there is no visual difference in the two filtered images. For VCNE, neurons in the same column in each cluster were processed simultaneously. Fifteen iterations were required for the processing. The result is shown in Figure 3.8e.

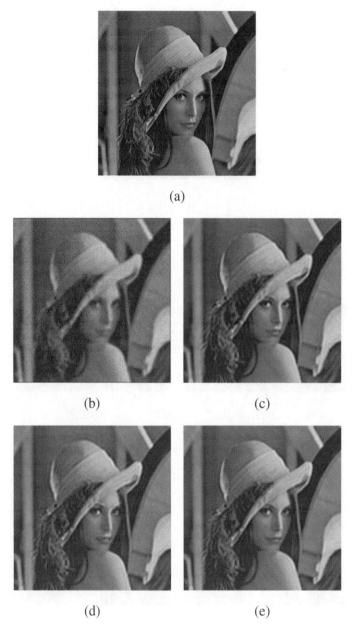

(a)

(b)   (c)

(d)   (e)

Figure 3.7 An image restoration example: (a) image *Lena*, (b) the distorted version of *Lena*, (c) restoration by DNE, (d) restoration by SCNE, and (e) restoration by VCNE.

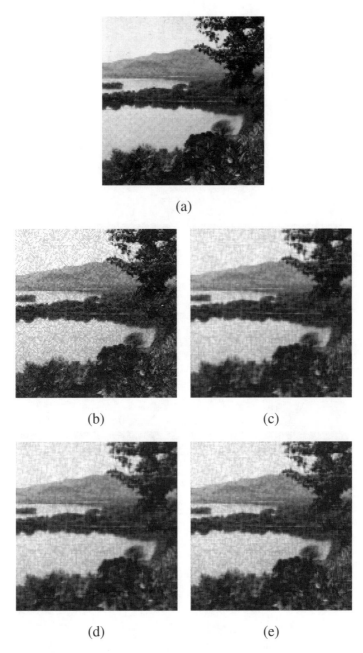

(a)

(b)   (c)

(d)   (e)

Figure 3.8 A statistical filtering example: (a) image *Lake*, (b) noise corrupted version of *Lake*, (c) filtering by DNE, (d) filtering by SCNE, and (e) filtering by VCNE.

3.7 CONCLUSIONS

In conclusion, a neural network with hierarchical cluster architecture can form a processing platform that is highly suitable for implementing image regularization algorithms. It is proposed that the incorporation of the local nature of the image formation model and the quadratic programming structure of the model-based regularization techniques enable the processing methods to be heavily parallelized and the processing algorithms to be effectively optimized. The parallel processing framework is much more general than the conventional processing techniques. It not only processes the well-known space-invariant data in real-time but brings the time-consuming space-variant, nonstationary, and other difficult cases into the real-time processing era.

References

[1] H. C. Andrews and B. R. Hunt. *Digital Image Restoration*. Englewood Cliffs, NJ: Prentice-Hall, 1977.

[2] W. K. Pratt. *Digital Image Processing*. 2nd Ed. New York: John Wiley & Sons, 1991.

[3] D. H. Ballard and C. M. Brown. *Computer Vision*. Englewood Cliffs, NJ: Prentice-Hall, 1982.

[4] J. K. Paik and A. K. Katsaggelos, "Image restoration using a modified Hopfield network," *IEEE Trans. Image Processing*, vol. 1, pp. 49–63, January 1992.

[5] Y.-T. Zhou, R. Chellappa, A. Vaid, and B. K. Jenkins, "Image restoration using a neural network," *IEEE Trans. Acoustics, Speech and Signal Processing*, vol. ASSP-36, pp. 1141–1151, July 1988.

[6] S. W. Lu and A. Szeto, "Hierarchical artificial neural networks for edge enhancement," *Pattern Recognition,* vol. 26, no. 8, pp. 1149–1163, 1993.

[7] J. K. Paik and A. K. Katsaggelos, "Edge detection using a neural network," in *Proc. ICASSP '90,* pp. 2145–2148 (Albuquerque, NM), 1990.

[8] C. Huang, "Parallel image segmentation using a modified Hopfield network," *Pattern Recognition Letters,* vol. 13, pp. 345–353, May 1992.

[9] T. Wang, X. Zhuang, and X. Xing, "Robust segmentation of noisy images using a neural network model," *Image and Vision Computing,* vol. 10, no. 4, pp. 233–240, May 1992.

[10] D. Chen, R. Jain, and B. Schunck, "Surface reconstruction using neural networks," *Proc. IEEE Conf. Computer Vision and Pattern Recognition—CVPR '92,* pp. 789–792, Champaign, IL, 1992.

[11] L. Guan and R. K. Ward, "Restoration of randomly blurred images via the maximum a posteriori criterion," *IEEE Trans. Image Processing*, vol. 1, no. 2, pp. 256–262, April 1992.

[12] L. Guan and R. K. Ward, "Restoration of stochastically blurred images by the geometrical mean filter," *Optical Engineering*, vol. 29, no. 4, pp. 289–295, April 1990.

[13] L. Guan and R. K. Ward, "Deblurring random time-varying blur," *J. Optical Society of America*, vol. 6, no. 11, pp. 1727–1737, November 1989.

[14] L. Guan, "A neural network approach to adaptive image enhancement," *SPIE Proc.*, vol. 1658, pp. 258–266, February 1992.

[15] L. Guan and X. Zhou, "Real-time image filtering: from optimal neuron evaluation to vector quadratic programming," in *Proc. IEEE Int. Conf. Systems, Man, and Cybernetics* (San Antonio, TX), pp. 694–699, 2–5 October 1994.

[16] J. J. Hopfield and D. W. Tank, "Neural computation of decisions in optimization problems," *Biol. Cybern.*, vol. 52, pp. 141–152, 1985.

[17] J. P. Sutton, J. S. Beis, and L. E. H. Trainor, "Hierarchical model of memory and memory loss," *J. Phys. A: Math. Gen.*, vol. 21, pp. 4443–4454, 1988.

[18] J. P. Sutton, J. S. Beis, and L. E. H. Trainor, "A hierarchical model of neurocortical synaptic organization," *Mathl. Comput. Modeling,* vol. 11, pp. 346–350, 1988.

[19] J. P. Sutton, "Mean field theory of nested neural clusters," *Proc. First AMSE Int. Conf. Neural Networks* (San Diego, CA), May 1991.

[20] L. Guan, "Image restoration by a neural network with hierarchical clustered architecture," *SPIE Proc.*, vol. 1903, San Jose, CA, pp. 72–83, February 1993.

[21] L. Guan, "A neural network with hierarchical cluster architecture in image restoration," *J. Electronic Imaging*, vol. 3, pp. 154–163, April 1994.

[22] L. Guan, "A unified neural framework for early visual information processing," *Proc. IEEE Int. Conf. Systems, Man, and Cybernetics*, vol. 2, (Le Touquet, France), pp. 327–332, 17–20 October 1993.

[23] L. Guan, "Optimal neuron evolution for image processing," in *Proc. ACNN '94: Australian Conf. Neural Networks*, Brisbane, Australia, pp. 157–160, January 1994.

[24] L. Guan, "Optimization of neural evolution in image restoration," *Proc. Int. Conf. Neural Networks and Signal Processing* (Guangzhou, China), pp. 302–307, November 1993.

[25] D. Bertsekas and J. Tsitsiklis. *Parallel and Distributed Computation. Numerical Methods.* Englewood Cliffs, NJ: Prentice Hall, 1989.

II

TECHNIQUES

4

STRATEGIES FOR REAL-TIME
MOTION ANALYSIS

Ronald L. Allen   *Department of Computer Science Engineering,*
University of Texas at Arlington

4.1 INTRODUCTION

Although engineers are confronted with a variety of applications that require real-time analysis of image motion, the technology remains problematic. The task is easy enough to describe. From a scene containing moving objects, we capture images, sequence them into a computer, and interpret them with algorithms whose design is driven by the need to complete an analysis within a time interval. Examples include autonomous vehicles, vehicle monitoring devices, target tracking systems, the many forms of digital video, and vision-based industrial robots. For these systems to perform correctly, they must not only accurately detect and estimate image motion, but they must do so in a timely and predictable fashion. This combination of requirements stresses every hardware and software component of current computing systems.

Real-time systems are notorious for the subtleties involved in their design, implementation, and maintenance [1]. Complications arise in an overwhelming number of areas, and they challenge the most accomplished computing generalist [2]. Operating systems, programming languages, and development tools must be carefully selected to ensure the verifiability of the delivered software [3, 4].

Working with images compounds these problems. Images have huge amounts of data; they severely overload the input/output channels of the vision computer. Working with sequences of images is worse still. And, as the rest of this chapter will show, the computational intricacy of motion analysis algorithms puts tough demands on vision computer processors. Getting the images into memory, finding what scene movements they reveal, and acting upon this result within a timeframe imposed by the application all present tremendous challenges in almost every area of computer system design.

Consider first that there are a range of complexities in image motion problems. A basic application might involve only the detection of significant motion within a scene containing rigid objects. But sometimes images subjected to analysis under a real-time constraint contain deformable objects. Also, from a sequence of images of a scene taken by a moving camera, it may be necessary to analyze the images in order to find the motion of the image acquisition device. This will be the situation, for instance, when a camera is attached to a mobile robot. Finally, from a sequence of images taken by a moving camera of a scene containing moving objects, one can attempt to determine the motion of the camera and the motion of the imaged objects.

It is easy to spot a difficulty with the last problem. If the motion of the moving camera matches the speed and direction of the moving objects, then—ignoring background effects—each image in the sequence will be the same. Although the objects are moving and the camera is moving too, image interpretation cannot detect that anything has changed. Unfortunately, the first two problems of image motion have very deep-rooted unsolvable elements in them as well. Problems of image motion characterization, even with fixed camera or objects, are generally ill-posed; they admit only partial and relative solutions.

To understand why this is so, it is important to distinguish among three vector fields: the *velocity field*, the *image motion field*, and the *optical flow field*. Each point on an object in a scene has a three-dimensional vector attached to it that gives its current motion. This is the velocity field; finding it is the ultimate goal of motion analysis. Projecting the velocity field onto the image plane gives the two-dimensional image motion field. The optical flow field, on the other hand, represents the changes in light intensity values in the image plane. These three are quite different (see Figure 4.1). This is shown by considering a perfectly smooth monochrome sphere rotating under constant illumination [5]. Although the scene and image motion fields are nonzero, the optical flow is zero. There are no changes whatsoever in the pixel values in the image.

What is given to the vision computer, however, is the optical flow. It is from the optical flow information that motion detection algorithms attempt to discover an estimate of the image motion field. And it is from the estimated motion field, in turn, that interpretation algorithms attempt to determine the motion of the objects in the scene or the motion of the imaging device. Objects and illumination conditions that produce ambiguities in motion determination, such as are shown in Figure 4.1, are clearly exceptional.

With the goal of analyzing image motion within a certain time limit, a real-time system designer might hope that, for a large variety of problems, there is a good correspondence between the optical flow field and the image motion field. The system can then generate some quick optical flow estimates. These estimates, in turn, can be compared to top-level structural information about the scene to give a velocity field. With this minimal computational load, the system has a reasonable chance of success: The computations are correct, the computational timeframe is

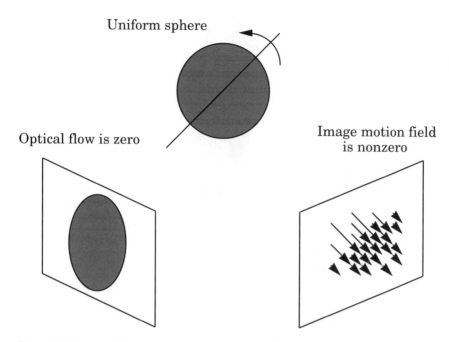

Uniform sphere

Optical flow is zero

Image motion field is nonzero

Figure 4.1 Vector fields in motion imaging. There are basic differences between the scene motion field, the image motion field, and the optical flow field. A uniformly gray rotating sphere has nonzero scene motion field and nonzero image motion field, but its optical flow field is zero.

acceptable, and the scheme is simple and predictable. Unfortunately, only in very special situations are the image motion and the optical flow fields the same.

Verri and Poggio [6] studied the difference between the image motion field and the optical flow field in order to find the conditions under which the two might be equal. Consider an object and its image as in Figure 4.2. The normal component of the image motion field is the component of the image motion field perpendicular to the edge of the object in an image, such as at point P in Figure 4.2. The normal component of the optical flow field is the component of the optical flow vector that is perpendicular to the edge. Verri and Poggio show that, in order for the normal optical flow vector to equal the normal image flow vector, the imaged object must have a diffused surface (i.e., it is Lambertian), the scene illumination must be uniform, and the object motion must be a translation. The authors [6] suspend each of these requirements and show that, in general, this results in a nonzero difference between the normal image flow and normal optical flow at an edge.

It is thus problematic to use the optical flow as a measure for the image flow. It is better to use the optical flow as a qualitative feature about the motion of scene objects and to rely on interpretation of the scene to arrive at velocity field estimates. However, insofar as an optical flow extraction technique relies on local

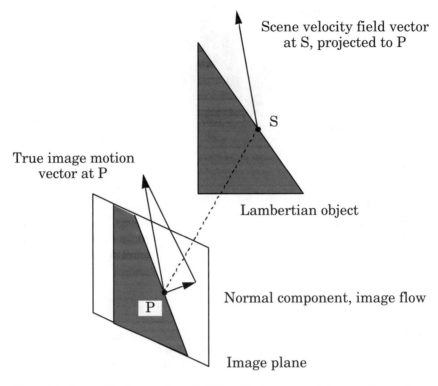

Figure 4.2 An equality theorem for optical flow. Under very special circumstances, the normal optical flow and normal image motion field components are equal: the object is Lambertian, the scene is uniformly illuminated, and the object's motion is a pure translation.

measurements at good quality edges, the normal optical flow does approximate the normal motion field. Then the inference of motion field from optical flow is well founded.

At the very start of a real-time motion system design, the quality of the images must be appraised with these negative results in mind. Additional computations are needed to resolve any possible disparity between the optical flow field and the image motion field. These calculations may become complicated and unpredictable, threatening the success of the real-time system.

There is a further problem in the correct computation of the optical flow itself. Ambiguity plagues even the most elementary attempt to measure motion in an image sequence. Consider an edge element in an image bounded by a small circular aperture, as in Figure 4.3. Any velocity field component of the object in the scene that is parallel to the direction of the edge cannot be discerned as optical flow. Only the normal component, perpendicular to the edge and in the

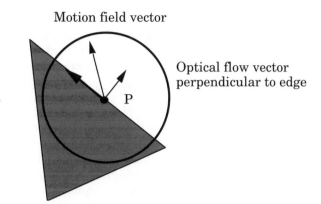

Figure 4.3 The aperture problem. The aperture problem causes the motion component parallel to the edge to be lost. The vision computer can only detect the component of the motion field normal to the edge.

direction of the edge gradient, is recoverable. Thus, there can be a fundamental ambiguity in the determination of the motion field in the neighborhood of an edge. This is known as the *aperture problem*. Let $I(x, y)$ be the pixel intensity at image location $P = (x, y)$ and **F** be the motion field vector at P. Then, in the presence of the aperture problem, only $\mathbf{F} \cdot \nabla I(x, y) = \mathbf{F} \cdot (\partial I / \partial x, \partial I / \partial y)$ can be found by analyzing temporal changes in pixel intensity near P.

If there is a corner in the image of the moving object, then the aperture problem disappears, assuming that the conditions exist so that the normal components of the motion field and the optical flow are equal (see Figure 4.4). We find the normal

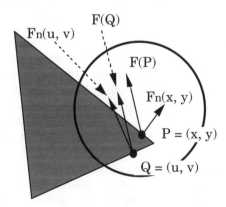

Figure 4.4 Overcoming the aperture problem. The aperture problem does not occur in the neighborhood of a corner. A corner of a Lambertian object under uniform illumination translates across the image. The true motion field can be recovered.

component of the optical flow at two points, $P = (x, y)$ and $Q = (u, v)$, that lie on edges forming the corner. The normal components of the optical flow, $Fn(x, y)$ and $Fn(u, v)$, are known from the motion of the edge locally; the edge gradients are known; and $F = F(Q) = F(P)$, because the object is translating. Then

$$Fn(x, y) = F \cdot \nabla I(x, y) \qquad (4\text{-}1a)$$

$$Fn(u, v) = F \cdot \nabla I(u, v) \qquad (4\text{-}1b)$$

and Eqs. (4-1a) and (4-1b) can be solved to find F because the gradients are not parallel.

It will be shown later that, in addition to corners, textured regions of the image are generally free of the aperture problem as well. It might seem at first that we only require a large enough aperture to capture an object edge in the image sequence for accurate estimation of the motion field. However, the intensity gradient, $\nabla I(x, y)$, is approximated in local neighborhoods—subapertures as it were—of edges. So the aperture problem arises in each such computation, and it is only dispensed with by later comparison with neighborhood information from image regions where the aperture problem does not arise.

The above simple examples illustrate a common two-step optical flow paradigm for finding the motion field in an image sequence [7]:

1. The normal component of the optical flow is determined for a number of local neighborhoods where the aperture problem may be present. If the special conditions for equality hold, then this is also the normal component of the motion field;

2. These results are recomputed by propagating information from regions free of the aperture problem to those found in the first step.

Once the motion field is reliably estimated, higher-level algorithms use it to interpret the scene and find the velocity field. By carefully selecting the motion estimation paradigm for the application, it is possible to avoid the problems outlined above and use this two-step approach to measure image motion in real-time.

The field of image sequence compression continues to draw strong industrial, government, and academic interest [8]. Commercial applications are surfacing right now: digital broadcast television, compact disk video, teleconferencing systems, multimedia, dynamic medical imagery. The Grand Alliance digital high-definition television (HDTV) standard has emerged after years of research, technical competition, debate, and political haggling.

These technologies require both the storage and transmission of enormous data sets. Image compression is the key. Achieving the compression ratios necessary for digital video involves the processing of individual images to remove spatial redundancies and a motion analysis of the sequence to remove temporal redundancies. There are standard methods for both compression techniques.

The Joint Photographic Experts Group (JPEG) specification standardizes still-image compression [9]. The steps in JPEG compression are:

1. Image data are broken into 8 × 8 blocks and processed with a forward discrete cosine transform (DCT).

2. Transform coefficients are quantized (with information loss) according to a quantization table with 64 entries.

3. Either Huffman coding or arithmetic coding is next run in a lowest-frequencies-first, zigzag fashion on the quantized transform coefficients. This step is lossless, and it attempts to maximize the entropy of the encoded coefficients.

JPEG decoding essentially reverses this procedure. While DCT-based coding is indeed efficient, digital video needs much bigger compression ratios to squeeze image sequences through relatively low bandwidth transmission channels.

Motion Picture Experts Group (MPEG) compression furnishes the current standard for image sequences. There are two versions. MPEG-1 is adequate for teleconferencing and compact disk video. It specifies a data rate of 2 Mb/s [10]. A more recent standard, MPEG-2, is targeted for HDTV. It specifies a bit rate of 10 Mb/s [11]. MPEG provides four types of compressed data stream images:

1. *DC-pictures* that allow serial digital devices, such as video cassette recorders, to perform quick searches.

2. *Intrapictures* (I-pictures) that are subject to less compression and readily available to search operations.

3. *Predicted pictures* (P-pictures) give good compression; however, they rely on the coding of a previous I-picture or P-picture.

4. *Interpolated* or *bidirection pictures* (B-pictures) that boast high compression ratios but rely on the coding of both a past and future I-picture or P-picture.

This diversity of compressed-image types makes MPEG a particularly accommodating standard for interoperation of the many commercial digital video devices now coming into use.

MPEG gives no motion estimation method. The standard only details how the encoder and decoder handle the motion displacements of 16 × 16 image blocks. MPEG's policy here is to let the real-time system designer pick the optimal motion estimation strategy for the application. This has spurred a number of research efforts in motion estimation and real-time data rate control [8].

Once the motion has been estimated, however, MPEG does standardize its representation. Each 16 × 16 image block has one or two associated motion vectors, depending on whether the image containing the block is predicted or interpolated. The motion vectors are always the differences between vectors associated with prior blocks. Because the optical flow is generally constant over small image regions, these differential motion vectors are either negligible or efficiently compressed.

MPEG grounds its two motion compensation techniques, prediction and interpolation, on the distinction between picture types. Compensation by prediction uses the fact that an image sequence—at least in local regions—is essentially a temporal translation of an earlier region. Only the slight perturbation must be encoded to predict the new frame. Interpolation uses a subsampled version of the acquired image, a correction term, a past image frame, and a future image frame to produce an image.

Other highly compressive sequential image coding methods are under development. Bit rates creep under 64 kb/s. More thorough motion estimation than commonly applied in MPEG-based systems is one approach [12]. Another is to model the objects in motion for the receiver so that their images do not need to be continually retransmitted. Research continues. Nevertheless, these methods do clearly promise to deliver digital video to public telephone networks and mobile radio systems in the near future.

Motion analysis is provably problematic as Verri and Poggio have shown [6]. Compounding this, the digital video domain appears to be one of the toughest applications because of the huge mass of data, the prevalence of small communication channel bandwidths, and the high expectations of commercial customers. Indeed, the public has grown up with motion picture cinema of superb quality. It expects nothing less, and it will never tolerate blocky scenery and jerky movements when the transition from analog to digital transpires. Fortunately, the necessity of computing the image motion field generally does not arise for digital video. The principal exceptions are some model-based motion analyses for very low bit rate compression [12]. Accurate transmitted estimates of the motion and velocity fields support the correct manipulation of the model image at the receiving end of the channel. This method aside, only the optical flow field is necessary; the transmitted dynamic imagery derived from it just has to look nice.

As we shall see below, we can take advantage of this simplification of the motion analysis problem. The applications sidestep the tough interpretation problems posed by the motion and velocity fields. Real-time digital video becomes feasible with special-purpose processors operating at low levels on the image intensity changes.

There are four basic strategies for detecting motion in image sequences using an optical flow approach: gradient, correspondence, spatio-temporal filtering, and phase-based methods. This chapter compares the methods by detailing their individual approaches to finding the optical flow field, circumventing the aperture problem, and detecting and estimating image motion in real-time.

4.2 GRADIENT APPROACHES

The gradient, or differential, algorithms attach a vector to each point in a displacement image. Then the optical flow from this gradient field is derived. Fennema and Thompson [13] used this approach years ago. They assume that the optical flow is constant in local image regions. As a result, the method only works for pure translational motion.

The classical gradient-based solution to finding the optical flow is due to Horn and Schunck [5, 14]. Making some assumptions that constrain the possible types of optical flow provides solvable systems of equations that produce optical flow information. Let $E(x, y, t)$ be the pixel values in an image sequence at location (x, y) of the image at time value t. Let $u(x, y)$ and $v(x, y)$ be the optical flow in the horizontal and vertical directions. Then, following Horn and Schunck, the illumination value at time $t + \delta t$ at point $(x + \delta x, y + \delta y)$, $\delta x = u\delta t$, $\delta y = v\delta t$, will be the same:

$$E(x + u\delta t, y + v\delta t, t + \delta t) = E(x, y, t) \qquad (4\text{-}2)$$

Expanding the left-hand side of (4-2) in a Taylor series gives the optical flow constraint equation

$$\frac{\partial E}{\partial x}u + \frac{\partial E}{\partial y}v + \frac{\partial E}{\partial t} = 0 \qquad (4\text{-}3)$$

We omit terms higher than first order. Equation (4-3) says that the u and v components of the optical flow lie on a line in the (u, v) plane given by the vector inner product

$$\left(\frac{\partial E}{\partial x}, \frac{\partial E}{\partial y}\right) \cdot (u, v) = -\frac{\partial E}{\partial t} \qquad (4\text{-}4)$$

We compute the optical flow in the direction of the intensity gradient (the normal optical flow) by finding the point (u, v) on the line given in (4-4) such that $v = u(\partial E/\partial y)/(\partial E/\partial x)$, shown in Figure 4.5.

The other component of the optical flow cannot be recovered from (4-4) because there is only one equation with two variables, u and v. This is the manifestation of the aperture problem in gradient-based optical flow methods. We need an additional constraint.

Assume that the motion field varies smoothly in the image. Then the second smoothness constraint comes from minimizing

$$e = e_s + \lambda e_c \qquad (4\text{-}5)$$

where

$$e_s + e_c = \int\int (u_x^2 + u_y^2 + v_x^2 + v_y^2)dx\,dy$$
$$+ \int\int (E_x u + E_y v + E_t)^2 dx\,dy \qquad (4\text{-}6)$$

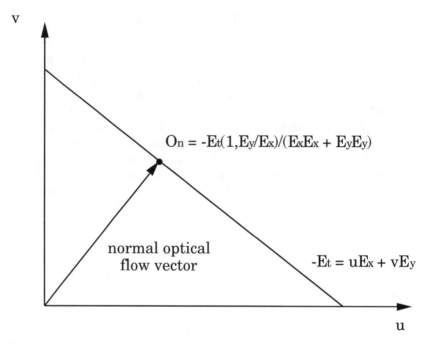

Figure 4.5 The aperture problem in gradient techniques. The optical flow constraint equation can be solved for (u, v) in the direction of the intensity gradient, $(\partial E/\partial x, \partial E/\partial y) = (E_x, E_y)$ to give the normal component O_n.

and u_x, and so on are partial derivatives. Here, λ is a parameter that controls the percentage of e_s and e_c in the total error e. Error e_s is out-of-smoothness measure, and e_c is the error in the optical flow constraint equation (4-3). From the calculus of variations, we arrive at

$$\nabla^2 u = \lambda \left(\frac{\partial E}{\partial x} u + \frac{\partial E}{\partial y} v + \frac{\partial E}{\partial t} \right) \frac{\partial E}{\partial x}$$

$$\nabla^2 v = \lambda \left(\frac{\partial E}{\partial x} u + \frac{\partial E}{\partial y} v + \frac{\partial E}{\partial t} \right) \frac{\partial E}{\partial y}$$

(4-7)

where ∇^2 is the Laplacian operator. Equations (4-7) can be solved by conventional Gauss-Seidel iterative methods [15].

A number of criticisms have been leveled at the smoothness constraint. For example, it clearly fails to hold when objects become occluded. Horn [5] suggests interpolation of the known values to areas where the smoothness condition does not hold. Various investigators have proposed other amendments to the constraint. Nagel [16] pointed out that keeping only first-order derivatives in the Taylor expansion leading to the constraint equation (4-3) essentially models local image intensities as a plane in the region of a pixel. This may be tolerable at edges, but it cannot hold at corners. The problem is that, although Horn and Schunck's derivation extracts normal optical flow, *it can only do so in areas where the aperture problem exists.* It cannot handle the very valuable image regions where the aperture problem does not exist, such as corners. Nagel changed the smoothness constraint to be a function of the gray values of image pixels, included second-order derivatives in his description of $E(x, y, t)$, and added an oriented smoothness constraint. As a result, his formulation of the gradient method succeeds in areas not affected by the aperture problem, that is, corners. Yachida [17] accepts the smoothness constraint as a first step, but modifies it by a refined estimate of optical flow. He propagates the starting approximations to nearby points using local constraints. This process is terminated when the displacement estimates in the local 5×5 window began to grow. In a critique of Yachida's result, Nagel and Enkelmann [18] expand on Nagel's idea to let variations in gray-scale values of pixels influence the smoothness constraints imposed during the computation of optical flow vectors. A number of thresholds for controlling the computations in this method are explored by Nagel and Enkelmann.

The controversy over the optical flow constraint equation (4-3) has never passed. Schunck himself critiqued its foundations in [19], when he pointed out that a divergence term needs to be included in (4-3), unless the motion of the object that is imaged is parallel to the image plane. If the object feature is moving toward or away from the camera, then the size of the feature will enlarge or shrink, respectively. This requires a density factor. To obtain his version of the constraint equation, Schunck had to assume that small texture tokens were available that could be tracked as the object in the scene moved. Nagel, in a polemic with Schunck, contended that any feature in the image plane has some spatial extent [20]. Unless this is accounted for in the very beginning of the optical flow analysis, then one is likely to incorrectly assume that feature sizes remain constant over time. Nagel derives a constraint equation that overcomes this difficulty.

Gradient methods usually employ only a very few frames in the temporal image sequence. Earlier implementation efforts only used a single pair of images to derive an instantaneous estimate of the optical flow displacement. Of course, the pioneering designs were based on less powerful input/output channels, weaker processors, and slower system buses than commonly available today. This does raise the possibility of applying today's powerful reduced instruction set computers (RISC) or special-purpose parallel machines to build gradient-method real-time systems using similar algorithms. Indeed, in the area of full-motion video compression for multimedia applications, difference images are extracted. Researchers are close to accomplishing software-based real-time encoding of dynamic imagery [21].

Even though real-time considerations push us in this direction, using short image sequences is very questionable. This eliminates object acceleration from the optical flow analysis. It increases noise sensitivity. It also hinders the computation of second-order derivatives, u_x and u_y of (4-6). Subbarao's research brought the benefits of long image sequences to light [22]. By allowing the optical flow to persist throughout the time sequence of images, Subbarao could dispense with the erratic derivatives and analyze special cases of nonrigid motion.

Numerous research efforts have built on the foundation laid by Horn and Schunck. Adiv found conditions where, in the presence of noise in the optical flow field, different objects can give rise to the same optical flow field and where two objects can give rise to contradictory information in the optical flow field [23]. Snyder discovered a mathematical foundation for all gradient-based optical flow methods [24]. He found three conditions that a smoothness constraint candidate must satisfy:

1. It must be invariant to a change in the imaging system's Cartesian coordinate system;

2. It must be positive definite;

3. It must not have mixed products of different components of the optical flow.

Enkelmann [25] begins his motion analysis by constructing pyramids of successively low-pass-filtered versions of the serial images. The constraints resemble Nagel's [20]. Based on the pioneering pyramid decomposition algorithm of Crowley and Stern [26], Enkelmann develops a coarse-to-fine method to get a solution for the optical flow field. The speedup in iteratively solving the motion equations is noteworthy for the real-time system builder. One drawback is that the preliminary pyramid decomposition is computation intensive. Moreover, there is a tendency for such multigrid methods to oscillate between solutions for the optical flow at different scales [27]. Such an oscillation can destroy the predictability required of a real-time image motion analysis system.

4.3 CORRESPONDENCE METHODS

Critical-feature-matching, or correspondence, methods are very similar to stereo-point correspondence algorithms in computer vision. The position disparity between image pairs determines the depth of a scene captured by a dual camera system. In contrast, motion analysis works on the time disparity between successive monocular images. Like the gradient method, the correspondence method generally uses a small number of images in the time sequence. However, the images are often more widely separated in time, because instantaneous derivatives do not need to be approximated.

The correspondence method is useful for the determination of shape and surface orientation from motion, digital video, and for tracking applications. Tracking systems include such applications as following an object through a prolonged sequence of images to study its path, moving the imaging device to physically follow the moving object, autonomous vehicles, robot navigation, and obstacle avoidance for robots.

Numerous real-time tracking implementations begin with a correspondence strategy. For example, Dickmanns and Graefe [28] developed a vision-based pendulum balancer, an automatic vehicle docking system, and an autonomous vehicle. Particularly impressive is the autonomous vehicle, named VaMoRs (Versuchsfahrzeug für autonome Mobilitèt und Rechnersehen). In August, 1987, it was driven over a new stretch of Autobahn near Munich, Germany. VaMoRs was able to negotiate 20 km of highway, reaching its maximum speed of 96 km/h. The vehicle can follow marked and unmarked lanes, and it can be driven under varying weather conditions.

In correspondence approaches, critical points, lines, or other features of objects in the first image are put into correspondence with similar features later in the sequence. The offset represented by the correspondence and the time interval between images together determine the optical flow of the objects in the image that possess those critical features. The matching process involved in verifying the correspondences among features in the correspondence model can suffer from combinatorial explosion—an anathema for real-time system designers.

There are two common real-time tactics for trimming the computational workload necessary for matching features between images:

1. Simple reduction in the number of critical features to achieve the timeliness that the application demands;

2. Reliance on multiresolution methods that employ coarse-to-fine approximation algorithms to obtain the estimate of optical flow.

Real-time applications generally employ the feature minimization strategy. Its obvious fault is that very strict assumptions about the visual scene must be made in order to begin the motion estimation. The second strategy has been primarily studied by researchers seeking to improve the robustness of the correspondence techniques.

Let us consider some real-time motion analysis applications that use feature minimization. Dickmanns and Graefe [29], for example, confined the features to small, critical regions of the scene. They modeled the roadway. They further constrained the matching search by considering only two consecutive images in the motion sequence; corresponding features are then quite closely spaced and quickly associated with one another. A coarse-grain parallel computer architecture serves to control their VaMoRs autonomous vehicle. The system has several general purpose processors (GPPs) and a central communication processor (SP). Feature-containing regions are partitioned among the GPPs. The GPPs post their analyses to the SP. The SP, in turn, updates the vehicle's current status and initiates control actions. By not wasting GPP processor cycles on irrelevant image data, Dickmanns and Graefe's applications were able to arrive at image sampling rates of up to 25 Hz [28] with less than ten processors. In another autonomous vehicle application, Chapuis et al. do not rely on a road model, and are able to perform real-time road mark tracking [30]. They obtained satisfactory results tracking the highway white line in image sequences lifted at speeds of 130 km/h. Nevertheless, to meet the system timing requirements with their standard Motorola 68020 microprocessor-based vision computer, only some ten image scan lines could be analyzed.

Much theoretical research has focused on finding the shape of objects from feature correspondences in dynamic images. This can be a critical issue for low-bit-rate compression applications in digital video [12]. There, one approach models image objects for storage and manipulation at the decoder side of the channel. This done, the moving object images do not need to consume further bandwidth; only the motion descriptions must be transmitted.

Significant progress has been made with correspondence strategies for finding the image motion and scene velocity fields. For point correspondences in three successive frames of a moving sequence, the problem of finding the structure of the points was solved by Ullman [31] in his doctoral dissertation. His work is reviewed by Ballard and Brown [32]. A number of researchers elaborated on Ullman's work. From two perspective views, Longuet-Higgins [33] and Tsai and Huang [34] found that eight point correspondences in motion scenes are sufficient to determine the 3-D motion and structure of an object. Some extensions and qualifications to Ullman's work are given by Huang and Lee [35]:

1. If only two orthographic views are given, then an infinite number of solutions to the structure from motion problem exist;

2. If only three point correspondences are available, then there are 16 solutions to motion and four solutions to structure from motion;

3. A linear algorithm is possible for the solution in (4-2) and to the four-point problem for which Ullman originally provided a nonlinear solution.

Negahdaripour [36] considered the problem of characterizing the objects that can give rise to ambiguities of shape and orientation when only two images are given. He posed his solution in the framework of a moving camera within a fixed scene. Thus, the results are directly applicable to problems of object tracking, design of autonomous vehicles, and obstacle avoidance. Specifically, Negahdaripour found that only hyperboloids of one sheet and some degenerate cases such as hyperbolic paraboloids, circular cylinders, and intersecting planes can cause an ambiguity in this scenario. In addition, the results are given for perspective, rather than orthographic, images.

If, by using the above methods, we can provide reasonably accurate estimates of the image motion and scene velocity fields, then there is the possibility of designing model-based digital video systems. Model objects may be derived from a known library of shapes: polygon meshes, wire frames, or deformable superquadrics, for instance [12]. Alternatively, image regions of interest may be accepted as the working objects. For example, Wang and Lee [37] cover the first image in a sequence with a deformable quadrilateral mesh. As the scene changes, edges are tracked between images to find the shape changes of the mesh elements. Better prediction of motion between image frames is possible with this method than with block-based techniques, such as MPEG.

As noted above, many correspondence-based approaches for motion analysis use hierarchical techniques. An early attempt to use correspondence for motion estimation by Wong and Hall used simple image intensities as features [38]. A brute force search and comparison over all possible corresponding pixels in the second image is extremely slow. Wong and Hall low-pass filtered the images to make a pyramid of several coarse resolution versions of the originals. Then they used a coarse-to-fine search for the best correlations of image brightness. Computational savings of some three orders of magnitude faster than exhaustive searching were reported. Glazer, Reynolds, and Anandan [39] used Laplacian-of-Gaussian bandpass [40] rather than low-pass filters, contending that this lessens the chances of false matches at coarse resolutions due to scaling and illumination differences between a pair of images. Burt, Yen, and Xu [41] developed a similar bandpass filtering approach using Burt and Adelson's Laplacian pyramid [42] for decomposing the images into direction- and velocity-tuned channels.

The above filtering and hierarchical search correspondence techniques [38, 39, 41] share a common fault. They can recover the full optical flow in the vicinity of a corner, where there is no aperture problem. But they cannot precisely obtain the normal optical flow in a region that contains a distinct straight edge [7]. This is due to the presence of many feasible matches between the two images of the time sequence along a straight edge (see Figure 4.6).

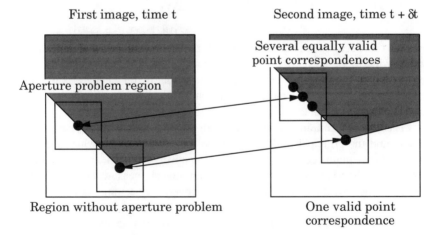

Figure 4.6 The aperture problem in correspondence methods. The optical flow is recovered in regions free of the aperture problem, but the normal component cannot be found along well-defined edges. Typically, a range of equally valid feature correspondences exist in such regions. This is a problem with the suggested MPEG block-based motion estimation technique.

Although the MPEG standard does not require a particular motion estimation method, it recommends one similar to that illustrated in Figure 4.6 [10]. The predictability and timeliness of a given real-time system may not be compromised by this problem. In that case, special-purpose VLSI chipsets and parallel hardware implementations of real-time motion analysis are available. In fact, desktop multimedia systems can be built around multimedia video processors, such as the Intel i750 Video Processor chip [43]. A full-motion analog-to-digital video conversion system was built around the Parallel Object Oriented Machine (POOMA) at Philips Research [44]. A POOMA has 100 nodes, each with local memory, some with I/O interfaces. Nodes are based on the Motorola 68020 processor. The encoder system assigns multiple frames to different processors for parallel computation in the motion estimation phase. Individual images are partitioned into regions and processed by separate nodes in the compression phase. Such implementations as these are impressive in the light of real-time performance, but their motion analysis methods suffer from aperture problem effects in the neighborhoods of edges.

Anandan [45, 46] succeeded in finding the normal optical flow for regions affected by the aperture problem. He also used the Laplacian pyramid to decompose two time-sequence images for a coarse-to-fine control strategy. However, he included a direction-dependent confidence measure in finding his correspondences between frames. Anandan first forms a Gaussian-weighted sum-of-squared-differences (SSD) map of the search window. The SSD map for a displacement of (x_0, y_0) in image I_0 to a search window about (x_1, y_1) in image I_1 is the sum

$$SSD(u, v) = \sum G(\Delta x, \Delta y)[I_0(x_0 + \Delta x, y_0 + \Delta y)$$
$$- I_1(u + \Delta x, v + \Delta y)]^2 \qquad (4\text{-}8)$$

over all $(\Delta x, \Delta y)$ such that $(u + \Delta x, v + \Delta y)$ is near (u, v), (u, v) lies in the search window of I_1, and $G(\Delta x, \Delta y)$ is the weighting function. Such match measures may be small for several (u, v) points that lie on an edge, as in Figure 4.6. Anandan's confidence measures, $C_{\min}$ and $C_{\max}$, are proportional to the two principal curvatures on the SSD surface (see Figure 4.7).

These are the minimum and maximum curvatures of the SSD surface in a region, and the principal directions are the unit vectors along which the minimum and maximum occur, $e_{\min}$ and $e_{\max}$, respectively [47]. The line of minimum curvature in the SSD map follows equally valid match measure values. The normal component of the optical flow can be recovered by examining the principal curvatures.

Scott also used an SSD map [48], but instead of principal curvatures, he computed the principal axes of the SSD map values. These are the orthogonal lines of best and worst fit through the centroid of the values [32]. These serve to find the normal component of the optical flow in regions affected by the aperture problem. Scott defends the principal axes method against the principal direction confidence measures. He argues that it is better able to handle multiple high-quality match positions than Anandan's multiresolution method.

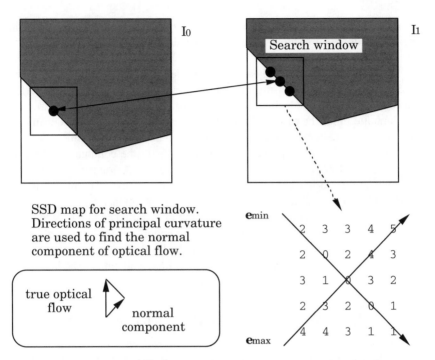

Figure 4.7 The sum-of-squared-differences principal curvatures. This method finds normal optical flow. Confidence measures C_{min} and C_{max} are scaled principal curvatures. The principal directions e_{min} and e_{max} distinguish between corners and lines and support the recovery of normal optical flow.

An approach using Kalman filtering, computationally similar to Anandan's and Scott's methods is described by Singh [7, 49]. Kalman filtering [50] is used to iteratively improve the estimates of image flow. Singh's procedure (see Figure 4.8) is to first compute the local optical flow, called *conservation information*, for each point in the image. Then, an earlier prediction is incorporated into this estimate. The prediction and the revised estimate are merged with optical flow data from

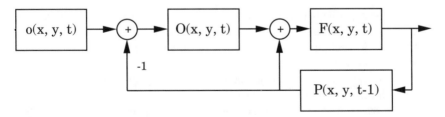

Figure 4.8 Simplified Kalman filtering scheme. Local optical flow information for the image, $o(x, y, t)$, is integrated with an earlier prediction, P, to form $O(x, y, t)$. From P, O, and estimates of optical flow at other regions, a true optical flow estimate F is found. A prediction is issued for the next iteration.

other neighborhoods (*neighborhood information*) to output a final estimate of the true optical flow. This output is saved to form the prediction to be used with the next estimate.

For real-time motion analysis, correspondence has proven to be the most widely applied strategy. In the case of autonomous vehicles, real-time performance is obtained by reducing the number of features tracked between frames. This limitation must be carefully considered, because cluttered scenes or images without critical features in the right location can cause the real-time system to fail. On the other hand, special hardware can supply the computational power needed for most digital video encoding and decoding. A common drawback is that applications do not adequately handle aperture effects. The reason is that these architectures tend to be limited to low-level operations. System designers trying to achieve high compression ratios with model-based coding may find that these pixel-level machines cannot conveniently support the top-level, goal-driven image interpretation needed for image motion field and scene velocity field determination. The next motion analysis method considered attempts to address some of the limitations of the correspondence method.

4.4 SPATIO-TEMPORAL FILTERING METHODS

A more recent approach is to consider the time sequence of two-dimensional images as a spatio-temporal image in three dimensions [51, 52]. Then, three-dimensional filters are applied to the volume image in space–time. If the filters are chosen to be oriented, localized, and sensitive to a graded range of spatio-temporal frequencies, then robust motion detection is possible. There are two basic strategies for using the three-dimensional spatio-temporal volume:

1. Motion detection in two spatial dimensions becomes a problem of detecting the orientation of a plane in the three-dimensional spatio-temporal volume;

2. Motion of textured objects in two dimensions becomes a problem of finding three-dimensional-oriented textures in the spatio-temporal volume.

The spatio-temporal filter method encompasses both approaches. Its broad strategy is to avoid the aperture problem at edges and yet still rely on low-level pixel operations. As such, it may be a candidate for implementation on advanced real-time systems using special-purpose video chips.

Adelson and Bergen [51] note that motion in the spatial domain can be identified with orientation in space–time. Figure 4.9 shows their idea. Suppose that a vertical bar is moving in the x direction of the x–y plane. Then, in the x-y-t volume, there will be a solid slice that can be detected with 3-D oriented edge filters.

Watson and Ahumada consider the case of a moving textured object [52]. The temporal and spatial frequencies of a drifting sinusoidal signal are related by

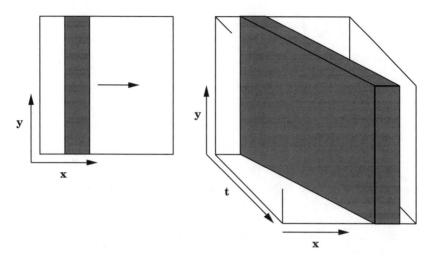

Figure 4.9 Object motion in space–time. Motion in the image generates a slab in the spatio-temporal volume. An oriented three-dimensional filter can detect the orientation of the surface.

$$u\omega_x = -\omega_t \qquad (4\text{-}9)$$

where u is the velocity of the sinusoid, ω_x is its spatial frequency, and ω_t is its temporal frequency. Suppose that a signal consists of many localized components of spatial frequency ω_x. Then, as the signal moves with velocity u in time, its temporal frequency will vary in the proportion (4-9). The set of such pairs form a line through the origin, and indeed (4-9) is the equation of a line of slope u in (ω_x, ω_t) space. This generalizes to two dimensions.

Suppose an object is a two-dimensional texture of x-spatial frequency ω_x and y-spatial frequency ω_y. As the texture moves with velocity vector (u, v), its temporal frequency will be

$$u\omega_x + v\omega_y = -\omega_t \qquad (4\text{-}10)$$

To see this, suppose that an image $f(x, y)$ is translating with velocity (u, v) in time. It has a spatio-temporal volume defined by

$$f(x, y, t) = f(x, y) * \delta(x - ut, y - vt), \qquad (4\text{-}11)$$

where $*$ is convolution and δ is the two-dimensional Dirac delta function. Taking the Fourier transform of both sides of (4-11) results in

$$\hat{f}(\omega_x, \omega_y, \omega_t) = \int_{-\infty}^{+\infty} \int_{-\infty}^{+\infty} \int_{-\infty}^{+\infty} f(x, y, t) e^{-j(x\omega_x + y\omega_y + t\omega_t)} \, dx \, dy \, dt \qquad (4\text{-}12)$$

$$= \int_{-\infty}^{+\infty} e^{-jt\omega_t} \int_{-\infty}^{+\infty} \int_{-\infty}^{+\infty} f(x, y)$$
$$* \delta(x - ut, y - vt) e^{-j(x\omega_x + y\omega_y)} \, dx \, dy \, dt \qquad (4\text{-}13)$$

$$= \hat{f}(\omega_x, \omega_y) \int_{-\infty}^{+\infty} e^{-jt\omega_t}$$

$$\cdot \int_{-\infty}^{+\infty} \int_{-\infty}^{+\infty} \delta(x - ut, y - vt) e^{-j(x\omega_x + y\omega_y)} \, dx \, dy \, dt \qquad (4\text{-}14)$$

$$= \hat{f}(\omega_x, \omega_y) \int_{-\infty}^{+\infty} e^{-jt\omega_t} \int_{-\infty}^{+\infty} \int_{-\infty}^{+\infty} e^{-jt(u\omega_x + v\omega_y)} \, dx \, dy \, dt \qquad (4\text{-}15)$$

$$= \hat{f}(\omega_x, \omega_y) \delta(t\omega_t) \delta(u\omega_x + v\omega_y)$$

$$= \hat{f}(\omega_x, \omega_y) \delta(u\omega_x + v\omega_y + t\omega_t) \qquad (4\text{-}16)$$

This describes the plane (4-10) in $(\omega_x, \omega_y, \omega_t)$ space, because $\hat{f}(\omega_x, \omega_y, \omega_t)$ is nonzero only where $\delta(u\omega_x + v\omega_y + t\omega_t) \neq 0$, i.e., where $u\omega_x + v\omega_y + t\omega_t = 0$. If an image consists of many oriented textures, then in the frequency domain, the ordered triples consisting of the associated x-spatial frequencies, y-spatial frequencies, and temporal frequencies of the textured patches of the object will form a plane.

Thus, a means of estimating the velocity of a textured object is to:

- Find the oriented textures of frequencies $(\omega_x, \omega_y, \omega_t)$ in the three-dimensional spatio-temporal volume. This can be done with a set of three-dimensional bandpass filters, for example;

- Plot the points in the spatio-temporal frequency domain;

- Find the plane that fits the data points;

- From relation (4-10), determine the actual (u, v) optical flow estimate for the textured object.

Figure 4.10 shows the concept of optical flow determination using the space–time frequency domain.

Singh and Allen [53] outline weaknesses in the gradient and the correspondence methods. As noted previously, the gradient method depends on estimating first- and second-order derivatives of pixel intensity. Because of this, image noise causes problems for the gradient method. The correspondence method can be beset with combinatorial explosions of matching possibilities between two time-sequence images. These problems are motivation for exploring the filtering schemes, but few researchers have actually used them for estimating motion [7].

Further motivation for study of the spatio-temporal filtering algorithms is the link they apparently share with biological vision systems. A number of researchers have established that the visual areas of the brain function as spatio-temporal bandpass filters [51, 52, 54–57]. Animal vision systems are generally greatly superior to machine vision systems for motion detection. Analyzing the brain structures that implement this biological motion analysis may provide clues as to how artificial systems might be built that approximate nature's power.

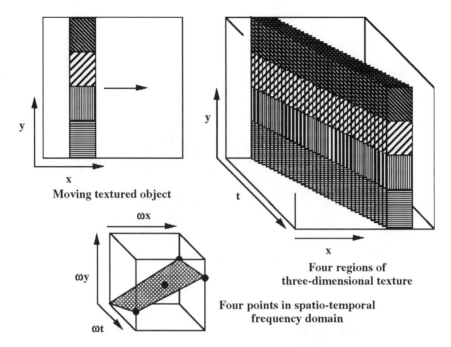

Figure 4.10 Spatio-temporal frequency method. Finding pattern optical flow (u, v) is possible using the spatio-temporal frequency domain. Filters sensitive to oriented filters are applied to the three-dimensional space–time volume. Responses are plotted as a set of data points in the spatio-temporal frequency domain, $(\omega_x, \omega_y, \omega_t)$ space. A plane can be fitted to the data points, determining (u, v) in (4-10).

In order to detect the edges in three dimensions, Heeger [58, 59] proposed the use of Gabor filters, which have been studied for use in low-level vision since Daugman [60] extended many of their properties to two-dimensional signals. A 3-D spatio-temporal Gabor filter is a sinusoid in a Gaussian window:

$$g_o(x, y, t) = \frac{1}{\sqrt{2}\pi^{3/2}\sigma_x\sigma_y\sigma_t} \exp\left[-\left(\frac{x^2}{2\sigma_x^2} + \frac{y^2}{2\sigma_y^2} + \frac{t^2}{2\sigma_t^2}\right)\right] \tag{4-17}$$

$$\cdot \sin(2\pi\omega_{x_0}x + 2\pi\omega_{y_0}y + 2\pi\omega_{t_0}t)$$

In (4-17), the spatio-temporal Gaussian window has an extent governed by σx, σy, and σt. The triple $(\omega_{x_0}, \omega_{y_0}, \omega_{t_0})$ gives the center frequency to which the filter is tuned. In (4-17) an odd, or sine-phase, Gabor filter is given; the corresponding even, or cosine-phase filter, $g_e(x, y, t)$ is obtained by replacing the sine component with a cosine component. Figure 4.11 shows a two-dimensional cosine-phase Gabor filter.

The filter (4-17) will have its largest response when centered on a texture to which the sinusoidal component is tuned and will respond to edges. Cosine-phase

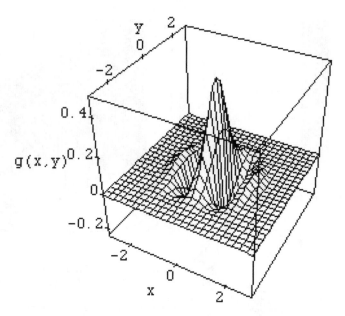

Figure 4.11 A two-dimensional even Gabor filter. The orientation of the filter may be changed. In three dimensions, such filters are sensitive to textures.

Gabor filters respond to blob-like areas of the 3-D image sequence. To obtain a motion-energy filter, Heeger forms $g(x, y, t) = g_o(x, y, t)^2 + g_e(x, y, t)^2$, a phase-independent filter that measures the Gabor energy filter of the spatio-temporal volume. The term $g(x, y, t)$ has frequency response [59] given by

$$
\begin{aligned}
G(\omega_x, \omega_y, \omega_t) = \frac{1}{4} \exp \Big\{ & -4\pi^2 \big[\sigma_x^2 (\omega_x - \omega_{x_0})^2 \\
& + \sigma_y^2 (\omega_y - \omega_{y_0}) + \sigma_t^2 (\omega_t - \omega_{t_0}) \big] \Big\} \\
+ \frac{1}{4} \exp \Big\{ & -4\pi^2 \big[\sigma_x^2 (\omega_x - \omega_{x_0})^2 \\
& + \sigma_y^2 (\omega_y + \omega_{y_0}) + \sigma_t^2 (\omega_t + \omega_{t_0}) \big] \Big\}
\end{aligned}
$$

(4-18)

Because $G(\omega_x, \omega_y, \omega_t)$ is a pair of Gaussians, it will have its largest response to a moving pattern with spatial frequencies $(\omega_{x_0}, \omega_{y_0})$ and temporal frequency ω_{t_0}. Several such filters are required for motion analysis to avoid the effects of image contrast. Heeger's procedure is as follows:

- The sequence of images is low-pass filtered and subsampled to form a Gaussian pyramid [42]. This multiple resolution decomposition will provide the spatial frequency tuning for the filters;

- A center-surround operator [40] filters each pyramid level to remove dc and low spatial frequencies;

- Twelve Gabor energy filters (4-17), all tuned to the same spatial frequency band but to different temporal frequencies and different spatial orientations, are applied to each pyramid level;

- Next, he computes the motion energy factor, which is the squared sum of the sine- and cosine-phase Gabor filter outputs;

- The resulting energies are convolved with a Gaussian to find a weighted approximation of the energy in the given range of frequencies;

- The velocity is estimated by minimizing an expression that predicts the response of the Gabor filters to a moving texture.

Heeger reports promising results in an experiment that simulates a camera flying over Yosemite Valley. The model gives estimates within 10% of the actual velocity of the camera and shows good robustness in the presence of noise. Heeger contends that the spatio-temporal filter model solves the aperture problem as well as the human visual system does because it extracts correct velocities when there are large contrasts in the image. Recall that the smoothness constraint of the gradient method conflicted directly with this. In fact, this method depends on large contrasts being present in the moving objects. Without textures present in the moving regions of the image sequence, the set of points plotted in the space–time frequency volume (e.g., Fig. 4.10) can form a line instead of a plane. This is the manifestation of the aperture problem for the spatio-temporal filtering method.

It should be noted that optical flow is essentially a problem of finding the motion of individual objects in a scene. Because the motion components are fundamentally local in nature, global transform methods, such as the Fourier transform, are unlikely to find application in motion detection. The Gabor filter method, however, uses filters that are frequency tuned and limited in spatial extent.

Other spatio-temporal filtering efforts include Jacobson and Wechsler's [61] application of the Wigner distribution [62]; an experiment using wavelets, targeted for real-time applications on a special computing platform by Singh and Allen [53]; and research by Bigün et al. for texture segmentation in aerial photographs of moving scenes [63].

The basic problem with the Gabor filtering approach, as Singh stresses [7], is the computational burden of computing the frequency responses of the images to the Gabor filters (4-13). Heeger's method of computing the Gabor energy filter responses is an $O(kn^2m)$ algorithm, where k is the size of the convolution kernel, m is the number of images in the sequence, and each image has n pixels [59]. Although the method furnishes outstanding motion estimates, the problem of algorithm timeliness casts doubt on its applicability for real-time applications.

Can the speed of the spatio-temporal filtering method be improved to approach real-time motion analysis requirements? This review of past techniques for motion analysis reveals that there are four basic tools that a proposed motion analysis method must consider: oriented edge detection, corner detection, texture detection, and multiresolution. By the Verri-Poggio result [6], an optical flow extraction technique that uses local approximations at pronounced image edges, will provide the normal optical flow, and this does approximate the normal motion field. Thus, a key feature of a proposed motion analysis method is some mechanism for assessing oriented edge quality and the impact of the Verri-Poggio theorem. The true optical flow can be found in the vicinity of a corner (Figs. 4.3 and 4.4). Once initial optical flow estimates are found within an image, these may be corrected by propagating values from image corners to regions where only the normal optical flow is known because of the aperture problem. To begin this, however, a candidate motion analysis scheme needs a corner detection tool. Texture detection and orientation estimation is a prerequisite for any method that attempts to use spatial frequency and temporal frequency information from image sequences. Except for the spatio-temporal filtering, motion analysis methods do not use this type of information. These low-level pixel operations can in principle be implemented in special-purpose VLSI or, possibly, with field programmable gate arrays.

Both Singh [7] and Heeger [59] consider the wavelet representation to be a possible replacement for the oriented-sensitive, spatial-frequency tuned Gabor energy filters. The wavelet representation has many strengths for image analysis [64, 65]. Among them are the desirable tools for motion analysis—edge, corner, and texture detection in a multiple resolution context. Orthogonal variants of wavelet multiresolution pyramids decompose the original image on an orthogonal basis set. This results in a decomposition that contains as many data points as the original image. There is no growth in data points maintained as, for example, in the Laplacian pyramid decomposition. Once decomposed into a wavelet pyramid, a signal or an image can be exactly reconstructed from the pyramid. This is true even for the orthogonal wavelet pyramids that allow no growth in the memory requirements for implementation. Exact reconstruction is important because it opens up the possibility of compression of images and the storing of object prototype libraries. Images of objects are stored in the form that will be used for the computations. The stored multiple resolution pyramid levels are the basis for coarse-to-fine registration and matching techniques.

Further, the orthogonal wavelet decomposition algorithms that generate wavelet pyramids are $O(n)$ algorithms. The reconstruction algorithms are similar and are of the same complexity. This self-similarity could be useful in parallel and VLSI implementations of motion detection schemes using orthogonal wavelets.

Yet another benefit of the wavelet representation is that the filters used are orientation sensitive. The orientation sensitivity of the filters is used to estimate the amount of image motion in the direction to which a typical filter is tuned. For example, Heeger [58] used twelve Gabor filters of differing orientation sensitivities and temporal frequency tuning for each level of the Gaussian pyramid. An issue is whether the horizontal and vertical orientation sensitivities of the orthogonal wavelet decomposition are sufficient for robust motion detection.

Filters that arise in applying wavelet methods are, like the Gabor filters, localized. This is important because, as indicated above, the objects moving in the scene cause edges, corners, and blobs to be present in the image sequence; all of these are local intensity variations. An important difference is that, in a true Gabor representation, the filters employed have the same spatial extent, even though their frequency tuning varies. In contrast, the wavelet filters that are tuned to lower frequencies have a larger spatial extent.

Although the wavelet representation has many advantages over the Gabor representations, there are some significant weaknesses as well. Orthogonal wavelets are usually avoided because of the lack of translation invariance in the decomposition [66, 67]. That is, the pyramid coefficients of a translated image are very much different from the original, untranslated image. This makes matching and registration of objects problematic. In motion analysis, it means that the moving objects in an image sequence will produce widely varying decomposition coefficients. The proposed algorithms must overcome this translation noninvariance in order for the motion estimation method to be stable.

Orthogonal wavelets further complicate coarse-to-fine matching and registration algorithms. A coarse representation of a signal at one level can have absolutely no positional correlation with its finer representation at the next (or any succeeding) level of scale. Thus, any method for registering object edges must admit the possibility of failure. Alternatively, it may be possible to show that the class of objects under consideration does not allow this failure. Details on these problems are given in [68, 69].

Finally, the orientation sensitivity of orthogonal wavelet image representations is strictly limited to horizontal and vertical edges. This limitation continues to three dimensions. Now the orientation sensitivity applies to planar surfaces orthogonal to a coordinate axis.

Despite the above limitations, an orthogonal wavelet image decomposition can serve as the framework for estimating image motion [70]. Instead of the usual iterative pyramid algorithm, a fast, direct derivation of coarse resolution space–time images with the wavelet decomposition is developed. The algorithms recommend coarse grain parallelism for the image sequence decomposition. Two spatiotemporal filtering methods are possible. The orientation of surfaces in $\mathbf{R}^3$ gives robust indication of image motion. However, the alternative method with oriented texture energies in the spatio-temporal image fares poorly when velocities vary.

4.5 PHASE-BASED APPROACHES

Phase-based methods are a recent hybrid [71, 72]. The input image is decomposed using a number of bandpass filters tuned to direction, scale, and speed. Here again, a multiple resolution processing step of the image sequence data is used. This approach uses differential methods applied to the phase instead of the image intensity of the image to get motion field estimates.

This requires a large number of filters and a large number of images in the sequence. Computation time will be the main problem in real-time implementations of phase-based methods. Further, they are most convenient for applications involving a single moving object. Given these constraints, the method has been shown to be quite accurate in comparison with the methods described above: the gradient, correspondence, and spatio-temporal filtering methods [73].

4.6 SUMMARY

The design of a real-time system must take into account many intricacies of the motion analysis problem to be successful. The discrepancies between the velocity field, the image motion field, and the optical flow are irrelevant in some applications and problematic in others. The aperture problem affects all motion analysis schemes and yet is often ignored by most reports on real-time implementations. However, it does little good to achieve system timeliness and predictability goals if the motion estimates themselves are wrong. These considerations led us on a protracted discussion of four motion analysis techniques from the perspective of real-time implementation.

Difference methods produce dense motion estimates, but they tend to be corrupted by noise. Correspondence methods are widely implemented in real-time systems: autonomous vehicles, tracking applications, and digital video systems. However, implementors often resort to great simplifications and very limiting constraints on system operation. These concerns, together with questions about correspondence predictability, timeliness, and aperture effects, have motivated research into spatio-temporal filtering methods. Here, there is some promise of settling high-level interpretation issues with low-level operations. But real-time applications will apparently need special hardware to perform the multiscale decompositions that the method presupposes. Phase-based approaches are new, relatively accurate, but work best in single object scenes.

References

[1] J. A. Stankovic, "Misconceptions about real-time computing," in *Real-Time Systems*. K. M. Kavi (editor), Los Alamitos, CA: IEEE Computer Society Press, 1992.

[2] P. A. Laplante. *Real-time Systems Design and Analysis: An Engineer's Handbook*. New York: IEEE Press, 1993.

[3] I. Lee, R. B. King, and R. P. Paul, "A predictable real-time kernel for distributed multisensor systems," *Computer*, vol. 22, no. 6, pp. 78–83, June 1989.

[4] W. A. Halang and A. D. Stoyenko. *Constructing Predictable Real Time Systems*. Norwell, MA: Kluwer Academic Publishers, 1991.

[5] B. K. P. Horn. *Robot Vision*. Cambridge, MA: MIT Press, 1986.

[6] A. Verri and T. Poggio, "Against quantitative optical flow," in *Proc. First Int. Conf. Computer Vision*, Washington, D.C.: IEEE Computer Society Press, pp. 171–200, April 1988.

[7] A. Singh. *Optic Flow Computation: A Unified Perspective.* Los Alamitos, CA: IEEE Computer Society Press, 1991.

[8] B. Girod, D. J. Le Gall, M. I. Sezan, M. Vetterli, and H. Yasuda, "Guest editorial: Introduction to the special issue on image sequence compression," *IEEE Trans Image Processing*, vol. 3, no. 5, pp. 465–468, September 1994.

[9] G. K. Wallace, "The JPEG still picture compression standard," *Communications of the ACM*, vol. 34, no. 4, pp. 31–44, April 1991.

[10] D. Le Gall, "MPEG: a video compression standard for multimedia applications," *Communications of the ACM*, vol. 34, no. 4, pp. 46–58, April 1991.

[11] *Signal Processing: Image Communication*, vol. 5, no. 1, February 1993.

[12] H. Li, A. Lundmark, and R. Forchheimer, "Image sequence coding at very low bitrates: a review," *IEEE Trans. Image Processing*, vol. 3, no. 5, pp. 589–609, September 1994.

[13] C. L. Fennema and W. B. Thompson, "Velocity determination in scenes containing several moving objects," *Computer Vision, Graphics, and Image Processing*, vol. 9, pp. 301–315, 1979.

[14] B. K. P. Horn and B. G. Schunck, "Determining optical flow," *Artificial Intelligence*, vol. 17, pp. 185–203, 1981.

[15] A. Ralston. *A First Course in Numerical Analysis.* New York: McGraw-Hill, 1965.

[16] H.-H. Nagel, "Displacement vectors derived from second order intensity variations in image sequences," *Computer Vision, Graphics, and Image Processing*, vol. 21, pp. 85–117, 1983.

[17] M. Yachida, "Determining velocity maps by spatio-temporal neighborhoods from image sequences," *Computer Vision, Graphics, and Image Processing*, vol. 21, pp. 262–279, February 1983.

[18] H.-H. Nagel and W. Enkelmann, "An investigation of smoothness constraints for the estimation of displacement vector fields from image sequences," *IEEE Trans. Pattern Analysis and Machine Intelligence*, vol. PAMI-8, no. 5, pp. 565–593, September 1986.

[19] B. G. Schunck, "Image flow: fundamentals and future research," *Proc. IEEE Conf. Computer Vision and Pattern Recognition*, pp. 560–571, June 1985.

[20] H.-H. Nagel, "On a constraint equation for the estimation of displacement rates in image sequences," *IEEE Trans. Pattern Analysis and Machine Intelligence*, vol. 11, no. 1, pp. 13–30, January 1989.

[21] B. Furht, "Multimedia systems: an overview," *IEEE Multimedia*, pp. 47–59, Spring 1994.

[22] M. Subbarao, "Interpretation of image flow: a spatio-temporal approach," *IEEE Trans. Pattern Analysis and Machine Intelligence*, vol. 11, no. 3, pp. 266–278, March 1989.

[23] G. Adiv, "Inherent ambiguities in recovering 3-D motion and structure from a noisy flow field," *IEEE Trans. Pattern Analysis and Machine Intelligence*, vol. 11, no. 5, pp. 477–489, May 1989.

[24] M. A. Snyder, "On the mathematical foundations of smoothness constraints for the determination of optical flow and for surface reconstruction," *IEEE Trans. Pattern Analysis and Machine Intelligence*, vol. 13, no. 11, pp. 1105–1114, November 1991.

[25] W. Enkelmann, "Investigations of multigrid algorithms for the estimation of optical flow fields in image sequences," *Computer Vision, Graphics, and Image Processing*, vol. 43, pp. 150–177, 1988.

[26] J. L. Crowley and R. M. Stern, "Fast computations of the difference of low-pass transform," *IEEE Trans. Pattern Analysis and Machine Intelligence*, vol. PAMI-6, pp. 212–222, 1984.

[27] C. Koch, H. T. Wang, R. Battiti, B. Mathur, and C. Ziomkowski, "An adaptive multi-scale approach for estimating optical flow: computational theory and physiological implementation," *IEEE Workshop on Visual Motion* (Princeton, NJ), pp. 111–122, 7–9 October 1992.

[28] E. D. Dickmanns and V. Graefe, "Applications of dynamic monocular machine vision," *Machine Vision and Applications*, vol. 1, pp. 241–261, 1988.

[29] E. D. Dickmanns and V. Graefe, "Dynamic monocular machine vision," *Machine Vision and Applications*, vol. 1, pp. 223–240, 1988.

[30] R. Chapuis, J. Gallice, F. Jurie, and J. Alizon, "Real time road mark following," *Signal Processing*, vol. 24, pp. 331–343, 1991.

[31] S. Ullman. *The Interpretation of Visual Motion*. Cambridge, MA: MIT Press, 1979.

[32] D. H. Ballard and C. M. Brown. *Computer Vision*. Englewood Cliffs, NJ: Prentice-Hall, 1982.

[33] H. C. Longuet-Higgins, "A computer program for reconstructing a scene from two projections," *Nature*, vol. 392, pp. 133–135, 1981.

[34] R. Y. Tsai and T. S. Huang, "Uniqueness and estimation of 3-D motion parameters of rigid bodies with curved surfaces," *IEEE Trans. Pattern Analysis and Machine Intelligence*, vol. PAMI-6, no. 1, pp. 13–27, January 1984.

[35] T. S. Huang and C. H. Lee, "Motion and structure from orthographic projections," *IEEE Trans. Pattern Analysis and Machine Intelligence*, vol. 11, no. 5, pp. 536–540, May 1989.

[36] S. Negahdaripour, "Multiple interpretations of the shape and motion of objects from two perspective images," *IEEE Trans. Pattern Analysis and Machine Intelligence*, vol. 12, no. 11, pp. 1025–1039, November 1990.

[37] Y. Wang and O. Lee, "Active mesh—a feature seeking and tracking image sequence representation scheme," *IEEE Trans. Image Processing*, vol. 3, no. 5, pp. 610–624, September 1994.

[38] R. Y. Wong and E. L. Hall, "Sequential hierarchical scene matching," *IEEE Trans. Computers*, vol. C-27, no. 4, pp. 359–366, April 1978.

[39] F. Glazer, G. Reynolds, and P. Anandan, "Scene matching by hierarchical correlation," *IEEE Computer Society Conf. Computer Vision and Pattern Recognition* (Washington, D.C.), pp. 432–441, 19–23 June 1983.

[40] D. Marr. *Vision*. New York: W. H. Freeman and Company, 1982.

[41] P. J. Burt, C. Yen, and X. Xu, "Multi-resolution flow-through motion analysis," *IEEE Computer Society Conf. Computer Vision and Pattern Recognition* (Washington, D.C.), pp. 246–252, 19–23 June 1983.

[42] P. J. Burt and E. H. Adelson, "The Laplacian pyramid as a compact image code," *IEEE Trans. Communications*, vol. 31, no. 4, pp. 532–540, April 1983.

[43] K. Harney, M. Keith, G. Lavelle, L. D. Ryan, and D. J. Stark, "The i750 video processor: a total multimedia solution," *Communications of the ACM*, vol. 34, no. 4, pp. 65–78, April 1991.

[44] F. Sijstermans and J. van der Meer, "CD-I full-motion video encoding on a parallel computer," *Communications of the ACM*, vol. 34, no. 4, pp. 82–91, April 1991.

[45] P. Anandan, "A unified perspective on computational techniques for the measurement of visual motion," in *Proc. First Int. Conf. on Computer Vision* (Washington, D.C.), pp. 219–230, June 8–11, 1987.

[46] P. Anandan, "A computational framework and an algorithm for the measurement of visual motion," *Int. J. Computer Vision*, vol. 2, pp. 283–310, 1989.

[47] M. P. do Carmo. *Differential Geometry of Curves and Surfaces*. Englewood Cliffs, NJ: Prentice-Hall, 1976.

[48] G. L. Scott. *Local and Global Interpretation of Moving Images*. London: Pitman Publishers, 1988.

[49] A. Singh, "Incremental estimation of image-flow using a Kalman filter," *IEEE Workshop on Visual Motion* (Princeton, NJ), pp. 36–43, 7–9 October, 1992.

[50] A. K. Jain. *Fundamentals of Digital Image Processing*. Englewood Cliffs, NJ: Prentice Hall, 1989.

[51] E. H. Adelson and J. R. Bergen, "Spatiotemporal energy models for the perception of motion," *J. Optical Society of America*, vol. A2, no. 2, pp. 284–299, 1985.

[52] A. B. Watson and A. J. Ahumada, "Model of human visual-motion sensing," *J. Optical Society of America*, vol. A2, no. 2, pp. 322–342, 1985.

[53] A. Singh and P. K. Allen, "A real time hierarchical model for optic flow determination via spatiotemporal frequency channels," in *Proc. DARPA Image Understanding Workshop* (Washington, D.C.), pp. 961–967, April 1988.

[54] C. L. Baker and M. S. Cynader, "Space-time separability of direction selectivity in cat striate cortex," *Vision Research*, vol. 28, pp. 239–246, 1988.

[55] J. P. Gaska, K. H. Foster, M. Nagler, and D. A. Pollen, "Spatial and temporal frequency selectivity of V2 neurons in the Macaque monkey," *Investigations in Ophthalmology and Visual Science (Supplement)*, vol. 24, p. 228, 1983.

[56] R. C. Emerson, M. C. Citron, W. J. Vaughn, and S. A. Klein, "Nonlinear directionally selective subunits in complex cells of cat striate cortex," *J. Neurophysiology*, vol. 58, no. 1, pp. 33–65, 1987.

[57] N. M. Grzywacz and A. L. Yuille, "A model for the estimates of local image velocity by cells in the visual cortex," *Proc. Royal Soc. London (B)*, vol. 239, pp. 129–161, 1990.

[58] D. J. Heeger, "Optical flow from spatiotemporal filters," *First Int. Conf. Computer Vision* (Washington, D.C.), pp. 181–190, June 8–11, 1987.

[59] D. J. Heeger, "Optical flow using spatiotemporal filters," *Int. J. Computer Vision*, pp. 279–302, 1988.

[60] J. G. Daugman, "Uncertainty relation for resolution in space, spatial frequency, and orientation optimized by two-dimensional visual cortical filters," *J. Optical Society of America*, vol. 2, no. 7, pp. 1160–1169, 1985.

[61] L. Jacobson and H. Wechsler, "Derivation of optical flow using a spatiotemporal-frequency approach," *Computer Vision, Graphics, and Image Processing*, vol. 38, pp. 29–65, 1987.

[62] B. Boashash, "Time-frequency signal analysis," in *Advances in Spectral Analysis and Array Processing*. S. Haykin (editor). Englewood Cliffs, NJ: Prentice Hall, pp. 418–517, 1990.

[63] J. Bigün, G. H. Granlund, and J. Wiklund, "Multidimensional orientation estimation with applications to texture analysis and optical flow," *IEEE Trans. Pattern Analysis and Machine Intelligence*, vol. 13, no. 8, pp. 775–790, August 1991.

[64] S. G. Mallat, "A theory for multiresolution signal decomposition: the wavelet representation," *IEEE Trans. Pattern Analysis and Machine Intelligence*, vol. 11, no. 7, pp. 674–693, July 1989.

[65] C. K. Chui. *An Introduction to Wavelets*. Boston: Academic Press, Inc., 1992.

[66] S. G. Mallat, "Review of multifrequency channel decompositions of images and wavelet models," Technical Report No. 412, Department of Computer Science, New York University, November 1988.

[67] E. P. Simoncelli, W. T. Freeman, E. H. Adelson, and D. J. Heeger, "Shiftable multiscale transforms," *IEEE Trans. Information Theory*, vol. 38, no. 2, pp. 587–607, March 1992.

[68] R. L. Allen and F. A. Kamanger, "Registration and matching using orthogonal wavelets," *Proc. IEEE-SP Int. Symp. Time-Frequency and Time-Scale Analysis*, (Victoria, BC, Canada), 4–6 October, 1992.

[69] R. L. Allen, "The wavelet multiresolution representation of images for pattern matching applications," M.S. Thesis, Dept. of Computer Science Engineering, University of Texas at Arlington, August 1990.

[70] R. L. Allen, "Motion estimation using the multiresolution analysis of $L^2(\mathbf{R}^3)$," *Proc. IEEE Southwest Symposium on Image Analysis and Interpretation* (Dallas, TX), pp. 124–129, 21–22 April, 1994.

[71] D. J. Fleet. *Measurement of Image Velocity*. Norwell, MA: Kluwer Academic Publishers, 1992.

[72] D. J. Fleet and A. D. Jepson, "Computation of component image velocity from local phase information," *Int. J. Computer Vision*, vol. 5, no. 1, pp. 77–104, 1990.

[73] J. L. Barron, D. J. Fleet, S. S. Beauchemin, and T. A. Burkitt, "Performance of optical flow techniques," in *Proc. 1992 IEEE Computer Society Conf. Computer Vision and Pattern Recognition* (Champaign, IL), pp. 236–242, 15–18 June.

5

MULTIMEDIA COMPRESSION
TECHNIQUES AND STANDARDS

Borko Furht   *Department of Computer Science and Engineering, Florida Atlantic University*

5.1 INTRODUCTION

Multimedia computing has emerged in the last few years as a major area of research. These computer systems have opened the wide range of potential applications by combining a variety of information sources, such as voice, graphics, animation, images, audio, and full-motion video. Looking at the big picture, multimedia can be viewed as the merging of three industries: computer, communications, and broadcasting.

Research and development efforts in multimedia computing have been divided into two groups. The first considerable effort has been centered on the stand-alone multimedia workstation and associated software systems and tools, such as music composition, computer-aided learning, and interactive video. However, the combination of multimedia computing with distributed systems offers even greater potential. New applications based on distributed multimedia systems include multimedia information systems, collaboration and conferencing systems, on-demand multimedia services, and distance learning.

The fundamental characteristic of multimedia systems is that they incorporate continuous media such as voice, video, and animated graphics. This implies the need for such systems to handle data with strict timing requirements and at high rate. The use of continuous media in distributed systems also implies the need for continuous data transfer over relatively long periods of time (e.g., playout of video stream from a remote camera). Additional important fundamental issues are: media synchronization, very large storage requirements, and the need for special indexing and retrieval techniques tuned to multimedia data types [1].

Figure 5.1 illustrates basic principles in dealing with continuous media (audio and video), and still images, and several examples of operations on these media. Audio and video information can either be stored and then used in an application, such as training, or it can be transmitted live in real-time. Live audio and video can be used interactively, such as in multimedia conferencing, or noninteractively, such as in TV broadcast applications. Similarly, stored still images can be used in an interactive mode (using operations such as browsing and retrieval) or in noninteractive mode (slide show).

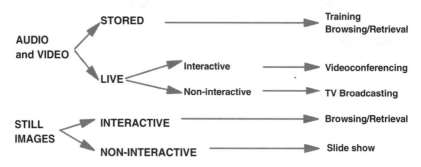

Figure 5.1 Various modes of operations on multimedia data.

It is interesting to note that multimedia stresses all the components of a computer system. At the processor level, multimedia requires very high processing power in order to implement software codecs, and multimedia file systems and corresponding file formats. At the architecture level, new solutions are needed to provide high bus bandwidth and efficient I/O. At the operating systems level, there is a need for high-performance to support new data types, real-time scheduling, and fast interrupt processing. Storage and memory requirements include very high capacity, fast access times, and high transfer rates. At the network level, new networks and protocols are needed to provide the high bandwidth, low latency, and jitter compensation required for multimedia. At the software tool level, there is a need for new object-oriented, user-friendly multimedia development tools, and tools for retrieval and data management, which are important in large, heterogeneous, networked and distributed multimedia systems.

Multimedia researchers are working in existing computer areas to transform current or develop new technologies suitable for multimedia. These research areas span computing and include: fast processors, high-speed networks, large-capacity storage devices, new algorithms and data structures, video and audio compression algorithms, graphics systems, human-computer interaction, real-time operating systems, object-oriented programming, information storage and retrieval, hypertext and hypermedia, languages for scripting, parallel processing methods, and complex architectures for distributed systems.

5.2 STORAGE REQUIREMENTS
FOR MULTIMEDIA APPLICATIONS

Audio, image, and video signals require vast amounts of data for their representation. Table 5.1 illustrates the mass storage requirements for various media types: text, image, audio, animation, video, and so on.

TABLE 5.1 Storage Requirements for Various Media Types

	Text	Image	Audio	Animation	Video
Object type	•ASCII •EBCDIC	•Bitmapped graphics •Still photos •Faxes	Noncoded stream of digitized audio or voice	Synched image and audio stream at 15–19 frames/s	TV analog or digital image with synched streams at 24–30 frames/s
Size and bandwidth	2 KB per page	•Simple: 64kB per image •Detailed: (color) 7.5 MB per image	Voice/Phone 8 kHz/8 bits (mono) 6–44 kB/s Audio CD 44.1 kHz/16 bit (stereo) 176 kB/s	2.5 MB/s for $320 \times 640 \times 16$ pixels/frame (16-bit color) 16 frames/s	27.7 MB/s $640 \times 480 \times 24$ pixels per frame (24-bit color) 30 frames/s

There are three main reasons why present multimedia systems require that data must be compressed. These reasons are related to: 1) large storage requirements of multimedia data, 2) relatively slow storage devices that do not allow playing multimedia data (specifically video) in real-time, and 3) the present network bandwidth, which does not allow real-time video data transmission.

As an example, a typical multimedia application may require the storage of more than 30 minutes of video, 2000 images, and 40 minutes of stereo sound on each laser disk side. This application would require about 50 GB of storage for video, 15 GB of storage for images, and 0.4 GB of storage for audio—a total of 65.4 GB of storage.

In another example, assuming color video frames with 620×560 pixels and 24 bits per pixel, it would be necessary to save about 1 MB per frame. For a motion video requiring 30 frames/s, 30 MB are required for one second of motion video. Even if there is enough storage available, we won't be able to play back the video in real-time due to the insufficient bit rate of storage devices. According to previous calculations, the required speed of a storage device should be 30 MB/s; however, today's technology provides about 600–900 kB/s transfer rate on CD-ROMs. Therefore, at the present state of technology of storage devices, the only solution is to compress the data before storage and decompress it before playback.

Modern image and video compression techniques offer a solution to this problem, which reduces these tremendous storage requirements. Advanced compression techniques can compress a typical image ranging from 10:1 to 50:1. Very high compression ratios of up to 2000:1 can be achieved in compressing video signals. Figure 5.2 illustrates storage requirements for a multimedia application consisting of various media types, assuming that the image is compressed by the ratio 15:1, and video by factors of 30:1 and 200:1. The total storage requirement for this storage-intensive application becomes a little over 2 GB, which is practical.

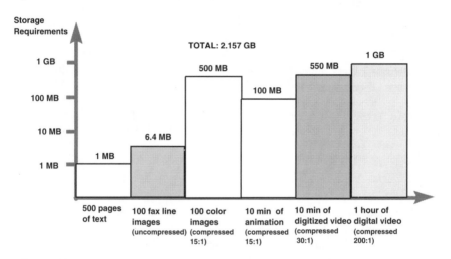

Figure 5.2 Storage requirements for a multimedia application, assuming that compression techniques are applied for images and video.

5.3 CLASSIFICATION OF COMPRESSION TECHNIQUES

Compression of digital data is based on various computational algorithms, that can be implemented either in software or in hardware. Compression techniques are classified into two categories: 1) lossless, and 2) lossy approaches [2]. Lossless techniques are capable of perfectly recovering the original representation. Lossy techniques involve algorithms that recover a presentation similar to the original one. The lossy techniques provide higher compression ratios and, therefore, they are more often applied in image and video compression than lossless techniques. The classification schemes for lossless and lossy compression are presented in Figures 5.3a and b, respectively.

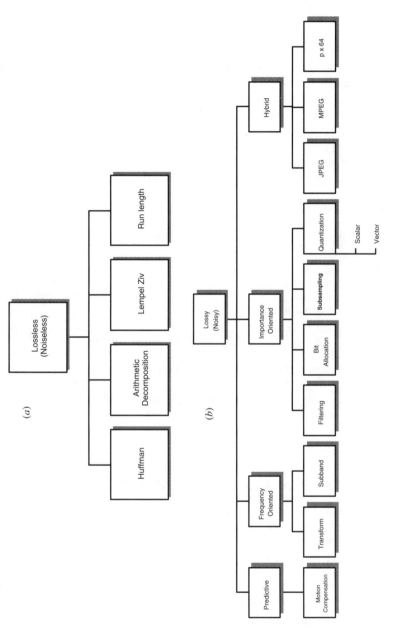

Figure 5.3 Classification schemes for (a) lossless, and (b) lossy compression techniques.

The lossy techniques are classified into: 1) prediction-based techniques, 2) frequency-oriented techniques, and 3) importance-oriented techniques. Predictive-based techniques, such as adaptive differential pulse-code modulation (ADPCM), predict subsequent values by observing previous values. Frequency-oriented techniques apply the discrete cosine transform (DCT), which relates to fast Fourier transform. Importance-oriented techniques use other characteristics of images as the basis for compression. For example, digital video interface (DVI^{TM}) technique uses color lookup tables and data filtering.

The hybrid compression techniques, such as JPEG, MPEG, and $p \times 64$, combine several approaches, such as DCT and vector quantization or differential pulse code modulation. Recently, standards for digital multimedia have been established based on these three techniques, as illustrated in Table 5.2.

TABLE 5.2 Multimedia Compression Standards

Short Name	Official Name	Standards Group	Compression Ratios
JPEG	Digital compression and coding of continuous-tone still images	Joint Photographic Experts Group	15:1 (full-color still-frame applications)
H.261 $p \times 64$	Video encoder/decoder for audiovisual services at $p \times 64$ kB/s	Specialist Group on Coding for Visual Telephony	100:1 to 2000:1 (video-based telecommunications)
MPEG	Coding of moving pictures and associated audio	Moving Pictures Experts Group	200:1 (motion-intensive applications)

5.4   IMAGE CONCEPTS AND STRUCTURES

A digital image represents a two-dimensional array of samples, where each sample is called a *pixel*. Precision determines how many levels of intensity can be represented, and is expressed as the number of bits/sample. According to precision, the images can be classified into:

Binary images, represented by 1 bit/sample. Examples include black and white photographs and facsimile images.

Computer graphics, represented by a lower precision, such as 4 bits/sample.

Gray-scale images, represented by 8 bits/sample.

Color images, represented with 16, 24, or more bits/sample.

According to the trichromatic theory, the sensation of color is produced by selectively exciting three classes of receptors in the eye. In an RGB color representation system, shown in Figure 5.4, a color is produced by adding the three primary colors: red, green, and blue (RGB). The straight line, where $R = G = B$, specifies the gray values ranging from black to white.

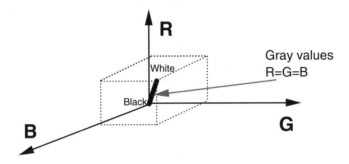

Figure 5.4 RGB representation of color images.

Figure 5.5 illustrates how a three-sensor RGB color video camera operates and produces colors at an RGB monitor [4]. Lights for sources of different colors are added together to produce the prescribed color.

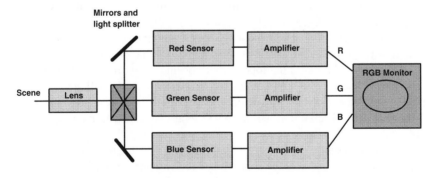

Figure 5.5 Three-sensor RGB color video camera.

Another representation of color images, YUV representation, describes luminance and chrominance components of an image. The luminance component provides a gray-scale version of the image, while two chrominance components give additional information that converts the gray-scale image to a color image.

The YUV representation is more natural for image compression. An image represented in RGB color can be converted into YUV systems using the following transformations [4]:

$$Y = 0.3R + 0.6G + 0.1B \qquad (5\text{-}1)$$

$$U = B - Y \qquad (5\text{-}2)$$

$$V = R - Y \qquad (5\text{-}3)$$

where Y is the luminance component and U and V are two chrominance components. When $R = G = B$, then $Y = R = G = B$, and $U = V = 0$, which represents a gray-scale image.

Another color format, referred to as YC_bC_r (similar to the YUV format) is intensively used for image compression. In YC_bC_r format, Y is the same as in the YUV system; however, U and V are scaled and zero-shifted to produce C_b and C_r, respectively, as follows:

$$C_b = \frac{U}{2} + 0.5 \qquad (5\text{-}4)$$

$$C_r = \frac{V}{1.6} + 0.5 \qquad (5\text{-}5)$$

In this way, chrominance components C_b and C_r are always in the range [0, 1].

Resolution of an image system refers to its capability to reproduce fine details [4]. Higher resolution requires more complex imaging systems to represent these images in real-time. In computer systems, resolution is characterized by the number of pixels (for example, VGA has a resolution of 640 × 480 pixels). In video systems, resolution refers to the number of line pairs resolved on the face of the display screen, expressed in cycles per picture height, or cycles per picture width. For example, the National Television Systems Committee (NTSC) broadcast system in North America and Japan, denoted 525/59.94, has about 483 picture lines. (The number 525 denotes the total number of lines in its rates, and 59.94 is its field rate in hertz). The high-definition TV (HDTV) system will approximately double the number of lines of current broadcast television at approximately the same field rate. The system will have 937 total lines and a frame rate of 65.95 Hz.

Figure 5.6 compares various image structures, showing the vertical and horizontal pixel counts [4], and the approximate total number of pixels.

The Comité Consultatif International de Télégraphique et Téléphonique (CCITT) has adopted two picture formats for video-based telecommunications: Common Intermediate Format (CIF) and Quarter-CIF (QCIF), described in detail in Section 5.6.

Full-motion video is characterized with at least a 24-Hz frame rate (or 24 frames/s), up to 30 or even 60 frames/s for HDTV. For animation, acceptable frame rate is in the range 15–19 frames/s, while for video telephony it is 5–10 frames/s. Videoconferencing and interactive multimedia applications require the rate of 15–30 frames/s.

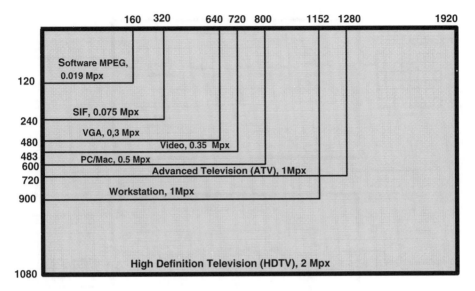

Figure 5.6 Various image structures.

5.5 JPEG ALGORITHM FOR FULL-COLOR STILL IMAGE COMPRESSION

Originally, the JPEG standard was targeted for full-color still frame applications, achieving 15:1 average compression ratio [3, 5]. However, JPEG is also applied in some real-time, full-motion video applications (Motion JPEG–MJPEG). The JPEG standard provides four modes of operation:

- *Sequential DCT-based encoding*, in which each image component is encoded in a single left-to-right, top-to-bottom scan

- *Progressive DCT-based encoding*, in which the image is encoded in multiple scans, in order to produce a quick, rough decoded image when the transmission time is long

- *Lossless encoding*, in which the image is encoded to guarantee the exact reproduction

- *Hierarchical encoding*, in which the image is encoded in multiple resolutions

5.5.1 Sequential JPEG Encoder and Decoder

The block diagram of the JPEG sequential encoder and decoder is shown in Figure 5.7.

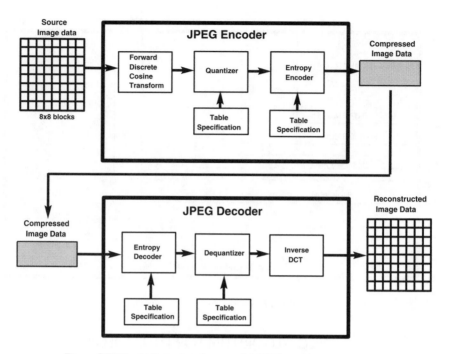

Figure 5.7 Block diagrams of sequential JPEG encoder and decoder.

JPEG Encoder

The original samples, in the range $[0, 2^P - 1]$, are shifted into the range $[-2^{P-1}, 2^{P-1} - 1]$. For a gray-scale image, where $p = 8$, the original samples in the range $[0, 511]$ are shifted into the range $[-128 + 127]$.

These values are then transformed into the frequency domain using the forward discrete cosine transform (FDCT) using the following equations:

$$F(u, v) = \frac{C(u)}{2} \cdot \frac{C(v)}{2} \sum_{x=0}^{7} \sum_{y=0}^{7} f(x, y) \cos \frac{(2x + 1)u\pi}{16} \cos \frac{(2y + 1)v\pi}{16} \quad (5\text{-}6)$$

where
$C(u) = \frac{1}{\sqrt{2}}$ for $u = 0$
$C(u) = 1$ for $u > 0$
$C(u) = \frac{1}{\sqrt{2}}$ for $v = 0$
$C(u) = 1$ for $v > 0$

The transformed 64-point discrete signal is a function of two spatial dimensions x and y, and its components are called *spatial frequencies* or *DCT coefficients*.

The $F(0, 0)$ coefficient is called the *dc coefficient*, and the remaining 63 coefficents are called the *AC coefficients*. A number of fast DCT algorithms are analyzed in [3].

For a typical 8×8 image block, most of the spatial frequencies have zero or near-zero values, and need not be encoded. This is illustrated in a JPEG example, presented in Section 5.5.2. This fact is the foundation for achieving data compression. In the next step, all 64 DCT coefficients are quantized using a 64-element quantization table, specified by the application. The quantization reduces the amplitude of the coefficients that have little or no contribution to the quality of the image, with the purpose of increasing the number of zero-value coefficients. Quantization also discards information that is not visually significant.

The quantization is performed according to the following equation:

$$F_q(u, v) = \text{Round} \left[\frac{F(u, v)}{Q(u, v)} \right] \tag{5-7}$$

where $Q(u, v)$ are quantization coefficients specified in the quantization table. Each element $Q(u, v)$ is an integer from 1 to 255, which specifies the step size of the quantizer for its corresponding DCT coefficient.

A set of four quantization tables are specified by the JPEG standard [3]. In the JPEG example in Section 5.5.2, a quantization formula is used to produce the quantization tables.

After quantization, the 63 ac coefficients are ordered into the "zigzag" sequence, as shown in Figure 5.8.

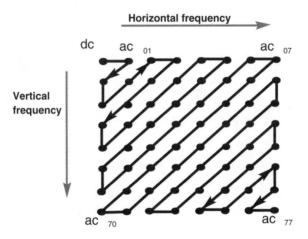

Figure 5.8 Zigzag ordering of ac coefficients.

This zigzag ordering will help to facilitate the next phase—entropy encoding—by placing low-frequency coefficients, which are more likely to be nonzero, before high-frequency coefficients.

This fact is confirmed by the experiment presented in [3] and results shown in Figure 5.9. These results show that when the coefficients are ordered zigzag,

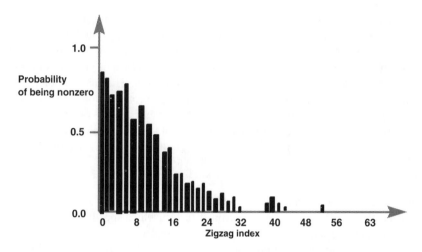

Figure 5.9 Probability of being nonzero of zigzag-ordered DCT coefficients.

the probability of coefficients being zero is an increasing monotonic function of the index.

The dc coefficients, which represent the average values of the 64 image samples, are coded using the predictive coding techniques, as illustrated in Figure 5.10.

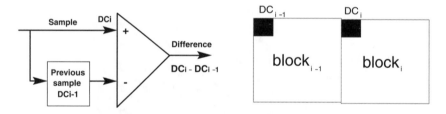

Figure 5.10 Predictive coding for dc coefficients.

The reason for predictive coding of dc coefficients is that there is usually a strong correlation between the dc coefficients of adjacent 8×8 blocks. As a consequence, the compression ratio will be improved.

Finally, the last block in the JPEG encoder is the entropy coding, which provides additional compression by encoding the quantized DCT coefficients into more compact form. The JPEG standard specifies two entropy coding methods: Huffman coding and arithmetic coding [3]. The baseline sequential JPEG encoder uses Huffman coding, which is presented next.

The Huffman coder converts the DCT coefficients after quantization into a compact binary sequence using two steps: 1) forming intermediate symbol sequence, and 2) converting intermediate symbol sequence into binary sequence using Huffman tables.

In the intermediate symbol sequence, each ac coefficient is represented by a pair of symbols, where:

Symbol-1	Symbol-2
(RUNLENGTH, SIZE)	(AMPLITUDE)

RUNLENGTH is the number of consecutive zero-lined ac coefficients preceding the nonzero ac coefficient. The value of RUNLENGTH is in the range of 0 to 15, which requires 4 bits for its representation.

SIZE is the number of bits used to encode AMPLITUDE. The number of bits for AMPLITUDE is in the range of 0 to 10 bits, so there are 4 bits needed to code SIZE.

AMPLITUDE is the amplitude of the nonzero ac coefficient in the range of [+1024 to −1023], which requires 10 bits for its coding. For example, if the sequence of ac coefficients is:

$$\underbrace{0, 0, 0, 0, 0, 0,}_{6} \ 476$$

the symbol representation of the ac coefficient 476 is

$$(6, 9) \ (476)$$

where RUNLENGTH = 6, SIZE = 9, and AMPLITUDE = 476.

If RUNLENGTH is greater than 15, then symbol-1 (15,0) is interpreted as the extension symbol with runlength = 16. There can be up to three consecutive (15,0) extensions.

In the following example,

$$(15, 0) \ (15, 0) \ (7, 4) \ (12)$$

RUNLENGTH is equal to $16 + 16 + 7 = 39$, SIZE = 4, and AMPLITUDE = 12.

The symbol (0,0) means *end of block* (EOB) and terminates each 8×8 block.

For dc coefficients, the intermediate symbol representation consists of:

Symbol-1	Symbol-2
(SIZE)	(AMPLITUDE)

Because dc coefficients are differentially encoded, this range is twice as large as the range for ac coefficients, and is [−2048, +2047].

The second step in Huffman coding is converting the intermediate symbol sequence into a binary sequence. In this phase, symbols are replaced with variable-length codes, beginning with the dc coefficients, and continuing with ac coefficients.

Each Symbol-1 (both for dc and ac coefficients) is encoded with a variable-length code (VLC), obtained from the Huffman table set specified for each image component. The generation of Huffman tables is discussed in [3]. Symbols-2 are encoded using a variable-length integer (VLI) code, whose length in bits is given in Table 5.3. For example, for an ac coefficient presented as the symbols

$$(1, 4) \ (12)$$

the binary presentation will be (i 1 1 1 1 1 0 1 1 0 1 1 0 0), where (1 1 1 1 1 0 1 1 0) is VLC obtained from the Huffman table, and (1 1 0 0) is VLI code for 12.

TABLE 5.3 Huffman Coding of Symbols-2

Size	Amplitude range
1	$(-1,1)$
2	$(-3,-2) \ (2,3)$
3	$(-7 \ldots - 4) \ (4 \ldots 7)$
4	$(-15 \ldots - 8) \ (8 \ldots 15)$
5	$(-31 \ldots - 16) \ (16 \ldots 31)$
6	$(-63 \ldots - 32) \ (32 \ldots 63)$
7	$(-127 \ldots - 64) \ (64 \ldots 127)$
8	$(-255 \ldots - 128) \ (128 \ldots 255)$
9	$(-511 \ldots - 256) \ (256 \ldots 511)$
10	$(-1023 \ldots - 512) \ (512 \ldots 1023)$

JPEG Decoder

In the JPEG sequential decoding, all the steps from the encoding process are inverted and implemented in reverse order, as shown in Figure 5.7.

First, an entropy decoder (such as Huffman) is implemented on the compressed image data. The binary sequence is converted to a symbol sequence using Huffman tables (VLC coefficients) and VLI decoding, and then the symbols are converted into DCT coefficients. Second, the dequantization is implemented using the following function:

$$F_q'(u, v) = F_q(u, v) \times Q(u, v) \tag{5-8}$$

Third, the inverse discrete cosine transform (IDCT) is implemented on dequantized coefficients in order to convert the image from frequency domain into spatial domain. The IDCT equation is defined as

$$F(x, y) = \frac{1}{4} \left[\sum_{u=0}^{7} \sum_{v=0}^{7} C(u)C(v)F(u, v) \cos \frac{(2x + 1)u\pi}{16} \cos \frac{(2y + 1)v\pi}{16} \right] \tag{5-9}$$

where
$C(u) = \frac{1}{\sqrt{2}}$ for $u = 0$
$C(u) = 1$ for $u > 0$
$C(u) = \frac{1}{\sqrt{2}}$ for $v = 0$
$C(u) = 1$ for $v > 0$

The last step consists of shifting back the decompressed samples in the range $[0, 2^P - 1]$.

Compression Measures

The basic measure for the performance of a compression algorithm is compression ratio (C_r), defined as

$$C_R = \frac{\text{Original data size}}{\text{Compressed data size}} \tag{5-10}$$

There is a trade-off between the compression ratio and the picture quality. Higher compression ratios may produce lower picture quality. Quality and compression can also vary according to source image characteristics and scene content. One measure for the quality of the picture, proposed in [5], is the number of bits per pixel in the compressed image (N_b), which is defined as the total number of bits in the compressed image divided by the number of pixels:

$$N_b = \frac{\text{Encoded number of bits}}{\text{Number of pixels}} \tag{5-11}$$

According to this measure, four different picture qualities are defined [5], as shown in Table 5.4.

TABLE 5.4 Picture Quality Characteristics

N_b(bits/pixel)	Picture Quality
0.25–0.5	Moderate to good quality
0.5–0.75	Good to very good quality
0.75–1.0	Excellent quality
1.0–2.0	Usually indistinguishable from the original

Another statistical measure that can be used to evaluate various compression algorithms is the root mean square (rms) error, calculated as

$$\text{rms} = \frac{1}{n}\sqrt{\sum_{i=1}^{n}(X_i - \hat{X}_i)^2} \tag{5-12}$$

where
X_i = original pixel values
$\hat{X}_i$ = pixel values after decompression
n = total number of pixels in an image

The rms shows the statistical difference between the original and decompressed images. However, in some cases, it may happen that the quality of a decompressed image with higher rms is better than one with lower rms.

In the next two sections, we will calculate these measures in several examples.

5.5.2   Sequential JPEG Encoding Example

In order to illustrate all the steps in baseline sequential JPEG encoding, we present step-by-step results obtained in encoding an 8×8 block of 8-bit samples, as illustrated in Figure 5.11. The original 8×8 block is shown in Figure 5.11a and, after shifting, the obtained block is given in Figure 5.11b. After applying the FDCT, the obtained DCT coefficients are given in Figure 5.11c. Note that, except for low-frequency coefficients, all the other coefficients are close to zero.

For the generation of the quantization table, we used the program proposed in [6]:

```
for i=0 to n;
  for j=0 to n;
      Q[i,j] = 1 + (1+i+j)*quality;
  end j;
end i;
```

The parameter "quality" specifies the quality factor and recommended range is from 1 to 25, where quality $= 1$ gives the best quality but the lowest compression rate, and quality $= 25$ gives the worst quality and the highest compression rate. In our example, we used quality $= 2$, which generates the quantization table in Figure 5.11d.

The coefficients obtained after implementing quantization are shown in Figure 5.11e. Note that a number of high-frequency ac coefficients are zero.

The zigzag ordered sequence of quantized coefficients is shown in Figure 5.11f, and the intermediate symbol sequence in Figure 5.11g. Finally, the encoded bit sequence obtained after implementing Huffman codes is shown in Figure 5.11h. The Huffman table used in this example is proposed in the JPEG standard for luminance ac coefficients [3], and the partial table needed to code the symbols from Figure 5.11g is given in Table 5.5.

Note that the dc coefficient is threatened by being from the first 8×8 block in the image and, therefore, it is coded directly (not using predictive coding as all the remaining dc coefficients). For this block, the compression ratio can be calculated as

$$C_r = \frac{\text{Original number of bits}}{\text{Encoded number of bits}} = \frac{64 \times 8}{98} = \frac{512}{98} = 5.22$$

and the number of bits/pixel in the compressed form is

$$N_b = \frac{\text{Encoded number of bits}}{\text{Number of pixels}} = \frac{98}{64} = 1.53$$

5.5.3   Sequential JPEG Experiments

In this section, we present results of experiments obtained by implementing the sequential JPEG algorithms for gray-scale images [7]. The JPEG algorithm has

140	144	147	140	140	155	179	175
144	152	140	147	140	148	167	179
152	155	136	167	163	162	152	172
168	145	156	160	152	155	136	160
162	148	156	148	140	136	147	162
147	167	140	155	155	140	136	162
136	156	123	167	162	144	140	147
148	155	136	155	152	147	147	136

(a)

12	16	19	12	11	27	51	47
16	24	12	19	12	20	39	51
24	27	8	39	35	34	24	44
40	17	28	32	24	27	8	32
34	20	28	20	12	8	19	34
19	39	12	27	27	12	8	34
8	28	−5	39	34	16	12	19
20	27	8	27	24	19	19	8

(b)

185	−17	14	−8	23	−9	−13	−18
20	−34	26	−9	−10	10	13	6
−10	−23	−1	6	−18	3	−20	0
−8	−5	14	−14	−8	−2	−3	8
−3	9	7	1	−11	17	18	15
3	−2	−18	8	8	−3	0	−6
8	0	−2	3	−1	−7	−1	−1
0	−7	−2	1	1	4	−6	0

(c)

3	5	7	9	11	13	15	17
5	7	9	11	13	15	17	19
7	9	11	13	15	17	19	21
9	11	13	15	17	19	21	23
11	13	15	17	19	21	23	25
13	15	17	19	21	23	25	27
15	17	19	21	23	25	27	29
17	19	21	23	25	27	29	31

(d)

61	−3	2	0	2	0	0	−1
4	−4	2	0	0	0	0	0
−1	−2	0	0	−1	0	−1	0
0	0	1	0	0	0	0	0
0	0	0	0	0	0	0	0
0	0	−1	0	0	0	0	0
0	0	0	0	0	0	0	0
0	0	0	0	0	0	0	0

(e)

(f)
61,−3,4,−1,−4,2,0,2,−2,0,0,0,0,0,2,0,0,0,1,0,0,0,0,0,0,−1,0,0,−1,0,0,
0,0,−1,0,0,0,0,0,0,0,−1,0,0,0,0,0,0,0,0,0,0,0,0,0,0,0,0,0,0,0,0,0,0,0

(g)
(6)(61),(0,2)(−3),(0,3)(4),(0,1)(−1),(0,3)(−4),(0,2)(2),(1,2)(2),(0,2)(−2),
(0,2)(−2),(5,2)(2),(3,1)(1),(6,1)(−1),(2,1)(−1),(4,1)(−1),(7,1)(−1),(0,0)

(h)
1110111101001001000001000110110110111001011111111011
11011101011111011011100011101101111101001010

Figure 5.11 Step-by-step procedure in JPEG sequential encoding of an 8 × 8 block:
(a) original 8× 8 block; (b) shifted block; (c) block after FDCT eq. (5-5); (d) quantization
table (quality = 2); (e) block after quantization eq. (5-6); (f) zigzag sequence;
(g) intermediate symbol sequence; and (h) encoded bit sequence (total 98 bits).

TABLE 5.5 Partial Huffman Table
for Luminance ac Coefficients

(RUNLENGTH, SIZE)	Code Word
(0, 0) EOB	1010
(0, 1)	00
(0, 2)	01
(0, 3)	100
(1, 2)	11011
(2, 1)	11100
(3, 1)	111010
(4, 1)	111011
(5, 2)	11111110111
(6, 1)	1111011
(7, 1)	11111010

been implemented and run on two SUN machines: SPARC 10 Model 41, characterized by 109 MIPS and 22 MFLOPS, and SPARC IPC, characterized by 17 MIPS
and 2.1 MFLOPS. We used the algorithm described in Section 5.5.2 to generate
different qualization tables, selecting the following values for parameter quality:
1, 2, 4, 8, 16, and 25. Several gray-scale images (320 × 200 pixels, 8 bits/pixel)
were compressed and decompressed using the JPEG algorithm.

Complete results for the gray-scale image "Lisa" are presented in [7]. The
empirical results are given in Table 5.6, and the original and decompressed images,
for different quality factors, are shown in Figure 5.12.

TABLE 5.6 Results of JPEG Compression for Gray-scale Image "Lisa" (320 × 240 pixels)

Quality Factor	Original Number of Bits	Compressed Number of Bits	Compression Ratio (C_r)	Bits/pixel (N_b)	RMS Error	Execution Times (ms) Sun Sparc 10/41	Sun IPC
1	512,000	48,021	10.66	0.75	2.25	0.59	6.31
2	512,000	30,490	16.79	0.48	2.75	0.59	6.22
4	512,000	20,264	25.27	0.32	3.43	0.58	6.39
8	512,000	14,162	36.14	0.22	4.24	0.59	6.44
15	512,000	10,479	48.85	0.16	5.36	0.58	6.45
25	512,000	9,034	56.64	0.14	6.40	0.58	6.32
DC only	512,000	7,688	66.60	0.12	7.92	0.57	6.25

From Table 5.6 and Figure 5.13, it is clear that compression ratios will produce
a lower quality image, and consequently the number of bits/pixel will decrease and
rms error will increase. Execution times, which include both encoder and decoder

Figure 5.12 Original image "Lisa" and after decompression for different quality factors: (a) original image; (b) quality = 1, C_r = 10.66; (c) quality = 2, C_r = 16.79; (d) quality = 15, C_r = 48.85; and (e) DC coefficient only, C_r = 66.60.

times, are very consistent at different quality levels. The average processing for SPARC has been over six times faster than for the IPC, which is consistent with the reported MIPS performance of these two machines.

5.5.4 JPEG Compression of Color Images

The described sequential JPEG algorithm can be easily expanded for compression of color images or, in a general case, for compression of multiple-component images. The JPEG source image model consists of 1 to 255 image components [5, 8] called *color* or *spectral bands*, as illustrated in Figure 5.13.

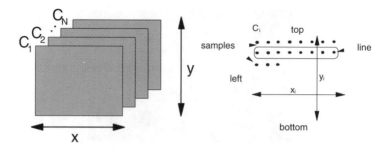

Figure 5.13 JPEG source image model.

For example, RGB and YUV representations both consist of three color components. Each component may have a different number of pixels in the horizontal (X_i) and vertical (Y_i) axes. Figure 5.14 illustrates two cases of a color image with three components. In the first case, all three components have the same resolutions, while in the second case, they have different resolutions.

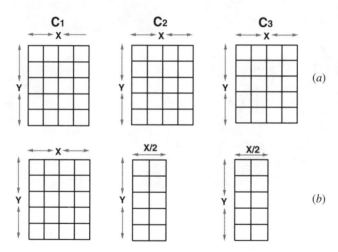

Figure 5.14 Color image with three components: (a) with same resolutions; (b) with different resolutions.

The color components can be processed in two ways:

a. *Non-interleaved data ordering* [5, 8], in which processing is performed component-by-component from left-to-right and top-to-bottom. In this mode, for an RGB image with high resolution, the red component will be displayed first, then the green component, and finally the blue component.

b. *Interleaved data ordering* [5, 8], in which different components are combined into so-called minimum coded units (MCUs).

Block diagrams of the encoder and decoder for color JPEG compression are identical to those for gray-scale image compression, shown in Figure 5.7, except that the first block into the encoder is a color space conversion block (for example, RGB-to-YUV conversion), and at the decoder side, the last block is the inversed color conversion, such as YUV to RGB.

Color JPEG Experiment

In this experiment, the execution time of a color JPEG algorithm has been analyzed [9]. The goal was to measure execution times of different blocks in the JPEG encoder and decoder and identify which blocks take more time. Originally, this experiment was performed in order to design some of the steps in the JPEG algorithm and parallelize the most effective parallel algorithm.

The color JPEG algorithm was run on an i486/33MHz machine with no math coprocessor. The 320 × 240 "Targa" image, with 24 bits/pixel, was compressed and then decompressed. The results are presented in Table 5.7.

TABLE 5.7 Color JPEG Experiment

Operation	JPEG Compression		JPEG Decompression	
	Time (s)	Percentage	Time (s)	Percentage
Read/Write File	0.75	11	0.34	6
RGB/YUV Conversion	1.40	21	1.14	19
Reorder from/for YUV	0.28	4	0.49	8
FDCT/IDCT	2.87	43	2.90	48
Quantization/ Dequantization	0.47	7	0.37	6
Huffman encode/decode	0.87	13	0.70	12
Write/Read File I/O	0.01	1	0.06	1
Total Time	6.65	100	6.00	100

From Table 5.7 it can be seen that the JPEG algorithm spends 48% of decompression time performing IDCT and, similarly, 42% of compression time performing FDCT. Color conversion also requires about 20% of total time execution, and Huffman coding about 12%.

Assuming a Pentium personal computer with math coprocessor, the expected performance of the JPEG algorithm can be improved about six times, which will mean about 1 s for decompression.

5.5.5 Progressive JPEG Compression

In some applications, an image may have large numbers of pixels and the decompression process, including transmission of the compressed image over the network, may take several minutes. In such applications, there may be a need to produce a quick, rough image quickly, and then improve its quality using multiple scans [3, 5, 8]. The progressive JPEG mode of operation produces a sequence of scans, each scan coding a subset of DCT coefficients. Therefore, the progressive JPEG encoder must have an additional buffer at the output of the quantizer and before the entropy encoder. The size of the buffer should be large enough to store all DCT coefficients of the image, each of which is 3 bits larger than the original image samples.

Figure 5.15 illustrates the differences in displaying a decompressed image in the progressive and sequential JPEG.

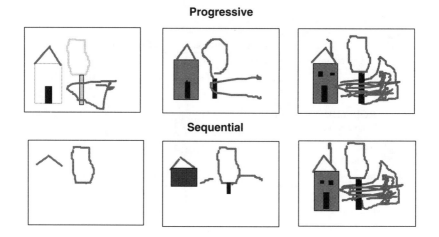

Figure 5.15 Progressive versus sequential JPEG coding.

Progressive JPEG compression can be achieved using three algorithms:

1. progressive spectral selection algorithm,

2. progressive successive approximation algorithm, and

3. combined progressive algorithm.

In the progressive spectral selection algorithm, the DCT coefficients are grouped into several spectral bands. Typically, low-frequency DCT coefficient bands are sent first, and then higher-frequency coefficients. For example, a sequence of four spectral bands may look like this:

band 1: dc coefficient only

band 2: ac_1 and ac_2 coefficients

band 3: ac_3, ac_4, ac_5, ac_6 coefficients

band 4: $ac_7 \ldots ac_{63}$ coefficients

In the progressive successive approximation algorithm, all DCT coefficients are sent first with lower precision, and then refined in later scans. For example, a sequence of three successive approximation bands may be as follows:

band 1: All DCT coefficients (divided by 4)

band 2: All DCT coefficients (divided by 2)

band 3: All DCT coefficients (full resolution)

The combined progressive algorithm combines both spectral selection and successive approximation algorithms. Figure 5.16 illustrates an image divided into eight combined scans. For example, in the first scan, only dc coefficients divided by 2 (will lower resolution) will be sent, and so on.

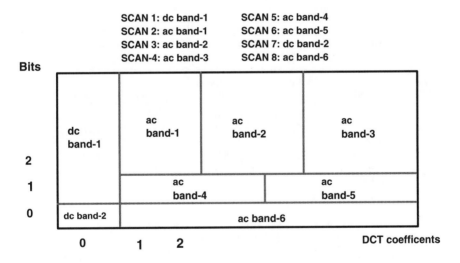

Figure 5.16 An example of image encoded using the combined progressive JPEG algorithm.

Progressive JPEG Experiment

In this experiment, we implemented both progressive algorithms, spectral selection (SS), and successive approximation (SA) to compress and decompress a 320×200 gray-scale image "Cheetah." In both cases, we used four scans, as follows:

	Spectral Selection	Successive Approximation
SCAN 1	DC, AC1, AC2	All DCT— divided by 8
SCAN 2	AC3–AC9	All DCT— divided by 4
SCAN 3	AC10–AC35	All DCT divided by 2
SCAN 4	AC36–AC63	All DCT— full resolution

The results of the experiments are presented in Tables 5.8 and 5.9. Figures 5.17 and 5.18 show results of sequential and progressive JPEG compression using EasyTech/codec, respectively. In the case of sequential JPEG, compression ratios obtained are in the range of 21 to 52. Assuming an image transmitted over a 64-kb ISDN network, the following four images are produced using progressive JPEG (Fig. 5.18). The first image of reduced quality appears on the screen very quickly, in 0.9 s. Each subsequent pass improves the image quality and it is obtained after 1.6, 3.6, and 7.0 s, respectively.

TABLE 5.8 Progressive Spectral Selection JPEG for Image "Cheetah": 320 × 240 pixels −> 512,000 bits

Scan Number	Bits Transmitted	Compression Ratio	Bits/pixel	RMS Error
1	29,005	17.65	0.45	19.97
2	37,237	7.73	1.04	13.67
3	71,259	3.72	2.15	7.90
4	32,489	3.01	2.66	4.59
Sequential JPEG	172,117	2.97	2.69	4.59

TABLE 5.9 Progressive Successive Approximation JPEG for Image "Cheetah": 320 × 240 pixels −> 512,000 bits

Scan Number	Bits Transmitted	Compression Ratio	Bits/pixel	RMS Error
1	26,215	19.53	0.41	22.48
2	34,506	8.43	0.95	12.75
3	63,792	4.11	1.95	7.56
4	95,267	2.33	2.43	4.59
Sequential JPEG	172,117	2.97	2.69	4.59

ORIGINAL

COMPRESSION FACTOR 21:1 (low)

COMPRESSION FACTOR 33:1 (medium)

COMPRESSION FACTOR 52:1 (high)

Figure 5.17 Sequential JPEG results using EasyTech/codec (courtesy of AutoGraph International).

Note that, in both algorithms, the first scan will be transmitted six to seven times faster than the sequential JPEG algorithm (26,215 bits in SA and 29,005 bits in SS versus 172,117 bits in sequential JPEG).

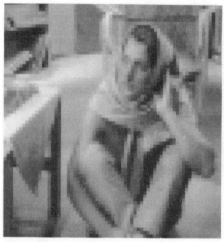

IMAGE AFTER 0.9 SECONDS   IMAGE AFTER 1.6 SECONDS

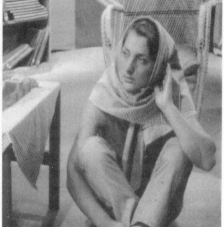

IMAGE AFTER 3.6 SECONDS   IMAGE AFTER 7.0 SECONDS

Figure 5.18 Progressive JPEG results using EasyTech/codec (courtesy of AutoGraph International).

5.5.6   Sequential Lossless JPEG Compression

The JPEG standard also supports a lossless mode of operation, by providing a simple predictive compression algorithm, rather than a DCT-based technique, which is a lossy one. Figure 5.19 shows the block diagram of the lossless JPEG encoder,

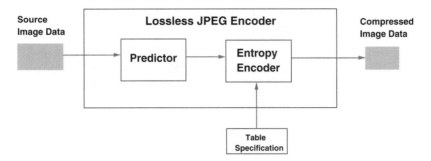

Figure 5.19 Block diagram of the lossless JPEG encoder.

in which a prediction block has replaced the FDCT and the quantization blocks from the baseline sequential DCT-based JPEG.

The predictor block works in such a way that a prediction of the sample $\hat{X}$ is calculated on the basis of previous samples A, B, and C, and then the difference $\Delta X = X - \hat{X}$ is computed, where X is the actual value of the sample (Figs. 5.20a and b). Then, the difference ΔX is coded using the Huffman arithmetic encoder.

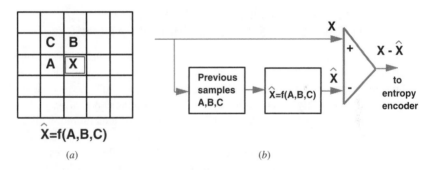

Figure 5.20 Lossless JPEG encoding: (a) Location of four samples in the predictor; (b) predictor block diagram.

Table 5.10 illustrates several different predictor formulas that can be used for lossless prediction.

Lossless JPEG compression typically gives around a 2:1 compression ratio for moderately complex color images.

5.5.7 Hierarchical JPEG Compression

Hierarchical JPEG mode of operation creates a set of compressed images beginning with the small images and then increasing resolution. This process is called *downsampling*, or *pyramidal coding* [3, 5, 8]. After the downsampling phase, each

TABLE 5.10 Predictors for Lossless
JPEG Compression

Selection Value	Predictor Formula
0	no prediction
1	$X = A$
2	$X = B$
3	$X = C$
4	$X = A + B - C$
5	$X = A + (B - C)/2$
6	$X = B + (A - C)/2$
7	$X = (A + B)/2$

lower-resolution image is scaled up to the next resolution (upsampling process), and used as a prediction for the following stage. Hierarchical JPEG encoder requires significantly more buffer space; however, the benefits are that the encoded image is immediately available at different resolutions [8].

5.6 $P \times 64$ COMPRESSION ALGORITHM FOR VIDEO-BASED TELECOMMUNICATIONS

The H.261 standard, commonly called $p \times 64$, is optimized to achieve very high compression ratios for full-color, real-time motion video transmission. The $p \times 64$ compression algorithm combines intraframe and interframe coding to provide fast processing for on-the-fly video compression and decompression. The $p \times 64$ standard is optimized for applications such as video-based telecommunications. Because these applications usually are not motion-intensive, the algorithm uses limited motion search and estimation strategies to achieve higher compression ratios. For standard video communication images, compression ratios of 100:1 to over 2000:1 can be achieved.

The $p \times 64$ compression standard is intended to cover the entire ISDN channel capacity ($p = 1, 2, \ldots, 30$). The $p \times 64$ video coding algorithm is intended for real-time communications allowing minimum delays. For $p = 1$ to 2, due to limited available bandwidth, only desktop face-to-face visual communications (videophone) can be implemented using this compression algorithm. However, for $p \geq 6$, more complex pictures are transmitted and the algorithm is suitable for videoconferencing applications.

5.6.1 CCITT Video Format

The $p \times 64$ algorithm operates with two picture formats adopted by the CCITT; common intermediate format (CIF), and quarter-CIF (QCIF) [10], as illustrated in Table 5.11.

TABLE 5.11 Parameters of CCITT Video Formats

Factors	CIF		QCIF	
	Lines/frame	*Pixels/line*	*Lines/frame*	*Pixels/line*
Luminance (Y)	288	352	144	176
Chrominance (C_b)	144	176	72	88
Chrominance (C_r)	144	176	72	88

Intended applications of this standard are for videophone and videoconferencing applications. The following examples illustrate the need for a video compression algorithm for these applications.

EXAMPLE 1   Desktop Videophone Application

Assuming channel capacity $p = 1$, the available network bandwidth is $B_A = 64$ kb/s. When using QCIF at 10 frames/s, the required bandwidth becomes

$$B_r = 144 \times 176 + 72 \times 88 + 72 \times 88 \times 8 \text{ bits } \times 10 \text{ frames/s } = 3 \text{ Mb/s}$$

As a consequence, a video compression algorithm must provide compression ratios of minimum:

$$C_r = \frac{B_r}{B_A} = \frac{3 \text{ Mb/s}}{64 \text{ kb/s}} = 47$$

EXAMPLE 2   Videoconferencing Application

Assuming $p = 10$ for a videoconferencing application gives required bandwidth of $B_r = 640$ kb/s. When using CIF format at 30 frames/s, the required bandwidth is

$$B_r = (288 \times 352 + 144 \times 176 + 144 \times 176) \times 8 \text{ bits } \times 30 \text{ frames/s}$$
$$= 36.4 \text{ Mb/s}$$

A video compression algorithm must provide a compression ratio of minimum:

$$C_r = \frac{B_r}{B_A} = \frac{36.4 \text{ Mb/s}}{640 \text{ kb/s}} = 57$$

5.6.2 $P \times 64$ Encoder and Decoder

The $p \times 64$ video compression algorithm combines intraframe and interframe coding to provide fast processing for on-the-fly video. The algorithm consists of: a) DCT-based intraframe compression, which, similar to JPEG, uses DCT, quantization, and entropy coding, and b) predictive interframe coding (DPCM) with motion estimation. The block diagram of the $p \times 64$ encoder is presented in Figure 5.21.

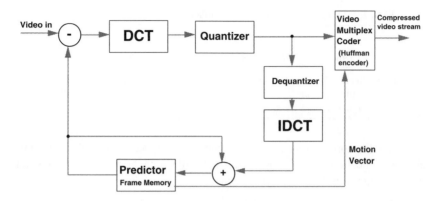

Figure 5.21 Block diagram of the $p \times 64$ encoder.

The algorithm begins by coding an intraframe block using the DCT transform coding and quantization, and then sends it to the video multiplex coder. The same frames are then decompressed using the inverse quantizer and IDCT, and then stored in the picture memory for interframe coding.

During the interframe coding, the prediction based on the DPCM algorithm is used to compare every macro block of the actual frame with the available macro blocks of the previous frame, as illustrated in Figure 5.22. Only the closest previous frame is used for prediction to reduce the encoding delay.

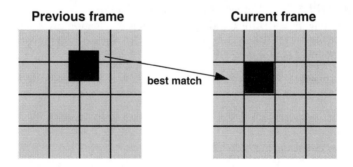

Figure 5.22 The principle of interframe coding in $p \times 64$ video compression algorithm.

Then, the difference is created as error terms, DCT-coded and quantized, and sent to the video multiplex coder with or without the motion vector. At the final step, entropy coding (such as Huffman coder) is used to produce more compact code.

For interframe coding, the frames are encoded using: a) DPCM coding with no motion compensation (zero-motion vectors), b) DPCM coding with nonzero motion vectors, and c) filtering of blocks by an optional predefined filter to remove high-frequency noise. At least one in every 132 picture frames should be intraframe coded. A typical $p \times 64$ decoder, shown in Figure 5.23, consists of the receiver buffer, the Huffman decoder, inverse quantizer, IDCT block, and the motion-compensation predictor that includes frame memory.

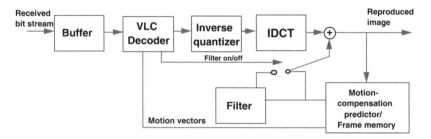

Figure 5.23 Block diagram of the $p \times 64$ decoder.

The motion estimation algorithms are discussed in Section 5.7.

5.6.3 Video Data Structure

According to the H.261 standard, a data stream has a hierarchical structure consisting of Pictures, Groups of Blocks (GOBs), Macro Blocks (MBs), and Blocks [10, 11]. A Macro Block is composed of four (8×8) luminance (Y) blocks and two (8×8) chrominance (C_r and C_b) blocks, as illustrated in Figure 5.24.

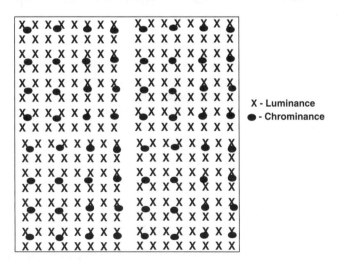

X - Luminance
● - Chrominance

Figure 5.24 Composition of a Macro Block: MB $= 4Y + C_b + C_r$.

A Group of Blocks is composed of 3 x 11 MBs. A CIF Picture contains 12 GOBs, while a QCIF Picture consists of 4 GOBs. The hierarchical block structure is illustrated in Figure 5.25.

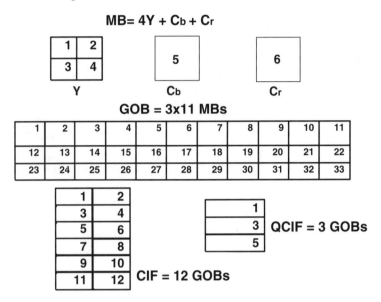

Figure 5.25 Hierarchical block structure of the $p \times 64$ data stream.

Each of the layers contains headers, which carry information about the data that follows. For example, a picture header includes a 20-bit picture start code, video format (CIF or QCIF), frame number, and so forth. A detailed structure of the headers is given in [10, 11].

The $p \times 64$ compression algorithm, or H.261 video codec, is very efficient for carrying visual services at $p \times 64$ kb/s ISDN networks with constant-bit-rate transmission. A new H.261 codec, proposed in [12], expands the existing H.261 codec to operate in ATM (asynchronous transfer mode) networks. A software-based video compression algorithm, called the popular video codec (PVC), proposed in [13], is suitable for real-time systems. The PVC coder simplifies the compression/decompression process of the $p \times 64$ algorithm by removing the transform and the motion estimation parts, and modifies the quantizer and the entropy coder.

5.7 MPEG COMPRESSION ALGORITHM
FOR MOTION-INTENSIVE APPLICATIONS

The MPEG compression algorithm is intended for compression of full-motion video. The compression method uses interframe compression and can achieve compression ratios of 200:1 by storing only the difference between successive frames. The MPEG approach is optimized for motion-intensive video applications, and its specification also includes an algorithm for the compression of audio data at ratios ranging from 5:1 to 10:1.

The MPEG first-phase standard (MPEG-1) is targeted for compression of 320×240 full-motion video at rates of 1 to 1.5 Mb/s in applications such as interactive multimedia and broadcast television. MPEG-2 standard is intended for higher resolutions, similar to the digital video studio standard CCIR 601, EDTV, and further leading to HDTV. It specifies compressed bit streams for high-quality digital video at the rate of 2–80 Mb/s. The MPEG-2 standard supports interlaced video formats and a number of features for HDTV. The MPEG-2 standard also addresses scalable video coding for a variety of applications that need different image resolutions, such as video communications over ISDN networks using ATM [8, 14]. The MPEG-4 standard is intended for compression of full-motion video consisting of small frames and requiring slow refreshments. The data rate required will be 9–40 kb/s, and the target applications include interactive multimedia and video telephony. This standard requires the development of new model-based image coding techniques for human interaction and low-bit-rate speech coding techniques [8].

Table 5.12 illustrates various motion-video formats and corresponding MPEG parameters.

TABLE 5.12 Parameters of MPEG Algorithms

Format	MPEG	Video Parameters	Compressed Bit Rate
SIF	MPEG	352×240 at 30 Hz	1.2–3 Mb/s
CCIR 601	MPEG-1	720×486 at 30 Hz	5–10 Mb/s
EDTV	MPEG-2	960×486 at 30 Hz	7–15 Mb/s
HDTV	MPEG-2	1920×1080 at 30 Hz	20–40 Mb/s

The MPEG algorithm is intended for both asymmetric and symmetric applications. Asymmetric applications are characterized by frequent use of the decompression process, while the compression process is performed once. Examples include movies-on-demand, electronic publishing, and education and training. Symmetric applications require equal use of the compression and decompression process. Examples include multimedia mail and videoconferencing.

When the MPEG standard was conceived, the following features were identified as important: random access, fast forward/reverse searches, reverse playback, audiovisual synchronization, robustness to errors, editability, format flexibility, and cost trade-off. These features are described in detail in [14].

The MPEG standard consists of three parts: 1) synchronization and multiplexing of video and audio, 2) video, and 3) audio.

5.7.1   MPEG Video Encoder and Decoder

In the MPEG standard, frames in a sequence are coded using three different algorithms, as illustrated in Figure 5.26.

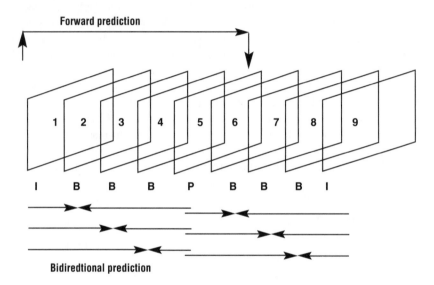

Figure 5.26 Types of frames in MPEG.

I frames (intra images) are self-contained and coded using a DCT-based technique similar to JPEG. I frames are used as random access points in MPEG streams and give the lowest compression ratios within MPEG.

P frames (predicted images) are coded using forward predictive coding, where the actual frame is coded with reference to a previous frame (I or P). This process is similar to H.261 predictive coding, except the previous frame is not always the closest previous frame, as in H.261 coding (see Fig. 5.22). The compression ratio of P frames is significantly higher than that of I frames.

B frames (bidirectional or interpolated images) are coded using two reference frames, a past and future frame (which can be I or P frames). Bidirectional, or interpolated, coding provides the highest amount of compression.

Note that, in Figure 5.26, the first three B frames (2, 3, and 4) are bidirectionally coded using the past frame I (frame 1), and the future frame P (frame 5). Therefore, the decoding order will differ from the encoding order. The P frame 5 must be decoded before B frames 2, 3, and 4, and I frame 9 before B frames 6, 7, and 8. If the MPEG sequence is transmitted over the network, the actual transmission order should be {1, 5, 2, 3, 4, 9, 6, 7, 8}.

The MPEG application determines a sequence of I, P, and B frames. If there is a need for fast random access, the best resolution would be achieved by coding the whole sequence as I frames (MPEG becomes identical to JPEG). However, the highest compression ratio can be achieved by incorporating a large number of B frames. The following sequence has proved very effective for a number of practical applications [8]:

$$\text{(I B B P B B P B B)} \quad \text{(I B B P B B P B B)} \ldots$$

In the case of 25 frames/s, random access will be provided through 9 still frames (I and P frames), which is about 360 ms [8]. On the other hand, this sequence will allow a relatively high compression ratio.

Motion Estimation

The coding process for P and B frames includes the motion estimator, which finds the best matching block in the available reference frames. P frames are always using forward prediction, while B frames are using bidirectional prediction, also called *motion-compensated interpolation*, as illustrated in Figure 5.27 [11].

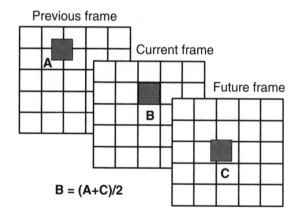

Figure 5.27 Motion-compensated interpolation.

B frames can use forward or backward prediction, or interpolation. A block in the current frame (B frame) can be predicted by another block from the past reference frame ($B = A \rightarrow$ forward prediction), or from the future reference frame ($B = C \rightarrow$ backward prediction), or by the average of two blocks ($B = (A + C)/2 \rightarrow$ interpolation).

Motion estimation is used to extract the motion information from the video sequence. For every 16×16 block of P and B frames, one or two motion vectors are calculated. One motion vector is calculated for P and forward- and backward-predicted B frames, while two motion vectors are calculated for interpolated B frames.

The MPEG standard does not specify the motion estimation technique; however, block-matching techniques are likely to be used [14]. The mean-absolute difference (MAD) block-matching technique for motion estimation obtains the motion vector by minimizing the following cost function [15]:

$$\mathrm{MAD}(dx, dy) = \frac{1}{256} \sum_{i=0}^{15} \sum_{j=0}^{15} \int \left| \int (i, j) - g(i - d_x, j - d_y) \right| \quad (5\text{-}13)$$

where

$f(i, j)$ = represents a 16×16 block (macroblock) from the current frame,

$g(i, j)$ = represents the same macroblock from a reference frame (past or future),

(dx, dy) = a vector representing the search location.

The simplest, but most computationally intensive search method—the exhaustive search—evaluates the cost function at every location in the search area.

Several algorithms have been developed to reduce the number of search points [16, 17, 18]. The three-step-search algorithm, proposed in [16] and implemented in [15], first calculates the cost function at the center and eight surrounding locations of the 32×32 block. The location that produces the smallest cost function becomes the center location for the next stage, and the search range is reduced by half.

Using a block-matching motion estimation technique, the best motion vector(s) is found, which specifies the space distance between the actual and the reference blocks. The difference between predicted and actual blocks, called the *error term*, is then calculated and encoded using the DCT-based transform coding. A block diagram of the MPEG-1 encoder, which includes motion predictor and motion estimation, is shown in Figure 5.28 [11].

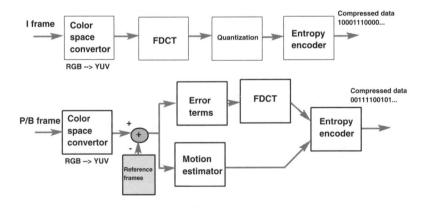

Figure 5.28 Block diagram of the MPEG-1 encoder.

A color image, as in H.261, is first converted into YUV format. Each image consists of the luminance component and two chrominance components. The luminance component has twice as many samples in the horizontal and vertical axes as the other two components, as in the H.261 standard. A typical MPEG decoder is shown in the block diagram in Figure 5.29.

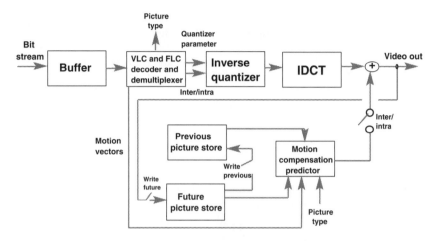

Figure 5.29 Block diagram of the MPEG-1 decoder.

5.7.2   Audio Encoder and Decoder

The MPEG standard also covers audio compression. MPEG uses the same sampling frequencies as compact-disk digital audio (CD-DA) and digital audio tape (DAT). Besides these two frequencies, 44.1 kHz and 48 kHz, 32 kHz is also supported, all at 16 bits. The audio data on a compact disk, with two channels of audio samples at 44.1 kHz with 16 bits/sample, requires a data rate of about 1.4 Mb/s [19]. Therefore, there is a need to compress audio data as well. The MPEG audio encoder and decoder are shown in Figure 5.30 [19, 8].

The input audio stream simultaneously passes through a filter bank and a psychoacoustic model. The filter bank divides the input into multiple subbands, while the psychoacoustic model determines the signal-to-mask ratio of each subband. The bit or noise allocation block uses the signal-to-mask ratios to determine the number of bits for the quantization of the subband signals, with the goal to minimize the audibility of the quantization noise. The last block performs entropy Huffman encoding and formats the data. The decoder performs entropy (Huffman) decoding, then reconstructs the quantized subband values, and transforms subband values into a time-domain audio signal. The detailed description of audio compression principles and techniques can be found in [19].

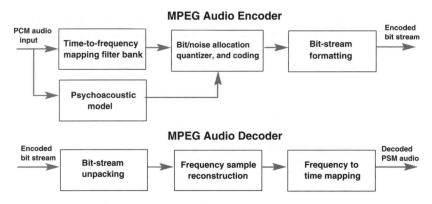

Figure 5.30 Block diagrams of the MPEG audio encoder and decoder.

5.7.3 MPEG Data Stream

MPEG specifies a syntax for the interleaved audio and video data streams. An audio data stream consists of frames that are divided into audio access units. Audio access units consist of slots, which can be either 4 bits at the lowest complexity layer (layer 1), or 1 byte at layers 2 and 3. A frame always consists of a fixed number of samples. The audio access unit specifies the smallest audio sequence of compressed data that can be independently decoded. The playing times of the audio access units of one frame are 8 ms at 48 kHz, 8.7 ms at 44.1 kHz, and 12 ms at 32 kHz [8]. A video data stream consists of six layers, as shown in Table 5.13.

TABLE 5.13 Layers of MPEG Video Stream Syntax

Syntax Layer	Functionality
Sequence layer	Context unit
Group of pictures layer	Random access unit: video coding
Picture layer	Primary coding unit
Slice layer	Resynchronization unit
Macroblock layer	Motion compensation unit
Block layer	DCT unit

At the beginning of the sequence layer, there are two entries: the constant bit rate of a sequence and the storage capacity that is needed for decoding. These parameters define the data buffering requirements. A sequence is divided into a series of group/s of pictures (GOP). Each GOP layer has at least one I frame as the first frame in the GOP, so random access and fast search are enabled. GOPs can be of arbitrary structure (I, P, and B frames) and length. The GOP layer is the basic unit for editing and MPEG video stream.

The picture layer contains a whole picture. The picture layer first contains information on the type of the frame present (I, P, or B), and the position of the frame in display order.

The bits corresponding to the DCT coefficients and the motion vectors are contained in the next three layers: slice, macroblock, and block layers. The block is an 8 × 8 DCT unit, the macroblock is the 16 × 16 motion compensation unit, and the slice is a string of macroblocks of arbitrary length. The slice layer is intended to be used for resynchronization during a frame decoding when bit errors occur.

5.7.4 MPEG Experimental Results

The Berkeley research group has developed the MPEG-1 video software decoder and made it public domain available for research communities [20, 21]. This software video decoder can decode and play 160 × 120 MPEG-1 video streams in real-time at 30 frames/s on the current generation of powerful reduced instruction set computer (RISC) workstations. It can also decode and play 320 × 240 video streams at about 16 frames/s, which is a factor of 2 of real-time. The code was also ported to a proprietary video processor at Philips research, where it is capable of decoding and playing in real-time 352 × 288 video frames.

The decoder has been ported to over 25 platforms and has been distributed to over 10,000 sites over the Internet. We ported this decoder in the Multimedia Laboratory at Florida Atlantic University, and analyzed its performance. The results are presented in this section.

The MPEG-1 decoder is implemented in C using the X-windows system. It is comprised of 12,000 lines of code. When analyzing the execution time of different blocks of the MPEG decoder, the results were obtained and are shown in Table 5.14 [20].

TABLE 5.14 Software MPEG Decoder
Analysis of Execution Time

Function	Time (%)
Parsing	17.4
IDCT	14.2
Reconstruction	31.5
Dithering	24.3
Misc. Arithmetic	9.9
Misc.	2.7

Interestingly enough, reconstruction and dithering require more than 50% of total time due to memory-intensive operations. On the other hand, IDCT only requires less than 15% of the total time. The conclusion is that the decoder can be speeded up significantly by developing techniques to reduce memory traffic in reconstruction and dithering.

In the following experiment, we analyzed the MPEG-1 decoder in decoding five motion-videos that are of different frame size and compressed with various compositions of I, P, and B frames. The results obtained are given in Table 5.15. Bit streams for the first three examples were created by the Xing software encoder, which only produces I frames (MJPEG). The last two streams were produced with a true MPEG encoder.

TABLE 5.15 Performance Analysis of Berkeley Software MPEG-1 Decoder

Video	Grand	Mjackson	Rom	Flower	Bicycle
Frame size	160×120	160×120	160×120	352×240	352×240
Total no. **of frames**	194	557	73	148	148
I/P/B **composition**	194/0/0	557/0/0	73/0/0	10/40/98	10/40/98
No. of **MBs/frame**	80	80	80	330	330
Compression **ratio**	40.3	47.4	17.9	52.9	47.4
Compression **ratio for I/P/B**	40.3/–/–	47.4/–/–	17.9/–/–	14.6/31.5/ 114.9	24.9/36.2/ 76.3
Compressed **bits/pixel**	0.60	0.51	1.34	0.45	0.45
Decoding time(s)	16.7	40.4	4.2	58.3	48.0
Average frame/s	11.6	13.8	17.4	2.5	3.1

In the final experiment, we measured the performance of the Berkeley MPEG-1 decoder running on different computer platforms, for two MPEG video streams. The results are presented in Table 5.16.

TABLE 5.16 Berkeley Software MPEG-1 Decoder Comparison of Different Computer Platforms

Video	Compression Ratio	Performance (Frames/s)			
		DEC AXP *3000/500* *@ 150 MHz*	*HP* *9000/750* *@ 66 MHz*	*SUN SPARC* *10/30* *@ 36 MHz*	*Intel* *486 DX/2* *@ 66 MHz*
Canyon 144×112	49	43.1	74.7	13.4	38.1
Flower 320×240	50	8.9	15.4	3.3	8.2

From Table 5.16, it can be concluded that most of the tested machines (except Sun SPARC I) can decode 144 × 112 video sequences in real-time (30 frames per second or more). However, for video sequences 320 × 240, the best performance is within a factor of two of real-time performance (HP9000/750 has achieved 15.4 frames/s).

Acknowledgments

The author would like to thank the following graduate students from the Multimedia Laboratory at Florida Atlantic University who successfully completed compression projects under the author's supervision, and provided a number of useful results presented in this chapter.

Doctoral students Mark Kessler and Jan Alexander; and master students Mauricio Cuervo, Lou Horowitz, and Henry Pesulima have developed sequential JPEG and provided results and images. Master students Shen Huang and Zhonggang Li have performed and obtained results for progressive JPEG compression, while master student Peter Monnes has analyzed JPEG performance. Master student Srikar Chitturi has ported and analyzed performance of the Berkeley software MPEG decoder.

Special thanks for typing, formatting, and finalizing this chapter goes to Donna Rubinoff, whose expertise and dedication were invaluable in the completion of this work.

References

[1] E. A. Fox, "Advances in interactive digital multimedia systems," *IEEE Computer*, vol. 24, no. 10, October 1991, pp. 9–21.

[2] B. Furht, "Multimedia systems: an overview," *IEEE Multimedia*, vol. 1, no. 1, 1994, pp. 47–59.

[3] W. B. Pennenbaker and J. L. Mitchell. *JPEG Still Image Data Compression Standard*. New York: Van Nostrand Reinhold, 1993.

[4] C. A. Poynton, "High definition television and desktop computing," in *Multimedia Systems*, edited by J. F. Koegel Buford, New York: ACM Press, 1994.

[5] G. Wallace, "The JPEG still picture compression standard," *Communications of the ACM*, vol. 34, no. 4, April 1991, pp. 30–44.

[6] M. Nelson. *The Data Compression Book*. San Mateo, CA: M&T Books, 1992.

[7] M. Kessler, J. Alexander, and B. Furht, "JPEG still image compression algorithm: analysis and implementation," Technical Report TR-CSE-94-07, Florida Atlantic University, Boca Raton, FL, March 1994.

[8] R. Steinmetz, "Data compression in multimedia computing—standards and systems," Parts I and II, *J. Multimedia Systems*, vol. 1, 1994, pp. 166–172 and 187–204.

[9] P. Monnes and B. Furht, "Parallel JPEG agorithms for still image compression," in *Proc. of Southeastcon '94* (Miami, Florida), April 1994, pp. 375–379.

[10] M. Liou, "Overview of the $p \times 64$ kbit/s video coding standard," *Communications of the ACM*, vol. 34, no. 4, April 1994, pp. 59–63.

[11] R. Aravind, G. L. Cash, D. C. Duttweller, H.-M. Hang, B. G. Haskel, and A. Puri, "Image and video coding standards," *AT&T Tech. J.*, vol. 72, January/February 1993, pp. 67–88.

[12] M. Ghanbari, "An adapted H.261 two-layer video codec for ATM networks," *IEEE Trans. Communications*, vol. 40, no. 9, September 1992, pp. 1481–1490.

[13] H.-C. Huang, J.-H. Huang, and J.-L. Wu, "Real-time software-based video coder for multimedia communication systems," *J. Multimedia Systems*, vol. 1, 1993, pp. 110–119.

[14] D. LeGall, "MPEG: a video compression standard for multimedia applications," *Communications of the ACM*, vol. 34, no. 4, April 1991, pp. 45–68.

[15] W. Lee, Y. Kim, R. J. Gove, and C. J. Read, "Media Station 5000: Integrating video and audio," *IEEE Multimedia*, vol. 1, no. 2, 1994, pp. 50–61.

[16] J. Koga, K. Iinuma, A. Hirano, Y. Iijima, and T. Ishiguro, "Motion compensated interframe coding for video conferencing," in *Proc. National Telecommunications Conf.* (Japan), 1981, pp. G5.3.1–5.3.5.

[17] J. R. Jain and A. K. Jain, "Displacement measurement and its application in interframe image coding," *IEEE Trans. Communications*, vol. 29, 1981, pp. 1799–1808.

[18] R. Srinivasan and K. R. Rao, "Predictive coding based on efficient motion estimation," *IEEE Trans. Communications*, vol. 33, 1985, pp. 888–896.

[19] D. Y. Pen, "Digital audio compression," *Digital Tech. J.*, vol. 5, no. 2, Spring 1993, pp. 28–40.

[20] K. Patel, B. C. Smith, and L. A. Rowe, "Performance of a software MPEG video decoder," in *Proc. First Int. ACM Multimedia Conf.* (Anaheim, CA), August 1993, pp. 75–82.

[21] L. A. Rowe, K. D. Patel, B. C. Smith, and K. Liu, "MPEG video in software: representation, transmission, and playback," *Proc. IS & TISPIE Symp. Electrical Imaging Science and Technology* (San Jose, CA), SPIE Press, 1994.

III

APPLICATIONS

6

REAL-TIME IMAGE PROCESSING
FOR AUTOMOTIVE APPLICATIONS

Giovanni Adorni   *Dipartimento di Ingegneria dell'Informazione,*
Alberto Broggi   *Università di Parma*
Gianni Conte
Vincenzo D'Andrea

6.1 INTRODUCTION

During the last 25 years profound changes have taken place in the transportation of goods and people, as well as a continuous increase in road traffic, which nowadays is very dense and complex. In contrast, the infrastructure (i.e., roads and highways) has not grown at the same rate due to economical and ecological constraints.

Several countries have launched research programs in this field to reduce traffic congestion and to increase safety. The Mobility 2000 program [1] and the Automated Highway System project [2] in the United States, the RACS [3] and AMTICS projects [4] in Japan, and the DRIVE [5] and EUREKA programs in Europe are examples of such initiatives.

PROMETHEUS (PROgraM for a European Traffic with Highest Efficiency and Unprecedented Safety) [6] is a pan-European EUREKA program initiated by the automotive industry in Europe and carried out in cooperation with the electronic and vehicle-component industry, with traffic management consultants, and with basic research at universities and research institutes.

PROMETHEUS (1987–1994) has been a vehicle-oriented program whereas the DRIVE program, supported by the European Community, is mainly oriented to infrastructure. Significant results obviously can be reached only if the two approaches can be concurrently pursued. Moreover, infrastructure-centered development would require strong cooperation between a variety of authorities responsible for road construction and maintenance. This cooperation is a potential source of conflicts, while vehicle-centered development is basically the responsibility of the automobile industry; in addition, it seemed more flexible.

The main goal of PROMETHEUS has been the use of state-of-the-art information and telecommunication technologies to support vehicle drivers, to optimize the effectiveness of navigation devices, and to link road traffic with other transport systems for the benefit of everybody. Among the techniques that have been exploited to reach the project goals, a great amount of attention was paid to computer vision.

Interest in computer vision systems in automotive applications has, over the last decade, been the object of a lot of discussion and even controversial conclusions. It is now well established, and this is also a result of the PROMETHEUS project, that the main goal of a vision system in everyday driving is to assist the driver by giving warnings and not to exclude the driver from the "vehicle control loop." The reasons for this choice are technical (i.e., hard real-time, harsh environment, etc.), legal (i.e., responsibility in case of misfunctioning), and functional (i.e., the human vision system is very sophisticated and extremely efficient). A different case is the application of a vision system to autonomous vehicles where the requirement of unmanned systems is mandatory, such as in hostile environments or military applications [7].

Interesting functionalities are offered by a vision system designed to give warnings to the driver in case of possible dangerous situations, or to give useful information for navigation [8]. Such warnings are the result of integrating data coming from a closed-circuit device (CCD) camera with different sources of information (e.g., infrared sensors, road map knowledge bases, etc.). Examples of useful information for the driver are

- warning about traffic rules;
- warning of obstacles in front of the vehicle;
- information about the vehicle position in the lane;
- information about the current road segment;
- suggestions about speed before the driver comes to a bend/junction.

This information can be computed by a set of heuristics and algorithms using different amounts of computation time. Therefore, because this information must be given to the driver in time in order to be useful, the vehicle speed is the parameter that decides what kind of information can be computed. Warnings can be generated using data from a vehicle movement sensor, and traffic rules can be stored in a road-map knowledge base or inferred by means of a vision system. For example, looking at the speedometer, if the car speed is greater than the maximum speed allowed in the road segment, then a warning is generated, where the maximum speed allowed in the actual road segment can be read on the road-map knowledge base or inferred by a vision system devoted to road traffic sign interpretation [9]. Information about the current road segment or about the vehicle position on the lane can be determined, for example, using the road/lane boundary-detection system described in this chapter. Such a system allows the construction of the vehicle local trajectory by means of simple geometric rules.

As already mentioned, the goal of our project has not been the definition of an autonomous vehicle. For this reason, the local trajectory is not computed to control the "actuators" of the vehicle: on the contrary, it is used to forecast the trajectory of the car. This forecast is verified by information from the road-map knowledge base related to the segment and, if necessary, the control goes to the driver assistance system, which sends warning messages to the driver.

To present warning/information to the driver in time to be useful, real-time response of the on-board vision system is mandatory. The architecture of a vision system for real-time application has specific requirements for high efficiency and speed. Practical systems must be able to attain these results at a moderate/low cost and with compact hardware. The architectural solution that is emerging is depicted in Figure 6.1 and it is composed of a CCD camera, a special-purpose processor, and a general-purpose computer system. The task of the special-purpose processor is to produce fast transformations of the image coming from the CCD camera. The result is then fed into a general-purpose computing system in order to obtain the appropriate warning and messages to the driver through the driver assistance system. The large amount of data involved, and the real-time requirement, prevent the use of a general-purpose computing system for the first stage of the system.

Figure 6.1 Architecture of the system.

This chapter discusses the use of a massively parallel architecture, PAPRICA [10], as the special-purpose processor, and presents the specific algorithms that are used to obtain the speed and efficiency required by automotive applications. A prototype of the discussed system is fully operative in the laboratory. It has also been demonstrated on board the MOB-LAB (MOBile LABoratory) vehicle (see Fig. 6.2) during the final PROMETHEUS Board Member Meeting (BMM'94) at the Mortefontaine track (Paris, October 1994) giving good performances on different functionalities [11, 12].

In this chapter, we illustrate two different functionalities for automotive applications as well as the chosen computational paradigms with their underlying theories, discussed in Section 6.2, and the special-purpose massively parallel architecture implementing the two functionalities, presented in Section 6.3. The first functionality, integrated on board the vehicle, is illustrated in Section 6.4, and consists of the real-time detection of the road/lane boundaries. The second func-

Figure 6.2 MOB-LAB vehicle.

tionality, currently being tested, is the application of optical flow field computation for obstacle detection, and it is illustrated in Section 6.5. Finally, Section 6.6 is a discussion of the system presented in this chapter as well as of the driver assistance system installed on board the MOB-LAB.

6.2 COMPUTATIONAL PARADIGM

Within the framework of computer vision-based automotive applications (i.e., road following), several different techniques have been used ranging from the use of a "focus of attention" for the analysis of interesting image areas (as, for example, in [13] and [14]), to the use of neural networks for the learning and detection of the road position [15, 16]; from the integration of a vision system for line marker detection and information coming from an inductive cable on the ground [17], to the use of multiple vision sensors for the measurement of the position of the vehicle on the lane, as well as the curvature of the lane in front of and behind the vehicle [18].

The approach discussed in this chapter makes use of techniques based on a massively parallel paradigm. The on-board integration of a massively parallel architecture has seldom been considered because it faces serious problems regarding cost and the size of the system. The use of a complex and general-purpose parallel architecture (as, for example, the MP2 MasPar used in the Carnegie Mellon's NAVLAB I [19–21]) is too expensive for widespread large-scale use. For this reason, the execution of low-level computations (efficiently performed by massively parallel systems) has been generally demanded for general-purpose processors, as in the case of VaMoRs [22].

One of the major drawbacks in the integration of general-purpose processors into portable or embedded systems is high power consumption [23, 24]. Power-consumption reduction can be achieved by lowering the power supply voltage, which is proportionally linked to the clock frequency. Unfortunately, this corresponds to a reduction in the computational power. This is one of the reasons that justify the use of a massively parallel architecture with a high number of simple and relatively slow processors into embedded systems [25].

A single-instruction, multiple-data (SIMD) massively parallel approach has been chosen for our system, leading to the development of a low-cost special-purpose application-oriented architecture, PAPRICA. As a consequence, the traditional algorithms and heuristics used for real-time problems on sequential architectures must be carefully redesigned according to the new specific data-parallel computational model.

Two computational paradigms that can be efficiently used on a massively parallel SIMD architecture are *cellular automata* and *mathematical morphology*.

6.2.1 Cellular Automata

Cellular automata are a computational paradigm for an efficient description of SIMD massively parallel systems [26, 27].

A d-dimensional cellular automaton (CA) is defined by four terms:

$$A \stackrel{\Delta}{=} < S, d, V, f >$$ (6-1)

where S is a finite set of symbols (or labels), d is the CA dimension, V is a neighborhood, and f is a local function (i.e., the local updating rule).

A cellular automata computation is described in terms of local interacting cells: the same local updating rule is active in each cell. This local structure, replicated in a regular lattice, is the basic ingredient of a CA. The symbols mark the state of the cells of A, and S is the set of all the possible states of each cell. The CA dimension d is the dimension of the regular lattice of cells: $L = Z^d$, where Z is the set of integers. A cell is a lattice point $x \in L$.

Because a CA works by associating states to cells, the natural space for a CA is S^L: i.e., the space of all the maps from L to S, associating a symbol s to every point x:

$$c : L \to S \qquad c(x) = s$$ (6-2)

where $c \in S^L$. The symbol s represents the state of the cell x, and c is called the *global configuration* of the CA, i.e., the coupling of a state to every cell.

The third element in the CA definition [see Eq. (6-1)] is a "neighborhood" V: a finite subset of the group of translations[1]: $V = \{v_i \mid i = 1, 2, \ldots, m\}$.

---

[1]The group is $(Z^d, +)$, and the group operation is ordinary vector composition. A translation $\tau \in T$ transforms the point $x \in L$ into $x' = x + \tau$, where $x' \in L$. With this definition, $(Z^d, +)$ is a commutative group.

When applied to a cell $x \in L$, a neighborhood V gives the set V_x of the points in L reached by a translation in V, starting from x:

$$V_x \stackrel{\Delta}{=} \{y = x + v \mid v \in V; \qquad x, y \in L\} \qquad (6\text{-}3)$$

Given the neighborhood V_x of a cell x, the local configuration c_{V_x} is the set of the states taken by all the cells belonging to V_x. In all the cells of the neighborhood, the local configuration takes the value of the global configuration in the cell itself:

$$c_{V_x}(x + v) \stackrel{\Delta}{=} c(x + v) \quad \text{where} \quad x \in L; \qquad v \in V; \qquad c_v \in S^V \qquad (6\text{-}4)$$

The local rule f of the CA is a map from the set of local configuration S^V in the set of symbols S:

$$f : S^V \to S \qquad f(c_V) = s \qquad (6\text{-}5)$$

This function associates a symbol from S to every local configuration of cells in S^V.

The time evolution of the CA (i.e., the computation) consists of the simultaneous application of f to every cell $x \in L$. The action of f consists of computing a new state for x, depending on the local configuration of the cells in V_x. Because c_{V_x} represents a set of m symbols (m is the cardinality of V), corresponding to the state of the cells in V_x, the action of f on the cell x can be written as follows:

$$f\left(c_{V_x}\right) \stackrel{\Delta}{=} f(s_1, s_2, \ldots, s_m) \qquad (6\text{-}6)$$

where $s_1, s_2, \ldots, s_m \in S$ are the states of the m cells in the neighborhood of x; i.e., $c_{V_x}(x + v_i) = s_i$; $v_i \in V$.

A CA can be described also by means of the variation of the global configuration under the application of the local function f in every cell. The global function G_f maps a global configuration in another, and depends on the choice of the local function f. The value of G_f for a given configuration c in a cell x is the value of f computed for the local configuration of the V-neighborhood of x:

$$G_f : S^L \to S^L \qquad \left[G_f(c)\right](x) = f(c_{V_x}) \qquad (6\text{-}7)$$

By constructing a CA with the above formalism, several properties are granted, such as continuity or invariance under lattice translation [28, 29].

When a CA is used for low-level computer vision, cells correspond to image pixels and the set S is the set of the possible gray values of a pixel. The dimension d is usually 2, associating the lattice to the image matrix (in this case, the lattice is finite). The neighborhood depends on the application, but usually it is a square centered on the cell, and V_N indicates the $N \times N$ square neighborhood. A widely used neighborhood is the 3×3 square, which can be described by means of nine translations:

$$V_3 \stackrel{\Delta}{=} \{(-1, -1), (0, -1), (1, -1), (-1, 0), (0, 0), (1, 0), (-1, 1), (0, 1), (1, 1)\}$$

or by means of a positional notation:

$$V_3 \stackrel{\Delta}{=} \{v_{NW}, v_N, v_{NE}, v_W, v, v_E, v_{SW}, v_S, v_{SE}\}$$

The local function f depends on the algorithm to be implemented by the CA. For example, a CA for uniform smoothing can be described by the following local function (in each cell, the pixel value is replaced by the average of the neighbors' gray values)

$$f(c_3) = \frac{1}{9} \sum_{u \in V_3} c_3(x + u) \tag{6-8}$$

where c_3 is the local configuration in V_3.

More complex applications of the CA computational paradigm to low-level computer vision on massively parallel architectures are given in Sections 6.4 and 6.5 of this chapter.

6.2.2 Mathematical Morphology

Mathematical morphology concerns the study of shapes by means of set theory, and it is commonly and efficiently used in image analysis tasks [30, 31]. Mathematical morphology has been extensively used in low-level computer vision applications because it allows the filtering and/or enhancement of only some characteristics of objects, depending on their morphological shape [32–34].

Within the mathematical morphology framework, a binary image A is defined as a subset of the two-dimensional Euclidean space E^2 ($Z \times Z$):

$$A = \{a = (a_i, a_j) \mid a_i, \qquad a_j \in Z\} \tag{6-9}$$

Three monadic transforms are defined on the generic image A: complement $(\cdot)^c$, reflection $(\check{\cdot})$, and translation $(\cdot)_t$, respectively:

$$A^c \triangleq \{x \in E^2 \mid x \neq a, \quad \text{for every } a \in A\} \tag{6-10}$$

$$\check{A} \triangleq \{x \in E^2 \mid x = -a, \quad \text{for some } a \in A\} \tag{6-11}$$

$$(A)_t \triangleq \{x \in E^2 \mid x = a + t, \quad \text{for some } a \in A\} \tag{6-12}$$

Following the definitions given in [32], some dyadic operators between sets are: dilation $\oplus$, erosion $\ominus$, opening $\circ$, closing $\bullet$, and matching $\oslash$, respectively:

$$A \oplus B \triangleq \{x \in E^2 \mid x = a + b, \quad \text{for some } a \in A, b \in B\} \tag{6-13}$$

$$A \ominus B \triangleq \{x \in E^2 \mid x + b \in A, \quad \text{for every } b \in B\} \tag{6-14}$$

$$A \circ B \triangleq (A \ominus B) \oplus B \tag{6-15}$$

$$A \bullet B \triangleq (A \oplus B) \ominus B \tag{6-16}$$

$$A \oslash Q \triangleq (A \ominus Q_1) \cap (A^c \ominus Q_0) \tag{6-17}$$

where $B \in E^2$ and Q is a couple $Q = (Q_0, Q_1)$, where both $Q_0, Q_1 \in E^2$, with the constraint that $Q_0 \cap Q_1 = \emptyset$. In the previous expressions A is the image to be processed, while B represents the *structuring element*, namely, another subset of E^2 whose shape parametrizes each operation. Moreover, if a structuring element

B is convex, it can be expressed with a chain of dilations of simpler sets:

$$B = \{[(B_1 \oplus B_2) \oplus B_3] \oplus \ldots\} \oplus B_n \tag{6-18}$$

6.2.3 Morphological Operations and Massively Parallel Cellular Systems

Several different special-purpose architectures have been developed in order to exploit the special nature of the computation performed by morphological operators. Part of them exploits spatial parallelism following the SIMD classification, in which a single pixel is computed by its own processing element (PE). The main problem of this kind of architecture lies in the interconnecting topology, which limits the size of practical structuring elements. Other architectures are formed by a number of specialized processors operating in pipeline on pixel values. A lot of work has also been devoted to the performance improvement of morphological operations on general-purpose serial architectures, using special data representations and by efficiently decomposing the structuring elements.

When a bit-mapped data representation is used, mathematical morphology operations involve repeated computations over large data structures; thus, any form of spatial parallelism improves the overall performances. Parallel architectures with spatial parallelism are formed by a high number of PEs devoted to the simultaneous computation of a single image area.

Starting with the original ideas of Unger [35], several processor arrays with a two-dimensional grid interconnection scheme and an SIMD processing paradigm have been conceived, designed, and implemented. This kind of architecture can be efficiently described by means of the cellular automata computational paradigm as well as by using mathematical morphology. Indeed, both approaches will be used in the description of the algorithms presented in Sections 6.4 and 6.5.

A chronological classification of the different research projects and implementations according to a three-generation taxonomy has been proposed in [36]. The early ILLIAC [37] and CLIP [38] machines belong to the first generation, which were mainly devoted to low-level image processing tasks. The second generation includes systems such as the ICL DAP [39], the Goodyear MPP [40], and the CLIP4 system [41], which have evolved to complete processing systems with dedicated operating systems and languages, and extended the application spectrum to high-speed scientific computations.

The triggering factors of the third generation were the availability and widespread use of the VLSI technologies of the 1980s and the natural mapping of a two-dimensional interconnection scheme over the planar structure of a silicon chip. This led to a number of different proposals and implementations (see, for example, [10, 42–46]). Most designs share original characteristics such as the two-dimensional mesh interconnection scheme and bit-serial computation while others, such as the Connection Machine [42], have increased the complexity of the interconnection network or widened the data path of the elementary PE, as in the

CLIP7 [47] or MasPar [48] systems. A recent commercially available machine, the AIS [45], has a one-dimensional interconnection scheme emulating, via a specialized memory interface, a two-dimensional mesh organization.

In order to run mathematical morphology applications in massively parallel architectures, each pixel is assigned to a PE, which computes its new value (depending on the neighborhood configuration, which reflects the specific structuring element). All the possible operations that the PEs can execute form the *instruction set*. Generally, the interconnecting topology limits the dimensions of practical structuring elements, typically reducing it to 3×3 [49], as in the Cytocomputer [50] and Goodyear MPP implementations. Thus, a generic structuring element needs to be decomposed into a chain of simpler and smaller ones, with the constraint of belonging to the instruction set.

In massively parallel architectures, the integration of a high number of simple PEs is generally preferred to the higher complexity of each single PE. The simple single-bit architecture of each PE provides hardware efficiency higher than that obtained by architectures with a higher word parallelism because the computations performed do not always involve multiple-bit operations. On the contrary, some cellular automata-based architectures, such as the CAM-6 [27] or the CAM-8 [51], process from 4-bit data up to 16-bit data in parallel, raising the problem of gray-level structuring element decomposition [52]. The efficiency of the computation depends on the instruction set, which must be accurately tuned [53].

6.3   PAPRICA SYSTEM

The main characteristics of the PAPRICA system [10, 54] (PArallel PRocessor for Image Checking and Analysis) are a conventional mesh-connected SIMD array that has been tailored to directly support a computational paradigm based on mathematical morphology and the processing support of data structures that can be larger than the physical size of the machine. The system also supports hierarchical nonmesh data structures and provides a low-cost experimental tool for research in the fields of image processing, VLSI design automation [54], and neural algorithms [55].

The kernel of PAPRICA architecture is a two-dimensional array of single-bit PEs with a direct 8-neighborhood. The instruction set can be described in terms of mathematical morphology operators, augmented with logical operations. Control flow operations are defined over the entire SIMD mesh, and hardware mechanisms are provided for the virtualization of large two-dimensional data structures. An additional mechanism allows the mapping of more complex hierarchical data structures on the same two-dimensional processing grid.

The PAPRICA system, shown in Figure 6.3 has been designed to operate as a coprocessor of a general-purpose host workstation equipped with a standard VME bus. The hardware system is based on a number of custom VLSI circuits; the current implementation comprises 256 PEs arranged in a 16×16 square matrix [56].

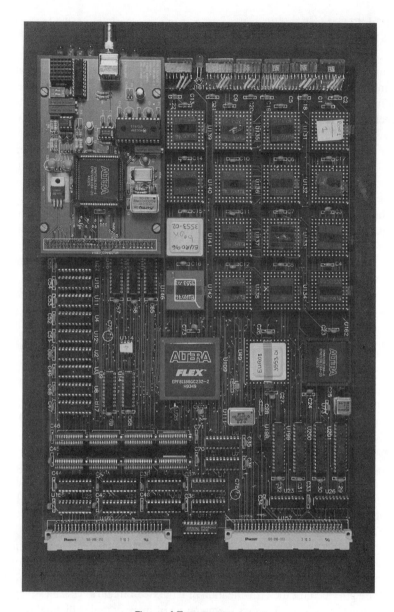

Figure 6.3 PAPRICA board.

The PAPRICA computational paradigm is based on the concept of matching operator $\oslash$, which is derived from the hit-or-miss transform [31]. This is a rather general approach and includes the other morphological operators [dilation $\oplus$, erosion $\ominus$, complement $(\cdot)^{c}$, translation $(\cdot)_{x}$, and transposition $(\check{\cdot})$] as special cases.

6.3.1 External Architecture

The PAPRICA instruction set can be partitioned into three different classes, namely:

- Elementary instructions, which are executed in parallel by every PE and perform logical and morphological operations. Each PAPRICA instruction is the cascade of a graphic operator $G(\cdot)$ and a logic operator $*$. A PAPRICA instruction format is

$$L_D = G(L_1) [*L_2 [\%A]]$$ (6-19)

  where L_D, L_1, and $L_2 \in [0\ldots63]$ are the identifiers of three binary layers.

  The graphic operator $G(\cdot)$ is one of the sixteen composite matching operators listed in Table 6.1, while the logical operator "$*$" is one of AND, OR, NOT, AND NOT, OR NOT, EXOR, one-bit ADD. The optional switch $\%A$ allows to OR of the result of instruction with an accumulator register A.

- Statements to implement the virtualization of the memory structure, allowing the emulation of several nonmesh computing architectures, such as pyramids.

- Control flow statements include UPDATE, FOR-ENDFOR, REPEAT-UNTIL, CALL-RET, JUMP, and IF(global flag)THEN-ELSE.

  Three global flags are computed for each Update Block, which are set according to the result of the last operator of that block. The SET, RESET, and NOCHANGE flags are respectively set if the complete image on the result layer is respectively white, black, or has not changed its value.

TABLE 6.1 List of PAPRICA Graphic Operators $G(L_1)$

Name	Description	Name	Description
NOP (L_1)	No OPeration	INV (L_1)	INVersion
NMOV (L_1)	North MOVe	SMOV (L_1)	South MOVe
WMOV (L_1)	West MOVe	EMOV (L_1)	East MOVe
EXP (L_1)	EXPansion	VEXP (L_1)	Vertical EXPansion
HEXP (L_1)	Horizontal EXPansion	NEEXP (L_1)	NorthEast EXPansion
ERS (L_1)	ERoSion	VERS (L_1)	Vertical ERoSion
HERS (L_1)	Horizontal ERoSion	NEERS (L_1)	NorthEast ERoSion
BOR (L_1)	BORder	LS2 (L_1)	LesS than 2

6.3.2 Programming Environment

The PAPRICA programming environment enables the writing application programs using the standard C language. The environment has been conceived in order to isolate applications from hardware implementation details: The same program can run on PAPRICA hardware, on a software simulator under UNIX or MS-DOS operating systems, or on a software simulator running on a CM2 Connection Machine [42].

An application is written using C with the help of two sets of functions. One function, the System Library, manages the interaction between the application and either the hardware or the emulator. The other function, the Macro Library, is an open set of functions that the user can use and augment to generate the PAPRICA code required by the target application.

PAPRICA was originally designed for the acceleration of tasks related to the design and verification of integrated circuit layouts and masks [54]. Nevertheless, the generality of the mathematical morphology computational paradigm allows an efficient use of the architecture in many tasks related to the processing of two-dimensional data structures with particular reference to real-time tasks, such as in automotive applications or mobile robotics [57]. In fact, its low production costs and its small physical dimensions allow the integration of this architecture on a vehicle or on a mobile robot.

6.4   ROAD/LANE BOUNDARY DETECTION

Two main approaches to real-time road/lane boundary detection from still images have been investigated, developed, and tested on the PAPRICA system. The computational paradigm for the extraction of the relevant features (road/lane boundaries) underlying the two approaches is based on massively parallel computations and on the exploitation of low-level processing. While in the former, the feature extraction process can be easily expressed by a set of cellular automata rules, in the latter, it can be efficiently explained with the help of the basic Mathematical Morphology operators and a few extensions to hierarchical morphology. The latter is the one chosen for the integration on board the MOB-LAB vehicle, because its extension to image sequence analysis is the one that achieves the best performances [11]. MOB-LAB is an open mobile laboratory suited to develop and test real-time systems, monitoring the trajectory of a vehicle running on extra-urban roads by means of computer vision systems.

The result of the enhancement process may be presented to the driver in two different ways, as shown in Figure 6.4, where the numbers on the arrows represent the image depth (bits/pixel):

- superimposed onto the original image highlighting the street boundaries, and displayed on an on-board monitor;

- computed by the PAPRICA host computer, which drives a set of LEDs on the on-board control panel.

Both approaches are discussed in the following subsections, with the emphasis on the approach itself and on its performance in terms of computational time and output quality.

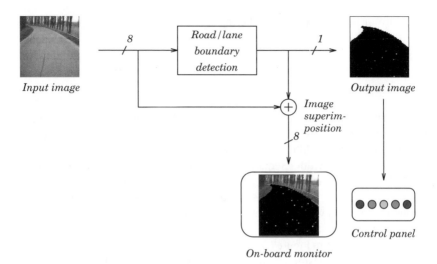

Figure 6.4 Data-flow diagram of the road/lane boundary detection system.

6.4.1 CA-Based Feature Extraction Approach

The CA-based feature extraction algorithm is composed of a set of classical filters, including clustering, edge detection, and correlation. Because automotive applications impose real-time constraints, traditional implementation of these filters requires a speed improvement.

The data-flow diagram of the CA-based feature extraction approach is shown in Figure 6.5, where the numbers on the arrows represent the image depth. The input image comes directly from the digitizer device, and consists of a 256×256 array of eight bit values (256 gray levels).

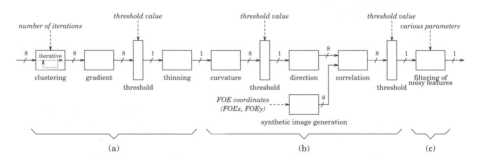

Figure 6.5 Data-flow diagram of the CA-based low-level process.

The features to be extracted (i.e., road/lane boundaries) are present in the original image as straight lines determined by high brightness discontinuities and pointing toward the focus of expansion (FoE) of the image. In order to extract such information, the following filtering sequence is used:

a. extract the brightness discontinuities;

b. retain only the straight lines that point toward the FoE;

c. discard the short segments, usually generated by noisy features.

As shown in Figure 6.5, sequence (a) has been implemented by preliminary clustering, followed by gradient-based filtering to detect the image edges, and then thresholding and thinning to obtain a final binary image containing segments with a single-pixel width. Sequence (b) was accomplished by the determination of the local curvature of the lines, followed by a thresholding operation in order to preserve only the straight lines. The feature extraction algorithm is obtained through correlation with a synthetic image that encodes the knowledge about the position of the FoE. Such a synthetic image is called *FoE image*. An example of FoE image is shown in Figure 6.6. It is worth noting that FoE position is computed with respect to the position of the camera. On board the MOB-LAB we used a camera installed on the front-left side of the vehicle. If we change the position of the camera, we have to also change the FoE image.

Figure 6.6 Example of an FoE image.

The last part of the sequence of Figure 6.5c, consists of simple morphological filters for the final elimination of noisy details.

Parallel and Local Feature Extraction

Ideally, each pixel determines if it belongs to the feature or not, that is, it measures the significance of the information contained in its neighborhood with respect to the local properties of the feature.

According to the notations introduced in Section 6.2.1, the image is mapped onto the two-dimensional lattice, and each pixel corresponds to a CA cell, where (x, y) represents the coordinates of a generic cell. The state s of cell u is partitioned into four substates:

$$s = \left(s_B, s_C, s_D, s_S \right) \tag{6-20}$$

where s_B, s_C, s_D, s_S represent the gray level of the pixel, the characteristic substate, the descriptive substate, and the significance substate, respectively.

A local rule f is first used to assign the descriptive substate s_D to each cell, using the brightness substate s_B of the cells belonging to its neighborhood V_N:

$$s_D(u) = f\left(s_B(v) \mid v \in V_N\right) \tag{6-21}$$

where the same symbols are used to indicate both the substate and the restriction of the global configuration to the substate components.

Due to its intrinsic connection to the specific feature to be extracted, the characteristic substate s_C is precomputed, applying the same function f to a virtual neighborhood configuration where the image brightness corresponds to the presence of the feature of interest.

Substates s_D and s_C are then compared and the pixel significance (with respect to the feature of interest) is encoded in a significance subtate s_S, which measures the distance between s_D and s_C:

$$s_S(u) = \left\| s_D(u) - s_C(u) \right\| \tag{6-22}$$

The determination of f and of s_C are the main points in the definition of the feature extraction algorithm.

Detection Process

With reference to automotive applications, the hypothesis used to define substates s_D and s_C is that the incoming images are acquired by a camera installed on the front-left side of a vehicle. In this case, the road/lane boundaries can be defined as the two straight lines starting from the bottom of the image and pointing to the FoE.

Each edge pixel is thus labeled with two 8-bit values representing the local direction d and the local curvature c of the line to which the pixel belongs. In the continuous case, it is

$$d(P) \triangleq \lim_{P' \to P} \frac{y' - y}{x' - x} \quad \text{and} \quad c(P) \triangleq \lim_{P' \to P} \frac{1}{R} \tag{6-23}$$

where symbols $P(x, y)$, $P'(x', y')$, and R refer to Figure 6.7a.

Due to the high discretization errors obtained in the analysis of a small neighborhood (which corresponds to the $\lim_{P' \to P}$), neighborhood dimensions (generally 3×3) should be increased in order to obtain higher precision. Unfortunately, the more extended the neighborhood (that is, the higher the distance between P and P'), the greater the difference between the actual result and the theoretical one, in which P and P' should be infinitely close. Experimental studies have derived the value of 11×11 as a good trade-off for the dimension of the neighborhood to be analyzed [58]. Therefore, calling $P^{(1)} = p(x^{(1)}, y^{(1)})$, $P^{(2)} = p(x^{(2)}, y^{(2)})$, ..., $P^{(n)} = p(x^{(n)}, y^{(n)})$ the sequence of n edge pixels, following the hypothesis of an 11×11 neighborhood, and assuming $i > 5$ and $i \leq n - 5$,

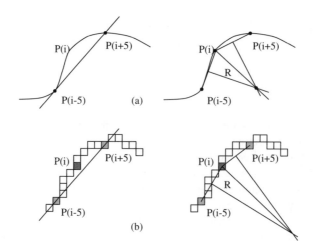

Figure 6.7 Direction and curvature: (a) continuous and (b) discrete cases.

$d(P^{(i)})$ and $c(P^{(i)})$ can be obtained as follows:

$$\begin{cases} d\left(P^{(i)}\right) = \dfrac{y^{(i-5)} - y^{(i+5)}}{x^{(i-5)} - x^{(i+5)}} \\[3mm] c\left(P^{(i)}\right) = \dfrac{2 \mid y^{(i-5)}x^{(i+5)} - x^{(i-5)}y^{(i+5)} \mid}{abc} \end{cases} \qquad (6\text{-}24)$$

$$\text{where} \quad \begin{cases} a = \sqrt{\left(x^{(i-5)}\right)^2 + \left(y^{(i-5)}\right)^2} \\[3mm] b = \sqrt{\left(x^{(i+5)}\right)^2 + \left(y^{(i+5)}\right)^2} \\[3mm] c = \sqrt{\left| x^{(i-5)} - x^{(i+5)} \right|^2 + \left| y^{(i-5)} - y^{(i+5)} \right|^2} \end{cases} \qquad (6\text{-}25)$$

as shown in Figure 6.7b. Because each pixel can access its eight neighbors, five iterations are needed to collect information about its 11×11 neighborhood, or, in this case, about the line morphology along an 11-step-long monodimensional neighborhood. The information about the curvature is now used to discard the pixels not belonging to a straight line through a thresholding operation.

The direction field $d(x, y)$, assigned to each preserved pixel, is thus identified by its descriptive substate s_D. The characteristic substate s_C is defined here as the slope of the geometrical line connecting pixel $p(x, y)$ to the FoE, indicated as $p(x_{FoE}, y_{FoE})$:

$$s_C(x, y) = \text{arctg}\, \frac{y_{FoE} - y}{x_{FoE} - x} \qquad (6\text{-}26)$$

Because the FoE image [the set of $s_C(x, y)$] depends only on two parameters (x_{FoE} and y_{FoE}), it can be generated and stored in the host memory. The computation of s_C is thus reduced to a simple loading from memory.

Significant substate s_S is thus computed as the distance between s_C and s_D, and the result is then thresholded to a medium value, in order to preserve the lines pointing close to the FoE. This includes the case in which car speed has a component perpendicular to the road/lane boundaries. A hysteresis process would reduce processing speed and produce results similar to the ones obtained with a mere threshold. The final step of the process is to eliminate segments shorter than an experimental fixed threshold.

6.4.2 Model-Driven Feature Extraction Approach

An image acquired from a moving vehicle can be considered as a patch of different areas: a portion of the street, obstacles, other vehicles, or shadows, surrounded by a specific background depending on the environment. The knowledge about such different areas enables the development of a segmentation algorithm that is simpler and faster than the traditional algorithms based on template matching [59], and also the one introduced in Section 6.4.1. This approach restricts the search area in a neighborhood of standard positions, and uses information on the shape of the road/lane region.

The model that contains the a priori knowledge on the feature to be extracted (i.e., road or lane boundaries) is encoded in the traditional data structure used in low-level processing, namely in a two-dimensional array of values. During our experiments, we used binary images representing two different regions: street and background. With this choice, in the final result the road or lane boundaries will appear as unfragmented lines, even if in the original input image they are partially occluded by obstacles. Henceforth, this image will be referred to as *synthetic image*. Figure 6.8 is an example of synthetic image encoding the knowledge of a model of a straight road.

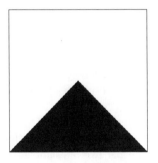

Figure 6.8 Example of a synthetic image.

Multiresolution Approach

Synthetic images and images coming from the camera (called *natural images*) cannot be directly compared with local computations, because the latter contains many more details than the former. Among all the known methods used to decrease the presence of details, it is necessary to choose one that would not decrease the strength of the feature to be extracted. For this purpose, a low-pass filter, such as an average filter reducing the brightness discontinuities, would reduce not only the presence of details, but also the relevance of the street boundaries, causing the detection to become more difficult. On the other hand, because the street boundaries exploit a long-distance correlation, a subsampling of both natural and synthetic images would lead to a comparison less dependent on the detail content. More generally, it is much easier to detect large-sized objects at a low resolution, where only their main characteristics are present, than at a high resolution, where the details of the specific instance of the represented object can make its detection difficult. Although the detection of objects works better at a low resolution, the complete recognition and description process can take place only at high resolutions, allowing the identification of even small details, due to the preliminary results obtained at a coarse resolution.

These considerations led to the use of a pyramidal data structure composed by the same image at different resolutions. It is worth noting that, when the computing architecture contains a number of PEs smaller than the number of image pixels (PE virtualization mechanism), a useful side effect, due to the reduction of the resolution, is the decrement in the number of computations to be performed [60].

The information content involved in a single local computation during the application of an iterative monoresolution cellular automaton depends on a portion of the original image whose linear dimensions depend directly on the number of iterations. Moreover, when a pyramidal computational paradigm is used, a further exponential dependency of that value on the number of subsamplings is introduced. Thus, the choice of a pyramidal computational paradigm, besides being supported by theoretical reasons, offers an advantage in terms of computational efficiency.

Detection Process

Figure 6.9 shows the data-flow diagram of the pyramidal algorithm, where the numbers on the arrows represent the image depth. Before each subsampling, the natural image is filtered. In this way, it is possible to decrease both the influence of noise and redundant details, and the distortion due to aliasing introduced by the subsampling process [61]. The image is partitioned into nonoverlapping square subsets of four pixels each; the filter consists of a simple average among the values of the pixels belonging to the same subset. The set of resulting values forms the subsampled image.

Once the minimum resolution has been reached (64×64, in the case of Fig. 6.9), the edges of the natural image are enhanced by the application of a few iterations of a clustering algorithm [62], and the two subsampled images are compared. The features encoded in the synthetic image are modified by an iterative algorithm (driven binary stretching, DBS) in order to get closer to the ones contained in the natural image (see Fig. 6.10). The result is then oversampled and further improved using the same DBS algorithm. These steps are iterated until the original resolution is reached.

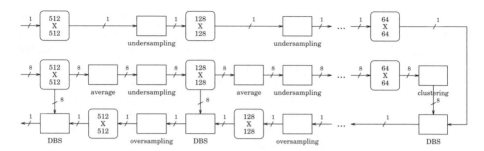

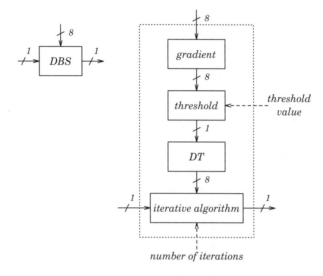

Figure 6.9 Data-flow diagram of the pyramidal algorithm.

Figure 6.10 Data-flow diagram of the DBS algorithm.

The goal of the DBS algorithm is to stretch (to adapt) the input binary synthetic image according to the data encoded into the gray-tone natural image, which will be used as a guide, and to produce as output a new version of the synthetic image.

In order to give a detailed description of the DBS algorithm, it is worth noting that the features of interest in the gray-tone image are the road/lane boundaries. Usually the boundary of a generic object is represented by brightness discontinuities in the image reproducing it, thus the first step is accomplished by the application of a gradient-based filter to the input image. Then, as shown in Figure 6.10, a threshold is applied to the gradient image, in order to keep only the most significant edges.

To stretch the synthetic image S toward the positions encoded in the thresholded image on a two-dimensional mesh-connected massively parallel architecture, an iterative algorithm is performed. Each border pixel of the synthetic image should move toward the position of the nearest foreground pixel of the thresholded image. For this purpose, a scalar field is defined on the image, representing the potential V associated to the pixel itself. The difference of two potential values $V(p) - V(q)$ represents the cost of moving pixel p toward position q. The iterative process will enable all the pixel movements associated with a negative cost. The scalar field should be such that a negative cost corresponds to the movement toward the nearest position of the foreground pixels of the thresholded image. Thus, $V(p)$ should depend on the minimum distance between pixel p and the foreground pixels of the thresholded image. It is easy to understand that the best description of the potential field is given by the distance transform (DT) [63], applied to the binary thresholded image[2].

The stretching algorithm can be expressed by means of the following two rules, where the *internal* and *external edges* of a binary image are defined as a difference between the original image and, respectively, its erosion and its dilation with the 3×3 8-neighbors structuring element.

1. Rule for the internal edge:
   - for each pixel of the internal edge of S, compute the maximum value of the DT associated with its four connected neighbors that does not belong to S;
   - remove from S all the pixels whose associated DT is greater than the value previously computed.

2. Rule for the external edge:
   - for each pixel of the external edges of S, compute the minimum value of the DT associated with its four connected neighbors that belong to S;
   - insert in S all the pixels whose associated DT is greater than the value previously computed, and all the pixels not belonging to the thresholded image whose associated DT is equal to the value previously computed.

Figure 6.11a shows the modulus of the DT coefficients (in the case of $\lambda = 0$), together with the input binary image, indicated with a gray texture (different square markings represent different states of input binary image). The output of the iterative DBS algorithm is presented in Figure 6.11b, where dark gray areas represent the stretching area. The specific requirement for the pixels that are moving toward a flat region, not belonging to the thresholded image, ensures that

---

[2]Due to a more efficient implementation-dependent data handling, the final version of the potential image DT is obtained by adding a constant λ to every coefficient, in order to work with only positive values: λ represents the maximum value allowed for gray-tone images. In this specific case, because 8-bit images are considered, $\lambda = 255$.

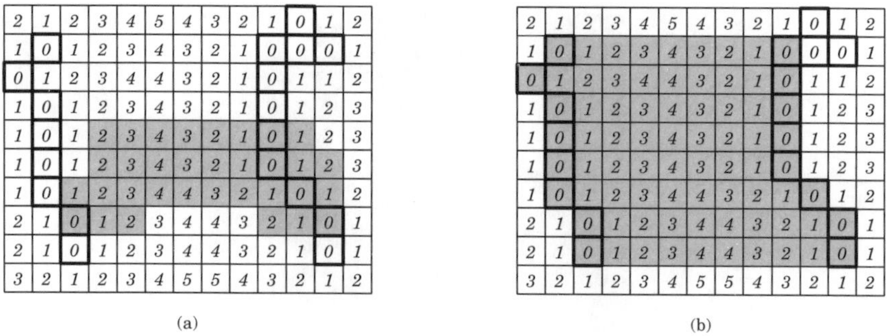

2	1	2	3	4	5	4	3	2	1	0	1	2
1	0	1	2	3	4	3	2	1	0	0	0	1
0	1	2	3	4	4	3	2	1	0	1	1	2
1	0	1	2	3	4	3	2	1	0	1	2	3
1	0	1	2	3	4	3	2	1	0	1	2	3
1	0	1	2	3	4	3	2	1	0	1	2	3
1	0	1	2	3	4	4	3	2	1	0	1	2
2	1	0	1	2	3	4	4	3	2	1	0	1
2	1	0	1	2	3	4	4	3	2	1	0	1
3	2	1	2	3	4	5	5	4	3	2	1	2

(a)

2	1	2	3	4	5	4	3	2	1	0	1	2
1	0	1	2	3	4	3	2	1	0	0	0	1
0	1	2	3	4	4	3	2	1	0	1	1	2
1	0	1	2	3	4	3	2	1	0	1	2	3
1	0	1	2	3	4	3	2	1	0	1	2	3
1	0	1	2	3	4	3	2	1	0	1	2	3
1	0	1	2	3	4	4	3	2	1	0	1	2
2	1	0	1	2	3	4	4	3	2	1	0	1
2	1	0	1	2	3	4	4	3	2	1	0	1
3	2	1	2	3	4	5	5	4	3	2	1	2

(b)

Figure 6.11 Example of a two-dimensional stretching: (a) input binary image; (b) stretched image.

the binary image does not follow the chain of maxima of the DT. With such a requirement, in the specific case of Figure 6.11, the maxima in the upper-right-hand side are not included in the resulting binary image.

Figure 6.12a shows the original image acquired from the moving vehicle, while Figures 6.12b and c show the results of the application of the two approaches presented respectively in Sections 6.4.1 and 6.4.2, in the case of road boundary detection. The preliminary experiments on the laboratory of the two different approaches, when processing 256×256 pixel images (8 bits/pixel) on PAPRICA simulators, showed that the former can filter a single image in about 1.36 s, while the latter (stopping the processing when a 64×64 binary image has been obtained) takes less than 0.8 s. We then decided to run the model-driven features extraction approach together with a top-down control for the selection of the most appropriate synthetic image on the PAPRICA board. Such an approach has also been extended to handle image sequences [11]. In this case, two main advantages (i.e., reduction of computational time and improvement of output quality) can be achieved by the substitution of the synthetic image with the binary image obtained by the computation of the previous frame.

Table 6.2 synthesizes the performance analysis of the system described in Section 6.4.2, according to the two modalities introduced at the beginning of the same section. It is worth noting that such performance has been obtained with five iterations of both DT process and DBS filter for each pyramid level. By means of the second modality (i.e., the driving of the set of LEDs on the on-board control panel) a lower resolution for image reconstruction (and LEDs driving) is required. During the tests on board the MOB-LAB, we stopped the resolution to 64×64. In this way, the $256^2 \rightarrow 16^2 \rightarrow 64^2$ filtering of a single frame is performed in less than 180 ms, allowing the computation of 5–6 frames/s.

Once the road/lane boundaries have been detected, the PAPRICA host computes the medial axis of the road/lane and presents to the driver through the control panel the deviation of the position of the vehicle with respect to this medial axis.

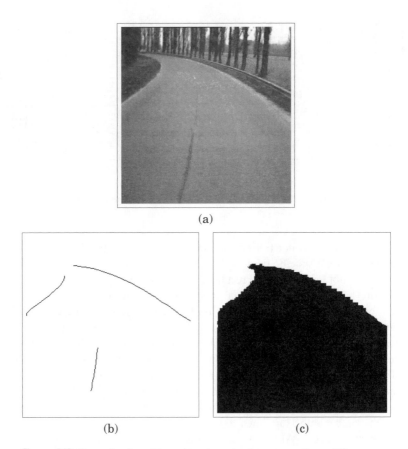

(a)

(b)   (c)

Figure 6.12 Example of road boundary detection by means of two different approaches: (a) input image; (b) CA-based approach; (c) model-driven–based approach.

TABLE 6.2 Performance Analysis of the Model-Driven Road/Lane Boundary Detection System

Operation	Image Dimension	Time (ms)
Undersampling	$256^2 \rightarrow 16^2$	155.7
DT, DBS & Oversampling	$16^2 \rightarrow 32^2$	3.55
DT, DBS & Oversampling	$32^2 \rightarrow 64^2$	18.55
DT, DBS & Oversampling	$64^2 \rightarrow 128^2$	69.13
DT, DBS & Oversampling	$128^2 \rightarrow 256^2$	296.87
Total (Control Panel modality)	$256^2 \rightarrow 16^2 \rightarrow 64^2$	177.80
Total (On-board Monitor modality)	$256^2 \rightarrow 16^2 \rightarrow 256^2$	543.80

6.5   OPTICAL FLOW FIELDS COMPUTATION

The study of motion in image sequence is a large and complex topic. In general terms, we remind the reader that a scene is a digitized representation of a continuous intensity variation in the world in view. We may observe that this scene is, in general, changing as the object in view, or the observer, or both, move with respect to each other, giving rise to optical flow (OF). OF associates a two-dimensional velocity with each point on the two-dimensional image plane. The shape from motion algorithms attempts to determine OF as a first step, and derive shape from it [64]. Intuitively, if the velocity of the observer is known, OF will reveal (object) surface information in some detail.

In this section we describe a cellular automata for OF computation, designed specifically to be implemented on PAPRICA architecture [57]. As in the previous case, we restrict the application domain to image sequences taken from a car moving along extra-urban roads. The target of the evaluation of the OF field is the detection of obstacles in front of the moving vehicle and the computation of the time to impact for approaching objects. Due to the automotive application, special care must be taken with the response time of the algorithm in order to have real-time performances of the entire system.

Given two subsequent frames of a sequence, the OF represents the displacement of the same feature between the two images. The feature can be triggered by local patterns, or can be determined at pixel level, as in our approach. The result of the computation is an image field where every position contains the feature displacement between the two frames. Feature correspondence is searched for in a fixed neighborhood of every pixel. If there are more than one correspondence, there must be a criterion for removing the ambiguity. In our approach, we choose the closest correspondence, or no correspondence at all, if there is more than one correspondence at the same distance.

6.5.1   Classical Approaches to OF
Computation

To better understand our approach, we will briefly analyze some existing works, emphasizing the differences with our work.

The method proposed by Horn and Schunck in [65] is an iterative one, based on the assumption of smooth variations in the OF field. The OF is obtained by the iterative solution of two differential equations (one for each OF component). Only two images are required and thus a restricted amount of memory is needed. Moreover, it is possible to construct the solution with algebraic computations only, which are well suited for PAPRICA architecture. The known problems of iterative solutions are that they can be very time-consuming, depending on the number of iterations, and quite sensitive to roundoff errors.

The algorithm proposed by Tretiak and Pastor [66] is based on the assumption that when the scene in two subsequent frames does not change, the brightness gradient is constant in space and time. The method works by imposing this hypothesis and looking for the points in the image where this condition is not fulfilled. In these points, the OF is computed on the basis of the second space–time derivative. To this end, it is necessary to use a spatial neighborhood of at least 5×5 cells—the two frames before and the two frames after the one being processed. Moreover, this method is based, as in the previous case, on the smoothness assumption on the space–time distribution of the light intensity. This requirement is equivalent to having a very high sampling frequency and little variation between two frames.

For our project, we need to operate on sequences of images taken in unconstrained illumination situations. The global brightness of the image may then change between two frames, causing false correspondences. One method, proposed in [67], is invariant to brightness changes during the sequence and is based on a double analysis of the sequence. The first pass obtains the brightness variations in the complete sequence; the second gets the OF components (with known brightness variations) and compensates for them. Unfortunately, this approach requires analyzing the whole sequence twice and has a high computational complexity.

Fast parallel OF algorithms have already been implemented on massively parallel computers. For example, Little, Bulthoff, and Poggio [68], have implemented a parallel OF algorithm on the CM2 Connection Machine. In this algorithm, the well-known "aperture problem" [69] is solved in a local fashion by taking advantage of the global communication mechanism of the Connection Machine. Unfortunately, global communication is not optimized on the PAPRICA architecture.

6.5.2 CA-Based OF Computation

The founding assumption of our CA-based method is that to obtain a fast computation, it is necessary to perform only simple operations, avoiding computation of analytical functions. To look for the highest correlation pair, the brightness of the central pixel is correlated with all the pixels of the neighborhood. If this pair can be determined without ambiguities, it is used for computing the OF direction.

We use a square neighborhood, centered on the central cell: V^l. The neighborhood is determined in terms of l "levels," each level being a square neighborhood contained in V^l. Thus V^3 contains three square neighborhoods: $3 \times 3, 5 \times 5$, and 7×7.

V^l is scanned by a "spiral" scan, level by level (see Fig. 6.13). The neighborhood V^l can be divided in l "reduced" neighborhoods, $U^1, U^2, \ldots, U^l$, each corresponding to a level of the spiral scan: $V^l = \bigcup_{k=1,\ldots,l} U^k$. Since V_n is an $n \times n$ neighborhood, the "reduced" neighborhood can be defined in terms of set differences:

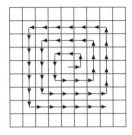

Figure 6.13 Example of spiral scanning.

$$U^1 = V_3$$
$$U^2 = (V_5 - V_3)$$
$$U^3 = (V_7 - V_5)$$
$$\cdots$$

where $V_i - V_5$ is the set of the elements of V_i not belonging to V_j.

Each U^k can also be described by a set of translations, each specified starting from the cell reached in the previous one. The translations belonging to level U^k are

$$U^k = \{(1,0), \overbrace{(0,1), \ldots, (0,1)}^{2k-1}, \overbrace{(-1,0), \ldots, (-1,0)}^{2k},$$

$$\overbrace{(0,-1), \ldots, (0,-1)}^{2k}, \overbrace{(1,0), \ldots, (1,0)}^{2k}\}$$

For instance, U^1, the 3×3 neighborhood, corresponds to the following set of translations:

$$U^k = \{(1,0), (1,0), (0,1), (-1,0), (-1,0), (0,-1), (0,-1), (1,0), (1,0)\}$$

It is easier to describe the CA local rule in terms of a procedure, rather than an analytical function. Figure 6.14 contains a *pseudocode* description of the rule, where the right side contains short comments. The two hypotheses of the rule are

- more than one correspondence at the same level means that the direction of the OF is ambiguous;

- small displacements are favored: a correspondence (or an ambiguity) at a level prevents correspondences at outer levels.

The rule starts by setting to zero the variable C_g, which will be used to store the level in which a correspondence is found (i.e., the OF intensity). Then a loop runs along all the levels, starting from inside.

For each level, the reduced neighborhood U^k is scanned in order, producing the spiral scan. The variable i gives the position in the spiral scan of a level.

```
C_g = 0                                          contains the level of the match
for k ∈ {1, 2, …, l} do                          indicates the current levels
   i = 0                                         the index scanning the current level
   C_k = 0                                       position of the match in the current level
   D_k = ∞                                       quality of the match
   F = 0                                         ambiguity
   for (v ∈ U^k) do                              level scan
      i = i + 1                                  position in the level
      δ = |c_{V^l}(x) − c_{U^k}(x + v)|          gray-value difference
      if (δ < ε_1) and (F = 0) and (C_g = 0) then    if it is a match
         if (C_k = 0) then                       if there is a simple match
            C_k = i                              sets the match position
            D_k = δ                             sets the quality of the match found
         fi
         if (C_k ≠ 0) and (|δ − D_k| < ε_2|) then   other matches with the same quality
            F = 1                                marks an ambiguity
         fi
         if (C_k ≠ 0) and (δ < |D_k − ε_2|) then   other matches with lower quality
            C_k = i                              sets the match position
            D_k = δ                             sets the quality of the match found
         fi
      fi
   rof
   if (C_k ≠ 0) and (F = 0) then                 a match without ambiguity
      C_g = k                                    sets the match at this level
   fi
rof
```

Figure 6.14 Local rule for finding the optical flow.

The gray-value difference between the center cell, $c_{V^l}(x)$, and the cell pointed to by the scan, $c_{U^k}(x + v)$, is stored in the variable δ. If this difference is below a threshold, ε_1, then there is a correspondence. If, at previous levels, there are correspondences ($C_g = 0$) or ambiguities ($F = 0$), no operation is performed. Otherwise, there are two possibilities:

- If there are no correspondences at this level ($C_k = 0$), then C_k (storing the match position in a level, i.e., the OF direction) takes the value of i, and D_k stores the gray-value difference δ for later comparisons.

- Otherwise, there is a comparison between the measured difference δ and the previous one D_k. Two cases are possible:

  - If δ and D_k are equal (within a range specified by ε_2), the variable F will mark an ambiguity.

– Otherwise, if the new correspondence δ is better than the previous D_k (within a range specified by ε_2), the variables C_k and D_k will mark the scan position as the correspondence found at this level.

After scanning a level, if there is a correspondence ($C_k \neq 0$) without ambiguities ($F = 0$), C_g takes the number of the level, k.

At the end of the scan, every cell will compute the OF from the direction and intensity stored in C_k and C_g. An example of CA-based OF computation, in the case of the image sequence of Figure 6.15, is shown in Figure 6.16.

Figure 6.15 Example of image sequence.　　**Figure 6.16** CA-based OF computation of the sequence of Figure 6.15.

The above-described CA is quite simple and fast. By using a neighborhood with three levels, a 256×256 pixel image with 8 bits/pixel is processed by PAPRICA in about 350 ms.

Nevertheless, as shown in Figure 6.16, a method based only on pixel level correspondences has several false matches. In order to avoid this problem, in [57] the method has been parametrized according to several variables, such as image subsampling, bits/pixel, scan levels. By means of these parameters it is possible to design a system for adapting the computation to the available computing power and the operational requirements. The system, integrating a data-driven process (OF computation) with an expectation-driven process, is currently being tested.

6.6 CONCLUSION

Extensive studies have been done in the last decade, and are still under way, to improve driving safety and comfort. These works, ranging from optimized road construction to variable traffic signs, from broadcasted traffic information to continuously improved vehicle design, contributed to reduce the accident rate, even in the still-increasing traffic. Beyond these approaches, there is also a demand to assist the driver directly in driving or in finding the way.

Car driving is a complex control task in which the driver acts as the central controller and performs sensor interpretation and navigation. In this control task, errors cannot be totally excluded, especially when the human capabilities in perception and reaction are exceeded. Errors, in this process, can lead to dangerous situations or even to accidents.

Driver assistance systems, or intelligent co-drivers, are aimed at reducing the driver's high workloads and mitigating the consequences of human limitations. Efficient contributions to increase driving comfort and safety are expected from these systems [70, 71]. A key characteristic of the intelligent co-driver is to act as an assistance system: the driver remains responsible and decisive for all driving tasks. Different levels of functionality of an intelligent co-driver can be defined [72]: 1) informing systems, providing the drivers with warning about specific driving situations, which the driver can quickly interpret, process, and transform into appropriate actions; 2) servo-systems, which alleviate the performance of actions initiated by the driver (e.g., servo-brake and servo-steering); 3) automatically intervening systems, which limit the consequences of nonlinearities of the controlled systems to keep the total system reaction within driver expectations (e.g., ABS); 4) automatically acting systems, which, on demand of the driver, perform actions according to the driver's rules.

The work described in this chapter is part of an intelligent co-driver developed in the framework of the EUREKA PROMETHEUS project by the Italian basic research group. The whole system, located at the level of informing systems in the previous taxonomy, is able to give warnings to the driver through a control panel in different driving situations, corresponding to different functionalities of the system. Such functionalities are

- Obstacle detection, by means of a real-time vision system integrating stereo techniques with a priori knowledge of the road environment [73].

- Road/lane detection, discussed in this chapter.

- Overtaking detection, devoted to alerting the driver during an overtaking maneuver if another vehicle is coming from the back. The detection of the incoming vehicle is performed by computing the optical flow of image sequences acquired from a single camera installed on the back of the vehicle [74].

- Safe distance computation, devoted to estimating safe distance from the preceding vehicle by means of data acquired through a single camera [75].

- Lateral distance detection of a reference line (e.g., guardrail or sidewalk edge), by means of millimeter-wave radar mounted on the dashboard [76].

During the final PROMETHEUS Board Member Meeting (BMM'94), 100 prototype vehicles were demonstrated on the Mortefontaine track (Paris, October

1994). The above-described functionalities, implemented by means of different technologies as well as different computational paradigms, showed good performances in the more than 1000 km covered by MOB-LAB during BMM'94.

This chapter described one of these functionalities, namely road/lane detection, as well as the chosen computational paradigms and the underlying theories. A second promising functionality discussed in this chapter, currently being tested, is the application of cellular automata-based optical flow field computation for obstacle detection. Obstacle detection has been one of the functionalities presented at BMM'94 on board the MOB-LAB, although the chosen approach was a stereo one, instead of the one discussed in this chapter, because of the real-time constraints.

Real-time constraints are fundamental for automotive applications for reducing the blindness of the intelligent co-driver even if, as discussed at the beginning of this chapter, a just-in-time response performance is acceptable.

The results collected during the tests on board the MOB-LAB demonstrate that, by means of the PAPRICA system, we are able to limit the blindness of the intelligent co-driver (running the road/lane detection functionality): In this case, the system blindness is a linear function of the speed obtained, multiplying the car speed by the response time of the system (see Table 6.2). More complex is the evaluation of the system blindness in the case of obstacle detection by means of optical flow computation. In this case, it is possible to estimate the maximum vehicle speed as a function of the system performance, as well as the system blindness that is, in turn, a function of the car speed and of the input image sequence resolution [57].

Acknowledgments

This work has been partially supported by CNR Progetto Finalizzato Trasporti under contracts 93.01813.PF74 and 93.04759.ST74, and by Italian Ministry of the University and Scientific Research under contract MURST 40% "Intelligent Systems." The Italian basic research activities of the PROMETHEUS project have been supported by the National Research Council through the "Progetto Finalizzato Trasporti II." The authors would like to thank Lucio Bianco, director of the "Progetto Finalizzato Trasporti II," the FIAT Research Center, and all the researchers involved in the PROMETHEUS project.

References

[1] Working Group on ATMS. "Advanced traffic management systems (ATMS)—Mobility 2000," in *The National Intelligent Vehicle Highway Systems Workshop* (Dallas, TX), March 1990.

[2] M. Nashman et al., "Real-time visual processing for autonomous driving," in *Proc. Int. Symp. on Intelligent Vehicles* (Tokyo), July 1993.

[3] Y. Shibano, T. Norikane, T. Iway, and M. Yamada, "Development of mobile communications system for RACS," in *Proc. Vehicle Navigation and Information Systems Conf.* (Toronto, Canada), September 1989.

[4] H. Okamoto, "Advanced mobile traffic information and communications system," in *Proc. Ann. Mtg. Transportation Research Board* (Washington, DC), January 1988.

[5] Commission of the European Communities, "R+D in advanced road transport telematics in Europe—DRIVE'91," in *Proc. Annual Meeting of Transportation Research Board* (DRIVE Central Office, Brussels), April 1991.

[6] G. Adorni, "Artificial intelligence for a safer and more efficient car driving," in *Proc. SPIE—Mobile Robots III*, vol. 1007, pp. 399–406 (Cambridge, MA), November 1988.

[7] E. Solem, "Robotics and the battlefield of the future," in *Proc. 3rd Conf. Military Robotics Applications* (Medicine Hat, Canada), September 1991.

[8] G. Adorni and A. Poggi, "Route guidance as a just in time multi-agent task," *Applied Artificial Intelligence*, vol. 10, no. 2, 1996.

[9] G. Adorni, A. Broggi, and V. D'Andrea, "A massively parallel approach to model-based object recognition," in *Proc. Int. Conf. Robotics, Vision and Parallel Processing for Industrial Automation*, pp. 300–306, (Ipoh, Malaysia), May 1994.

[10] A. Broggi, G. Conte, F. Gregoretti, C. Sansoè, and L. M. Reyneri, "The PAPRICA massively parallel processor," in *Proc. MPCS—IEEE Int. Conf. Massively Parallel Computing Systems*, pp. 16–30, (Ischia, Italy), 2–6 May 1994.

[11] G. Adorni, M. Bertozzi, and A. Broggi, "Massively parallel road/lane detection," in *Proc. AATTE—Fourth Int. Conf. Applications of Advanced Technologies in Transportation Engineering* (Capri, Italy), 27–30 June 1995.

[12] A. Broggi, G. Conte, F. Gregoretti, R. Passerone, C. Sansoè, and L. M. Reyneri, "Massively parallel hardware support for the MOB-LAB," in *Proc. AATTE—Fourth Int. Conf. Applications of Advanced Technologies in Transportation Engineering* (Capri, Italy), 27–30 June 1995.

[13] E. D. Dickmans and B. D. Mysliwetz, "Recursive 3-D road and relative ego-state recognition," *IEEE Trans. Pattern Analysis and Machine Intelligence*, vol. 14, pp. 199–213, 1992.

[14] K. P. Wershofen and V. Graefe, "A real-time multiple lane tracker for an autonomous road vehicle," in *Proc. EURISCO '91*, (Corfu), June 1991.

[15] T. M. Jochem, D. A. Pomerleau, and C. E. Thorpe, "MANIAC: a next generation neurally based autonomous road follower," in *Proc. Int. Conf. Intelligent Autonomous Systems: IAS-3* (Pittsburgh, PA), February 1993.

[16] D. A. Pomerleau, *Neural Network Perception for Mobile Robot Guidance*. Boston: Kluwer Academic Publishers, 1993.

[17] K. Aoki, T. Suzuki, and A. Tachibana, "A fully automated intelligent vehicle system based on computer vision for automated highway system," in *Proc. 1st World Congress on Applications of Transport Telematics and Intelligent Vehicle-Highway Systems*, pp. 1925–1932 (Paris, France), November–December 1994.

[18] B. Ulmer, "Autonomous automated driving in real traffic," in *Proc. First World Congress on Applications of Transport Telematics and Intelligent Vehicle-Highway Systems*, pp. 2118–2125 (Paris, France), November–December 1994.

[19] T. M. Jochem and S. Baluja, "A massively parallel road follower," in *Proc. CAMP'93—Computer Architectures for Machine Perception*, pp. 2–12, (New Orleans), December 1993.

[20] T. M. Jochem and S. Baluja, "Massively parallel, adaptive, color image processing for autonomous road following," in *Massively Parallel Artificial Intelligence*. (H. Kitano, ed.), AAAI Publisher and The MIT Press, 1993.

[21] C. Thorpe, M. Herbert, T. Kanade, and S. Shafer, "The new generation system for the CMU Navlab," in *Vision-Based Vehicle Guidance*, (I. Masaki, ed.), pp. 30–82. Berlin: Springer Verlag, 1991.

[22] V. Graefe and K.-D. Kuhnert, "Vision-based autonomous road vehicles," in *Vision-based Vehicle Guidance*, (I. Masaki, ed.), pp. 1–29. Berlin: Springer Verlag, 1991.

[23] A. Chandrakasan, S. Sheng, and R. Brodersen, "Low-power CMOS digital design," *IEEE J. Solid-State Circuits*, vol. 27, no. 4, pp. 473–484, 1992.

[24] B. Courtois, "CAD and testing of ICs and systems: where are we going?" Technical report, TIMA & CMP, January 1993.

[25] G. H. Forman and J. Zahorjan, "The challenge of mobile computing," *Computer*, vol. 27, no. 4, pp. 38–47, 1994.

[26] H. Gutowitz (ed.). *Cellular Automata: Theory and Experiment*. Cambridge, MA: MIT Press, 1991.

[27] T. Toffoli and N. Margolous. *Cellular Automata Machines*, Cambridge, MA: MIT Press, 1987.

[28] K. Culik II, L. P. Hurd, and S. Yu, "Computation theorethic aspects of cellular automata," *Physica D*, vol. 45, pp. 431–440, 1990.

[29] D. Farmer, T. Toffoli, and S. Wolfram (eds.). *Cellular Automata*, Amsterdam: North-Holland, March 1983.

[30] G. Matheron. *Random Sets and Integral Geometry*. New York: John Wiley, 1975.

[31] J. Serra, *Image Analysis and Mathematical Morphology*. London: Academic Press, 1982.

[32] R. M. Haralick, S. R. Sternberg, and X. Zhuang, "Image analysis using mathematical morphology," *IEEE Trans. Pattern Analysis and Machine Intelligence*, vol. 9, no. 4, pp. 532–550, 1987.

[33] R. van den Boomgaard and R. van Balen, "Methods for fast morphological image transforms using bitmapped binary images," *Computer Vision, Graphics, and Image Processing: Graphical Models and Image Processing*, vol. 54, no. 3, pp. 252–258, May 1992.

[34] X. Zhuang and R. M. Haralick, "Morphological structuring element decomposition," *Computer Vision, Graphics, and Image Processing*, vol. 35, pp. 370–382, September 1986.

[35] S. Unger, "A computer oriented toward spatial problems," *Proc. IRE*, vol. 46, pp. 1744–1750, 1958.

[36] T. Fountain, *Processor Arrays: Architectures and Applications*. London: Academic Press, 1987.

[37] W. L. Bouknight et al., "The ILLIAC IV system," *Proc. IEEE*, vol. 60, pp. 369–388, 1972.

[38] M. Duff, D. M. Watson, T. Fountain, and G. Shaw, "A cellular logic array for image processing," *Pattern Recognition*, vol. 15, pp. 229–247, 1973.

[39] S. Reddaway, "DAP—a distributed array processor," in *Proc. 1st Ann. Symp. Computer Architectures*, pp. 61–65 (Florida), 1973.

[40] K. Batcher, "Design of a massively parallel processor," *IEEE Trans. Computers*, vol. C-29, pp. 836–840, 1980.

[41] T. Fountain and V. Goetcherian, "CLIP4 parallel processing system," *IEE Proc.*, vol. 127E, pp. 219–224, 1980.

[42] W. D. Hillis. *The Connection Machine*. Cambridge, MA: MIT Press, 1985.

[43] I. N. Robinson and W. R. Moore, "A parallel processor array architecture and its implementation in silicon," in *Proc. IEEE Custom Integrated Circuits Conf.*, pp. 41–45 (New York), 1982.

[44] NCR Corporation, Dayton, OH. *Geometric Arithmetic Parallel Processor*, 1984.

[45] L. A. Schmitt and S. S. Wilson, "The AIS-5000 parallel processor," *IEEE Trans. Pattern Analysis and Machine Intelligence*, vol. 10, no. 3, pp. 320–330, May 1988.

[46] T. Sudo, T. Nakashima, M. Aoki, and T. Kondo, "An LSI adaptive array processor," in *Proc. IEEE Int. Solid-State Circuits Conf.*, pp. 122, 123, 307, 1982.

[47] T. Fountain and K. Matthews, "The CLIP 7A image processor," *IEEE Trans. Pattern Analysis and Machine Intelligence*, vol. 10, no. 3, pp. 310–319, May 1988.

[48] MasPar Computer Corporation, Sunnyvale, CA. *MP-1 Family Data-Parallel Computers*, 1990.

[49] F. Gerritsen and P. Verbeck, "Implementation of cellular logic operators using 3×3 convolution and table lookup hardware," *Computer Vision, Graphics, and Image Processing*, vol. 27, 1984.

[50] R. M. Lougheed and D. L. McCubbrey, "The cytocomputer: a practical pipelined image processor," in *Proc. 17th Ann. Symp. Computer Architectures*, pp. 271–277, (Seattle, WA), 1980.

[51] N. Margolus and T. Toffoli, "Cellular automata machines," in *Lattice Gas Methods for Partial Differential Equations* (G. D. Doolen et al., eds.) pp. 219–249, Redwood City, CA: Addison Wesley, 1990.

[52] F. Y.-C. Shih and O. R. Mitchell, "Decomposition of gray-scale morphological structuring elements," *Pattern Recognition*, vol. 24, no. 3, pp. 195–203, 1991.

[53] A. Broggi, "Speeding-up mathematical morphology computations with special-purpose array processors," in *Proc. 27th IEEE Computer Society Int. Conf. System Sciences*, vol. I (T. N. Mudge and B. D. Shriver, eds.), pp. 321–330 (Maui, Hawaii), January 1994.

[54] G. Conte, F. Gregoretti, L. Reyneri, and C. Sansoè, "PAPRICA: a parallel architecture for VLSI CAD," in *CAD Accelerators*. (A. P. Ambler, P. Agrawal, and W. R. Moore, eds.) Amsterdam: North Holland, pp. 177–189, 1991.

[55] G. Adorni, V. D'Andrea, and G. Destri, "A massively parallel approach to cellular neural networks image processing," in *Proc. Third Int. Workshop on Cellular Neural Networks and Their Applications*, pp. 423–428 (Rome, Italy), December 1994.

[56] F. Gregoretti, L. M. Reyneri, C. Sansoè, and L. Rigazio, "A chip set implementation of a parallel cellular architecture," *Microprocessing and Microprogramming*, vol. 35, pp. 417–425, 1992.

[57] G. Adorni, A. Broggi, G. Conte, and V. D'Andrea, "A self-tuning system for real-time optical flow detection," in *Proc. 1993 IEEE System, Man, and Cybernetics Conf.*, pp. 7–12, (Le Toquet, France), 1993.

[58] H. Freeman and L. Davis, "A corner-finding algorithm for chain-coded curves," in *IEEE Trans. Computers*, vol. C-26, pp. 297–307, 1977.

[59] D. H. Ballard and C. M. Brown. *Computer Vision*. Englewood Cliffs, NJ: Prentice Hall, 1982.

[60] A. Broggi, "Performance optimization on low-cost cellular array processors," in *Proc. MPCS—IEEE Int. Conf. Massively Parallel Computing Systems*, pp. 334–338, (Ischia, Italy), May 2–6 1994.

[61] W. K. Pratt, *Digital Image Processing*. New York: John Wiley & Sons, 1978.

[62] A. Broggi and A. Gandini, "Parallel image clustering: a real-time application for a special-purpose architecture," in *Proc. 8th SCIA—Scandinavian Conf. Image Analysis*, vol. 1, (K. A. Hogda, B. Braathen, and K. Heia, eds.) pp. 297–304 (Tromsoe, Norway), 25–28 May 1993. IAPR—Int. Assoc. for Pattern Recognition; NOBIM—Norwegian Society for Image Processing and Pattern Recognition.

[63] G. Borgefors, "Distance transformations in digital images," *Computer Vision, Graphics, and Image Processing*, vol. 34, pp. 344–371, 1986.

[64] S. Ullman. *The Interpretation of Visual Motion*. Cambridge, MA: The MIT Press, 1979.

[65] B. Horn and B. Schunck, "Determining optical flow," *Artificial Intelligence*, vol. 17, no. 1–3, pp. 185–204, 1991.

[66] O. Tretiak and L. Pastor, "Velocity estimation from image sequences with second order differential operators," in *Proc. 7th IEEE Int. Conf. Pattern Recognition*, pp. 16–19, 1984.

[67] J. Ducan and T. Chou, "On the detection of motion and the computation of optical flow," *IEEE Trans. Pattern Analysis and Machine Intelligence*, vol. 14, no. 3, 1992, pp. 346–352.

[68] J. Little, H. Bulthoff, and T. Poggio, "Parallel optical flow computation," in *Proc. Image Understanding Workshop* (Los Angeles, CA), February 1987, pp. 417–431.

[69] D. Marr and S. Ullman, "Directional selectivity and its use in early visual processing," in *Proc. Royal Society of London, B*, vol. 211, pp. 151–180, 1981.

[70] U. Palmquist, "Intelligent cruise control, a key component towards improved traffic control," in *Proc. IEEE Intelligent Vehicle 93* (Tokyo, Japan), July 1993, pp. 20–28.

[71] D. Reister et al., "Systems engineering approach for rational implementation of PROMETHEUS achievements," in *Proc. 25th ISATA* (Florence, Italy), June 1992.

[72] T. B. Sheridan, "Supervisory control," in *Handbook of Human Factors*. New York: John Wiley, 1987.

[73] S. Denasi, C. Lanzone, P. Martinese, G. Pettiti, G. Quaglia, and L. Viglione, "Real-time system for road following and obstacle detection," in *Proc. SPIE on Machine Vision Applications, Architectures, and Systems Integration III*, pp. 70–79 (Boston, MA), October 1994.

[74] M. Tistarelli, "Vision-based overtaking control to aid car driving," in *Proc. 2nd National Conf. of PFT2*, pp. 2539–2549 (Genoa, Italy), May 1995.

[75] C. Braccini, A. Grattarola, and L. Crovato, "Cruise control," in *Proc. 2nd National Conf. PFT2*, pp. 2551–2555 (Genoa, Italy), May 1995.

[76] C. Cugiani, L. Giubbolini, and R. Tascone, "Millimeter-wave guard rail tracking system for the vehicle lateral control," in *Proc. IEEE 4th Int. Conf. Vehicle Navigation and Information System*, pp. 521–524 (Ottawa, Canada) October 1993.

7

BIOLOGICALLY MOTIVATED IMAGE CLASSIFICATION SYSTEM

N. Petkov   *Department of Computing Science,*
University of Groningen

7.1 INTRODUCTION

Understanding natural vision and cognition is a problem that is recognized as a grand challenge to science and technology [1]. For its solution the cooperative efforts of scientists from areas as diverse as neurophysiology/neuroanatomy, psychology, biophysics, and computer science will be needed. This paper presents a study in which results of neurophysiological research on the visual cortex of primates give the basis for computer simulations whose real-time implementation is enabled by high-performance computing and in which scientific visualization plays an important role. Gaps in our knowledge of the function of the visual cortex are bridged by an artificial neural network (ANN), which exhibits self-organization properties resembling the self-organization properties of natural systems.

As to the role of computer simulations in the above-mentioned effort, in computational neuroscience they are believed to be useful in finding explanations for and predictions of phenomena that might take place in the brain. Such simulations may provide a basis for testing competing theories of perception, development, learning, and cognition and may also help suggest neuroanatomical, neurophysiological, and behavioral experiments aimed at filling the gaps in our understanding of the concerned phenomena [2]. The goal of the study presented in this paper is less ambitious: In the tradition of engineering, it is concerned primarily with the practical problem of building an artificial system that exhibits perceptual and cognitive properties comparable with those of natural vision systems.

I next elaborate on the basic knowledge and techniques that are used as enabling "ingredients" in this study; these are: neurophysiological findings, scientific visualization, artificial neural networks, and high-performance computing.

7.1.1 Some Neurophysiological Findings

The system described in this paper was inspired by two facts known from neuro-physiological research on the visual cortex of primates. The first fact is that many neurons in the primary visual cortex react strongly, in one way or another, to oriented lines, segments, and edges [3, 4] (see also the references in [4]). The second fact is that in certain areas of the visual cortex of monkeys, more specifically in the inferior temporal sulcus, cells have been found that respond selectively to faces but not to other visual stimuli [5–11].

As to the first above-mentioned fact, the extensive neurophysiological studies carried out in the past three decades have resulted in a considerable understanding of the organization and function of the primary cortex and led to computational models of primary cortical cells based on so-called *receptive field functions* [12–17]. On the basis of these results, one can compute quantities that correspond to the activities of visual cortical cells when an arbitrary input image is projected on the retina.

In Section 7.2, a cortical filter model is presented that is related to the above-mentioned models and the models we have used in previous works [18–23] but aims at coming closer to reality as it is known from the results of neurophysiological and neurobiological research. This model involves linear filtering based on receptive field functions of so-called *simple cells* and subsequent half-wave rectification (thresholding). The particular values of the receptive field function parameters used in this (updated) version of the model are chosen to match the values that are observed most frequently in neurophysiological measurements on simple cortical cells [12].

As to the second fact mentioned above, at present there exists no computational model of face-selective cells. The problem here is not just to conceive a computational scheme that would enable one to detect the presence of a face in an input image—this problem and the related problem of person identification by face image were and are among the most intensively studied computer vision problems for which various computational schemes have been proposed (see e.g., [24–36] for different approaches and [37] for a collection of works and further references). The real challenge is to find out the scheme employed in natural vision systems to recognize faces and actually not only faces but other arbitrary objects as well.

The solution to this problem is additionally complicated by a gap in our knowledge of how the activities of primary cortex cells are used in subsequent visual cortex structures. While at present it is well understood that an activation of a single cell of the concerned type signals the presence of an edge or a line of particular orientation, size, and position, the way in which the joint activities of many such cells signal complex structures is still not known. To use the words of D. Hubel [4], "If our perception of a certain line or curve depends on simple or complex cells, it presumably depends on a whole set of them, and how the information from such sets of cells is assembled at subsequent stages in the path to build up what we call percept of lines or curves (if indeed anything like that happens at all) is still a complete mystery." The artificial neural network structure given in Section 7.3 is proposed as a substitution for the cortical structures that connect the primary visual cortex with the hierarchically higher areas of the visual cortex and that presumably carry out the mentioned assembling of information. Its role in this study is that of bridging a gap in our knowledge of the visual cortex instead of filling it.

A most important aspect of the problem of finding out the scheme employed by the brain for object recognition is whether this scheme is predetermined genetically or whether it arises by means of self-organization under the influence of experience. The fact that face-selective cells are found in infant monkeys [11] and that newborn babies are able to distinguish between faces and other patterns, including geometrically incorrect face caricatures [38], may speak in support of genetical "hard-wiring" of the recognition system for such special visual patterns as faces, which are important for the survival of an infant individual. This study, however, is based on the belief that, at least as far as common objects different from special visual patterns such as faces are concerned, 1) self-organization and experience play a more important role in hierarchically higher cortical areas— otherwise, it would be difficult to explain our ability to recognize objects, such as cars and TV sets, that are products of modern age—and 2) that class-specific cells, similar to face-selective cells but selective to other object classes, emerge in these areas of the visual cortex under the influence of experience. Consequently, the Kohonen artificial neural network model used in this paper has been chosen among ANN models that exhibit self-organization properties.

7.1.2 Scientific Visualization

As mentioned above, at present it is not clear how the activities of primary cortical cells are assembled at subsequent cortical levels to represent compound patterns such as lines, curves, and other even more complex visual patterns. Computing the whole set of such activities, which is estimated to have 10^8–10^9 elements, and giving it to an artificial neural network cannot be a solution to the problem, because currently available ANN models fail when given large input data sets of raw unstructured data. Structuring the input data and the neural network itself turns out to be an important step in achieving the useful properties expected from an artificial neural network, such as self-organization, convergence, correct classification, and so on.

In an attempt to approach the problem of plausible structuring of the set of computed primary cortex cell activities, one may try to take a closer look at this set. Apparently, it would be impossible to encompass the interdependence of the computed quantities by simply inspecting their numerical values, one at a time. This situation is not much different from the situation arising in other application areas of high-performance computing. In computational fluid dynamics, for instance, very large three-dimensional vector fields specifying the velocity of a fluid at different positions are computed for a large number of instants. However, only a fraction of the bulk of computed data is of interest; these are combinations of velocity values at nearby positions that form particular patterns indicating the presence of turbulences.

Scientific visualization has been demonstrated to be a very helpful means for evaluating results in computational research by making use of the unique pattern recognition capabilities of the human visual system to discover patterns of interest in large data sets [39]. One can apply these capabilities to the set of quantities computed as a model of the activity of the primary visual cortex and thus use them in a scientific simulation problem whose solution would uncover the basic mechanisms according to which these capabilities arise.

The visualization and data structuring approach adopted in this study is to group together the quantities computed as models of the activities of cortical cells in two-dimensional subsets, called *cortical images*, according to the similarity of the receptive field functions used to compute them. (While this is certainly not the only possible way of choosing subsets for visualization and neural network input, it is a straightforward one to begin with.) The observed gross effect of the cortical filters that generate such cortical images is enhancement of intensity transitions of particular size and orientation. If the receptive field function size is appropriately chosen (visualization plays an important role in the process of determining the appropriate size), one can get a set of cortical images that are 1) simple enough, typically containing a few disjoint oriented elongated areas—this simplicity is important for the subsequent neural network processing—and 2) yet (as a set) characteristic of the input image—this is important for achieving correct classification.

7.1.3   Self-Organizing Artificial Neural Networks

As mentioned in the beginning, self-organization is believed to be an important property of natural vision systems, especially at hierarchically higher levels. An artificial system, which is expected to exhibit perceptual and cognitive properties similar to those of natural systems, should therefore also be able to self-organize itself, in particular to form its own classifications of the presented data. Such properties are characteristic of various artificial neural network models. This study is concerned with ANN models that incorporate unsupervised learning, notably the Kohonen self-organizing networks [40–43].

The self-organizing neural network classifier presented in Section 7.3 consists of two layers of Kohonen networks. In the first layer, one Kohonen network is taken for each cortical filter channel; the output of such a channel, a cortical image, is the input to an associated Kohonen network. The collective output of these first-layer networks is used as an input for a second-layer Kohonen network in which clusters of output units correspond to classes of objects. In the learning phase, a set of cortical images generated by the cortical filters from a set of input images is presented to the set of first-layer Kohonen networks, which are iterated through a learning process until convergence and self-organization occur. The learning in the second layer starts after the learning in the first layer is completed.

This system proved to be capable of learning various visual patterns and subsequently correctly classifying similar (but not identical) patterns without incorporating any model knowledge. In Section 7.3, results of experiments with this network structure are given in which different classes of objects, such as faces, armchairs, teacups, and bottles, invoke activity in different clusters of output units.

7.1.4 Computational Demands

The approach proposed below is computationally rather intensive even in the current small-size version of the system. The real-time image classification, where "real-time" means classification within a reasonable time comparable with the response time of a natural system for the same task, requests the power of a Gflop/s supercomputer. In Section 7.4, I elaborate on the computational demands of the system. Possible extensions and improvements of the system are commented on and an estimation is made of the computational power of an artificial system that would be able to mimic natural vision.

7.2 CORTICAL FILTERS AND IMAGES

7.2.1 Receptive Fields and Receptive Field Functions

The receptive field of a visual neuron is the part of the visual field, typically measured in spatial angle, within which a stimulus can influence the response (i.e., the firing rate) of the neuron. The receptive field function, which is defined on the two-dimensional visual field denoted in the following by Ω, describes the response of a neuron to a small spot of light as a function of position. In practice, a background signal called the *conditioning stimulus* [44] is used to elicit a certain intermediate-level response from a cell, and its response to the light spot stimulus is measured relative to this level. Both excitory and inhibitory effects can be measured in this way. Note that, due to the use of a conditioning stimulus, the receptive field function *cannot* be considered as the impulse response, which by definition is the response to a light spot stimulus on a dark background *only*. Nevertheless, the receptive field function is useful, in that for a wide class of visual neurons, notably the so-called simple cells in the primary visual cortex, it can be used to compute a first approximation of the response of a neuron to composite stimuli.

7.2.2 Semilinear Model

The term *simple cells*, whereby "simple" is contrasted to "complex" and "hypercomplex," was introduced to refer to the possibility of dividing the receptive fields of such cells into separate excitory and inhibitory zones [3, 4]. The following model is widely used (see e.g., [16, 17]) to compute the response r of a simple cell characterized by a receptive field function $g(x, y)$ to a composite visual signal $s(x, y)$, $(x, y) \in \Omega$; that is, a signal that is not merely a light spot at a given position but rather a superposition of such spots with different luminances at different positions resulting in a two-dimensional signal (image):

1. An integral

$$\tilde{s} = \iint_{\Omega} s(x, y)g(x, y) \, dx \, dy \qquad (7\text{-}1)$$

is evaluated in the same way as if the receptive field function $g(x, y)$ were the impulse response of a linear system and

2. the result $\tilde{s}$ is submitted to half-way rectification (more generally to thresholding) to compute the response r of the cell:

$$r = \tilde{s} \quad \text{if} \quad \tilde{s} > 0 \qquad (7\text{-}2)$$
$$r = 0 \quad \text{if} \quad \tilde{s} \leq 0 \qquad (7\text{-}3)$$

7.2.3 Receptive Field Functions of Simple Cells

As to the particular form of the function g, it has been the subject of neurophysiological research for more than 35 years. A finding that set the beginning of intensive research in this area was that there are a large number of cells in the primary visual cortex that react most strongly to oriented lines and edges instead of spot stimuli as cells in the preceding stages of the visual path do [3]. In particular, the receptive fields of one particular type of such cells, subsequently called *simple cells*, were found to consist of a number of oriented altering parallel excitory and inhibitory zones. Experimental work done in the past 35 years led to a more precise description of simple cortical cells by receptive field maps (two-dimensional response tables) and different families of functions have been demonstrated to fit such maps well [12–15]. In this study, we use the following family of functions to model simple cells:

$$g_{\xi,\eta,\sigma,\gamma,\Theta,\lambda,\varphi}(x, y) = e^{-\frac{(x'^2 + \gamma^2 y'^2)}{\sigma^2}} \cos\left(2\pi \frac{x'}{\lambda} + \varphi\right) \qquad (7\text{-}4)$$

$$x' = (x - \xi)\cos\Theta - (y - \eta)\sin\Theta$$
$$y' = (x - \xi)\sin\Theta + (y - \eta)\cos\Theta$$

where the arguments x and y specify the position of a light spot[1] in the visual field and ξ, η, σ, γ, Θ, λ, and φ are parameters that as a set of values are different for different simple cells. These parameters and their effect on the function g are next explained in more detail.

---

[1]More precisely, a flashing light spot is used in receptive field mapping experiments. In order to simplify matters, in the following it is assumed that g models the long-term response of simple cells.

The pair (ξ, η), which has the same domain Ω as the pair (x, y), specifies the center of a receptive field within the visual field, Figure 7.1. In the following, integers are used as values of x, y, ξ, η, σ, and λ. Of course, the concrete values have to be related to the size of the images if different image sizes are used. All images shown in this paper are of size/resolution 512×512. It is notable that while the pairs (x, y), which correspond to the positions of retinal light detectors, sample the visual field Ω uniformly, the sampling of Ω by the pairs (ξ, η), which correspond to primary cortical cells, is densest near the center of the visual field. In this study, Ω is taken to be a regular grid of size 512×512, more precisely $\Omega = \{-256, \ldots, 255\}^2$, and (x, y) as well as (ξ, η) are allowed to take all possible pairs of values in this set.

The parameter σ, which is measured in the same units as x, y, ξ, and η, determines the (linear) size of the receptive field, Figures 7.1c–d. The response of a cell to a light spot in position (x, y) that is at a distance greater than 2σ from the center (ξ, η) of the receptive field can practically be neglected; this dependence is well modeled by the Gaussian factor $e^{-[(x^2 + \gamma^2 y^2)/\sigma^2]}$. Neurophysiological research has shown that the diameters of the smallest to the largest receptive fields are in a ratio of at least 1:30 [12]. For practical reasons, only one value of σ is used in this pilot study, $\sigma = 32$. As already mentioned above, any particular value has to be related to the image size (here 512×512).

The support of the Gaussian factor $e^{-[(x^2 + \gamma^2 y^2)/\sigma^2]}$ and consequently the receptive field has an elliptic form. Its eccentricity is determined by the parameter γ, called the *spatial aspect ratio* (Figure 7.2). In neurophysiological measurements on simple cells, this ratio has been found to vary in a very limited range of $0.25 < \gamma < 1$ [12]. The value $\gamma = 0.5$ is used in this study.

A notable characteristic of receptive field functions of simple cells are the altering parallel excitory and inhibitory zones, which in Eq. (7-4) are modeled

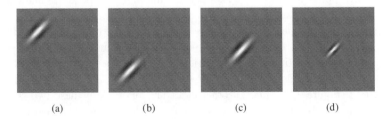

(a)	(b)	(c)	(d)

Figure 7.1 Receptive fields of different positions (a,b,c) and sizes (c,d). The gray level of the background label positions in which a light spot stimulus has no effect on the firing rate of a cell. Lighter or darker colors indicate excitory and inhibitory zones, respectively. The receptive fields are centered at points with coordinates (ξ, η) as follows: (a) $(-120,120)$; (b) $(-120,-120)$; (c) $(0,0)$; (d) $(0,0)$. (The size/resolution of the shown images is 512×512 with point $(0,0)$ centered in the middle.) The receptive field size parameter is $\sigma = 35$ for (a,b,c) and $\sigma = 20$ for (d). The values of the other parameters of the function are chosen as follows: $\gamma = 0.5$, $\lambda = 2\sigma$, $\Theta = \frac{1}{4}\pi$, $\varphi = 0$.

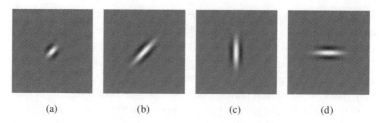

(a)   (b)   (c)   (d)

Figure 7.2 Receptive fields of different eccentricities: (a) $\gamma = 1$; (b,c,d) $\gamma = 0.5$, and orientations: (a,b) $\Theta = \frac{3}{4}\pi$; (c) $\Theta = 0$; (d) $\Theta = \frac{1}{2}\pi$. Values of the other parameters: $(\xi, \eta) = (0, 0)$, $\sigma = 35$, $\lambda = 2\sigma$, $\varphi = 0$. (Image resolution 512×512.)

by the harmonic factor $\cos(2\pi\frac{x'}{\lambda} + \varphi)$, $x' = (x - \xi)\cos\Theta - (y - \eta)\sin\Theta$. The parameter Θ is an angle ($\Theta \in [0, \pi]$) that specifies the orientation of the normal to the parallel excitory and inhibitory stripe zones (this normal is the axis x'), Figures 7.2b–d. In neurophysiological measurements, the orientation bandwidth of simple cells has been found out to be in the range $13°$–$20°$ [12], which suggests that, for computer simulations, taking something between 15 and 9 discrete values of Θ that are evenly distributed in the range $[0, \pi)$ should be sufficient from an information-theoretical point of view. For practical reasons, eight values of Θ are used in this study.

The parameter λ, measured in the same units as x, y, ξ, η, and σ, is the wavelength[2] of the harmonic factor $\cos(2\pi\frac{x'}{\lambda} + \varphi)$. Alternatively, $2\pi/\lambda$ is the spatial frequency or, equivalently, the magnitude of the wavevector. The ratio σ/λ determines the number of parallel excitory and inhibitory zones that can be observed in the receptive field of a cell, Figure 7.3. The parameters λ and σ are closely correlated; on the set of all simple cells, the ratio σ/λ, which determines the spatial-frequency bandwidth of a cell, varies in a very limited range of 0.4–0.9, which corresponds to two to five excitory and inhibitory stripe zones that can be observed [12]. One value, $\sigma/\lambda = 0.5$, is used in this study.

Finally, the parameter $\varphi \in (-\pi, \pi)$, which is a phase offset in the harmonic factor $\cos(2\pi\frac{x'}{\lambda} + \varphi)$, determines the symmetry of the function g: for $\varphi = 0$ and $\varphi = \pi$, the function g is symmetric/even with respect to the center (ξ, η) of a receptive field (Figure 7.3a–b); for $\varphi = -\frac{1}{2}\pi$ and $\varphi = \frac{1}{2}\pi$, g is antisymmetric/odd (Figure 7.3c), and all other cases are mixtures of these two (Figure 7.3d). In this study, the values 0 (corresponding to "center-on" symmetric receptive fields), π (corresponding to "center-off" symmetric receptive fields), and $-\frac{1}{2}\pi$ and $\frac{1}{2}\pi$ (corresponding to antisymmetric receptive fields with opposite polarity), are used for the parameter φ. This means that, for every choice of the values of

---

[2]Note that, due to the Gaussian factor, one cannot speak of a single wavelength of the whole receptive field function: the magnitude of the image of the function g in the frequency domain consists of two Gaussians of size proportional to $1/\sigma$ that are symmetrically arranged around the center and centered at spatial frequencies $2\pi/\lambda$.

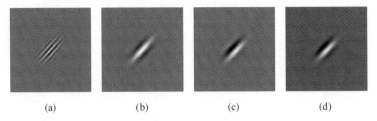

(a)　　　　　　(b)　　　　　　(c)　　　　　　(d)

Figure 7.3 Receptive fields functions of different spatial frequency bandwidth (a,b) and symmetry (b,c,d). The spatial frequency bandwidth and the related number of parallel excitory and inhibitory zones are controlled by the ratio σ/λ: (a) $\sigma/\lambda = 1.5$; (b,c,d) $\sigma/\lambda = 0.5$. One can use as a rule of thumb the fact that the number of stripe zones is equal to approximately six times the ratio σ/λ. The symmetry of the receptive fields is controlled by the parameter φ: (a,b) $\varphi = 0$ (symmetric/even "center-on" receptive fields); (c) $\varphi = \frac{1}{2}\pi$ (antisymmetric/odd receptive field); (d) $\varphi = \frac{1}{4}\pi$ [a mixture of (b) and (c)]. Values of the other parameters: $(\xi, \eta) = (0, 0)$, $\sigma = 35$, $\gamma = 0.5$, $\Theta = \frac{3}{4}\pi$. (Image resolution 512×512.)

the other parameters, in particular of (ξ, η), σ, and Θ, four types of functions with the respective symmetry properties are used. Such a choice might well correspond to certain results of neurophysiological research that: cells of different polarity [4] as well as pairs of cells with phase difference of $\frac{1}{2}\pi$ [45] have been observed.

As to the importance of simple cells for the visual system, it is believed that they play a role in the process of form perception, in that they act as detectors of oriented intensity transitions such as edges, lines, and bars that are believed to be major components of form. In particular, a cell with a symmetric receptive field ($\varphi = 0$ or $\varphi = \pi$) will react strongly to a bar that coincides in direction and width with the central lobe of the receptive field. A cell with an antisymmetric receptive field ($\varphi = -\frac{1}{2}\pi$ or $\varphi = \frac{1}{2}\pi$) will react strongly to an edge of the same orientation if the first excitory zone is on the light side of the transition and the first inhibitory zone on the dark side. Consequently, image processing operators inspired by the function of simple cells have been proposed as line and edge detectors [16, 17] and combinations of symmetric and antisymmetric operators have been demonstrated to be useful for the detection of texture [46].

7.2.4   Cortical Images

Substituting a given receptive field function $g_{\xi,\eta,\sigma,\gamma,\Theta,\lambda,\varphi}(x, y)$ in Eqs. (7-1)–(7-3), one can compute the response $r_{\xi,\eta,\sigma,\gamma,\Theta,\lambda,\varphi}$ of a simple visual cortical cell modeled by this function to an input image $s(x, y)$. Figure 7.4 shows four input images for which a number of such quantities are computed and shown[3] in Figures 7.5

---

[3] Negative cortical images are shown; this means that black and white colors correspond to high and low (zero) activity, respectively.

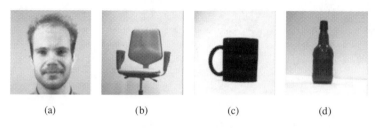

    (a)   (b)   (c)   (d)

Figure 7.4 Input images representing the classes: (a) faces; (b) armchairs; (c) teacups; (d) bottles. (Image resolution 512×512.)

through 7.8, grouped together in so-called *cortical images*. The quantities grouped in one such image are computed with receptive field functions of the same values for all parameters but the pair (ξ, η); the latter specify the pixel to which the value of such a quantity is assigned. The filters that generate such images are referred to as *cortical filters* or *channels*.

Roughly speaking, the effect of such a filter is to enhance luminance transitions of a given orientation and at a given scale. For instance, the left and right boundaries of the head in the input image shown in Figure 7.4a are enhanced in the cortical images shown in Figure 7.5a–d. The horizontal boundaries between the head and the background, and between the forehead and the hair as well as the upper and lower horizontal boundaries of the eyes are enhanced in Figure 7.5i–l. The upper-left boundary of the head, the two eyes, and other features are enhanced to different extents in the cortical images shown in Figure 7.5m–p, and so forth.

As illustrated by Figures 7.5 through 7.8, in the majority of the cases, the counterpart cortical images computed from different input images are quite different. In some cases, individual cortical images, computed from different input images, can be similar, but this is never the case for all cortical images simultaneously. This property of sets of cortical images and the fact that single cortical images computed with receptive fields of appropriate size are rather simple patterns make such sets of images suitable as input to a self-organizing neural network classifier with appropriate structure.

As one can easily mention, there is a certain redundancy in the computed cortical images, in that the same or similar transitions are enhanced in different cortical images (compare, for instance, the images in Figure 7.5i–l). Elsewhere we have proposed nonlinear mechanisms, such as cross-orientation competition and lateral inhibition, in order to reduce this redundancy and make the cortical images more suitable for interpretation and further processing [20–23, 47, 48]. These mechanisms turn out to be quite useful in achieving the mentioned goals and there is also certain neurophysiological evidence that such mechanisms are actually employed in natural vision [49]. Unfortunately, these mechanisms are computationally very intensive, which makes them inhibitive for the development of a system with reasonable response times. Therefore, these mechanisms are not applied in this study. Instead, in Eqs. (7-2) and (7-3), a threshold value

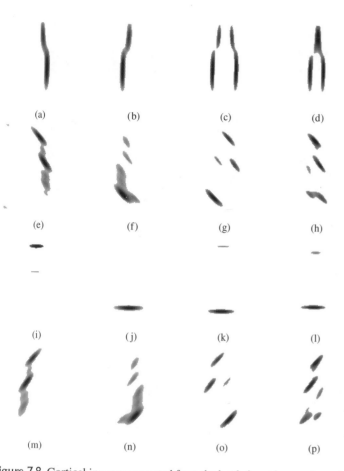

(a)   (b)   (c)   (d)

(e)   (f)   (g)   (h)

(i)   (j)   (k)   (l)

(m)   (n)   (o)   (p)

Figure 7.8 Cortical images computed from the bottle input image shown in Figure 7.4d, applying receptive field functions of different orientation and symmetry. The images shown in one row are computed with the same value of the orientation parameter as follows: (a–d) $\Theta = 0$; (e–h) $\Theta = \frac{1}{4}\pi$; (i–l) $\Theta = \frac{1}{2}\pi$; (m–p) $\frac{3}{4}\pi$. The value of the phase/symmetry parameter φ for the images in the first and second columns, which represent the responses of cells with antisymmetric receptive fields of opposite polarity, is $-\frac{1}{2}\pi$ and $\frac{1}{2}\pi$, respectively. The value of φ for the images in the third and fourth columns, which represent the responses of cells with symmetric center-on and center-off receptive fields, is 0 and π, respectively. The values of the other parameters are as follows: $\sigma = 32$, $\gamma = 0.5$, $\sigma/\lambda = 0.5$. (Image resolution 512×512.)

entation cortical images that are used as input patterns to the neural network sifier are more difficult to interpret when visualized separately.

In deciding which size of the receptive field is appropriate, there are two tradicting aspects. On one hand, the use of very small receptive fields ($\sigma < 8$

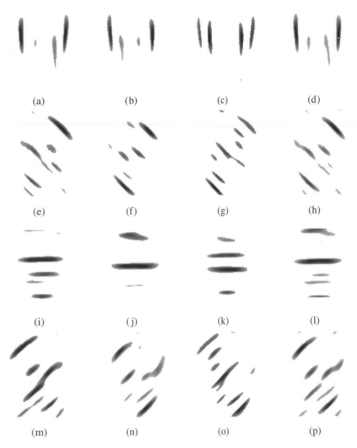

(a)   (b)   (c)   (d)

(e)   (f)   (g)   (h)

(i)   (j)   (k)   (l)

(m)   (n)   (o)   (p)

Figure 7.5 Cortical images computed from the face input image shown in Figure 7.4a, applying receptive field functions of different orientation and symmetry. The images shown in one row are computed with the same value of the orientation parameter as follows: (a–d) $\Theta = 0$; (e–h) $\Theta = \frac{1}{4}\pi$; (i–l) $\Theta = \frac{1}{2}\pi$; (m–p) $\Theta = \frac{3}{4}\pi$. The value of the phase/symmetry parameter φ for the images in the first and second columns, which represent the responses of cells with antisymmetric receptive fields of opposite polarity, is $-\frac{1}{2}\pi$ and $\frac{1}{2}\pi$, respectively. The value of φ for the images in the third and fourth columns, which represent the responses of cells with symmetric center-on and center-off receptive fields, is 0 and π, respectively. The values of the other parameters are as follows: $\sigma = 32$, $\gamma = 0.5$, $\sigma/\lambda = 0.5$. (Image resolution 512×512.)

greater than zero is applied to all pixel values of a cortical image. This threshold value is computed as a fraction (0.25) of the maximum pixel value of the four cortical images, which are computed with receptive field functions of the same size and orientation but of different symmetry.

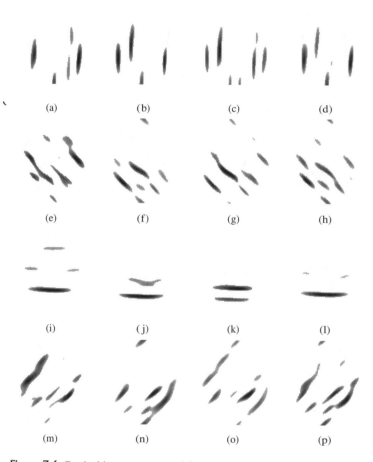

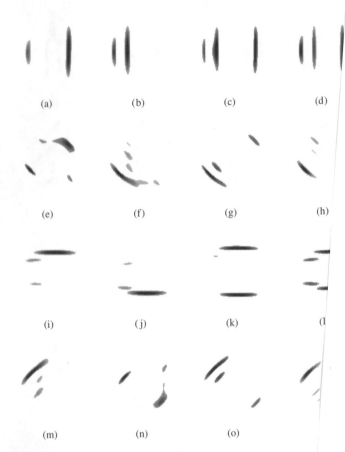

Figure 7.6 Cortical images computed from the armchair input image shown in Figure 7.4b, applying receptive field functions of different orientation and symmetry. The images shown in one row are computed with the same value of the orientation parameter as follows: (a–d) $\Theta = 0$; (e–h) $\Theta = \frac{1}{4}\pi$; (i–l) $\Theta = \frac{1}{2}\pi$; (m–p) $\frac{3}{4}\pi$. The value of the phase/symmetry parameter φ for the images in the first and second columns, which represent the responses of cells with antisymmetric receptive fields of opposite polarity, is $-\frac{1}{2}\pi$ and $\frac{1}{2}\pi$, respectively. The value of φ for the images in the third and fourth columns, which represent the responses of cells with symmetric center-on and center-off receptive fields, is 0 and π, respectively. The values of the other parameters are as follows: $\sigma = 32$, $\gamma = 0.5$, $\sigma/\lambda = 0.5$. (Image resolution 512 × 512.)

7.2.5   Appropriate Receptive Field Size

Before elaborating on the problem that receptive field size is "appropriate," the notion of a composite cortical image (Figure 7.9, page 209) is first introduced

Figure 7.7 Cortical images computed from the teacup input image Figure 7.4c, applying receptive field functions of different orienta symmetry. The images shown in one row are computed with the s of the orientation parameter as follows: (a–d) $\Theta = 0$; (e–h) $\Theta = $ $\Theta = \frac{1}{2}\pi$; (m–p) $\frac{3}{4}\pi$. The value of the phase/symmetry parameter images in the first and second columns, which represent the respo cells with antisymmetric receptive fields of opposite polarity, is $\frac{1}{2}\pi$, respectively. The value of φ for the images in the third and f columns, which represent the responses of cells with symmetric and center-off receptive fields, is 0 and π, respectively. The valu other parameters are as follows: $\sigma = 32$, $\gamma = 0.5$, $\sigma/\lambda = 0.5$. (resolution 512 × 512.)

as an image that is computed as a pixel-wise maximum super cortical images as those shown in Figures 7.5 through 7.8. referred to as *single-orientation* cortical images. Composite used only for visualization. They are useful for this purpose,

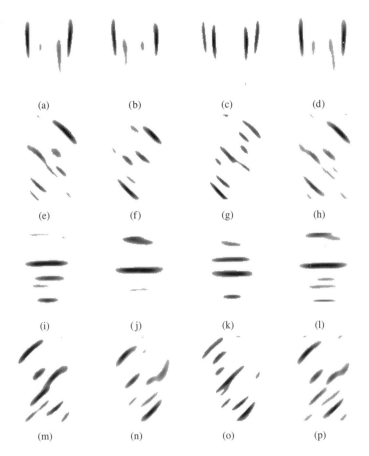

Figure 7.5 Cortical images computed from the face input image shown in Figure 7.4a, applying receptive field functions of different orientation and symmetry. The images shown in one row are computed with the same value of the orientation parameter as follows: (a–d) $\Theta = 0$; (e–h) $\Theta = \frac{1}{4}\pi$; (i–l) $\Theta = \frac{1}{2}\pi$; (m–p) $\Theta = \frac{3}{4}\pi$. The value of the phase/symmetry parameter φ for the images in the first and second columns, which represent the responses of cells with antisymmetric receptive fields of opposite polarity, is $-\frac{1}{2}\pi$ and $\frac{1}{2}\pi$, respectively. The value of φ for the images in the third and fourth columns, which represent the responses of cells with symmetric center-on and center-off receptive fields, is 0 and π, respectively. The values of the other parameters are as follows: $\sigma = 32$, $\gamma = 0.5$, $\sigma/\lambda = 0.5$. (Image resolution 512×512.)

greater than zero is applied to all pixel values of a cortical image. This threshold value is computed as a fraction (0.25) of the maximum pixel value of the four cortical images, which are computed with receptive field functions of the same size and orientation but of different symmetry.

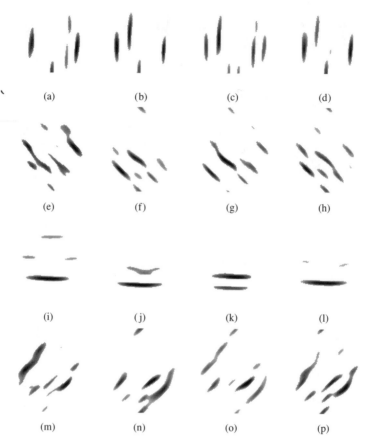

Figure 7.6 Cortical images computed from the armchair input image shown in Figure 7.4b, applying receptive field functions of different orientation and symmetry. The images shown in one row are computed with the same value of the orientation parameter as follows: (a–d) $\Theta = 0$; (e–h) $\Theta = \frac{1}{4}\pi$; (i–l) $\Theta = \frac{1}{2}\pi$; (m–p) $\frac{3}{4}\pi$. The value of the phase/symmetry parameter φ for the images in the first and second columns, which represent the responses of cells with antisymmetric receptive fields of opposite polarity, is $-\frac{1}{2}\pi$ and $\frac{1}{2}\pi$, respectively. The value of φ for the images in the third and fourth columns, which represent the responses of cells with symmetric center-on and center-off receptive fields, is 0 and π, respectively. The values of the other parameters are as follows: $\sigma = 32$, $\gamma = 0.5$, $\sigma/\lambda = 0.5$. (Image resolution 512×512.)

7.2.5 Appropriate Receptive Field Size

Before elaborating on the problem that receptive field size is "appropriate," the notion of a composite cortical image (Figure 7.9, page 209) is first introduced

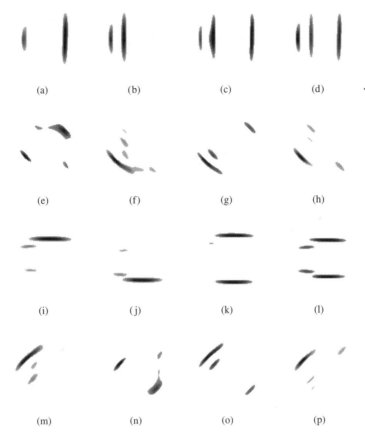

Figure 7.7 Cortical images computed from the teacup input image shown in Figure 7.4c, applying receptive field functions of different orientation and symmetry. The images shown in one row are computed with the same value of the orientation parameter as follows: (a–d) $\Theta = 0$; (e–h) $\Theta = \frac{1}{4}\pi$; (i–l) $\Theta = \frac{1}{2}\pi$; (m–p) $\frac{3}{4}\pi$. The value of the phase/symmetry parameter φ for the images in the first and second columns, which represent the responses of cells with antisymmetric receptive fields of opposite polarity, is $-\frac{1}{2}\pi$ and $\frac{1}{2}\pi$, respectively. The value of φ for the images in the third and fourth columns, which represent the responses of cells with symmetric center-on and center-off receptive fields, is 0 and π, respectively. The values of the other parameters are as follows: $\sigma = 32$, $\gamma = 0.5$, $\sigma/\lambda = 0.5$. (Image resolution 512×512.)

as an image that is computed as a pixel-wise maximum superposition of simple cortical images as those shown in Figures 7.5 through 7.8. The latter will be referred to as *single-orientation* cortical images. Composite cortical images are used only for visualization. They are useful for this purpose, because the single-

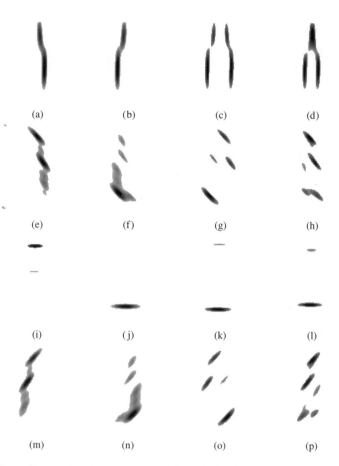

Figure 7.8 Cortical images computed from the bottle input image shown in Figure 7.4d, applying receptive field functions of different orientation and symmetry. The images shown in one row are computed with the same value of the orientation parameter as follows: (a–d) $\Theta = 0$; (e–h) $\Theta = \frac{1}{4}\pi$; (i–l) $\Theta = \frac{1}{2}\pi$; (m–p) $\frac{3}{4}\pi$. The value of the phase/symmetry parameter φ for the images in the first and second columns, which represent the responses of cells with antisymmetric receptive fields of opposite polarity, is $-\frac{1}{2}\pi$ and $\frac{1}{2}\pi$, respectively. The value of φ for the images in the third and fourth columns, which represent the responses of cells with symmetric center-on and center-off receptive fields, is 0 and π, respectively. The values of the other parameters are as follows: $\sigma = 32$, $\gamma = 0.5$, $\sigma/\lambda = 0.5$. (Image resolution 512×512.)

orientation cortical images that are used as input patterns to the neural network classifier are more difficult to interpret when visualized separately.

In deciding which size of the receptive field is appropriate, there are two contradicting aspects. On one hand, the use of very small receptive fields ($\sigma < 8$

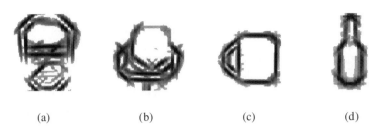

(a)   (b)   (c)   (d)

Figure 7.9 Composite cortical images computed as pixel-wise maximum superposition of single-orientation cortical images. Each of the images (a) through (d) is computed as a superposition of the images shown in the first two columns of Figures 7.5 through 7.8, respectively.

for 512×512 images) delivers cortical images with high information content: visualizing a composite cortical image of, say, a face, allows an observer not only to classify the input image as that of a face, but also to identify a particular person. The high information content is, however, an obstacle for a self-organizing neural network classifier: for instance, most of the "features" observable in a cortical image computed from a face input image (numerous fine line segments) will be due to the hair and using an input image in which the hair is just combed differently will lead to a feature pattern that is "perceived" as completely different by a self-organizing artificial neural network.

On the other hand, choosing a very large receptive field size ($\sigma > 64$ for 512×512 images) results in cortical images with too-small information content to be useful for classification. When visualizing composite cortical images computed with very large receptive field sizes, it is difficult even for a human observer to correctly classify the objects in the input images and one cannot expect that a simple artificial neural network classifier will perform better.

Here, "appropriate" size means that the resulting single-orientation cortical images 1) should be simple, containing a relatively small number of features (typically a few elongated activity lines per image), and 2) at the same time, as a set, sufficiently characteristic of the input image to allow successful automatic classification (the latter requirement is controlled by visualizing composite cortical images). Our experiments show that for the classification of objects that fill the input image frame, taking σ to be approximately $\frac{1}{16}$ of the image size gives satisfactory results. Therefore, in the particular application described here, the value $\sigma = 32$ was chosen for images of size 512×512.

7.2.6 Subsampling and Its Relation to Complex Cells

The cortical images computed according to the above-sketched scheme are rather large (512×512), which makes them impractical for experimenting with artificial neural networks. Inspecting these images, one can notice that the areas of activity are relatively thick. This is due to the convolution[4] of the input image with the particular receptive field functions used. A sharp edge will, for instance, be smeared over a certain area and less sharp intensity transitions will appear correspondingly thicker. In order to determine a subsampling factor to be used for reduction of the image size, one can estimate the effect of smearing as follows:

Let us assume that there is a sharp edge transition in the input image. For an antisymmetric receptive field function, for instance, the quantity $r'_{\xi,\eta,\sigma,\gamma,\Theta,\lambda,\varphi}$, which is computed from the input image according to the above-sketched scheme, will be large if the orientation Θ coincides with the normal to the edge and if the center (ξ, η) of the receptive field lies on the edge. If (ξ, η) lies within a certain distance of the edge, the quantity $r'_{\xi,\eta,\sigma,\gamma,\Theta,\lambda,\varphi}$ will still be nonzero. This distance depends on the receptive field size as determined by the parameter σ and the main wavelength λ (the first zero crossing of the harmonic factor is at a distance of approximately $\lambda/2$ from the center (ξ, η) of the receptive field). Because we use parameter values such that $\sigma = \lambda/2$, one can conclude that $\lambda/2$ or, equivalently, σ is the distance to the edge within which a sharp edge will be smeared. The subsampling factor to be used for image reduction is determined by this distance of smearing. Of course, one should subsample by a factor that is a fraction of the smearing distance, e.g., $\sigma/4$, in order not to miss high values (features).

In the application reported here, 512×512 cortical images computed with the parameter value $\sigma = 32$ are subsampled by a factor of $\sigma/4 = 8$ along the rows and then along the columns and thus reduced to images of size 64×64. The thinnest activity areas in these 64×64 images are still two pixels wide but the values of the concerned two pixels may differ considerably. Therefore, the 64×64 images are subsampled by a further factor of two to reduce them to size 32×32. In order not to miss the higher value in a group of two pixel values, when subsampling, we take the higher value of two neighboring pixels along the rows or columns of the 64×64 image. The ultimately obtained images of size 32×32 are relatively small (and thus practical for experimenting with artificial neural networks) and carry at the same time enough significant information that can be used for object classification.

One should mention that there is a certain correspondence between the pixel values of the ultimate (subsampled) images and the activities of so-called *complex cells* in the primary visual cortex. Similar to simple cells, complex cells react to oriented intensity transitions such as lines, bars, and edges but, in contrast to simple cells, their receptive fields cannot be divided in excitory and inhibitory zones. The behavior of a complex cell can be qualitatively explained, thinking of

---

[4]If $g(x, y)$ in the integral on the right side of Eq. (7-1) is substituted by the actual form of the function $g_{\xi,\eta,\sigma,\gamma,\Theta,\lambda,\varphi}(x, y)$ according to Eq. (7-4), the integral takes the form of convolution of the input image $s(x, y)$ with the function $g_{\xi,\eta,\sigma,\gamma,\Theta,\lambda,\varphi}(x, y)$. Note, however, that one can speak of convolution only if the parameters $\sigma, \gamma, \Theta, \lambda, \varphi$ do not depend on ξ and η. This assumption is an oversimplification, as pointed out in the final section of the chapter.

such a cell as a unit that combines (e.g., computes the maximum or an AND-like function of) the responses of a number of simple cells with the same orientation and receptive field size but responsible for nearby positions (i.e., having displaced receptive fields) along a line perpendicular to the receptive field stripe zones [4]. Effectively, in the previously proposed subsampling scheme, each pixel value of the ultimate 32×32 images is computed as the maximum of the values of two pixels of the respective 512×512 (simple-cell responses) image, which are at a distance $\sigma/4$. At this place, it is worth mentioning that in monkey cortex the number of simple cells is relatively small as compared to the number of complex cells; a possible explanation of this fact might be that each main dendritic branch of a complex cell might perform the function of a simple cell [4].

7.3 TWO-LAYER SELF-ORGANIZING ANN CLASSIFIER

7.3.1 Kohonen Self-Organizing Networks

A Kohonen network [40–43] consists of one layer of interconnected nodes. There is no separate layer of input nodes—all inputs connect to every node in the network. There is no output layer, either—each of the nodes is itself an output unit. The nodes can be arranged in a one-, two-, or higher-dimensional array. This dimensionality is important regarding the interconnections between the nodes: a learning process can start with complete connectivity (at this stage the dimensionality of the node array has no influence) and ends in a state in which each node connects to only a limited number of other nodes in a certain neighborhood, eventually only to its nearest neighbors on the corresponding one-, two-, or higher-dimensional grid (the importance of the dimensionality of the node array in this final state is apparent).

In this work, a one-dimensional array of nodes (Figure 7.10) is used as a building block of a composite-structured neural network. The reason for this choice is that the one-dimensional case seems to be best understood with respect to properties such as self-organization and convergence [50]. In the following the general

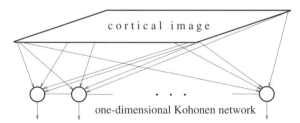

Figure 7.10 A one-dimensional Kohonen network is associated with each cortical filter channel, accepting a single-orientation cortical image as an input. The edges that interconnect the nodes symbolize neighborhood relations.

concept of the Kohonen algorithm is briefly sketched, using as an illustration the particular application in which a cortical image is used as an input to a network.

An array of coefficients $\{w_{\xi,\eta}^{(i)} \mid (\xi, \eta) \in \Omega'\}$, called the *weights*[5] (although they are not used for weighting input values but are rather subtracted from them), is associated with each node; here the superscript $i = 1, 2, \ldots, n$ denotes the number of a node in a network and the pair (ξ, η) denotes a pixel of a (subsampled) cortical image that is used as an input to the network.

The output of the network for a given input pattern (in this case a cortical image) $\{r_{\xi,\eta}' \mid (\xi, \eta) \in \Omega'\}$ is determined[6] by computing a distance $d^{(i)}$ between the input pattern and the weight array $\{w_{\xi,\eta}^{(i)} \mid (\xi, \eta) \in \Omega'\}$ for each node i as follows:

$$d^{(i)} = \sum_{(\xi,\eta)\in\Omega'} (r_{\xi,\eta}' - w_{\xi,\eta}^{(i)})^2, \qquad i = 1, 2, \ldots, n \qquad (7\text{-}5)$$

The node for which the minimum distance is obtained is determined as the winner— its weight array is, in a way, most similar to the input pattern—and is activated, that is, it outputs a value 1 while the other nodes output 0's.

In the learning phase, when an input pattern $\{r_{\xi,\eta}' \mid (\xi, \eta) \in \Omega'\}$ is presented, a winner node $i \in \{1, 2, \ldots, n\}$ is determined and its array of weights $\{w_{\xi,\eta}^{(i)} \mid (\xi, \eta) \in \Omega'\}$, as well as the arrays of weights of the nodes $j = i - k_i, \ldots,$ $i + k_i$ in a certain neighborhood of it, are updated as follows:

$$w_{\xi,\eta}^{(j)} := w_{\xi,\eta}^{(j)} + \nu(r_{\xi,\eta}' - w_{\xi,\eta}^{(j)}), \qquad j = i - k_i, \ldots, i + k_i, \qquad (\xi, \eta) \in \Omega' \qquad (7\text{-}6)$$

In this way the weight array of the winner node and the weight arrays of its neighbors[7] are corrected to become more similar to the input pattern. The coefficient ν $(0 < \nu < 1)$, called the *gain*, usually decreases with each repeated submission of the input pattern, thus slowing the rate of weight adaptation. Similarly, the neighborhood k_i also decreases, thus localizing the domain of adaptation and the ensuing domain of activity in subsequent submissions of similar patterns.

When an input pattern is presented a number of times (learning cycles) to such a network, the weight array of one of the nodes (the winner) will become similar to the input pattern. The weight arrays of the nodes in a certain neighborhood of the winner will also become similar to the input pattern. As a consequence, when a similar input pattern is presented subsequently, it will most probably activate a unit in the concerned neighborhood. In this way, the nodes that are activated by similar patterns tend to cluster in the network, a property of the network

---

[5]In the following, Ω' and $\{r_{\xi,\eta}' \mid (\xi, \eta) \in \Omega'\}$ denote the "subsampled visual field" and reduced cortical image (of size 32×32), respectively.

[6]The parameters σ, γ, Θ, λ, and φ used to compute and denote a cortical image are skipped to improve readability.

[7]Here the weight arrays of the winning node i and its neighbors $i - k_i, \ldots, i + k_i$ are updated in the same way. More generally, the effect of updating can be made to depend on the distance of a node to the winning node, e.g., decrease with increasing distance.

referred to as *self-organization*. Usually, not single patterns but rather sequences of patterns[8] are presented a number of times. The desired properties that are expected to occur (if the set of input patterns is "good enough," whatever this might mean) are convergence of the weights to certain values and the already mentioned self-organization.

7.3.2   The First Layer

The above-described Kohonen network model is applied to single-orientation cortical images, whereby a separate network is used for each single-orientation cortical channel. One such network is associated with each of the $m = 32$ cortical channels, whereby the number 32 results from the use of eight values of the orientation parameter Θ and four functions of different symmetry per orientation, which correspond to the four values of φ that are used $(-\frac{1}{2}\pi, 0, \frac{1}{2}\pi, \pi)$. These $m = 32$ networks form the first layer of the proposed self-organizing classifier (Figure 7.11).

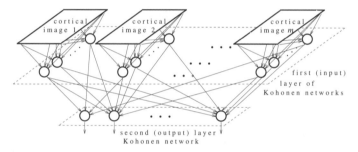

Figure 7.11 The two-dimensional activation pattern produced by the set of networks in the first layer is used as an input pattern to a second-layer (output) network.

As to the number of nodes n, it is chosen depending on the target application, taking into account the following considerations: 1) n has to be greater than the number of target classes that have to be discriminated and 2) n should not be very large to prevent a very sparse assignment of nodes to classes and a large ensuing number of learning epochs needed to achieve convergence. In this work, the number of nodes used for each first-layer network is taken to be $n = 20$. This number is chosen according to the above-mentioned considerations and a particular test application in which five classes of objects (images of faces, armchairs, teacups, bottles, and pens) had to be discriminated.

For each network, the learning sequence consisted of 30 single-orientation cortical images computed from 30 corresponding input images (six images for

---

[8]The presentation of a sequence of learning patterns is referred to as a *learning epoch*.

each of the following classes: faces, armchairs, teacups, bottles, and pens). Convergence was achieved amazingly fast—typically in a few learning epochs[9]. As to self-organization, the nodes that are activated by images of the same class tend to build clusters, but interleaved nodes of different classes or nodes that are never activated, as well as mixed-class nodes, can also be observed. The first-layer networks also show the ability to generalize, which means that in most cases the nodes can be activated by more than one representative of the same class.

7.3.3 The Second Layer

The existence of mixed-class nodes means that, if one would use just one single-orientation cortical channel with one associated Kohonen network, one can get misclassifications. This is not amazing, because as already pointed out, individual cortical images are not necessarily characteristic of the classes of the corresponding input images. However, the *set* of cortical images is characteristic of the class to which an input image belongs.

The proposed two-layer network structure is based on this assumption and expected to function as follows: Each of the first-layer networks associated with the corresponding cortical channels makes its own classification of the cortical image it receives. It is not the individual activation patterns of the first-layer networks that are characteristic of the class of the input image but rather their collective activation pattern. One can think of the first-layer networks associated with different cortical channels as voting for different classes. These votes are counted by another network arranged in the second layer and the class that collects the largest number of votes wins.

The second-layer network has a structure that is similar to the structure of the individual networks in the first layer, in that it is also one-dimensional, with the same number of nodes n and the same neighborhood relations. The only difference is that, while the inputs to the first-layer networks are cortical images of size $k \times k$ ($k = 32$ in this particular case), the inputs to the second-layer network are $m \times n$ binary activity patterns produced by the m first-layer networks, each of n nodes ($n = 20, m = 32$ in this case).

The learning process for the second layer is started after the learning in the first layer is completed. The learning sequence consists of 30 activity patterns induced in the nodes of the first layer for the corresponding 30 input images. Similar to the convergence behavior of the first-layer networks, the learning process takes not more than ten epochs.

The classification of the learned input patterns is always correct; this means images from different classes always activated different nodes in the second layer.

---

[9]A starting neighborhood of five nodes on the left and five nodes on the right of each node is used and each time a node is selected as a winner, the number of its neighbors on each side is reduced by one. The starting value of the gain v is chosen to be 0.8, decreasing it by 0.005 while $v \geq 0.4$ and by 0.002 if $v < 0.4$.

As to test patterns, until now the system was tested only for the classification of face test images taken under similar conditions [18], which it succeeded in classifying correctly.

7.4 SUMMARY OF RESULTS AND FUTURE PLANS

7.4.1 Summary of Results

In this chapter it was demonstrated that neurophysiological findings can be useful to set up artificial systems that exhibit properties that resemble the perceptual and cognitive abilities of natural systems. In particular, a set of so-called cortical images, modeling the activities of cells in the primary visual cortex, is computed from each input image and used as an input to a self-organizing artificial neural network classifier based on the Kohonen algorithm. When presented with a number of input images as learning patterns, the system is capable of building its own internal representations, which well correspond to our own perception of correct class membership. Similar patterns that are input subsequently are correctly classified.

A most remarkable feature of such a system is that it does not incorporate any model knowledge about the objects that have to be learned and then classified; this means that no model, such as the fact that a face has two eyes, a nose, a mouth, and so on, is used. The system computes its own (biologically motivated) internal representations of objects and uses them later on to classify new objects. It is notable that the output units of the classifier system correspond to classes of objects and not to particular input objects.

7.4.2 Possible Improvements in the Use of Cortical Images

The research done until now has raised more questions and problems than given answers. Here are some of them concerning the use of cortical images and the simulation of the function of the primary cortex:

1. A straightforward generalization of the scheme proposed in Section 7.2 is to compute a multidimensional array $\{r'_{\xi,\eta,\sigma,\gamma,\Theta,\lambda,\varphi}\}$ where the parameters $\sigma, \gamma, \Theta, \lambda, \varphi$ are allowed to take all values that are observed in neurophysiological studies. In this study we compute and visualize subsets (slices) within each of which the values of the parameters $\sigma, \gamma, \Theta, \lambda$, and φ are fixed. A problem that can be identified here is that of *defining and experimenting with alternative plausible subsets*.

2. It is known from neurophysiological experiments that the size of the receptive fields (represented in our model by the parameter σ) changes with the position in the visual field [represented in our model by the pair (ξ, η)],

growing from very small near the center of the fovea to very large near the periphery of the visual field (see, for instance, [4] and references therein).

A related problem is that, while the parameters ξ and η take their values in the same domain of (angle) values as the coordinates x and y of the pixels in an image $s(x, y)$, the distribution of a finite number of such values is different: in contrast to x and y whose discrete values are typically taken to be equidistant, the density of the discrete values of ξ and η near the center of the visual field is much larger than in the periphery. We currently implement a log-polar mapping of the visual field onto the set of cortical activities and receptive field size that is increasing with the distance (angle) to the center of the visual field.

3. Besides simple and complex cells, so-called *hypercomplex* or *end-stopped cells* [4] and the recently found so-called *periodic-pattern-selective* or *grating cells* [51] are distinguished in the neurophysiology of the primary visual cortex. The response of an end-stopped cell is maximal for a given length of an oriented line segment or edge and drops quickly if the line segment or edge is extended on one or both sides. A grating cell reacts to a system of parallel lines or bars with a given orientation and periodicity but does not react to single lines or bars. We currently investigate the possibility of incorporating cortical images computed on the basis of end-stopped and grating cells into the proposed system.

7.4.3   Possible Improvements in the Neural Network Classifier

As to possible improvements in the function of the neural network classifier, one can mention the following problems and possible solutions.

1. First of all, one has to conceive and add to the system schemes for the compensation of translations, rotations, and size scaling of the objects to be classified. The above proposed scheme of low-pass filtering and subsequent subsampling of cortical images compensates only for translations smaller than the subsampling factor.

   A possible solution to this problem might be one in which the computed cortical images are shifted synchronously (i.e., all cortical images are shifted in the same direction at the same distance) within a given search space and a winning node is computed for each possible shift. The actual winner is determined among the individual winners for the different shifts. More generally, deformable template matching schemes can be used [52].

   The potential of log-polar representations for the compensation of rotations and scalings is also currently being investigated.

2. Another problem concerns Kohonen's learning algorithm. In its simple form, it allows the overwriting of patterns by new patterns, even in the case

in which there are nodes that have not yet been assigned a pattern. We currently experiment with a scheme in which an individual threshold value is assigned to each node and eventually updated in the process of learning. Updating of the pattern that is stored in a winner node is allowed only if the computed distance is smaller than the threshold distance already assigned to the node. Otherwise, another node for which the computed distance is not minimal but for which the distance is smaller than the respective threshold distance is determined as the winner whose weight array will be changed.

3. The patterns that were used for learning in the above-mentioned experiments arise from objects on a smooth background. More generally, the segmentation problem has to be solved, but such a segmentation may itself imply recognition of the object. As far as the learning patterns are concerned, supervised segmentation can be applied, being ignorant of the nature of the mechanism that corresponds to the supervising agent.

As to the segmentation of an input image in a classification task, one can model this capability by an iterative process in which segmentation and recognition are coupled. A useful aspect of the Kohonen network model is that a particular input pattern can be associated with each output node. This pattern occupies a certain area of the visual field so that in a next step of the iterative process one can take only this area of the visual field to compute cortical images.

7.4.4 Computational Demands

On the basis of this approach, a system is being set up for which it would be sufficient to put an object in front of a camera and tell the system (by a keystroke) to memorize it; this action would initiate grabbing a few images of the object, computing the corresponding sets of cortical images and using them as learning patterns for the self-organizing classifier. In a classification task, when the same or a similar object is put in front of the camera and the system is requested to classify it (by another keystroke), the system would grab one or a few images, compute the corresponding sets of cortical images and use them as input for the classifier to assign a class membership to the object.

In the present implementation of the system in the AVS programming environment on a 66 MHz up-to-date workstation, approximately one minute is needed to compute a set of 32 cortical images for each input image. On the Connection Machine CM-5 of the University of Groningen, which has 16 processing nodes and 64 vector units, this computation takes three seconds. (The particular implementation would allow this time to be kept constant up to a set of 256 cortical images.) With the most current up-to-date processor technology and parallel processing, it is in principle possible to reduce the processing time to a fraction of a second, which would roughly correspond to the response time of natural vision systems. Of course, this does not mean that the system will perform as well as natural systems. The quality of classification will depend critically on further improvements of the model. Some of the problems of the current model addressed above can be estimated to be a source of computational effort exceeding the amount of computations in the current model and its implementation by orders of magnitude.

The already mentioned dependence of the receptive field size on the position in the visual field $[\sigma = \sigma(\xi, \eta)]$ means, for instance, that the integral in Eq. (7-1) cannot be computed as convolution via fast Fourier transform (FFT) and inverse FFT, as it is done in the current implementation, but has to be directly evaluated; this may give rise to an increase of the integral computation time by a factor greater than ten. The optimal mapping technique mentioned with respect to the compensation of translations and other pattern deformations is computationally very intensive, in particular when it has to be applied to a very large number of prestored patterns [52]. The iterative scheme for determining a winning node and the modeling of the interaction between the process of recognition and the process of segmentation may become another source of a very large number of computations.

One can conclude that the real-time implementation of the approach will remain a challenge to computer technology for a number of years ahead.

7.4.5 Computational Perspective

Because the ultimate goal is to set up a system that can perform (almost) as well as a natural system does, it is interesting to make a rough evaluation of the computational power that may be needed for that.

The visual cortex consists of approximately 10^8–10^9 neurons, whereby each neuron is connected via synaptic connections with 10^4 other neurons in average; this implies a total number of synaptic connections on the order of 10^{12}–10^{13}. (For more details on the structure and functional organization of the visual cortex of primates, the reader is referred to [4, 53–57] and references therein.)

When active, a visual neuron fires at a rate of 4 to 40 spikes (impulses) per second, whereby the firing rate indicates the level of activity. Assuming that a train of several, say four, impulses is needed to be fired by a neuron in order to communicate its level of activity to other neurons, one can infer from the above firing rates that a visual neuron is capable of communicating one to ten (on average, five) different levels of activity per second to other neurons. These activity levels are conveyed via axons and axonal branches ending in synaptic transitions. The efficiency of activity transfer at a given synapse can be modeled by a weight associated with the synapse. In a very rough model adopted in most artificial neural network paradigms, each synaptic event of activity-level transfer requires one multiplication for the weighting process and one addition for accumulation of the activities that come to a neuron via different synapses (see, e.g., [58–60, 43]).

With 10^{12}–10^{13} synapses, each transferring an average of five activity levels per second and a transfer event requiring at least two arithmetic operations, one comes to an estimate of 10^{13}–10^{14} operations per second that would be necessary to mimic the function of the visual cortex. This should be considered as a lower-bound estimation, because the actual processes that lead to the activation of a neuron are much more complex than the simple multiply-and-accumulate scheme mentioned above. (The implicit assumption is that the complexity of these processes more than compensates for the fact that the visual neurons do not have to be active all at the same time.)

From the above considerations, one can conclude that vision and cognition are correctly recognized as grand challenge problems whose solution will require (parallel) computers with Tflop/s performance [1] (Tflop/s $= 10^{12}$ floating-point operations per second). Mimicking natural vision, i.e., executing the above-mentioned 10^{13}–10^{14} operations per second, will, however, need the speed of even more powerful computers, possibly of Pflop/s computers (Pflop/s $= 10^{15}$ flop/s).

Acknowledgments

I would like to thank John G. Daugman for his friendly comments on the interpretation of neurophysiological findings concerning face-selective cells and the developmental psychology of face recognition. In particular, the respective references were taken from his summary and bibliography of the main literature in this area [61].

I also gratefully appreciate the programming work carried out by my graduate students Thomas Nicolas, Olivier Javaud, and Henk Klijn Hesselink.

References

[1] *Grand Challenges 1993: High Performance Computing and Communications.* The FY 1993 U.S. Research and Development Program (Report by the Committee on Physical, Mathematical and Engineering Sciences) Federal Coordinating Council for Science, Engineering and Technology, Office of Science and Technology Policy, 1993 (68 pp.).

[2] T. J. Sejnowski, C. Koch, and P. S. Churchland, "Computational neuroscience," *Science*, vol. 240, 1988, pp. 1299–1305.

[3] D. Hubel and T. Wiesel, "Receptive fields, binocular interaction, and functional architecture in the cat's visual cortex," *J. Physiol. (London)*, vol. 160, 1962, pp. 106–154.

[4] D. H. Hubel, "Explorations of the primary visual cortex, 1955–1978," (1981 Nobel Prize lecture), *Nature*, vol. 299, 1982, pp. 515–524.

[5] D. I. Perrett, P. A. J. Smith, D. D. Potter, A. J. Mistlin, A. S. Head, A. D. Milner, and M. A. Jeeves, "Visual cells in the temporal cortex sensitive to

face view and gaze direction," *Proc. Roy. Soc. London B.*, vol. 223, 1985, pp. 293–317.

[6] D. I. Perrett, M. H. Harries, R. Bevan, S. Thomas, P. J. Benson, A. J. Mistlin, A. J. Chitty, J. K. Hietanen, and J. E. Ortega, "Frameworks of analysis for the neural representation of animate objects and actions," *J. Experimental Biology*, vol. 146, 1989, pp. 87–113.

[7] D. I. Perrett, J. K. Hietanen, M. W. Oram, and P. J. Benson, "Organization and functions of cells responsive to faces in the temporal cortex," *Phil. Trans. Roy. Soc. London B: Biolog. Sci.*, vol. 335, 1992, pp. 23–30.

[8] E. T. Rolls, G. C. Baylis, and C. M. Leonard, "Role of low and high spatial frequencies in the face-selective responses of neurons in the superior temporal sulcus," *Brain Research*, vol. 25, 1985, pp. 1021–1035.

[9] E. Rolls, "Neurophysiological mechanisms underlying face processing within and beyond the temporal cortical visual areas," *Phil. Trans. Roy. Soc. London B: Biolog. Sci.*, vol. 335, 1992, pp. 11–21.

[10] R. Desimone and C. G. Gross, "Visual areas of the temporal cortex of the macaque," *Brain Research*, vol. 178, 1979, pp. 363–380.

[11] C. Gross, "Representation of visual stimuli in inferior temporal cortex," *Phil. Trans. Roy. Soc. London B: Biolog. Sci.*, vol. 335, 1992, pp. 3–10.

[12] J. G. Daugman, "Uncertainty relations for resolution in space, spatial frequency, and orientation optimized by two-dimensional visual cortical filters," *J. Opt. Soc. Am. A*, vol. 2, no. 7, 1985, pp. 1160–1169.

[13] J. P. Jones and L. A. Palmer, "An evaluation of the two-dimensional Gabor filter model of simple receptive fields in cat striate cortex," *J. Neurophysiology*, vol. 58, 1987, pp. 1233–1258.

[14] J. G. Daugman, "Complete discrete 2-D Gabor transforms by neural networks for image analysis and compression," *IEEE Trans. Acoustics, Speech, and Signal Processing*, vol. 36, no. 7, 1988, pp. 1169–1179.

[15] D. G. Stork and H. R. Wilson, "Do Gabor functions provide appropriate descriptions of visual cortical receptive fields," *J. Opt. Soc. Am. A*, vol. 7, no. 8, 1990, pp. 1362–1373.

[16] F. Heitger, L. Rosenthaler, R. von der Heydt, E. Peterhans, and O. Kübler, "Simulation of neural contour mechanisms: from simple to end-stopped cells," *Vision Research*, vol. 23, no. 5, 1992, pp. 963–981.

[17] B. S. Manjunath and R. Chellappa, "A unified approach to boundary perception: edges, textures, and illusory contours," *IEEE Trans. Neural Networks*, vol. 4, no. 3, 1993, pp. 96–108.

[18] N. Petkov, P. Kruizinga, and T. Lourens, "Biologically motivated approach to face recognition," in *New Trends in Neural Computation, Proc. Int. Workshop on Artificial Neural Networks, IWANN '93*, J. Mira, J. Cabestany, and A. Prieto (eds.) June 9–11, 1993, [Sitges (Barcelona), Spain], *Lecture Notes in Computer Science*, vol. 686. Berlin: Springer Verlag, 1993, pp. 68–77.

[19] N. Petkov, T. Lourens, and P. Kruizinga, "Lateral inhibition in cortical filters," *Proc. Int. Conf. Digital Signal Processing and Int. Conf. Computer Applications to Engineering Systems*, July 14–16, 1993 (Nicosia, Cyprus), pp. 122–129.

[20] N. Petkov and T. Lourens, "Human visual system simulations—an application to face recognition," in *Proc. 1993 European Conf. Circuit Theory and Design*, H. Dedieu (ed.) August 30–September 3, 1993 (Davos, Switzerland). Amsterdam: Elsevier, 1993, pp. 821–826.

[21] N. Petkov, T. Lourens, and P. Kruizinga, "Orientation competition in cortical filters—an application to face recognition," *Computing Science in The Netherlands 1993*, Nov. 9–10, 1993 (Utrecht) Amsterdam: Stichting Mathematisch Centrum, 1993, pp. 285–296.

[22] N. Petkov and T. Lourens, "Interacting cortical filters for object recognition," in *Proc. Asian Conference on Computer Vision 1993*, K. Sugihara (ed.), November 23–25, 1993 (Osaka, Japan), pp. 583–586.

[23] T. Lourens, N. Petkov, and P. Kruizinga, "Large scale natural vision simulations," *Future Generation Computer Systems*, vol. 10, 1994, pp. 351–358.

[24] A. J. Goldstein, L. D. Harmon, and A. B. Lesk, "Identification of human faces," *Proc. IEEE*, vol. 59, 1971, p. 748.

[25] T. Kanade, "Picture processing by computer complex and recognition of human faces," Technical Report, Kyoto University, Dept. of Information Science, 1973.

[26] Y. Kaya and K. Kobayashi, "A basic study on human face recognition," in *Frontiers of Pattern Recognition*. S. Watanabe (ed.), 1972, p. 265.

[27] J. Buhmann, J. Lange, and C. von der Malsburg, "Distortion invariant object recognition by matching hierarchically labeled graphs," *Proc. IJCNN'89*, 1989, pp. 151–159.

[28] A. L. Yuille, "Deformable templates for face recognition," *J. Cognitive Neuroscience*, vol. 3, no. 1, 1991, pp. 59–70.

[29] B. S. Manjunath, R. Chellappa, and C. von der Malsburg, "A feature based approach to face recognition," in *Proc. 1992 IEEE Computer Society Conf. on Computer Vision and Pattern Recognition*, (Champaign, IL), June 1992, pp. 373–378.

[30] M. Lades, J. C. Vorbrüggen, J. Buhmann, J. Lange, C. von der Malsburg, R. P. Würtz, and W. Konen, "Distortion invariant object recognition in the dynamic link architecture," *IEEE Trans. Computers*, vol. 42, no. 3, 1993, pp. 300–311.

[31] M. Turk and A. Pentland, "Face recognition using eigenfaces," in *Proc. IEEE Computer Society Conf. Computer Vision and Pattern Recognition* (Maui, HI), June 1991, pp. 586–591.

[32] Zi-Quan Hong, "Algebraic feature extraction of image for recognition," *Pattern Recognition*, vol. 24, no. 3, 1991, pp. 211–219.

[33] O. Nakamura, S. Mathur, and T. Minami, "Identification of human faces based on isodensity maps," *Pattern Recognition*, 1991, pp. 263–272.

[34] G. Cottrell and M. Fleming, "Face recognition using unsupervised feature extraction," in *Proc. Int. Neural Network Conf.*, Oxford: Pergamon, 1990.

[35] H. Boattour, F. Fogelman Soulié, and E. Viennet, "Solving the human face recognition task using neural nets," in *Proc. INNC '90*, (Paris), Dordrecht: Kluwer, September 1990, pp. 322–325.

[36] V. Bruce and M. Burton, "Computer recognition of faces," in *Handbook of Research on Face Processing*, A. W. Young and H. D. Ellis (eds.). Amsterdam: Elsevier, 1989, pp. 487–506.

[37] A. W. Young and H. D. Ellis (eds.). *Handbook of Research on Face Processing*. Amsterdam: Elsevier, 1989.

[38] C. Goren, M. Sarty, and P. Wu, "Visual following and pattern discrimination of face-like stimuli by newborn infants," *Pediatrics*, vol. 56, 1975, pp. 544–549.

[39] B. McCormick, T. A. DeFanti, and M. D. Brown (eds.), "Visualization in scientific computing" (NCF report), *ACM SiGGRAPH Computer Graphics*, vol. 21, no. 6, November 1987.

[40] T. Kohonen, "Self-organized formation of topologically correct feature maps," *Biol. Cybern.*, vol. 43, 1982, pp. 59–69.

[41] T. Kohonen, "Analysis of a simple self-organizing process," *Biol. Cybern.*, vol. 44, 1982, pp. 135–140.

[42] T. Kohonen. *Self Organization and Associative Memory*, 3rd ed. Berlin: Springer-Verlag, 1990.

[43] R. Beale and T. Jackson. *Neural Computing*. Bristol: Adam Hilger, 1990.

[44] P. O. Bishop, J. S. Coombs, and G. H. Henry, "Receptive fields of simple cells in the cat visual cortex," *J. Physiology* (London), vol. 231, pp. 31–60.

[45] D. Pollen and S. Ronner, "Phase relationships between adjacent simple cells in the visual cortex," *Science*, vol. 212, 1981, pp. 1409–1411.

[46] J. Bigün, "Gabor phase in boundary tracking and region segregation," in *Proc. Int. Conf. Digital Signal Processing and II Int. Conf. Computer Applications to Engineering Systems* (Nicosia, Cyprus), July 14–16, 1993, pp. 229–234.

[47] N. Petkov, "Cortical images, self-organising neural networks and object classification," in *Shape Analysis*, M. Suk (ed.) (Ablex Publishing, 1994, in preparation), 41 pages.

[48] O. Javaud and T. Nicolas, "Neural network for face discrimination: Kohonen's features map applied to cortical images," M.Sc. Thesis, Department of Computer Science, University of Groningen, June 1994.

[49] M. Concetta Morrone, D. C. Burr, and L. Maffei, "Functional implications of cross-orientation inhibition of cortical visual cells. I. Neurophysiological evidence," *Proc. R. Soc. London*, vol. B 216, 1982, pp. 335–354.

[50] M. Cotrell, J. C. Fort, and G. Pages, "Two or three things that we know about the Kohonen algorithm," in *Proc. of the European Symposium on Artificial Neural Networks 94* (Brussels), M. Verleysen (ed.), April 20–22, 1994. Brussels: D facto, 1994, pp. 235–244.

[51] R. von der Heydt, E. Peterhans, and M. R. Dürsteler, "Periodic-pattern-selective cells in monkey visual cortex," *J. Neuroscience*, vol. 14, no. 4, 1992, pp. 1416–1434.

[52] P. Kruizinga and N. Petkov, "Optical flow applied to person identification," in *Proc. 1994 EUROSIM Conf. Massively Parallel Processing*, J. C. Zuidervaart and L. Dekker (eds.), June 21–23, 1994 (Delft, The Netherlands) Amsterdam: Elsevier, 1994, 8 pages.

[53] S. W. Kuffler, J. G. Nichols, and A. R. Martin. *From Neuron to Brain*. Sunderland, MA: Sinauer Associates Inc., 1984.

[54] D. C. van Essen, "Functional organisation of the primate visual cortex," in *Cerebral Cortex*, A. Peters and E. G. Jones (eds.), vol. 3. New York: Plenum, 1985.

[55] M. S. Livingstone and D. H. Hubel, "Segregation of form, color, movement, and depth: anatomy, physiology, and perception," *Science*, vol. 240, 1988, pp. 740–749.

[56] E. A. De Yoe and D. C. van Essen, "Concurrent processing streams in monkey visual cortex," *Trends in Neuroscience*, vol. 11, May 1988, pp. 219–226.

[57] S. Zeki and S. Shipp, "The functional logic of cortical connections," *Nature*, vol. 335, 1988, pp. 311–317.

[58] J. A. Feldman and D. H. Ballard, "Connectionists models and their properties," *Cognitive Science*, vol. 6, 1982, pp. 205–264.

[59] D. E. Rummelhart et al. *Parallel and Distributed Processing*, vol. 1: *Foundations*; Ch. 8, "Learning internal representations by error propagation," D. E. Rummelhart, G. E. Hinton and R. J. Willams, pp. 318–364, Cambridge, MA: MIT Press, 1986.

[60] P. Smolensky. "On the proper treatment of connectionism," *Behavioral and Brain Sciences*, vol. 11, 1988, pp. 1–23.

[61] J. G. Daugman. *Computational, Neural, and Psychological Aspects of Face Recognition, Literature Survey and Bibliography*. Cambridge, England: Computing Laboratory, Cambridge University, 1994.

8

TESTING THE ROBUSTNESS
OF AN UNDERWATER VISION SYSTEM

Jan O. Hallset   *Hitec A/S, Norway*

8.1   INTRODUCTION

This chapter describes a vision system for our PISCIS project and reports on the testing of its robustness. PISCIS is a proposed project for the use of an untethered autonomous underwater vehicle (AUV) for pipeline inspection. The vision system is termed PVS (the PISCIS vision system). It will assist the AUV in finding and following pipelines. A salient feature of the PVS is that it is designed to find all pipelines within the field of view and, thus, the AUV can follow any of them. Robust image interpretation is important, as humans cannot interact with the PVS and correct errors. Furthermore, the image quality is reduced by backscatter, light absorption, a nonuniform background (the seabed), and marine material on the pipelines. The PVS is fixed to a vehicle and must rely on a heading sensor and an altitude sonar to match image features with pipeline models. The models are retrieved from a map based on the vehicle's position.

The PISCIS vehicle is shown inspecting a pipeline in Figure 8.1. The camera's field of view (FOV) is indicated with the dark square, the light source's coverage with the shaded circle, and an altitude sonar with a vertical "ray" at the back of the vehicle. A video will be recorded, possibly using the same camera as the PVS, while the AUV is moving along the pipeline. A human operator will later do the actual pipeline inspection by replaying the video.

After being launched somewhere near the pipeline, the AUV has to transit to the pipeline's origin. The AUV will then follow the pipeline by means of the PVS. During the mission, the AUV must circumvent subsea installations, and then continue tracking a pipeline on another side of an installation. Finally, upon mission completion, the AUV must land at a predetermined base. In the

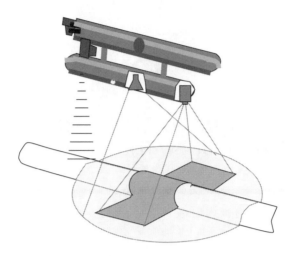

Figure 8.1 Pipeline inspection.

transit, circumvention, and landing phases, the vehicle is assisted by a map-based navigation system rather than the PVS. The PISCIS project is described in more detail in [1] and [2]. The background for the project can be found in [3] and [4].

The task of the PVS is to use a camera to continuously find the position and heading of all nearby pipelines relative to the AUV. The positions and headings are used in a control loop to move the vehicle to a chosen pipeline. They are also used to keep the vehicle over this chosen pipeline during the inspection.

To make a simple and low-cost system, it is profitable to use the same charge coupled device (CCD) camera for both videorecording and relative positioning. The three alternative systems for recognition and relative positioning are magnetic trackers, sonars, and structured light sensors. They are all either bulky, expensive, or use too much energy compared to a CCD-camera in a pressure housing.

Little has been published on complete systems that use cameras for un-derwater object-tracking. However, the PVS has been inspired by two land-based systems for road-following: the VITS vision system for the autonomous land vehicle (ALV), which has a color camera and a laser range scanner, is pre-sented in [5]; the similar VaMoRs system, equipped with tele- and wide-angle cameras, is presented in [6]. Both projects have been extensively tested un-der realistic outdoor conditions and can, therefore, contribute invaluable expe-rience.

Section 8.2 presents the environment the PVS faces. Section 8.3 presents the PVS itself, and the following Sections 8.4 to 8.6 present the details of the PVS's segmentation, matching, and interpretation stages. Section 8.7 reports experimen-tal results, emphasizing testing of robustness. Section 8.8 presents a summary and discussion.

8.2   THE PVS ENVIRONMENT

The PVS is designed to operate in an underwater environment, which is highly unstructured and cannot be controlled. Six basic problems arise from operating in this environment:

1. The outlines of pipelines are broken by marine growth, mud, or sand cover. The background, that is, the seabed, is nonuniform and may introduce false image features that make image analysis difficult.

2. Ambient light decreases rapidly as a function of water depth and the vehicle has to bring its own light source, as illustrated in Figure 8.1. The light intensity from this source will decrease with the distance to the seabed, as the light energy then will be spread over a larger area. Worse still is that the visual range is reduced by light absorption, resulting in faint light and, thus, low contrast at ranges of a few meters.

3. The light intensity will vary slowly over the covered area. It will be relatively constant for a given distance in the center of the scene and will then drop abruptly at the edges. The problem is made worse because the surface reflectance is not the same for all the objects or the background. The two problems are difficult to handle and will probably have to be ignored. However, they are minimized since marine material will smooth the objects and the background.

4. By using an active light source, the quality of images is degraded by backscatter from the water. The image will have small, bright spots caused by reflections (backscatter) from organic material floating in the water between the scene of interest and the camera. This effect is predominant in shallow waters.

5. The system is fixed to a moving vehicle. The vehicle will find and follow pipelines at known locations. This suggests that models of pipelines should be retrieved from a pipeline map and made available to the PVS based on the vehicle's position.

6. Scenes with many, possibly overlapping, objects are difficult to interpret. The problem gets worse if there are similar objects, or objects that look the same from a given viewpoint. Underwater pipelines are not expected to overlap, but they can have the same diameter and, thus, look the same. Their known relative position and heading must be used to differentiate between them.

The PVS that is presented in the following, and described fully in [2], will handle these difficulties by adapting known image analysis techniques to the underwater environment. It is argued in Section 8.4 that edge-based image segmentation is well suited. Edge points should be assembled into short lines, which again are used for recognition of a pipeline's outline. The assumption is that enough short lines will be generated to enable recognition of the pipeline's heading and position, even though the outline is broken.

8.3   THE PISCIS VISION SYSTEM

The PVS takes its inputs from a camera, an altitude sonar, a heading sensor, a position sensor, and a pipeline map, and presents its results to the PISCIS mission control system (PMC), as shown in Figure 8.2. The PVS is a classical pipelined vision system. Its four main modules are found in the figure: a segmentation pipeline with a filter, an edge, and an MHough function; a Predict module for finding pipeline segments within the FOV; a Match module that matches image lines with pipeline segments; an Interpret module for validating matches. An overview of the PVS is given in the following (refer to Figure 8.2) before further details are given in Sections 8.4 to 8.6.

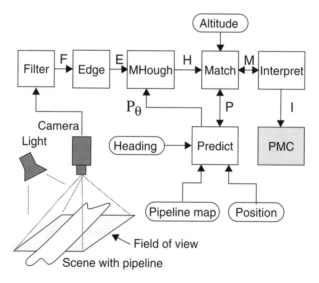

Figure 8.2 The PISCIS vision system.

The PVS's light source can reach pipelines on the seabed if the altitude is less than 5 m. The Predict module must, in addition, find that there are possible pipelines within the FOV. Assume that these two preconditions are satisfied. Then the vehicle state-variables position, altitude, and heading will be read simultaneously with an image-frame from the camera. Thereafter, lines are extracted from the image by the segmentation module functions: The digitized image is smoothed by the Filter function. The smoothed image F will be turned into an edge-point image E by the Edge function. The MHough function requires input from the Predict module in addition to E.

The Edge and MHough functions are based on known algorithms that are adapted to the underwater environment: 1) the edge-detection algorithm is based on the Sobel operator ([7], p. 337); 2) the MHough algorithm is based on a modification of the Hough transform ([7], p. 130). The first algorithm enables the PVS to find image edge-points as the contrast in the scene varies with the AUV's distance to the scene. The second algorithm finds the position and orientation of short line segments from these edges. The lines are found even though there are spurious edge-points caused by backscatter from the water and natural features in the environment.

The Predict module will find a list P of pipeline segments from the pipeline map, based on the vehicle's position. The segments in P are rotated to vehicle coordinates by the Predict module based on the vehicle's heading. A list P_q of the vehicle-relative headings of the segments in P are input to the MHough function. It will search for image lines in the directions given by P_q and produce a list of lines H, which will be scaled to vehicle-relative coordinates by the Match module, based on the vehicle's altitude.

All the pipeline segments that are found to be within the camera's FOV will be retrieved from the pipeline map. There may be retrieved segments that are outside the FOV due to the vehicle's position uncertainty. The segments will, therefore, be matched one by one with image lines. The matching process could have failed because of too many false segments if all were simultaneously matched. Another consequence of the uncertain pipeline-segment position is that the matching in the PVS must be based solely on the pipeline heading and diameter, which are assumed to be known.

The Match module will match one and one segment from P with the scaled image lines and store the result in a list M as (P_i, L_i)-pairs of image-line clusters and pipeline-segment parameters. There may exist false lines that do not belong to any pipeline segment. The PVS simply ignores spurious lines that cannot be matched to a pipeline segment. The matching algorithm is a variant of Agglomerative clustering ([8], pp. 230–235).

The chosen matching method will, in general, result in false or ambiguous matches caused by segments that have the same diameter and heading, as shown in Figure 8.3a. The figure shows an image from a simple scene with two parallel pipelines, P_1 and P_2. They will look exactly the same in an edge image. This is indicated in Figure 8.3b by the two sets of line clusters L_1 and L_2. The matching stage will end up with four matches: (P_1, L_1), (P_1, L_2), (P_2, L_1), (P_2, L_2).

The Interpret module resolves the ambiguity after matching by assuming that the relative positions of pipelines are accurate. It will search for the set of (P_i, L_i)-pairs that in combination gives the "best" geometric fit of pipeline segments and line clusters. Pairs that increase an error function too much are rejected. By observing the relative position in Figure 8.3, it is obvious that the correct matches are (P_1, L_1) and (P_2, L_2). The two other matches are discarded. The accepted pairs are the final interpretation of an image. The Interpret module will deliver the valid matches in the list I to the PMC.

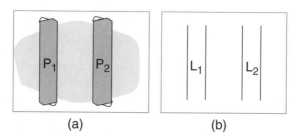

Figure 8.3 (a) A scene with two parallel pipeline segments with the same diameter; (b) the resulting line image.

8.4   SEGMENTATION

The segmentation stage is the basis for image analysis and must be reliable. It faces four problems: 1) the outlines of pipelines will be distorted or broken by marine growth and mud or sand cover; 2) furthermore, it is expected that their interior will be covered with patches of marine material; 3) their color is expected to be blurred by marine material; 4) the color balance is shifted with the distance to the object. A natural balance can only be obtained within a distance of 2 to 3 m [9] as the absorption of the red wavelength is higher than that of the blue/green wavelength.

From the above discussion, it can be concluded that the boundary of pipelines should be used for recognition. The boundary will, of course, be distorted, but it is expected that big objects like pipelines always will have a distinguishable contour and that they can be recognized by their contrast against the seabed: The marine life and marine material on the pipeline will differ from that on the seabed. Thus, the best viewpoint for recognition is from above, such that the seabed can be seen on both sides of the pipeline. Boundary detection has the additional advantage that fast, high-level analysis is possible because the number of edge-points usually is at least two orders of magnitude less than the original number of image pixels.

Boundary detection starts by finding edge-points in an image that can be grouped, or rather linked, into boundaries. There are, in general, two problems that must be handled: 1) The contrast in an image can change, which makes it difficult to find a threshold that can be used to discriminate between edge- and non-edge-pixels. If it is too high, edges that are searched for are lost. If the threshold is set too low, unwanted edges are introduced by noise in the image. The threshold should ideally be found directly from the image data; and 2) the boundary-linking algorithm may be led astray by spurious edges or be stopped at missing edge-points.

The proposed segmentation pipeline, which solves these two problems for the PVS, can be seen in Figure 8.2 and is described in the next three sections. It consists of a preprocessing stage including an average filter, an edge-detection stage that can set a threshold automatically, and a modified Hough line-detector that is robust.

8.4.1 Preprocessing

An auto-iris lens is used to keep the light-intensity in a scene constant as the AUV's distance to the seabed changes. Note that the contrast still will change even though the average intensity will be fine. A difficulty with these lenses, as with all lenses, is to retain a sharp and detailed image at high aperture. This should not be a problem, as the PVS is to detect large pipeline objects, where details are of less interest.

A second problem with auto-iris lenses is that they may use a too-small aperture when there are spots of high light intensity in a scene. This will result in an image with low contrast, as the automatic iris control is based on measuring the average intensity in the scene. If this proves to be a problem, a lens with a controllable iris can be chosen and more sophisticated control can be achieved. However, underwater images are dominated by a sandy seabed and surfaces with marine material, and it is unlikely that there will be highly reflecting surfaces causing such spots.

An averaging filter will reduce the effect of backscatter and the slight gain differences in the individual cells of a CCD-camera. Backscatter spots, which are smaller than the mask size (3×3 pixels) of the averaging filter, will be smoothed. However, the effects of heavy backscatter or large, bright spots on objects are difficult to handle. The engineering solution is to make the best of it and reduce the effect of the backscatter by separating the light source and the camera [10].

8.4.2 Edge Detection

There are numerous ways of computing the gradient for edge detection ([11], pp. 491–556). It seems that most detectors perform well on images with a high signal-to-noise ratio, and poorly on images with a low one. Alas, there are practically no objective measures available to specify the performance of a detector ([12], p. 116).

The Sobel operator is popular because of its computational simplicity. Kitchen and Malin [13] have compared it with other similar operators and found that it has the most uniform magnitude response as a function of edge direction. This is important when searching for boundaries that can have any direction in an image.

The problem of finding an edge threshold remains, and a new method for doing this is proposed here. It is based on a suggestion by Lacroix [14]. She proposes to calculate the edge magnitude for all image pixels and to keep the x percent of them that have the highest magnitude. The problem is that too many or too few edge-points may be accepted. More serious is that edges will be found in images where there are none.

In the method that is proposed here, it will be assumed that x percent of the edge-points, those with the least magnitude, are noise. The assumption is that it is easier to guess the maximum content of edges than how many there really are.

Underwater images are expected to have relatively few man-made objects that can generate edges, and a reasonably safe value for x is 60 to 70%. It is further assumed that the magnitude of the noise edges has a Gaussian distribution with a mean m and a standard deviation s. Denote the Sobel magnitude of a pixel by e_i, the number of pixels in an image by n, and the edge threshold by t. Edge pixels are those in which

$$e_i > t = m + 3\sigma \tag{8-1}$$

where m and s are given by

$$m = \frac{1}{n} \sum_i e_i$$
$$\sigma^2 = \frac{1}{n} \sum_i (e_i - m)^2 \tag{8-2}$$

When the noise has a Gaussian distribution, only 0.5% of the noise edges will be misjudged as "real" edges. The threshold will be found based on perhaps 70% of the background, but there will be few edges found in this 70%. If there are no objects in the image, and the background is modestly uniform, there will be equally few edges found in the remaining 30% of the image. However, a few outliers must always be expected in images of natural scenes.

A problem is that boundaries, after thresholding, will appear to be more than one pixel thick. Several algorithms have been proposed that place the boundary point where the magnitude has a peak value in the gradient-direction. In [15] the performances of some of the algorithms are compared and the resulting outputs are surprisingly similar. The PVS uses the Sobel operator for finding the edge magnitude and gradient, which are the inputs to the boundary-point detection scheme [15, 16]. This straightforward scheme [2] will produce an edge-point image with one-pixel-thick boundaries.

The proposed thresholding method is fast and surprisingly robust, but it will, as all other methods, encounter problems with images that have extremely low contrast. This can happen if an image is saturated with light or if it gets too little light. This must be handled by the PMC by not allowing the vehicle to get too near to or too far from the pipelines on the seabed.

8.4.3 Line Detection

A pipeline segment will occur in an edge image as two parallel lines, which are separated by the diameter of the segment (see Figure 8.3). Furthermore, it is assumed that the segments can extend beyond the edges of the image such that closed contours cannot be found.

Apparent lines in the edge-point image will have gaps because marine material will distort the outline of the segments and the image will contain unwanted edge-points, which must be rejected. They are caused by backscatter and natural features in the environment. The Hough transform offers, according to [17], an almost unique ability to handle images containing noise, and missing and extraneous data.

The use of the Hough transform has three problems: 1) lines will be indicated by clusters of almost the same (q, d) values, rather than a single strong value. A method for detecting these clusters and finding the most probable line from one has to be found. The interaction between the cluster size, the number of clusters, and the threshold is not obvious; 2) although line angles and the perpendicular distances from the image center are readily found, there is no indication of line length and position; 3) the basic transform searches for all possible lines in the edge image, which is time-consuming and unnecessary when the directions of expected lines are known. This problem is, of course, easy to solve by restricting q to be within the range of expected line angles.

The algorithm, which is proposed in the following, will solve these three problems. The modified transform will be referred to as *MHough*.

The basic Hough transform keeps track of which lines a certain edge pixel can be part of. The MHough transform will do it the other way around by keeping track of which pixels can be included in a line with a given length, midpoint, and angle.

MHough may be seen as a search algorithm that uses line templates. It will reduce the processing time by restricting the line-template angles to the directions of expected pipelines. MHough will start by assuming that every edge pixel that is not already part of a line can be a line center. It will then place a template line with a fixed length and a fixed angle q over that edge pixel at (x_c, y_c), as shown in Figure 8.4. MHough will count the number of edge-points under the template. If the number exceeds a given percentage of the template length, these pixels will be accepted as a line. The accepted line will now have a known position, length, and angle. The accepted edge pixels will be marked such that they will not be counted for inclusion in another line.

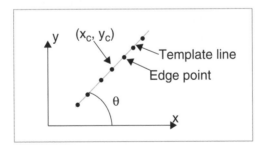

Figure 8.4 A line template laid "over" points in an edge image.

This way of setting a threshold may not seem to be any different from picking a "good" threshold in the basic Hough transform, but it is. A line is now based on a given percentage of edge pixels within a known length. Long "dotted" lines will not be accepted together with short "solid" ones. The result of the MHough transform will be a list of fixed-length lines with midpoint and heading parameters of (x_i, y_i) and q_i.

8.5 MATCHING

This module matches image lines with pipeline-segments from the pipeline map. Matching is done in vehicle coordinates and image lines must be scaled, based on the vehicle altitude, to their real-world size before comparison. Two alternatives for matching have been considered. The first is a classical tree-search method proposed in [18]. This method will have problems with keeping the image-processing time down. This is caused by the combinatorial explosion when there are many segments and image lines.

The PVS uses an alternative method for matching. It is a variant of the Agglomerative Clustering Algorithm (ACA) described by Duda and Hart ([8], pp. 230–235). Figure 8.5 shows the main steps of the basic ACA.

```
1. Let c' = n and Kᵢ = {xᵢ}, i = 1,...,n.
2. If c' ≤ c, stop.
3. Find the nearest clusters Kᵢ and Kⱼ.
4. Merge Kᵢ and Kⱼ.
5. Delete Kⱼ, and decrement c' by one.
6. Goto 2.
```

Figure 8.5 The basic Agglomerative clustering algorithm.

In the above algorithm, it is assumed that there are n samples that are to be merged into exactly c clusters. The algorithm starts by letting all samples x_i be a cluster kernel K_i. It then finds the two nearest clusters K_i and K_j, according to some criterion, and merges these two into the cluster K_i. K_j is deleted and the cluster counter c' is decremented by one. The merging of clusters is continued until the desired number of clusters c is reached.

The ACA must be modified if the number of clusters is unknown as it is here. This can be done by choosing a suitable "nearest" criterion, which must be cast such that the merging is stopped when the remaining clusters are too far separated. The criterion must be based on one or more of the pipeline segment parameters: the position, the length, the heading, and the diameter. The exact position of a segment is not known and the segment will, in addition, usually extend over the whole image such that the length cannot be used. However, it is assumed that the vehicle-relative heading q_m and the diameter d_m are known. Thus, these two parameters can be used for clustering.

The PVS does the clustering in two steps by first pairing two and two image lines, which both must have the heading q_m and be separated by d_m. This is illustrated in Figure 8.6 where first l_1 and l_2 is made into the pair p_1, and l_3 and l_4 into p_2. The pairs will now be the center lines of short candidate pipeline segments, which can be merged with other candidates into a longer segment center line. Figure 8.6 shows that p_1 and p_2 are aligned and, thus, they can be combined into a

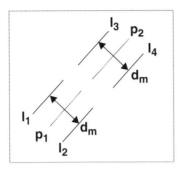

Figure 8.6 Pairing of image lines into pipeline segment kernels.

longer line. The result of the matching will be one or more such long lines for each pipeline segment. Note that the pipeline segments are matched one and one with the image lines. Thus, when there are two segments that have the same q_m and d_m, they will be matched with the same image lines. The Interpret module (Section 8.6) will resolve the conflicting matches based on the segments' relative position.

The pairing of lines and the clustering of these pairs into longer center lines are guided by a series of tests. These tests are similar to the ones presented by Grimson and Lozano-Perez ([18], p. 451). Three tests are used to find the line pairs:

1. The first is on the angle deviation between q_m and an image line's heading q_i. Two image lines must be found to form a pair. The deviation must be less than a threshold t_q:

$$|\theta_i - \theta_m| < t_\theta \qquad (8\text{-}3)$$

2. The second test is on scale. The distance between two image lines should be about the same as d_m. A threshold t_{dd} will be set for the maximum allowed deviation. It will be scaled by d_m as the error in the diameter found from the image and is expected to be proportional to the error in the altitude measurement. Denote the signed perpendicular distance from the origin of the vehicle's coordinate system to the two lines by r_i and r_j, where r_i is found by

$$r_i = y_i \cos\theta_i - x_i \sin\theta_i \qquad (8\text{-}4)$$

The following condition must then be met if the two lines are to be paired into a center line candidate:

$$\|r_i - r_j| - d_m\| < t_{dd} \cdot d_m \qquad (8\text{-}5)$$

3. The third test is on the distance between the two image lines that are to be paired. The midpoints of the two lines must not be too far separated and a scalable threshold t_{md} will be set for the maximum allowed distance. The assumption is that close lines are more probably generated by the same pipeline segment than lines that are far apart. The least possible distance will be the pipeline's diameter; thus, it is reasonable to let t_{md} be scaled

by d_m. Denote the midpoints of the two lines by (x_i, y_i) and (x_j, y_j), respectively. To be paired, the two must meet the following condition:

$$\sqrt{(x_i - x_j)^2 - (y_i - y_j)^2} < t_{md} \cdot d_m \qquad (8\text{-}6)$$

The parameters (x_p, y_p, q_p) of a pair that met the conditions in (8-3), (8-5), and (8-6) are given by

$$x_p = \frac{x_i + x_j}{2}$$

$$y_p = \frac{y_i + y_j}{2} \qquad (8\text{-}7)$$

$$\theta_p = \frac{\theta_i + \theta_j}{2}$$

Every possible pair of lines will be found guided by the three tests given above. An image line will be allowed to be part of only one pair, and lines that cannot be paired will be ignored.

The clustering will be started with one of the found pairs as a cluster kernel. The kernel will be merged with other pairs into a longer line that will be a possible pipeline segment center line. The clustering will be guided by two tests that check the lengthwise-distance d_{lw} and the crosswise-distance d_{xw} between a cluster's midpoint and a pair's midpoint. The cluster and the pair can be merged if d_{lw} is less than a threshold and d_{xw} is less than another. Both the lengthwise threshold t_{lwd} and the crosswise threshold t_{xwd} are scaled by d_m just as t_{dd} and t_{md} are.

Figure 8.7 shows the parameters of a cluster and a pair. Denote the parameters of the cluster by (x_c, y_c, q_c, n_c) where n_c is the number of pairs in the cluster.

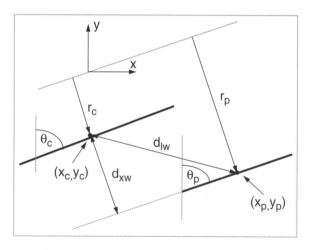

Figure 8.7 The parameters of a cluster and a pair.

Denote the parameters of one of the pairs already in the cluster by (x_q, y_q, q_q), and the parameters of a pair that is a candidate for merging by (x_p, y_p, q_p). Assume that (8-4) is used to find r_c for the cluster and r_p for the pair. The cluster and the pair can then be merged if the two following conditions are met:

$$d_{xw} = |r_c - r_p| < t_{xwd} \cdot d_m \tag{8-8}$$

and

$$d_{lw} = \sqrt{(x_q - x_p)^2 - (y_q - y_p)^2} < t_{lwd} \cdot d_m \tag{8-9}$$

The lengthwise distance is approximated as the diagonal distance as in (8-9). Pairs will be merged with the cluster until no more pairs can be included in it. A new pair will then be picked as a cluster kernel and new clusters will made in the same way. This will continue until there are no more pairs that can be clustered. The parameters of the cluster are updated every time a new pair is included in it and the pair will be marked as a part of that cluster such that it cannot be included in another one. The cluster parameters, which are the result of the matching stage, are updated by:

$$x_c = \frac{x_c \cdot n_c + x_p}{n_c + 1}$$

$$y_c = \frac{y_c \cdot n_c + y_p}{n_c + 1}$$

$$\theta_c = \frac{\theta_c \cdot n_c + \theta_p}{n_c + 1} \tag{8-10}$$

$$n_c = n_c + 1$$

The importance of the test against d_{lw} is illustrated in Figure 8.8, which contains four pipeline segments. Assume that they all have the same diameter. Segment a_b is a branch of segment a, and b_b is a branch of segment b. Furthermore, segment b_b is parallel with and an extension of a_b, but their endpoints are separated by the distance d. The two segments would always have been merged without the test of d against $t_{lwd} d_m$.

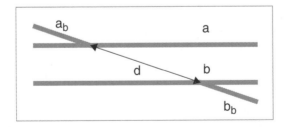

Figure 8.8 A pipeline configuration where two short pipeline segments can be merged into a long false one.

Note that step 3 in the ACA (Fig. 8.5) has been simplified. The criteria for merging as given in (8-8) and (8-9) are of the "near enough" type rather than "nearest." This can be done because it is expected that pipelines will not overlap and, thus, clusters will be well separated. As a consequence of this, the clustering process will be faster. The alternative would have been to find the "distance" between every possible pair of clusters before the pair with the least "distance" could have been merged.

8.6 INTERPRETATION

The name of this module is probably somewhat presumptuous as it indicates that the module has some, perhaps primitive, intelligence. What the module really will do is to search for the combination of matches with the best fit between image line clusters and pipeline segments. The set of matches that has the least error will be accepted as a valid interpretation and the rest of them will be discarded. The Interpret module will check that all segments of the interpretation are inside the FOV before it finds the fit error.

8.6.1 Interpretation Based on "Coupled Constraints"

Grimson and Lozano-Perez ([18], pp. 487–492) describe the rationale for a method, referred to as "coupled constraints." They want to find an assignment of image patches with model faces and propose to find an initial interpretation by finding a range of probable assignments between two faces and two patches. This range will be further constrained when a third face and patch are assigned. By including more patches and faces, the range of possible assignments will be quickly reduced. If the range becomes empty, the interpretation can be discarded. The method, which will be proposed here, will use the idea of coupled constraints as the basis for a blind search for the best range of assignments. The search problem is illustrated in Figure 8.9.

Figure 8.9a shows three pipeline segments s_1–s_3 that are found to be within the FOV by the Predict module. Assume that s_1–s_3 have the same diameter, that s_1 and s_2 have the same heading, and that the Match algorithm finds three image line clusters c_1–c_3 corresponding to s_1–s_3. A cluster is shown in Figure 8.9a as a point that indicates its midpoint. The Match module will find a list M of five matches, which can be seen in Figure 8.9b. A match m_i from M will consist of a pair (c_i, s_i), where c_i contains the parameters of an image cluster and s_i the parameters of the corresponding pipeline segment. The five matches are: s_3 is represented by and matched with c_3; c_1 is matched with both s_1 and s_2. This happens as the Match module clusters image lines with segments solely based on their heading and diameter; c_2 will be matched with s_1 and s_2 for the same reason. The Interpret

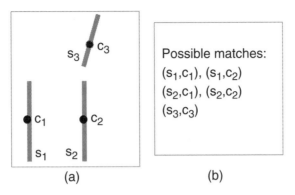

Figure 8.9 A possible set of matches between image clusters c and pipeline segments s.

module must solve two problems in order to find a valid interpretation from the five matches:

1. There is an offset between the origin of the image line clusters and the pipeline segments that is caused by the position uncertainty of the vehicle. Thus, the relative positions of segments must be compared with the relative positions of their corresponding line clusters. As an example, consider the two matches (s_1, c_2) and (s_2, c_1) in Figure 8.9: the signed distance between s_1 and s_2 is the negative of the signed distance between c_2 and c_1. Thus, the combination of the two is inconsistent and the two matches must be discarded as a valid interpretation.

   Assume now that the valid interpretation is the three matches in Figure 8.10: (c_1, s_1), (c_2, s_2), and (c_3, s_3). This solution will be found by checking that the signed distance between s_1 and s_2 are about the same as the signed distance between c_1 and c_2. The (c_3, s_3)-match must also be consistent with (c_1, s_1). The differences in signed distances are given as the dd_i-values in Figure 8.10. Note that their sizes are strongly exaggerated.

   This method, where the matches must be consistent with each other if they are to be accepted as a valid interpretation, has the flavor of Grimson and Lozano-Perez's "coupled constraints." The method can be more formally stated when it is assumed that the signed distance is found with a function D. We would like to find the segment s_r for which the accumulated distance-difference DD_r has its minimum. It is given by the following equation:

$$DD_r = \sum dd_i \tag{8-11}$$

   where the distance difference dd_i is defined as:

$$dd_i = \| D(s_r, s_i) - D(c_r, c_i) \| \tag{8-12}$$

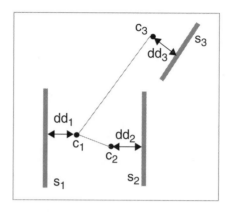

Figure 8.10 Position independent matching.

Wild points will be removed by defining a threshold t_{dd} and requiring that:

$$dd_i = MIN(dd_i, t_{dd}) \qquad (8\text{-}13)$$

2. The second problem concerns how to find dd_i. An image line cluster is described by its (x, y)-midpoint [see (8-10)] while a pipeline segment is described by a line. Their headings are assumed to be the same as where the cluster is found, based on the segment's heading. We would like to find the point on each segment in a possible interpretation that results in the minimum DD_r. This will be done by appointing one and one segment in M as a reference segment r, and computing DD_r at all possible positions along r. If DD_r is less than the current DD_{min}, it will be noted as the new DD_{min} together with the current position along r. The noted position will, after all the segments in M have been traversed, give the valid interpretation: Namely, the segment in M that has $dd_i < t_{dd}$ for that position.

The error distance dd_i can be detailed by referring to Figure 8.11. The center lines of two segments r and m can be seen, where r is the reference segment and m is another segment of a match in M. The two corresponding image clusters have the midpoint coordinates (x_{ir}, y_{ir}) and (x_{im}, y_{im}). The endpoints of the segments are respectively $(p1_r, p2_r)$ and $(p1_m, p2_m)$. The point on r, for which the dd_i's are to be computed, is shown as (x_r, y_r). The two segments can be part of a valid interpretation if the distance dd_m meets the following condition:

$$dd_m = \sqrt{(x_n - x_m)^2 + (y_n - y_m)^2} < t_{dd} \qquad (8\text{-}14)$$

where

$$x_n = x_r + (xi_m - xi_r)$$
$$y_n = y_r + (yi_m - yi_r) \qquad (8\text{-}15)$$

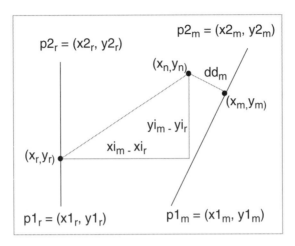

Figure 8.11 The parameters used for checking if a reference segment *r* and a segment *m* can be parts of the same interpretation.

and (x_m, y_m) is the point on *m* that is nearest to (x_n, y_n) when the finite length of *m* is accounted for ([2]).

8.6.2   Limitations of the Interpretation Strategy

A problem arises when only one pipeline segment is within the FOV, and two are found by the Prediction module. This will happen if pipeline A has been tracked for some time, and the position uncertainty has increased. Then pipeline B may also be inside the FOV according to the navigation system. However, from historical data and physical restrictions, it is clear that a sudden jump from A to B cannot occur, and that a match with pipeline B must be rejected.

A second problem is illustrated with Figure 8.12 where a pipeline with two branches can be seen. Imagine that both branches are found to be within the FOV, but that the real FOV is limited, as shown by the light-shaded squares at positions A and B in the figure. It will then be impossible to distinguish between an image taken at position A and B.

The solution to the two problems, described above, is to introduce prediction ([6]). For the PISCIS vehicle, this will mean that the PMC must predict, based on the vehicle dynamics and the pipelines' positions in the previous image, where they are expected to occur in the next one. The PVS must use the predicted positions of the pipeline segments to restrict the search for the valid interpretation. A problem is, of course, how to find the pipelines' positions the first time: The PMC must then make the vehicle search for the pipelines at positions where ambiguous

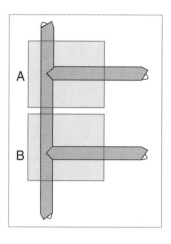

Figure 8.I2 An ambiguous pipeline configuration where images taken at position A and B, with an FOV as indicated by the shaded squares, cannot be distinguished.

configurations cannot occur. The implementation of the prediction scheme will be the next natural step when experiences have been gained with the robustness of this PVS version.

8.7   TESTING THE PVS

Sections 8.7.1 and 8.7.2 will show that the PVS can find the center lines of pipelines based on "sensor" input and the four images in Figures 8.13 and 8.14. Section 8.7.3 will show that the PVS can do this under rotation and scaling errors and skewed light. Section 8.7.3 uses the three scenes in Figures 8.13 and 8.17.

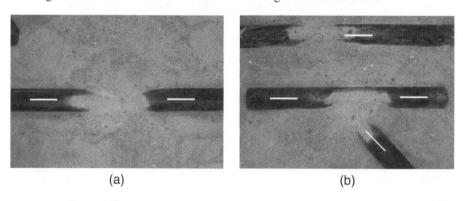

(a)   (b)

Figure 8.I3 Found pipeline center lines for (a) Scene1 and (b) Scene2.

The center lines are found by telling the PVS that it is at 4 m altitude, and giving it a proper heading and scaling factor for each image and position. The altitude and heading are assumed to be exact, while the position is assumed to be known within an error circle. The three images that are used have 8-bit gray-level resolution and a size of 256×182 pixels.

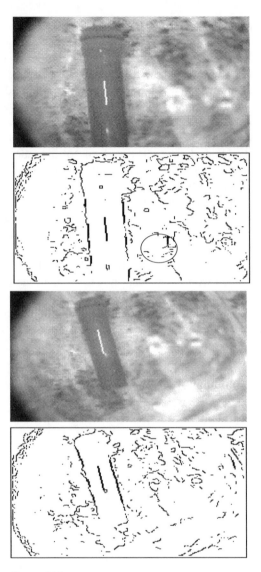

Figure 8.14 Two views of an underwater scene from the Ocean Basin Laboratories. They show a gray plastic tube on the rusty steel-plated bottom of the basin. The gray level images are the original ones with the center lines that the PVS detects. The black and white ones show the edge-points that the Edge algorithm finds, the lines that the MHough algorithm finds, and the center line. The edge-points are one pixel thick while the lines are two pixels thick.

Images are by their nature diverse and, thus, a complete test of the PVS cannot be done. The test must be restricted to the processing of "representative" images. It has been a problem that real underwater scenes are unavailable. The test will, however, show that the PVS can handle effects that are expected to be present under water. They have, like real underwater images, highly varying contrast, "pipelines" with a broken outline, and a nonuniform background. Four images will be used: 1) The first image, which will be referred to as Scene1, is shown in Figure 8.13a. It is a black plastic tube that is laid out on a background of sand. The midpoint of the tube is partly covered with sand; 2) Scene2 in Figure 8.13b is a slightly more complex configuration of three plastic tubes; 3) The two images in Figure 8.14 show a gray plastic tube deployed in the Ocean Basin Laboratory (OBL) at MARINTEK in Trondheim, Norway. OBL is basically a freshwater tank that is 50×80 m wide and 10 m deep. Note that the center lines that the PVS has found are drawn into Figures 8.13 and 8.14.

The pipeline map shown in Figure 8.15, which is used in the test of the PVS, makes up a rather small world. The map shows two branched pipelines laid out on a flat seabed. All the pipeline segments in the map have a diameter of 1 m. The map is purely artificial and preprogrammed as a fixed list of pipeline segments into the PVS. The segments that are found within the left-most circle will be matched with Scene2, and the segments within the right-most circle will be matched with Scene1 and the two underwater images in Figure 8.14.

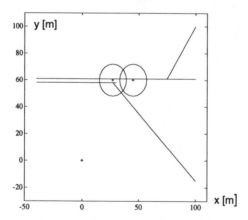

Figure 8.15 A simple world model of pipelines, with the AUV at the two circled positions.

Some problems are ignored in the test. Plastic tubes are used for building the lab scenes instead of the concrete and steel pipes that are expected to appear under water. This was done because plastic tubes were at hand, concrete and steel tubes were not. The lab scenes will, therefore, appear with better contrast between the pipes and the background than in real underwater scenes. Light distribution is not the same for the lab scenes and for underwater scenes. However, it is shown in Section 8.7.3 that the PVS can handle an uneven light distribution.

The parameters of the PVS, previously presented in Sections 8.4 to 8.6, have been set to fixed values and are the same for all three scenes. The choice of these parameters are discussed thoroughly in [2]. This section shows that the chosen values give a reasonably robust PVS, although a lower number of parameters would have been preferred in order to make the PVS more robust. However, it seems that a high number of parameters are the curse of most vision systems ([19], p. 118).

8.7.1 The PVS Used on "Dry" Images

Figure 8.16 shows that the MHough function has found lines at 0 relative to the image's horizontal axis for Scene1, and at both 0 and 45 for Scene2.

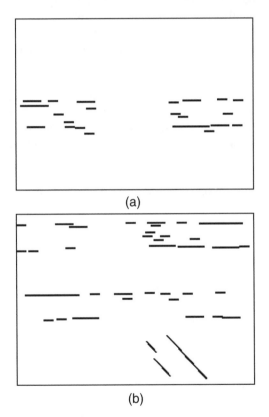

(a)

(b)

Figure 8.16 Line images after using the MHough algorithm on the edge-point images of (a) Scene1 and (b) Scene2.

There are two observations that can be made based on the two line images in Figure 8.16: 1) The number of false lines are reduced to a minimum by restricting the search for lines to the expected directions of pipes. This again reduces the computational burden and complexity of the following matching stage; 2) The line images are not an exact representation of the pipe boundaries. They have many of the expected properties of underwater line images: many of the lines in the interior of the pipes are clearly caused by spurious edge-points, the boundaries of the pipes have holes and are even completely missing at places where the pipes are covered with sand, and the boundaries are somewhat misplaced. Thus, if the PVS can find pipe center lines from these line images, it is probable that it can find pipes from real underwater scenes.

Figure 8.13 shows the center lines for Scene1 and Scene2, that are found based on the line images in Figure 8.16. The white center lines are drawn directly by the PVS. The found matches for Scene1 and Scene2 are quite satisfactory because there are no apparently false center lines. The problem that the same segments are assigned to several center lines and vice versa appears to have been solved by the Interpret module. In [2], it is shown that it indeed finds a set of matches based on the known relative position of the segments. The remaining matches are discarded.

Figure 8.13a shows that the PVS has found two center lines for the single pipeline segment in the scene. It is no surprise that two matches are found because the pipe in Scene1 is broken in two by a sand cover. The two parts that can be seen will naturally have the same diameter and heading and, thus, will both be plausible matches. However, if the two lines had been closer, they might have been merged into one. This merging is guided by t_{lwd}. As the two center lines are consistent, there will be no problems for the PMC to use them for pipeline-following.

Figure 8.13b shows that the PVS has found one center line for the upper segment, two for the middle, and one for the lower. The sand cover for the upper pipe is slightly shorter than the one for the lower and, thus, the result is that the upper two parts get merged because they are closely enough guided by t_{lwd}, while the middle ones remain separated. As with Scene1, this will not cause problems for the PMC because the detected center lines are consistent.

8.7.2 The PVS Used on Two Underwater Images

Figure 8.14 is from the Ocean Basin Laboratories. It shows a gray plastic tube that is deployed on the bottom of the basin. The figure presents two views of the tube with the center lines that the PVS detects. The center lines are shown as short, white line segments. The two images are taken with a camera vertically mounted on a moving underwater vehicle. The heading and altitude was not measured and, thus, suitable headings and scales are derived from the images in Figure 8.14. The position in the world map of Figure 8.15 is set to (45,60) where a single pipe will be within the FOV.

This test shows that the PVS can find pipes in underwater images taken with a camera that is fixed to an underwater vehicle. The images have low contrast and appear to be dim. Still, the PVS manages to calculate a suitable threshold for edge-point detection and to detect lines that can be combined into a valid interpretation of the scene. The images are a good illustration of the powerful concept of using the expected heading of the pipes, together with a minimal line length to ignore unwanted edge-points: There is only one apparent false line in each of the two images even though there are many unwanted edge-points. These two lines are circled. However, it is expected that there will be more than one false line in most images; see, for example, Figures 8.16 and 8.17.

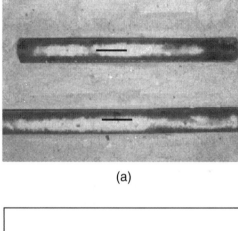

(a)

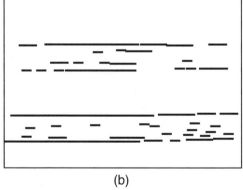

(b)

Figure 8.17 (a) Scene3 with two parallel pipe segments, and (b) the corresponding line image found by the PVS.

8.7.3   The Robustness of the PVS

There are many parameters in the PVS, and it is important to choose them such that the PVS will be robust; that is, it ought to function over a wide range of image acquisition conditions. A complete dynamic test of the PVS's robustness will require that it is attached to an underwater vehicle and run along a pipeline. This has not been possible, but it will be shown here that the PVS can handle changes in the image acquisition conditions expected to occur in an underwater environment.

In Sections 8.7.1 and 8.7.2, it was demonstrated that the PVS is robust against varying contrast from image to image, and against position uncertainties. This section will show tests of how the PVS handles three additional types of errors: 1) rotation errors around the vehicle's three axes; 2) scaling errors caused by uncertainties in the altitude measurement; 3) shadows and uneven light distribution caused by a skewed light source.

These tests will be done on Scene1 and Scene2 from Figure 8.13, and on the image in Figure 8.17, which will be referred to as Scene3. Scene3 presents two parallel pipes matched with pipe segments found at position (0,60) in Figure 8.15. Figure 8.17a shows the center lines detected by the PVS, when none of the three error types are present. The center lines are illustrated with short, black line segments. Note that the pipe segments are partly covered with sand along their center lines. This is done to make the interpretation task more difficult for the PVS. It finds a plausible interpretation of the scene, although the sand cover will generate false lines, as can be seen from Figure 8.17b.

Rotation

The PISCIS vehicle, which the PVS will be attached to, can rotate around its three axes. The pitch around the y-axis and the roll around the x-axis cannot be controlled. The PVS must tolerate these rotations, expected to be less than 10°. This expectation is based on the fact that the PISCIS vehicle is designed to be stable in pitch-and-roll [20]. The third rotation is the yaw around the z-axis, which can be controlled and measured with a heading sensor. The PVS can use the measured heading directly, and does not have to tolerate large uncertainties in its value. In fact, it uses the known heading actively in its pipeline-recognition algorithms. However, the vehicle is to follow a pipeline and must know its heading relative to the pipe. This relative heading cannot be derived accurately by comparing the expected pipe-heading with the measured vehicle-heading. There will be heading errors in both the pipeline map and the heading sensor, and the PVS must, in addition to detecting the pipe's position, estimate the pipe's vehicle-relative heading. Thus, it is important to detect how many combined heading errors the PVS can handle, but first, the robustness against pitch-and-roll errors will be demonstrated.

Pitch–and–Roll Errors.   Figure 8.18 visualizes the laboratory configuration of the light and the camera. They are both at a height of 0.85 m above the laboratory

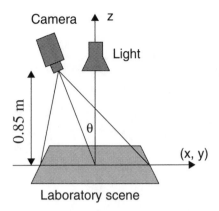

Figure 8.18 Camera and light configuration for the pitch-and-roll test.

scene and are aligned along the image's x- or y-axis. The light points along the z-axis down to the middle of the scene, while the camera has a roll or pitch angle of q relative to the z-axis.

Figure 8.19a presents an image of Scene3, with the pipe center lines discovered by the PVS after the camera had been tilted $10°$ around the image's y-axis (the vehicle's y-axis). The tilting of the camera simulates the pitching of the vehicle. In Figure 8.19b, the pitch is $20°$. It can be observed that the PVS detects the pipe center lines even with the considerable pitch of $20°$. There are two reasons for this robustness: 1) The pitching does not change the scene geometry very much, although the distortion is clearly visible in both images. The threshold parameters in the PVS are generous and will tolerate a certain distortion; 2) When the pitch becomes large, it is more important that there always is an image column having the correct scale. Thus, the PVS has a good chance of finding center lines around this column when pipes are parallel with the x-axis. This means that the PVS will encounter problems when the pitch is large and, in addition, a scene contains pipe segments at an angle with the x-axis.

Figures 8.19c and d show Scene3 and the pipe center lines found by the PVS after the camera had been rolled $10°$ and $20°$, respectively, around the vehicle's x-axis. It can be observed that the PVS discovers the pipe center lines even with the roll of $20°$. This is no surprise, as there are almost no visible distortions of the scene in the two images. This is due to the fact that the pipe segments are perpendicular to the roll direction. The roll will cause an apparent change in the diameter of and the distance between the pipe segments. However, the tolerated error in the diameter is set to 20% (t_{dd} is 0.2) and, thus, the roll must be very large in order to cause such an error. The same argument goes for the distance between two pipe segments where the error can be 26% (t_{xwd} is 0.26).

The conclusion from the above discussion is that the PVS is robust against roll-and-pitch distortion of a scene. The PVS performs well on all the images in Figure 8.19 and, thus, it is a reasonable assumption that it can handle both a pitch and a roll of at least $10°$.

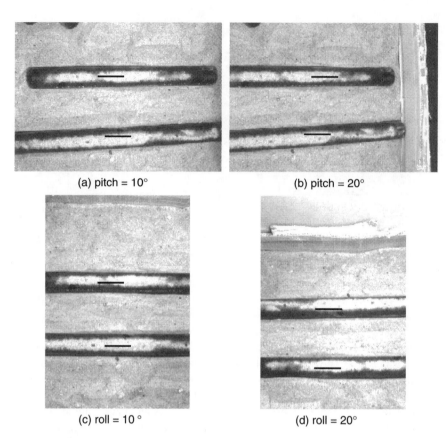

(a) pitch = 10°   (b) pitch = 20°

(c) roll = 10 °   (d) roll = 20°

Figure 8.19 Scene3 seen through a camera that is pitched (a) 10° and (b) 20°, and rolled (c) 10° and (d) 20°.

Heading Errors.   If the heading sensor is a compass, it can be expected to have an accuracy of 2° to 3°. The accuracy of pipeline maps is not available. However, it is possible to deploy pipelines with the same heading accuracy as that of a compass, as most vessels are equipped with more sophisticated navigation instruments than a compass. Thus, the combined heading error of the compass and the map will not be expected to exceed 5°.

The test of the PVS's robustness against heading errors is based on processing Scene1, Scene2, and Scene3. The three scenes have been rotated in five steps from 5° to −5° around the original heading of the images. The PVS starts to fail in finding valid interpretations at higher rotation values. The stepping has been done by rotating the original image array rather than taking images of the scenes with different camera rotations. The method used is faster and makes it easier to get accurate rotation values.

The result of processing the rotated images is shown in Figures 8.20a–e and the correct heading of the three scenes in Figure 8.20c. The rotation angle D_q at each row of the figure must be read as the combined heading error of the compass and a pipe-segment model. The numbers in parentheses are the corresponding rotation-error estimates that the PVS derives from each scene in that row. Each estimate is calculated from the set of valid matches for a scene. Each match is basically a center line based on a number of image-line pairs n_i with midpoint coordinates (x_{ij}, y_{ij}). An estimate of each center line's rotation can be found by fitting a line through these midpoints, in a least-squares sense and finding its estimated heading q_i. Assume that the corresponding pipe segment's map-heading is q_i. The rotation estimate for one match is then the difference between g_i and q_i. The rotation estimate D_q for the whole set of valid matches will be taken as a weighted sum of the individual differences. The following set of equations will then produce the D_q values given in the parentheses of Figure 8.20:

$$a \tan \bar{\theta}_i = \sum_j \frac{(y_{ij} - \bar{y}_i) \cdot (x_{ij} - \bar{x}_i)}{(x_{ij} - \bar{x}_i)^2}$$

$$\Delta \bar{\theta} = \frac{1}{n} \sum_i (\theta_i - \bar{\theta}_i) \cdot n_i \tag{8-16}$$

$$\text{where} \quad n = \sum n_i$$

The first thing that can be observed from Figure 8.20 is that the estimates of the rotations are not particularly accurate. However, they have the right sign and increase when the real rotation increases. Note also that the images in Figure 8.20c show a slight estimated heading error, even though the headings of the pipe in those three images are supposed to be the same as in their models. This can be attributed to the fact that it is difficult to align the pipes with an accuracy of more than $1°–2°$, when building the scenes in the lab.

The second observation that can be made from Figure 8.20 is the fact that the interpretations seen as center lines move around relatively much as a function of the rotation. However, the PVS manages to detect center lines for all combinations of scenes and rotations, and the found center lines are always plausible.

This discussion indicates that the PVS can handle heading errors up to $5°$, although far from perfect. However, the PMC will use D_q, found by the PVS, to adjust the vehicle's estimated heading relative to the pipelines. This means that the heading error will be bounded by the error in D_q. From Figure 8.20, it is calculated that the standard deviation of the error in D_q is 1.13. Thus, it is a reasonable assumption that the PVS will be robust against heading errors as it can contribute in reducing them to $1°$ to $2°$. When the heading error has been reduced to that level, the PVS will be able to make stable scene interpretations, as the ones in Figure 8.20c.

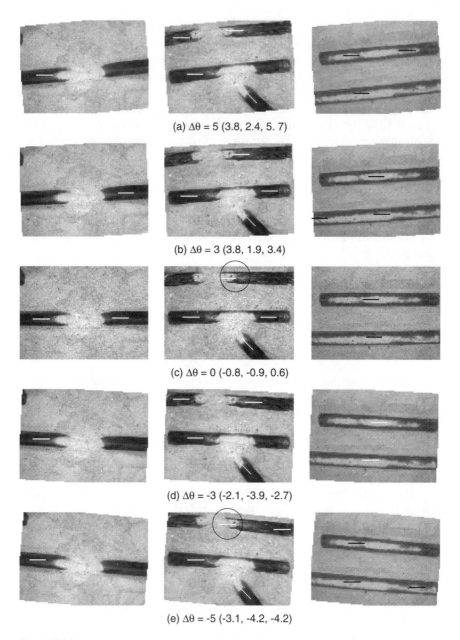

(a) $\Delta\theta = 5$ (3.8, 2.4, 5. 7)

(b) $\Delta\theta = 3$ (3.8, 1.9, 3.4)

(c) $\Delta\theta = 0$ (-0.8, -0.9, 0.6)

(d) $\Delta\theta = -3$ (-2.1, -3.9, -2.7)

(e) $\Delta\theta = -5$ (-3.1, -4.2, -4.2)

Figure 8.20 The pipe center lines that the PVS finds for Scene1, Scene2, and Scene3 are dependent on the rotation error $\Delta\theta$. It is assumed that rotation error is zero in row (c). The numbers outside the parentheses in rows (a) to (e) are the real rotation, while the ones inside the parentheses are the estimated rotation that the PVS finds. (The contrast is low for two of the center lines in Scene2 and, thus, they have been pointed out with circles.)

Scaling Errors

The altitude measurement with a sonar is not expected to be more accurate than 10% of the altitude. This means that the scale of image features in the PVS can be expected to vary by the same 10% (see [2]). A sonar's accuracy is about 1%. The problem is that a single point is assumed to be measured and, thus, the roughness of the seabed causes uncertainty in trusting whether this measurement is valid over the whole FOV. Another complicating factor occurs when the top of the pipe segment is much higher than the seabed. Assume, for example, that the vehicle is at an altitude of 5.0 m over the seabed and that a pipe with a diameter of 1.0 m is within the FOV. This means that there may be 20% difference in the altitude between the seabed and the top of the pipe. If the PVS is to handle such large pipe diameters, the single-point altitude measurement must be replaced with a multipoint measurement. The detected altitude used by the PVS will then be the mean of these multiple measurements.

In the test presented here, the large-pipe-diameter problem has been ignored.

The test of the PVS's robustness against scaling errors is based on processing Scene1, Scene2, and Scene3. The results of the test are shown in Figure 8.21a–e. The scaling constant c_c (see [2]) has been changed in steps of 5% in an interval of $\pm 15\%$, relative to its ideal value of 0.01. It can be seen that the PVS manages to detect the correct center lines in all but the $+15\%$ case in Figure 8.21a. For all the other cases, the detected center line moves slightly around as c_c changes, but they are always near the apparent center lines of the pipes. The center lines detected in Scene2 deserve some further discussion.

When c_c is less than 0.01, the upper pipe is interpreted as two segments instead of one. However, this is no problem as they both are consistent interpretations (see Section 8.7.1).

The other observation that can be made is, when c_c is larger than 0.01, the middle pipe is detected with one center line instead of two. However, the remaining center line is a valid detection of the pipe.

To conclude from the above discussion: the PVS is robust against scaling errors. It performs well within a $\pm 10\%$ variation of the c_c scaling factor when fed with Scene1, Scene2, and Scene3. Thus, it is a reasonable assumption that it can handle at least such a variation.

Skewed Light

The light source and the camera ought to be separated in order to reduce the effect of backscatter. Based on numbers given in [10], it is suggested in [2] that the light and the camera must be separated by 25% of the distance to the scene. The problem with this separation is that it makes the light distribution uneven and induces shadows in the scene. Alas, the PVS has to accept this, as the backscatter is expected to be a problem best handled in this way.

Figure 8.22 presents the light and camera configuration used in this test of the PVS's robustness against skewed light. The light is aligned with the camera along

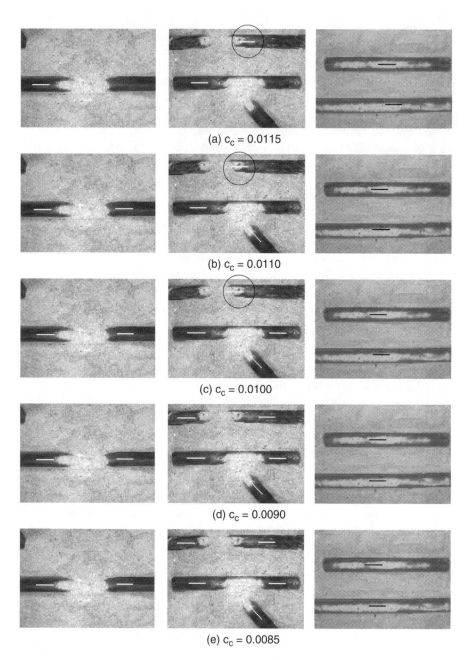

(a) $c_c = 0.0115$

(b) $c_c = 0.0110$

(c) $c_c = 0.0100$

(d) $c_c = 0.0090$

(e) $c_c = 0.0085$

Figure 8.21 The pipe center lines that the PVS detects for Scene1, Scene2, and Scene3 are dependent on the scaling constant c_c. The images in rows (a) and (b) shows a too-high constant, (c) the correct one, and (d) and (e) a too-low one. The contrast is low for three of the center lines in Scene2 and, thus, they have been pointed out with circles.

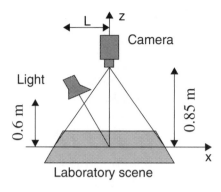

Figure 8.22 Camera and light configuration for the skewed light test.

the x-axis. The light is at a height of 0.6 m above the scene, while the camera is at 0.85 m. The camera points along the z-axis down to the middle of the scene, while the light is separated from the camera by some distance L. The vertical position of the light is given by physical restrictions of the laboratory setup.

The image of Scene3 in Figure 8.23a is taken with the light source at $L = -0.18$ m along the x-axis. The PVS manages to detect the center lines of both the pipe segments. Figure 8.23b shows that the PVS locates the center lines when the

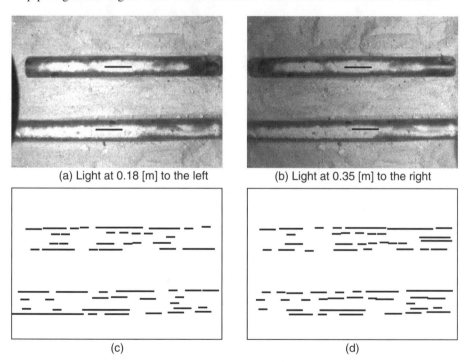

(a) Light at 0.18 [m] to the left   (b) Light at 0.35 [m] to the right

(c)   (d)

Figure 8.23 Scene3 with two different separations of the light source and the camera. Refer to Figure 8.22 for an explanation of the light and camera configuration.

light is moved to $L = 0.35$ m. The line images in Figures 8.23c and d demonstrate that the PVS derives a rich set of lines in both images. However, there are rather fewer lines at the left end of Figure 8.23d. This indicates that a separation of 0.35 m is around the maximum of what the PVS can handle.

Figures 8.24a and b display two side views of Scene3, with the light source at L of -0.18 and 0.35 m, respectively. The PVS manages to detect the pipe center lines in Figure 8.24a, but it fails badly in b. The cause of this failure can be discovered by looking at the line image in Figure 8.24d. Here, the shadowing induces false pipe-boundary lines and causes true ones to be lost. Furthermore, there are false boundaries in the background caused by sand ridges that cast shadows. The PVS finds a valid interpretation of lines from some of the false boundaries. This happens as the shadowing either increases the apparent diameter of the real pipes, or removes boundaries in the shadow zone. The net result is that line pairs cannot be formed because they are rejected when tested against the t_{dd} threshold.

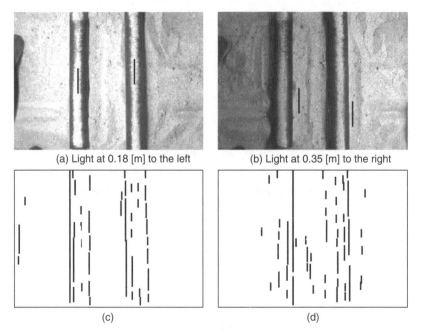

(a) Light at 0.18 [m] to the left   (b) Light at 0.35 [m] to the right

(c)   (d)

Figure 8.24 A side view of Scene3 with two different separations of the light source and the camera. Refer to Figure 8.19 for an explanation of the light and camera configuration.

This discussion can be summarized by stating that the PVS is robust against uneven light distribution, but can fail because of shadows. The interesting aspect lay in how far the light and the camera can be separated in percent of the altitude. Figure 8.22 shows that they will be separated by 30% when the light is at an x-position of -0.18 m and by 58% when it is at 0.35 m. Both these values are larger than the wanted separation of 25%. Thus, it must be concluded that the PVS is robust against skewed light, as it handles both uneven light distribution and shadowing without problems in the 30% case.

However, it may be a good idea to make the light distribution as even as possible, because this means that the PVS can handle scenes with a lower contrast compared to an uneven distribution. More important is that the shadows, which induce false boundaries, will be suppressed. An even distribution can be achieved by the rather classic symmetric-light arrangement illustrated in Figure 8.25a. The shadows induced by the right light will be removed by the left one, and vice

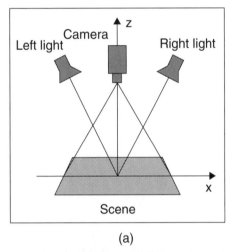

(a)

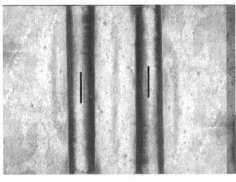

(b)

Figure 8.25 (a) A symmetric light arrangement that reduces/removes the shadows in a scene; (b) the effect of introducing a symmetric left light in the scene of Figure 8.24b. The PVS can now find the correct pipe center lines (see text).

versa. The effect of this simple arrangement is illustrated by applying it to the scene in Figure 8.24b, where PVS previously failed. The symmetric light has been synthesized by rotating the image in Figure 8.24b 180° and adding it to the original image. The resulting image with an even light distribution is shown in Figure 8.25b. Now, the PVS detects the correct pipe center lines. Thus, it can be suggested that the PVS will handle even large separations of the camera and the light source, as long as the source is symmetric.

8.8   CONCLUSION

The application of a vision system (the PVS) in a proposed pipeline inspection AUV has been presented. The PVS is used for pipeline tracking: The pipeline's position and heading relative to the vehicle is found by the PVS and used to guide the vehicle along the pipe.

The PVS has been presented, and the essential scheme for the inclusion of orientation, altitude, and position sensors has been given. It has been pointed out that robust image interpretation is important in the unstructured underwater environment. Here, automatic edge-thresholding and a modified Hough transform have been proposed for robust segmentation. The resulting robust interpretation has been ensured with a matching stage that accounts for the vehicle position uncertainty by doing position-independent matching. This may lead to ambiguous matches. The final interpretation stage discards improbable combinations of matches.

It has been shown here that the proposed PVS can interpret moderately complex configurations of pipelines, even when the vehicle's position is not exact. Furthermore, it has been shown that the PVS is robust against scaling errors, rotation errors, varying contrast from image to image, shadowing, and uneven light distribution.

However, it has been pointed out in [2] that there are things that can and should be improved: The error handling could be better and the number of parameters in the PVS should have been reduced. These improvements are not crucial in a prototype vehicle, where reliability is of less priority, but they are essential in a future production version of the PISCIS.

The PVS is not fundamentally different from other model-based vision systems, it is simply adapted to an underwater vehicle and environment. Consequently, state sensors must be present so that the PVS can relate images to its view of the real world, a light source must be added, and image-processing algorithms must be adapted to the unstructured environment. The object-model database, or rather pipe-segment map, is spatially indexed, and distant segments (models) are not considered for recognition. This is in contrast to most other experimental systems where all models are considered equally probable.

The scenes that PVS can interpret seem to be simple compared to what others have reported [20]. However, the quality of underwater images are poor compared to images from indoor scenes. Thus, priority has been given to robustness rather than the interpretation of complex scenes. This is reasonable, as pipelines are big objects and relatively few can turn up within a scene.

How to tailor or adapt algorithms in computer vision is dependent on the image quality and the task at hand. If the image quality is bad, all methods will fail. Here, it was assumed that the light and the camera with an auto-iris lens provide images of adequate quality. Furthermore, pipelines must have a visible outline and not be covered by sand and heavy marine growth.

The strategy in this work has been to tailor methods that counter the degraded quality of underwater images. Section 8.7 shows that the methods are well suited, and they will provide a sound basis for interpreting underwater scenes with pipe-segment configurations.

Acknowledgments

This work was done by members of the staff of The Foundation for Scientific Research at The Norwegian Institute of Technology (SINTEF). The project has in part been funded by The Royal Norwegian Council for Scientific and Industrial Research (NTNF).

References

[1] J. O. Hallset and O. J. Rodseth, "PISCIS—An AUV for pipeline inspection," in *Proc. 7th Int. Symp. Unmanned Untethered Submersible Technology*, (Durham, NH), 23–25 September, 1991, pp. 51–59.

[2] J. O. Hallset. "A vision system for an autonomous underwater vehicle." Dr. ing. thesis, The Norwegian Institute of Technology, Trondheim Norway, ITK report 1992:109-W.

[3] O. J. Rodseth, "Research on autonomous underwater vehicles in Norway." Seminar on Autonomous Underwater Vehicles, The Association for Structural Improvement of the Shipbuilding Industry (Tokyo), November 1990.

[4] O. J. Rodseth and J.O. Hallset, "ROV90–A prototype autonomous inspection vehicle," in *Proc. First Int. Offshore and Polar Engineering Conf.* (Edinburgh), 11–15 August 1991, pp. 42–47.

[5] M. A. Turk, D. G. Morgenthaler, K. D. Gremban, and M. Marra, "VITS—A vision system for autonomous land vehicle navigation," *IEEE Trans. Pattern Analysis and Machine Intelligence*, vol. 10, no. 3, May 1988, pp. 342–361.

[6] E. D. Dickmanns, B. Mysliwetz, and T. Christians, "An integrated spatio-temporal approach to automatic visual guidance of autonomous vehicles," *IEEE Trans. Systems, Man, and Cybernetics*, vol. 20, no. 6, November/December 1990, pp. 1273–1284.

[7] R. C. Gonzalez and P. Wintz. *Digital Image Processing.* New York: Addison Wesley, 1987.

[8] R. O. Duda and P. E. Hart. *Pattern Classification and Scene Analysis.* New York: John Wiley and Sons, 1973.

[9] D. MacKay, "Choosing an underwater TV system," *Underwater Systems Design*, January/February 1991, pp. 13–25.

[10] J. J. Jaffe, "Computer modelling and the design of optimal underwater imaging systems," *IEEE J. Oceanic Engineering*, vol. 15, no. 2, April 1990, pp. 101–111.

[11] W. K. Pratt. *Digital Image Processing*. New York: John Wiley and Sons Inc.

[12] R. C. Jain and T. O. Binford, "Ignorance, myopia, and naivete in computer vision systems," *Computer Vision, Graphics, and Image Processing*, vol. 53, no. 1, January 1991, pp. 112–117.

[13] L. J. Kitchen and J. A. Malin, "The effect of spatial discretization on the magnitude and direction response of simple differential edge operators on a step edge," *Computer Vision, Graphics, and Image Processing*, 1988, pp. 243–258.

[14] V. Lacroix, "A three-module strategy for edge detection," *IEEE Trans. Pattern Analysis and Machine Intelligence*, vol. 10, no. 6, November 1988, pp. 803–810.

[15] M. M. Fleck, "Some defects in finite-difference edge finders," *IEEE Trans. Pattern Analysis and Machine Intelligence*, vol. 14, no. 3, March 1992, pp. 337–345.

[16] J. Canny, "A computational approach to edge detection," *IEEE Trans. Pattern Analysis and Machine Intelligence*, vol. 8, no. 6, November 1986, pp. 679–698.

[17] J. Illingworth and J. Kittler, "A survey of the Hough transform," *Computer Vision, Graphics, and Image Processing*, vol. 44, no. 44, 1988, pp. 87–116.

[18] W. E. L. Grimson and T. Lozano-Perez, "Recognition and localization of overlapping parts from sparse data," in *Three-Dimensional Machine Vision*. T. Kanade (editor). Norwell, MA: Kluwer Academic Press, pp. 451–510.

[19] M. A. Snyder, "A commentary on the paper by Jain and Binford," *Computer Vision, Graphics, and Image Processing*, vol. 53, no. 1, January 1991, pp. 118–119.

[20] M. Oshima and Y. Shirai, "An object recognition system using three dimensional information," in *Three-Dimensional Machine Vision*. T. Kanade (editor). Norwell, MA: Kluwer Academic Press, pp. 355–397.

9

THE ART AND SCIENCE OF MULTIMEDIA

Mihai Nadin   *University of Wuppertal*
                   Germany

9.1 INTRODUCTION

As multimedia unfolds, we understand that it is more the expression of technology at work than of fundamental science. This is not uncharacteristic of the entire real-time imaging field—and to a large extent of the vast majority of new practical human experiences having the computer at their core. The peculiarity of this development should serve as encouragement to proceed, parallel to continuing with innovation and experimentation, in the direction of articulating a stimulating, open-ended theory of the field. Such a theory could open new avenues and help foster further innovation. It may be too early to proceed with a "grand scheme" multimedia science, but some foundation can be set. The task is far from superfluous. Given the inter- and cross-disciplinary nature of interactive multimedia, students, as well as practitioners and innovators, are faced with the need to understand concepts and principles of many disciplines that are supposed to converge here. In this spirit, the contributions the reader can expect from this chapter are: defining the field; characterizing current and possible applications; drawing attention to the critical component that we identify as the underlying aesthetics; showing how a heterogeneous generic configuration is designed and implemented; dealing with the critical issues of authoring and navigation; introducing a method for real-time image acquisition; and, finally, addressing issues of the evolving networked multimedia. For clarity's sake, examples are provided, solutions diagrammed, and applications discussed. While real-time imaging is the ongoing premise, the focus is rather on what makes it possible—and sometimes how it is possible—not what it is, which is probably its most changing aspect.

9.2   TIME AND DATA TYPES

There are as many definitions of multimedia as the many flavors it comes in. One characteristic of multimedia is the richness in data types, in particular, time-defined types. Moreover, the set of data types being open (i.e., more can become available at any time), it follows that richness is not only a characteristic, but a challenge. Richness in data types facilitates flexibility in conveying information, especially pertinent to dynamic phenomena. It also ensures the various functions of multimedia and its broader field of applications. Among the data types currently integrated in real-time imaging platforms are text; computer-generated images; electronic photography; imported still images; analog and digital video (in standard formats); as well as high-definition TV (analog and digital) in real-time or prerecorded; sound (real-time input or prerecorded, in analog or digital format); real-time images from electronic microscopy, radioastronomy, seismology, or manufacturing processes; animation (on film, video, or computer-generated); film in its known formats; haptic data via transducers; and more. There is no limit, especially if we examine multimedia not in its canned forms (CD-ROM primarily) but as a dynamic system that can be used in almost any kind of human activity. Although to date games and documentary applications—historic accounts in the form of "electronic books" of events or accomplishments subject to interactive queries, exemplary case studies in medicine, geology, physics, and so on—as well as teleconferencing probably dominate the field, interactive multimedia is already *deployed* in many other activities. It covers e-mail, telemedicine, design, engineering, CAD/CAM, and entertainment. Businesses adopted the technology not only to improve marketing, but also for more effective information processing. Education is rapidly integrating it in the dissemination of subject matter for which the book, slides, the overhead projector, and video are no longer adequate. Training based on interactive multimedia applications running over client-server networks is now a practical solution to a problem businesses and state agencies have faced for a long time. And, of course, the military made multimedia part of a new way to conceive and solve tasks in an age of fast changes in methods and means of warfare.

Regardless of the intended function, one thing should be clear from the outset: The fact that interactive multimedia integrates various data types is a curse and a blessing at the same time. One-dimensional, homogeneous communication means the computer required a more easily manageable discipline. In the multimedia space of many means, the coordination becomes extremely difficult. What might have been, for better or worse, an issue of culture and intuition in the simpler world of computer graphics or desktop publishing simply escapes human control. Unless we realize what we have to do to cope with complexity, chances are that *more* will not translate into *better*.

9.2.1 Hardware Structure

General-purpose computers, as well as specialized computers providing high-performance processing, gave to real-time imaging the power and diversity expected in more complex endeavors. Advanced graphics (including imaging), video, fast and effective rendering (extended to 3-D), not to mention the ever richer feature set of image display methods and technologies, are part of the multimedia technological advancement.

The dominant real-time imaging structure still unites a geometry engine and a raster processor. Along the pipeline of polygon processing, huge amounts of data flow to the display component, where texture mapping, transparency, local shading, and so on are integrated into what finally appears as an interactive image. Further progress, from the operating system concepts down (multithreading, for instance), and obviously in the area of parallel processing, will eventually make real-time *more real*. The most seductive (as well as the really bare-bones) multimedia configuration is based on the traditional real-time imaging structure. Nevertheless, in order to address the goals for which the static image, and even computer animation, are less adapted, this configuration was extended in a combination where software and additional hardware (all kinds of boards) compensated for limitations inherent in the computer graphics structure. Of determining importance was progress in high-capacity storage, as well as in the early adoption of standards defining what became the generic CD-ROM medium. As a publishing medium, CD-ROM and its relatively limited number of variations (CD-ROM/XA for fully lip-synchronized, interleaved motion and sound, CD-I, CD-V, Photo-CD) made possible a viable alternative to proprietary formats. As a result, technical characteristics of the medium—access time, in the first place—remain an area open for competitive solutions, while format engages providers of content in a competition of using the storage capacity for significant work and for making available appropriate supporting software tools (for navigation, indexing, retrieval, etc.).

9.2.2 A New Generic Medium

To account for the diversity of the various components of multimedia is already a very difficult task. Text on a page of an illustrated magazine or in a book (scientific treatise, popular encyclopedia, art publication) is unlike such text in the context of a multimedia "page," be it an e-mail message that integrates moving images and sound or a motion clip. One can look at the author reading his poem, can hear the voice, can change the typeface of the displayed text (if one chooses to have it displayed); one can add music (already existing or synthesized "on the fly"). One can animate words, replace the reader with an actor who might do more justice to the poem. One can transform words into abstract shapes. We can, of course, visualize the world described poetically, regardless of whether it is a realistic rendition or an abstraction. All this has been shown in experimental or commercial products. The limit is that of our knowledge or imagination. Our respect for what we hear and see, our visual and musical abilities, and—yes—the multimedia platform we use affect the outcome. The same applies to applications that are not artistic or educational in nature.

Those cheap machines that integrate a CD-ROM, maybe even a laser disk player, and which their manufacturers call "the first multimedia station," are not yet what they are proclaimed to be. If they were, they could support a design application suitable for architecture, product design, or event design (remember the Olympics?). The video sequence that an architect captured at the site of a commissioned building can be integrated into the architectural design; each new sketch can be turned into a 3-D rendition, placed on tape, and viewed from all possible angles. Fly-over, our obsession since the inception of computer animation, is as easy as movement through the not-yet completely designed—not to say constructed—home, hotel, or university. Interactive programs, as well as noninteractive immersive virtual reality of multimedia intent, support "walk-throughs." Motion is the feature (usually relying on some animation capability) supporting digital immersion. The balance sheet of the endeavor—e.g., how much such a building costs, how much a change in design or materials would affect time and cost—is part of such an interactive multimedia environment. So is the possibility of inquiring into other databases in order to validate one or another design decision. A multimedia database is a powerful dimension of this new level of real-time imaging in action. New products or events involving thousands of people—better yet, hundreds of thousands or even millions—can be designed in a multimedia environment. An events-designer literally "sees" what was planned in a multimedia rendition before the event takes place, and maximizes the intended effect of each sequence. Certainly, if trivialized, multimedia turns out to be merely a sleeker form of presentation—instead of one slide projector, use ten (and never forget fade-in, fade-out effects from a dissolve unit); and instead of a video presentation, use a wall of monitors into which images from various tapes are fed simultaneously. You know the rest.

Many innovative projects integrating video, film, 3-D images, and—why not?—virtual reality methods and gear, result in multimedia artifacts never experienced before. To a great extent, the project for the fixing of the Hubble telescope was a multimedia development with a virtual reality component. Technologically, all parts exist for endeavors of such and even higher complexity. We can "write" digital images to videotape; we can integrate video into digital computer graphics and animation. We can edit video, film, and digital sequences from a multimedia station. We can output to hard disks, to digital or analog video, to film, to printed matter, and to holography. But in order to achieve quality and value, we need to understand what all this means [1].

The business community is interested in getting interactive multimedia presentations over networks. Powerful servers and effective visual database management programs reflect this interest. Imagine a business meeting where one can effectively show how the on-line point-of-sale financial results translate into an animation of redesigned products ("Forget the blue, it doesn't sell! And change the length!"), or a new store design (to avoid bottlenecks at checkout, or to minimize loss through shoplifting at Christmas time); or how a TV ad for a new product makes it into children's games. A simulated world of the new genetics of individual diet can effectively translate into the action taken by those concerned about how they look or how much they weigh; how swimming, walking, or simply becoming aware of the control they have on their own decisions affects their health and life expectancy. Or, for the more demanding souls and minds, there can be generic shows of artists revered by the public, or of the works we would like to hang on our walls at home, of the music or poetry we'd like to experience. Again, all this is technologically possible today. The challenge is in understanding the aesthetic implications of "speaking" and "writing" in the multidimensional language of multimedia—time being the critical dimension.

Interactive multimedia can serve as a design tool and visualization medium. It can be an originator of communication (using heterogeneous sources of information) and political activism, or a medium for electronic publishing (laser disks, CD-ROM, CD-I, video in both analog and digital formats, and so on). It is a participatory medium, not a single device of mixed output. Interactive multimedia is an exceptionally powerful educational environment: It allows for active discovery in the process of teaching and learning, supporting individualized "navigation" in the wealthy world of knowledge and experience.

9.2.3   The Gnoseological Platform

From among the many forms in which multimedia enters our practical experiences, the scientific endeavor leading to new knowledge stands out. Indeed, as knowledge in our age becomes more and more computational, the acquisition of knowledge and its experimental validation require gnoseological platforms on which real-time scientific goals can be effectively pursued. Fundamentally, the gnoseological platform made possible by real-time imaging has already benefited and changed science. It affords a new medium for representation, a medium for experimentation (simulation), and a new medium for designing (including the design of new experiments) based on the knowledge computationally acquired.

Knowledge in computational form succeeds where previous analytical attempts—many based on inductive procedures (from observations translated into data to information processing)—failed. Chaos theory is an example. As crude as the graphics routines were when Lawrence, Feigenbaum, Mandelbrot, et al. made their observations, without computers, our realization of chaotic behavior (population growth, fluid dynamics, the physics of weather patterns, etc.) would have been delayed. On real-time systems, initial knowledge was often refined, fractals emerged, and the new science from which they stem was put to use in imaging technologies (for instance, in compression algorithms). Computational science became possible once computer representations (or *visualizations*, as they are called) (in a medium richer than graph paper, photography, film, video, and even holographs) allowed for the development of a body of knowledge otherwise impossible. Radioastronomy illustrates this quite convincingly. The birth of a new galaxy is really not a static subject but a dynamic process requiring powerful visualization methods. Regardless of how spectacular all these are, we are already past this level. Although multimedia is far from being the reality some claim to design and others to manufacture and sell—we will return to this soon—it has already established the next *level* of possibilities and expectations on the gnoseological platform afforded by real-time imaging.

Scientific metaphors are as much metaphors as those of poetry. Only their intention is different. On the interactive multimedia gnoseological platform, hypotheses can be formulated visually, or even in some syncretic form that combines moving images, sounds, alphanumeric sequences, and so forth. Genetic research, as much as artificial life (AL) inquiries, is finding in multimedia a richer "language." This composite "language" results from the cooperation and coordination of other languages. The production of meaning in this language is quite different from any other semantics we are aware of.

Science and Aesthetics

Despite the many differences among these three different forms of computational acquisition, representation, and communication of knowledge, one important aspect appears to be shared among them: They all assume and rely on an underlying aesthetic component. More precisely, in all previous forms of knowledge, such as in the language of theories, in mathematical or logical formulations, or in the positivist approach of experiments, the aesthetic component is reducible to what is called *elegance* (of formulations, formulae, experiments). Mathematicians, physicists, chemists, and many others in the sciences have written about the beauty of theories that seem to parallel their appropriateness or even validate their truth. But once science becomes computational, and computation offers powerful real-time imaging, the underlying aesthetic becomes more complex. Moreover, because decisions of an aesthetic nature, such as selection of color codes (e.g., for representation of abstract entities) or visual conventions (for dynamic phenomena), have to be made prior to the scientific formulation, it is clear that such aesthetic decisions "tint" the knowledge. Therefore, it is not unusual today to have on the teams of research facilities—some of the supercomputing centers are known for this—people qualified to handle questions of aesthetics. In the world of graphics and visualization, graphic designers are sufficiently qualified to support scientists in their attempts to visually formulate new hypotheses. That in some cases images coming from the gnoseological platform are still ugly, or far from clear, is a phenomenon experienced inside and outside the scientific community. With the advent of animation, the situation became even more critical. Multimedia, which integrates real-time, is faced with even bigger challenges. As a still new experience, it has probably failed on aesthetic grounds as often as, if not more frequently than, on technological and scientific grounds. This is the reason why, before attempting to think of a multimedia configuration regardless of its intended functionality (entertainment, education, business, medicine, gnoseological platform, etc.), one needs to account for its intrinsic aesthetic characteristics.

Indeed, the complexity of the tasks necessitating the deployment of interactive multimedia is paralleled—make no mistake about this!—by the aesthetic complexity on whose account multimedia finally succeeds or fails. Having asserted this, some further considerations regarding the matter have to be made.

9.3 WHAT WE KNOW AND WHAT WE HAVE TO DISCOVER

Since Gutenberg (and the Chinese well before him), we learned how to deal with the printed text. Since Niepce and Daguerre, we learned heliography, that is, how to "draw with light,"—how to take photographs. Since Muybridge, Dickson, and the Lumière brothers (at the end of the 19th century), we learned to work with film; and later on, with Nipkow, Leblanc, and Zworykin, to use television. Our experience with computer graphics, for over 25 years now, has also taught us many things about a new medium, as well as a new way of thinking. We have integrated the experiences of printing and computer graphics, making desktop publishing a reality. We have integrated scientific data acquisition, design knowledge, and imaging into powerful visualization. Aesthetic structure gave coherence to our knowledge, more and more made up of fragments of specialized research.

When all seemed clear and settled, a new perspective opened: interactive multimedia. Curiously, while the graphics pipeline (described in the introductory lines) as it evolved in a rather *static* environment is still maintained, the new perspective opened by multimedia is fundamentally *dynamic*. Interactive multimedia is one among other new technologies resulting from progress in computation. And it is one of the fastest growing, both in terms of the technology and in business terms. Unfortunately, it reached this status of success even before its many originators could take the time to understand what it is. They rushed to patent almost trivial aspects instead of asking themselves some fundamental questions. (Compton's *New Media Hypercard Handbook* is the best-known example.) For many, it is just a gimmick, a buzzword that brings in grant money and new clients. For others, it is a new name for what they did before but now with faster computers, more memory, and better output devices.

9.3.1 The Challenge of Dynamics

For those really serious about what they do and how they use their talent, knowledge, and money, it is a field still in the process of defining itself. This process is not easy. We know a lot about printing, photography, typography, graphics, video, and film. Each carries aesthetic assumptions already integrated in our culture.

Each field established expectations of quality. Experience in these media showed that type is not reducible to the rules of calligraphy, a picture is not a drawing, a movie is much, much more than a sequence of moving photos. While there are common qualities, usually defined as aesthetic characteristics—symmetry, rhythm, harmony of colors or shapes—each of these media has its own condition. The constraints of type—even when taking into consideration the vast difference between the hot type of yesteryear and today's digital type—are dissimilar in nature from the constraints of photographic film. The qualifiers "slow" or "high-speed" to describe sensitivity and granularity are only at the tip of the iceberg. So are the many different ways of processing and printing. The dynamic quality of cinematography is, despite appearances, unlike in nature from the dynamic quality of a video. Film resolution, understood as part of the intrinsic aesthetic condition of the medium, is yet to be matched by any other visual media we are aware of.

Multimedia, as already stated, is different from the particular media it integrates. In interactive multimedia, text and image and movement, the worlds of the digital and of the analog, sources of images, sounds (from reality or synthesized), animation, and everything else that people use in expressing themselves can be united. Interactive multimedia is effective when all its components are well designed and their integration results in an expressive unity, subject to the active participation in the work, regardless of its functionality, by the viewer. Interactivity means the integration of the viewer in the work.

9.3.2   The Multimedia Book

The outcome of good interactive multimedia recalls the gestalt principle: The resulting dynamic entity is more than the sum of its parts. Nonlinearity and nonsequentiality, which are intrinsic to any visually oriented activity (integrating sound or not), confer upon interactive multimedia possibilities that no other medium or tool have when taken independently.

The new kind of thinking required by multimedia is not the result of combining what some knew about type, what others knew about photo or video cameras, what yet others knew about computer graphics and animation, optical storage, and hypercard (or any other hypertext embodiment). While film scripting and editing comes closer to multimedia, it is still not at the same level of complexity. I was once commissioned to find out what it would take to create a CD-ROM of one of Isaac Asimov's stories about the future (*I, Robot*). A book publisher, who quite conveniently owns the rights to the story, wanted to step into the world of interactive multimedia. The product had to allow an animated fictional character to navigate the reader through the text, making visual each part of the world Asimov described. It also had to introduce the writer himself (at that time seriously ill, but enormously interested in a "new book" of interactions and anticipatory characteristics). A game—that is, the making of a robot from parts described in the text—was also desired. This introduced an interactive dimension, a challenge to the "reader." Finally, if the "reader" so wished, the story would be printable from the disk so that the pleasure and intellectual reward of a literate understanding of the text would continue the digital multimedia journey. To accomplish all these in a proper way, one had to design an interactive digital book shell, not just illustrate Asimov's text. The project, if approached properly, is neither technologically nor aesthetically trivial. Such a project changes our cultural notion of a book, of reading, of interaction. It goes well beyond the mediocre Sony and Voyager products marketed as multimedia, and beyond finally what the publisher actually produced. To trivialize instead of adding new dimensions to past values is a danger that interactive multimedia should avoid at any price.

9.3.3 Conflicting Demands

To design multimedia means many things. Obviously, it means to understand everything that can fuse in the new syncretic language, to be aware of technical and communicational aspects, to be sensitive to the viewers' cognitive characteristics, and to be willing to challenge stereotypes. As someone has said, the public at large (and technology innovators in particular) is more familiar with bad design, and conditioned to prefer it. This is what we receive through all media most of the time. Still, for multimedia to succeed, it has to develop means and methods of expression that ensure an effective trade-off between functional expectations and aesthetic goals. Information-driven design is the place to start. Indeed, defining what the specific problem addressed in a given case is, the designer acknowledges two sets of choices: a) what has to be achieved; b) how to achieve the goal. Functional considerations can be formalized in an information processing language. Aesthetic considerations are formal in nature, but functional in the context we work in. Contrast, for instance, is a powerful aesthetic element. Used appropriately, it enhances functionality. Used excessively, it can detract attention from other elements.

There is no list of aesthetic goals that can be checked off with the expectation that, once each element is in place, the whole is right. But there is an aesthetic rationality that starts with a general expectation of elegance—the Latin root of the word associates *elegance* to selection, choosing—and cultivates simplicity. A multimedia design needs to promote integrity. Corruption of expressive means—colors, shapes, rhythms, and others—is as bad as corruption of data. In order to achieve integrity, the means of expression have to be kept to an expressive minimum. In order to achieve this minimum, which depends on the context, the designer works through stages of refinement. In so doing, each formal element is evaluated for how appropriate (or not) it is within the broad scope of the multimedia work.

Multimedia being a mixed medium, its design starts by acknowledging *time* dependency. Scale, contrast, and proportion are all time-sensitive. The language of multimedia might be visually dominant; however, it is not reducible to only what we see but also when and how what we see—and timing—enhance each other. Under certain circumstances, an image can be purposely fuzzy (not enough contrast) if the sound or other time element (movement) compensates. On paper, lack of contrast is deadly. In multimedia, it can be a powerful way to attract attention to something that otherwise would pass by in the flow of images.

Aesthetic integration is of extreme importance. This means to acknowledge not only how various data types are properly processed but also how a "house" is built from the many different "bricks" available in the digital realm. We will probably have to expand the gestalt body of knowledge that deals with images (figure/ground strategy, for instance) to see how the composite multimedia can take advantage of the "hard-wired" characteristics of human holistic perception. Perceptual structuring (which is what *gestalt* means) makes us aware of the role of proximity (what is close to what, but in terms of an expanded notion of closeness, i.e., which sound is close to a fast-moving laser beam), similarity, continuity, and closure. This can translate into design strategies for grouping components of multimedia, for introducing hierarchies, or for building on shared conventions of aesthetic relationship (color contrast related to sound contrast, for instance).

9.3.4   The Road to Interactivity

Regardless of the purpose for which it is used, interactive multimedia needs to be well conceived, appropriately designed, and technologically comprehensible and manageable. This last expectation raises, among other things, critical aspects of the role interfaces play in interactive multimedia [2]. Production tools already come with a language of operations, in extension of the platform-dependent user interface. Presentation tools introduce new conventions. Ideally, there should be no real gap between the two, except that the viewer/participant should not be subjected to learning yet another interface (or to reading hundreds of pages of manuals). All these expectations are a tall order. Multimedia requires integration of technological means, design at a higher level of the heterogeneous ways and means people use to express themselves, and dynamic qualities. It is nonsequential; that is, it is a configurational space of expression and communication. It implies an appropriate understanding (cognitive, cultural, and sociological) of how people relate to such a wealth of means of expression, and of the dangers of manipulation and disconnectedness from reality. Finally, and perhaps the most difficult expectation, it implies an understanding of interactivity as a way of unleashing human creativity, and of eventually making us all spiritually richer through vastly shared experiences.

9.4   A CONFIGURATION SHELL

Having looked at interactive multimedia from a functional perspective—from the gnoseological platform to the minimal computer–CD-ROM player (or battery of players) combination—and from the perspective of the underlying aesthetics, we can conclude that various applications will require various configurations. There is no such thing as an off-the-shelf multimedia system that can satisfy each and every demand. The major effort in designing a multimedia configuration is in determining the set of data types and the aesthetic constraints culturally acknowledged with respect to each type. In addition, issues of interfacing—process interfaces, as well as user interfaces—become critical to providing the best return on the investment. Generally speaking, while multimedia became possible exactly because faster real-time imaging machines (at the core of this platform) are cost effective, these platforms almost always incorporate expensive proprietary technologies. In addition, awareness of intellectual property is a significant factor in pricing visual databases from which multimedia applications will, in time, extract more and more information.

After exemplifying many varieties of applications, we can suggest a shell configuration—actually, a design that was implemented for purposes as diverse as design and production of multimedia products (including laser disks and CD-ROM), design research, modeling and simulation, and even knowledge acquisition and dissemination. Without going into detail, we have to explain some of the concepts and technologies incorporated in the configuration.

9.4.1 Analog and Digital

In order to videorecord computer graphics animation, one has to address the issue of converting digital data into analog signals that meet standard display characteristics. A computer graphics monitor is predominantly a red-green-blue (RGB) component display of noninterlaced 1280×1024 signal, scanning at 75 Hz. Broadcast video, using the 1941 NTSC (National Television Standards Committee) standard, or the two European systems known as PAL (Phase Alternative Line) and SECAM (Sequential Color and Memory—applied mainly in France) of more recent times, is a composite interlaced 525- (in the United States) or 625- (in Europe) line signal, scanning at 30 Hz. The problem at hand is the conversion from the computer graphics display to video broadcast. Conversely, the problem is how to convert a video signal—in the standard formats mentioned—into digital data. In its generality, this problem extends to high-definition (analog and digital) television and recording technologies, seen either as input or output or both. Evidently, moving images are quite demanding in terms of memory and synchronization. Live video usually includes sound, and this adds another level of complexity.

Keeping the entire approach simple, let us follow a concrete situation. Computer graphics animation is sent through a frame buffer to video-encoding hardware (see Figure 9.1). Digital frames are thus converted into an analog-component (RGB) signal. A scan converter brings down the scan rate of the component signal obtained as output from the buffer to the horizontal and vertical refresh rate of a video monitor. Within the same process, the resolution is corrected downwards. A video encoder (NTSC, PAL, or SECAM) encodes the signal, translating the

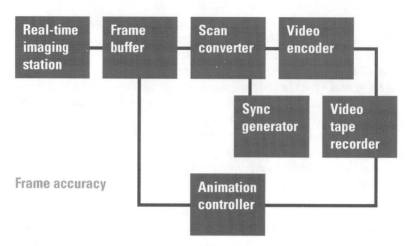

Figure 9.1 Digital-to-analog video.

component (RGB) noninterlaced signal into composite interlaced. A so-called *sync generator* synchronizes video output with broadcast timing standards. *Gen lock*, that is, locking the signal to the timing of the deflection ("electron gun") of the TV, is a function of extreme importance for video quality. A video camera could, under certain circumstances, take the desired image from the computer screen directly. But short of providing frame-accurate recording, the video quality will not be more acceptable than a Polaroid picture compared to a quality photograph.

Another possible avenue is storing animation frames on analog or digital videodisk recorders (frame storage devices). Being also frame-accurate and offering large storage capacity, such devices help in handling the memory bottleneck of live video processing. Up to 80,000 frames (and recently, up to 60 minutes of live video) can be recorded. These media are either write-once-read-many (WORM) or even rewritable.

On the video-to-computer side, an almost parallel sequence has to be followed (see Figure 9.2). Again, some solutions are standard (and in the meantime integrated in some desktop stations). Others are proprietary.

Similar paths must be provided for the processing of sound. Usually, sound synthesis and interfaces to electronic instruments are also provided. The low-cost digital-to-audio converter chip was replaced by computer-based audio at 16-bit, 44.1-kHz digitization, which is the resolution of a standard audio CD. In recent years, some of these functions were integrated into computer stations (from the pioneering NeXT station of mixed memories to Silicon Graphics, Sun, Hewlett-Packard, and to the Apple Quadra machines). Analog-to-digital (A/D) converter circuits and digital signal processors (DSP) are among standard features of machines designed with multimedia applications in mind. The real-time performance

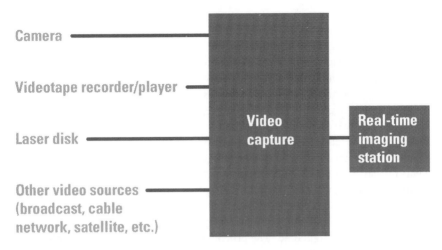

Figure 9.2 Analog video to digital.

of the digital signal processors (e.g., the 24-bit DSP 56001 from Motorola, or the 32-bit DSP 3210 chip from AT&T) ensures processing of sound as it is inputted (via microphone, synthesizer, interface, electronic instruments, video channels, etc.). It must be pointed out that, with the increased attention to voice recognition, the expectation is that this technology will become a standard in interactive multimedia. The DSP chip clearly helps in the task.

9.4.2   Voice and Handwriting Recognition

While searching through huge image and sound databases, it is quite counterintuitive (and counterproductive) to be constrained by keyboard input. Nevertheless, the state of the art is still some steps away from commands based on voice recognition. Even handwriting recognition is not yet so effective as to justify a pen-based computer as the front end for the search engine. Be this as it may, chances are very good that in not-too-distant a future (two to five years), the new interactive multimedia configuration will routinely use them. Actually, in order to reflect the awareness of further progress in areas such as voice or handwriting recognition as well as in other aspects of multimedia, a very useful design concept is modularity. Not that we would simply pull out the keyboard and replace it with a microphone at some moment in the future, but we could preserve the integrity of the configuration and work on the new interfaces, drivers, and routines that allow for better solutions. Together with the notion of modularity, we should build upon the expectation of networked multimedia, that is, distributed interactive multimedia. Of course, this layer introduces constraints and standards of broadband high-speed communication (and the appropriate protocols), which extend beyond the scope of this text.

9.4.3   A Multimedia Publisher Environment

The configuration I am presenting is an attempt to integrate the desktop, videotop, soundtop, and production means necessary to output in a variety of media. Omitted are specific input and output devices that a scientist would use in the gnoseological platform or a business executive in a presentation (slide projector controllers, dissolve units, LCD displays, or large screen projectors, etc.). The configuration is broken into two modules: *editing* and *recording* (Figures 9.3 and 9.4). Other modules can be added as the nature of the activity requires. Instruments for monitoring the process, in particular level and quality of signals, are indicated. Their presence (or absence) does not affect the functionality. Switching can be performed via physical patches or through soft-patching in a programmable router.

In these two diagrams, provisions were made for monitors and measuring devices that, although they do not affect functionality, are of critical importance for the quality of the outcome. The principle is that of viewing images before and after each processing step. Regardless of how well hardware and software work, conversions always result in loss of detail or in various forms of shifting (colors, shapes, timebase, etc.). Even the first generation (original image or master copy) will not automatically guarantee the integrity of sound, of the visual, or of their combination if the production does not adhere to strict rules of quality control and does not provide various correction facilities. Rendering of animation sequences often poses major issues of color saturation (they appear as "dirty" on TV monitors) or brightness (luminance). A graphic designer, used to the medium of mixed pigments and print, is simply not equipped to address the complexities of video design. Video producers have problems in realizing the distinction between a tape (non-random-access medium, of constraints specific to the magnetic medium) and a laser disk or, even better, CD-ROM.

We mention all these aspects mainly in order to specifically point to areas where the underlying aesthetics is subject to corruption. Some of this corruption is reversible—a digitally scanned image can be corrected until it carries the values of the unaffected original. In other cases, such as in digitizing a live video image, the corruption might not be correctable, or the reference might become unavailable. The consequence differs from application to application. It is evident that gaining knowledge about phenomena requires extreme precision and faithfulness to detail, insofar as they taint the knowledge. For presentation purposes, the choice is somewhat broader. The unity among time-defined data types needs to be preserved in ways appropriate to the multimedia goal. But even in this case, there are distinctions to be made among different times involved. Synchronization is implicit in the process; timelines are explicit in multimedia scripts; real-time (of occurrences, natural phenomena, etc.) is part of the larger temporal scheme of human life and experience. None can be treated without the understanding of how they might affect each other or the interactive quality of the multimedia experience.

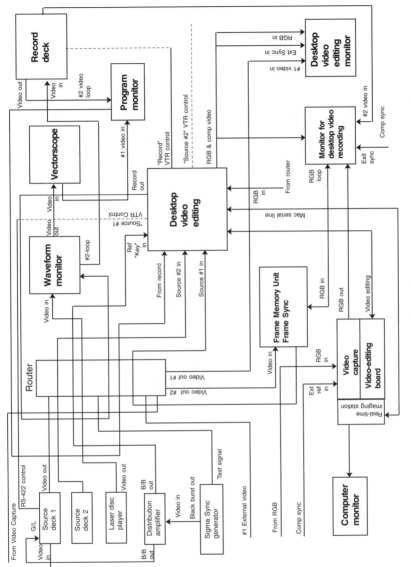

Figure 9.3 Editing module.

275

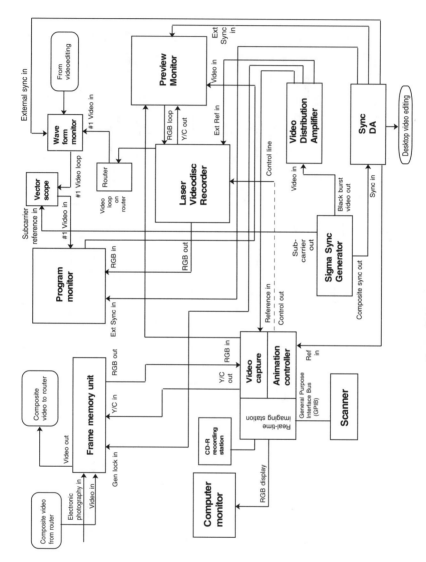

Figure 9.4 Recording module.

276

9.5 AUTHORING AND NAVIGATION

Multimedia is often a real-time participatory interactive process. It can also be interactive communication, a publication or a distribution medium, or a combination of these. Until the day data—regardless of their type—can be saved to a CD-ROM device within a multimedia application similarly to how we "write" data to a floppy or a hard disk, many more gigabytes and terabytes will have to pass through the pipelines leading to current publishing techniques. Nevertheless, for low-volume situations, as they can occur in scientific applications, or for extremely customized products, alternatives to proofing and limited publishing are already available as an extension of the desktop computer. The so-called *compact disk-recordable* (CD-R) offers such an alternative. As a matter of routine, almost as the desktop computer brought printing to the individual writer, multimedia brings electronic publishing to the author.

Multimedia publication is of interest here not through its ever-changing technology, but rather in view of the many implications it has on managing and formatting data, as well as in providing means for successful navigation. It really does not matter whether the data wind up on a glass master or on a polycarbonate substrate with prepatterned grooves topped by a photosensitive dye (this is the CD-R technology). What does matter is that heterogeneous contents—video, slides, sound, animation, etc.—are fused into a multimedia product that will be accessed by its viewers through regular CD-ROM players. These viewers will not know about the standard spiral file format (the ISO 9660, with its strict file-naming conventions) shared by CD-ROM, CD-audio, CD-I, and similar products (such as the Sony Data Discman and the Kodak Photo-CD), but they will definitely realize how much more economical the medium is. From archival storage to testing work in progress (interface, interactivity, integration of various data types, etc.), functions of a full-fledged CD-ROM are provided in CD-R. Once larger volume is considered, the work can be economically recorded to full CD-ROM. Multimedia publications, compared to paper, are 100 to 1000 times cheaper. As we cannot afford any more printed full-color catalogs of art, maps, furniture, cars, tourist offerings, new fashion collections, and so much more, we *can* afford them in CD-ROM. Clinical data, teaching materials, and all kinds of catalogs can be published and interactively accessed. But for this to happen, one must either buy commercially available authoring programs or develop such programs in order to do justice to the content published. The same applies to retrieval tools. Publishing software would need to meet precise expectations of those needing it: user interface, emulation of CD-ROM on hard disk, compliance with the ISO 9660 file-naming conventions—along with the possibility to ignore them, e.g., when only in-house archiving is performed—format variety, control over physical location of files, and so on. The software will also have to meet expectations of a more general nature: the ability to integrate all the desired data types; good scripting facilities; the possibility to support external commands might become necessary, that is, the program should allow for additions of features (or extensions). Last, but not least, the publisher should be allowed to distribute run-time files created in the software.

Multimedia is a nonsequential, nonlinear medium. These characteristics should be accounted for in the publishing software. *Nonsequential* means that various components do not have to be provided in the sequence of writing (letters, words, sentences); moreover, they do not have to be accessed as linear tape is. Random access to video changes the condition of the medium, regardless of whether multimedia only integrates video or is outputted as video. It confers upon the medium dynamic qualities that make video interactive.

Navigation through the wealth of multimedia is far more demanding than reading a book, watching a tape, or listening to music. Pretty early in the evolution of multimedia, attempts were made to apply the experience of navigation to text-based contents. This is why hypertext—the visionary nonlinear reading and interpretation of text suggested at the end of World War 2 by Vannevar Bush [3] in his prophetic "As We May Think"—was examined as a candidate for handling complexities well beyond those of large collections of static information. In the meantime, hypertext was embodied in some commercial products (Apple's Hypercard™, Asymetrix's Toolbook™, and others).

9.5.1 Docent™

For large collections of images associated with a comprehensive database, with video, and with sound, several ways to search, retrieve, and access can be defined. In what follows, I shall describe a simple hypermedia model inspired by the classic function of a docent (in a science or natural history museum, for instance). A docent is a guide knowledgeable about the contents of a collection. Docents continuously improve their knowledge. They can actively take notes as new data about the collection become available. They author articles or lectures on subsets of the collection. Assuming a collection of images on a laser disk (slides, video, sound), Figure 9.5 explains the hypermedia situation to be handled by a docent.

On a more general level, we can think of a hypermedia document and how information pertinent to it can be stored in card format (since the card, discussed in Vannevar Bush's article, is the paradigm adopted, regardless of the computer platform). Whether laser disk, CD-ROM, hard drive, floppies, slides with indexed positions on a remote random-access slide projector, the content is indexed on cards. Accordingly, the space of addresses is what the program searches through. Hypermedia extends the idea of hypertext to include still and moving images and sound [4]. Figure 9.5 shows the relationship between the Docent and a videodisk. The Docent contains the database that can be searched. The text can contain links to still images, motion picture clips, and sounds that are stored on some random-access medium (videodisk, CD-ROM, remote-random-access slide

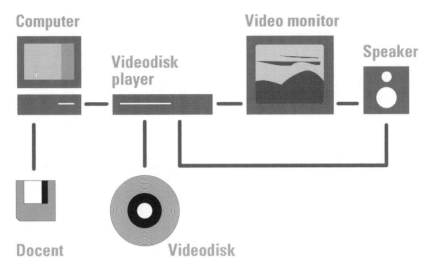

Figure 9.5 Matching a database to a collection of images on a videodisk.

projector, etc.). A link may point to a still image on the videodisk, or to a motion sequence that includes sound. A single image may actually be a still frame from a motion sequence. One single Notebook Note Card can include text and recorded voice comments, as well as links to still images and motion sequences with sound (see Figure 9.6).

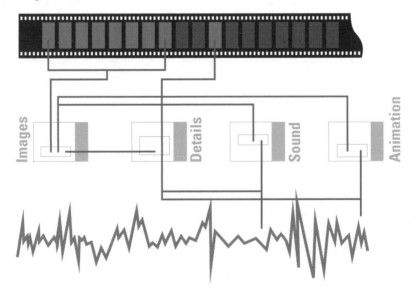

Figure 9.6 Multimedia datacards.

A Docent and its associate image database is a hypermedia document. Reading hypermedia documents is accomplished with the aid of links that create and define the web of the hypermedia document. The process of following links is called *navigation* or *exploration*. Hypermedia links can create very richly detailed presentations that simultaneously engage several of the viewer's sensory modalities—visual, auditory, and kinesthetic (see Figure 9.7).

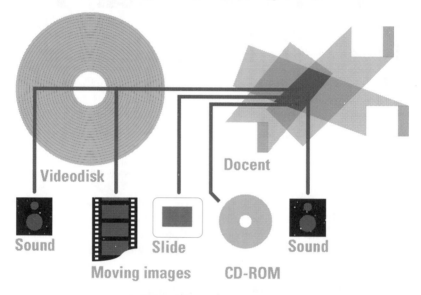

Figure 9.7 Hypermedia links.

Datacards within the Docent contain all of the information the Docent knows about images on the videodisk. Each datacard contains fields. (Every datacard has the same number of fields and the same kind of information.)

Design Objectives

The primary design objective of Docent was to avoid creating overly complex navigation and information structures. The aim was to end up with a program that made it easy to navigate through large collections of text and images, while at the same time providing powerful search tools for locating desired images. When creating hypertext and hypermedia programs, there is a tendency to create environments that make it easy to "get lost" while examining links, making it difficult to get back to a particular point. Avoiding this phenomenon—the "Where am I?" problem—was a major organizational principle behind Docent. The use of "breadcrumb trails" is a typical hypermedia and hypertext navigation tool. As you look through the information, the system remembers where you've been, creating implicit links between bits of information. Usually, however, this means that it is necessary to backtrack along the trail to get to an intermediate point along the trail. (Jumping back to the beginning is usually quite easy.)

The organization of Docent is such that it is possible to jump from one part of the program to another very easily. Exploration using Docent is supposed to offer two major conveniences:

1. Employ structural search requests using Boolean logic without assuming that the users know what it is (while not penalizing those who do)

2. Provide an intuitive point of entry; that is, by not assuming that those searching already know what they are looking for (name of the book, melody of the song, color of a flower, etc.)

Boolean Operators. In order to extract knowledge from a database, Boolean operators (AND, OR, etc.) are frequently used. While an art historian might look for a work identified by the artist's name, the medium (oil, watercolor, ink, etc.), and genre (landscape, portrait, still-life), a salesperson might need to match specifications of size, material, price, and availability of spare parts catalogued in electronic format. Getting the search to come as close as possible to how people formulate their objectives requires an interface that is intuitive, but also sufficiently precise. Driven by an iconic interface, as seen in Figure 9.8, the Docent allows the user to define search criteria. These are evaluated by the program as they are

Figure 9.8 The iconic interface of Docent.

entered. If a criterion is not available, the user is promptly informed. For the informed user, multiple search criteria can be entered (such as sequences of OR, AND, etc.). Performance of the search engine is only marginally affected by the multiple criteria. Searching can be performed in Automatic procedure or Manual (the search starts once the user initiates it).

Point of Entry. Regardless of the content of the database, and even of its function, the point-of-entry issue is critical and helps the user find out what is available. A Search Index was put in place in order to inform the user about each Search Category (database fields). In other words, the Docent tells the user what will be recognized as a criterion.

9.5.2 Docent Notes

A major objective in designing the Docent was making possible a record of searches and allowing for activities such as annotations, notetaking, and authoring. As already mentioned, this is done in a utility called Notes (no relation to the Lotus product). Each successful search can be "written" to Notes. That means that subsets of images, sounds, video, or a combination can be selected. If the videodisk is about art history, the subset is like the set of slides a professor prepares in advance for a given subject ("Portraits by Rembrandt" or "Expressionist Landscapes" or "The Mother in Luciente's Paintings"). For collections of images regarding design (CAD, for instance), engineering, architecture, or fashion, the subsets extract all that relates to an intended function. Each time the subset is "written" to Notes, database information is automatically copied there, too. This allows for interactive multimedia lecturing, with prompts provided on the screen as the lecture is delivered. If in need of changing the order within a selected set, the lecturer can interactively "shuffle" the "slides," or get back to any image desired. Figure 9.9 shows the Notebooks within a Docent.

All Notes texts can be exported, together with digitized images, from the videodisk to a desktop platform. Thus, a full authoring system for interactive multimedia "performance" is provided. This "reading" software emulates all the functions of the "writing," that is, "publishing software". It can be used to generate product catalogs, interactive networked presentations, articles, or new multimedia presentations.

9.5.3 MetaDocent™

The MetaDocent creates Docents for different kinds of large collections of data, regardless of their kind. It is a high-level program that compiles a text database pertinent to multimedia components regardless of where these are physically located (on hard disks, videotapes, laser disks, CD-ROM). Basically, a MetaDocent is built on top of an empty Docent. It allows an informed developer to specify field names, describe field types, and to determine formats and search criteria. The

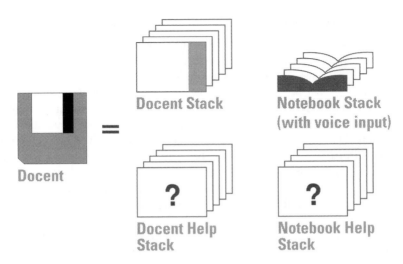

Figure 9.9 Notebooks within a Docent.

program verifies proper length of records and proper parsing of search indexes. Functionality of Notebooks is also defined at this level. An import facility from databases checks for the integrity of the data. Search indexes and external indexes are automatically generated. Once the MetaDocent finishes creating a particular Docent, a Yank function removes all that pertained to the labor (like builders removing scaffolding after they finish a house).

From Entry Level to High End

As succinct as this presentation had to be, it shows how one can derive a hypermedia environment from a hypertext structure. The role played by the user interface is critical, especially in view of the many complexities multimedia production has. The MetaDocent can be used as an authoring tool for creating CD-ROM, videodisks, or combinations in which all data types are present.

Many other tools available in the market offer functionality appropriate to a variety of applications. Between low-end (entry-level) programs incorporating Quicktime or Video for Windows (for integrating video sequences or sound tracks) and high-end authoring systems, the difference is not only in price. At the high end, programmability is a characteristic. It can be embodied in visual programming, that is, manipulation of icons "underneath" which code is hidden. Such code can be for calls to hardware devices or responses to user inputs (interactivity). Chances are that the major computing platforms (Windows, OS/2, Macintosh, UNIX) will evolve in the direction of acknowledging standard formats while simultaneously maintaining the competitive edge of proprietary solutions. Object-oriented programming will probably play an important role in this direction.

Nonpersistent Data Modes

To follow a link in hypertext means to find a word or a significant language construct relevant to a search or interpretation. But when the source node consists of nonpersistent data, to follow the link is at least deceiving. In addition, the critical issue of synchronization (e.g., the time relations among elements in a composite multimedia component) needs to be addressed. Interactive training modules or interactive kiosks of all types bring their own set of requirements to expression. On-screen responses are different from menu-driven instructions or tests. Cross-platform compatibility is probably another characteristic that will have to be addressed. While it is true that hypermedia is in many ways the meeting point of multimedia and hypertext, in many more ways it is a new qualitative aspect of real-time computing in the sense that it has complex timing schemes at its core. Such schemes are critical in maintaining the integrity of data and providing a coherent semantic framework. Once multimedia enters the world of networks, of client–server, and of distributed computing architectures, such demands become critical.

9.6   DIGITAL LIBRARY

Multimedia is celebrated for the spectacular innovation that brings it into the public eye. From on-line shopping (predicted to grow twenty-fold within the next three years) to the Multimedia University, the public is experiencing advanced combinations of text, graphics, video, animation, and sound. But there are many more down-to-earth multimedia applications. In the course of developing multimedia systems and concepts, I realized that the very critical issues of preservation and access are more than what became known as the lucrative field of *document management*. Progress has indeed been made in converting the paper archives of the past into the new digital archives, fully indexed and easily accessible. Scanners have been hard at work; so were digitizers of all kinds. The new archives are of many orders of magnitude better adapted to their function (often prescribed by law). But there are some limitations; not the least, loss in "touch and feel," probably irrelevant for business data, but not at all for preserving manuscripts, books, and artifacts affected by physical and chemical agents.

Along this line of cultural interest, I worked on major preservation projects, including some that extended to prestigious libraries (the Vatican Library, the Library of Corvey Castle in northern Germany) whose collections need to be preserved and made available to a larger public. Multimedia proved to be of significance in more than one way. In order to preserve, one has to define alternative media. These are all quite heterogeneous. To replace the film medium of microfiches (black-and-white or color), we had to find substitutes that are of no lesser quality (in maintaining faithfulness to the original), less subject to change over time, and easily accessible. Solutions differ as the contents differ. After creating a laser disk containing Vatican Library incunabulae (Vat. Lat. 39), after several attempts with

CD-ROM (incorporating the Docent), and after taking the expensive path of printing high-quality facsimiles, the concept of the Digital Library finally crystallized. In short, this concept provides:

1. fast, real-time image acquisition in HDTV format;
2. transfer from HDTV format to a variety of media (from 35 mm slides to printing plates);
3. integration in full-fledged multimedia with video, sound, text database, animation.

The end result of the digital acquisition phase was a digital original that can be rendered compatible with any imaginable display technology [5]. What is most attractive in this multimedia solution is that the *object* (book, manuscripts) becomes a locus of interaction. Its digital facsimile can be endlessly approached, studied from many angles, distributed over networks, and integrated into the broader context to which it belongs. True, in the process of experimenting with this concept, we ran into the problems of standards: digital vs. analog, European vs. American formats, aspect ratio. Nevertheless, it became clear that, from a suitable HDTV format, it was rather trivial to derive videodisks (at HDTV resolution as well as in NTSC, PAL, SECAM), CD-ROM at full resolution and size subsampled, printed output, and separation films with overlay proofs. What remains to be tested is distribution over networks and a video-server for a client–server configuration that will replace the library as we know it with access to collections too frail to withstand further damage in the course of being examined by readers. This dimension of multimedia, that is, the ability to disseminate values unapproachable not too long ago, is in line with the interactive communication potential it has. To make accessible what Vannevar Bush defined as our "bewildering store of knowledge" is one of the most exciting potentials of multimedia [6].

9.7 HOW AND WHAT DO WE INTERCONNECT?

Multimedia triggered innovation in many directions. It also set expectations for which further technological progress and theories are necessary. From among the many directions this progress will take, one can single out interconnection. It is clear that graphical display technology can be further improved through special-purpose architectures. The evolution of many multimedia applications make it unequivocal that the path is from software to the bus to the motherboard. It is like salmon going upstream to spawn. This improvement path is probably more effective than the current strategy of connecting general-purpose machines. Nevertheless, a third possibility is even more exciting, and within the spirit of multimedia: connection of various specialized machines. Maybe new graphics primitives will affect the architecture of the real-time imaging station. Maybe parallelism will be better adapted to tasks of animation. But even if one machine will embody the best there is for imaging, we will still not have addressed the wide variety that can result from interconnecting various specialized machines. Casual transfer of high-resolution images at real-time rates necessitated the new client workstations that can display images from video-servers. Such servers, still in their infancy, need to have scalable power and vast (really vast!) database storage (no matter how good our compression schemes). They have to be endowed with bandwidth connections for fiber or wireless networking. Such servers need to coordinate distributed processing of clients (capable of special functions) and to synchronize it with its own parallel processors. Extremely high floating-point performance will be required in some cases (for instance, in advanced modeling)—advanced graphics (3-D rendering, for example) in others. Distribution of tasks means very good communication between the various processing units is necessary. The geometry specialized chip, the raster chip, the one dedicated to texture mapping (including solid texture) would have to coordinate their efforts better than the processors of polygons or pixels now in use.

Obviously, swapping video e-mail or addressing video-rich databases is not yet in need of this advanced technology. Not even video-on-demand for digital cable TV systems needs more than what we have on LAN servers. Time-dependency of multimedia data is a characteristic of the medium that was only superficially addressed in all the attempts to bring it to the networks. As long as our "intelligence" in dealing with data on networks is on the network (switching hubs, frame relay, and various other network gear), we will be limited even in understanding what else multimedia can do. My argument is that very knowledgeable clients and a powerful specialized server will eventually make possible what no networking-based technology, as we now use it, can. But until then, we have to continue navigating through the maze of fiber distributed data interface (FDDI) and asynchronous transfer mode (ATM) and whatever, while learning more and more that the multimedia we experience and generate is probably no more of a beginning than what the UNIVAC once was for the computer revolution.

References

[1] W. J. Grosky, "Multimedia information systems," *IEEE Multimedia*, Spring 1994, pp. 21–29.
[2] T. M. Maybury (Editor). *Intelligent Multimedia Interfaces*. Cambridge MA: MIT Press, 1994.
[3] V. Bush, "As we may think," *The Atlantic Monthly*, vol. 176, no. 1, pp. 101–108, 1945.
[4] J. Nielsen. *Hypertext and Hypermedia*. San Diego: Academic Press, 1990.
[5] A. C. Luther. *Digital Video in the PC Environment*, 2nd edition, New York: McGraw Hill, 1989.
[6] E. Barrett (Editor). *The Society of Text: Hypertext, Hypermedia, and the Social Construction of Information*. Cambridge MA: MIT Press, 1989.

GLOSSARY

accumulation error. An image error caused mainly by the discretization process.

activity packet. *See* **templates**.

address bus. *See* **bus**.

aliasing image. A distortion introduced by the subsampling process.

associative memory. A hardware scheme that employs a storage device that achieves multiple-data processing via a built-in search capacity. Also called *content-addressable memory*.

asynchronous event. An event that occurs at unpredictable points in the flow-of-control and is usually caused by external sources such as a clock signal.

block-matching. A motion estimation technique in which the pattern of the image segment around the point under tracking at time $t - \Delta t$ is used as the reference pattern for searching the displacement at time t.

binary images. Images represented by 1 bit/sample. Examples include black/white photographs and facsimile images.

bus. The wires that connect the CPU and main memory. The bus is used to exchange memory location information ("addresses") and data between the CPU and main memory in binary-encoded form. The width of the bus is determined by the number of bits or wires provided for the binary code. Usually the address and data wires are referred to as the address bus and data bus, respectively.

cellular automata. A computational paradigm for an efficient description of SIMD massively parallel systems.

center weighted median. A type of weighted median filter that is found by repeating only the value at the window center.

central processing unit (CPU). In a computer, it provides for arithmetic and logical operations.

CISC. *See* **complex instruction set computer**.

color images. Images represented with 16, 24, or more bits/sample.

compass gradients. A set of eight images that, when used in windowed convolution, provides an edge filter.

complex instruction set computer (CISC). A processor that is characterized by a large number of complex instructions involving long microprograms, numerous multilevel addressing modes, and sophisticated CPUs. *Contrast* **reduced instruction set computer**.

compute-bound. Computations in which the number of operations is large in comparison to the number of I/O instructions.

computer graphics. Images represented by a lower-precision, as 4 bits/sample.

content-addressable memory. *See* **associative memory**.

convolution. *See* **windowed convolution**.

coprocessor. A second, independent processor used to expand a CPU's macroinstruction set so that complicated operations need not be coded in high-level languages.

correspondence motion detection. Motion analysis using the time disparity between successive monocular images. Also called *matching*. Contrast **gradient** and **spatio-temporal filtering motion detection** methods.

CPU. *See* **central processing unit**.

CPU utilization. A measure of the percentage of non-idle processing.

data bus. *See* **bus**.

dataflow architectures. An MIMD architecture where control flow is determined by the availability of data. *See also* **token**, **templates**.

DCT. *See* **discrete cosine transform**.

decoding. In a CPU, determining which set of microinstructions corresponds to a given macroinstruction.

deterministic system. A system where, for each possible state and each set of inputs, a unique set of outputs and the next state of the system can be determined. *See* **event determinism** and **temporal determinism**.

DFT. *See* **discrete Fourier transform**.

digital image. A function of two discrete variables.

dilation. Dual of erosion.

direct memory access (DMA). An input/output scheme where access to the computer's memory is afforded to other devices in the system without CPU intervention. *Contrast* **memory-mapped I/O** and **programmed I/O**.

direct mode. A memory addressing scheme in which the operand is the data contained at the address specified in the address.

discrete cosine transform (DCT). An image transform similar to the discrete Fourier transform, but that provides better separation for images with strong pixel-to-pixel correlation.

discrete Fourier transform (DFT). An operation that separates an image into its frequency components. *See also* **fast Fourier transform**.

disjunctive normal form. A representation of a Boolean expression that involves a logical sum of products (maximum of minima).

DMA. *See* **direct memory access**.

dynamic priority system. A preemptive priority system where the task priorities can change during program execution. Contrast fixed priority system.

edge filter. An operation that takes in a gray-scale image and yields a binary image whose 1-valued pixels are meant to represent an edge within the original image.

embedded system. A software system that does not have a generalized operating system interface and is used explicitly to control specialized hardware.

erosion. A basic morphological image operation used to construct binary filters. Its dual is dilation.

event. Any occurrence that results in a change in the sequential flow of program execution. *See* **asynchronous event** and **synchronous event**.

event determinism. This means that the next state and outputs of a system are known for each set of inputs that trigger events.

execute. In a CPU, the process of acting upon a microinstruction sequence.

fast Fourier transform (FFT). A fast version of the discrete Fourier transform.

fast Hadamard transform. A way of improving compression using the Hadamard matrix via factorization.

FFT. *See* **fast Fourier transform**.

firm real-time system. A real-time system where some fixed small number of deadlines can be missed without total system failure.

fixed priority system. A preemptive priority system where the task priorities cannot be changed once the system is implemented. *Contrast* **dynamic priority system**.

fixed rate system. A software system where interrupts occur only at fixed frequencies.

flat dilation. *See* **moving maximum**.

flat erosion. *See* **moving minimum**.

floating-point number. A term describing the computer's representation of a real number.

gnoseological platform. A computer-based framework for cognition.

gradient motion detection. Differential motion detection algorithms that attach a vector to each point in a displacement image. The optical flow from this gradient field is then derived. *Contrast* **correspondence** and **spatio-temporal motion detection** methods.

granulometric size distribution. A distribution generated by counting the pixels in each succeeding filtered image using a granulometry.

granulometry. A sequence of openings using structuring elements that are of increasing size.

gray-scale moving median filter. A moving median filter for images that are not binary.

Hadamard matrix. A special matrix used in a lossy compression scheme. *See also* **fast Hadamard transform**.

hard real-time system. A real-time system where failure to meet even one deadline results in total system failure.

hierarchical encoding. Image encoding in which the image is encoded in multiple resolutions.

hit-or-miss transform. In morphological image processing, a nonincreasing Boolean function used for image restoration.

hypercube processor. A processor configuration that is similar to the linear array processor except that each processor element communicates data along a number of other higher dimensional pathways.

image. A collection of digital picture elements, or pixels, stored as x, y coordinates (or x, y, and z) along with other information such as color, intensity, etc.

image motion field. The two-dimensional projection of the velocity field onto the image plane.

image plane. The collection of two-dimensional coordinates from an image.

image regularization. The process of shaping the raw image data (natural image) into a format suitable for image analysis or visualization.

increasing Boolean function. *See* **positive Boolean function**.

interleaved data ordering. Data ordering in which different components are combined into so-called minimum coded units (MCUs).

interrupt. A hardware signal that alters the sequential nature of the fetch-decode-execute cycle by transferring program control to special interrupt handler routines.

interrupt controller. A device that provides additional interrupt handling capability to a CPU.

interrupt latency. The inherent delay between when an interrupt occurs and when the CPU begins reacting to it.

Joint Photographic Experts Group (JPEG). A lossy compression technique that is an industry standard for image information storage and retrieval.

JPEG. *See* **Joint Photographic Experts Group**.

linear array processor. A processor architecture that has one PE for each column in the image, and enough memory directly connected to each PE to hold the entire column of image data for several distinct images. Also called *vector processor*.

linear granulometries. In a granulometry, the resulting opening sequences using vertical and horizontal line segments of increasing length.

look-up table. An optimization technique that allows for the computation of continuous functions using mostly fixed-point arithmetic.

lossless compression. An image compression scheme where decompression yields the exact image that was compressed. *Contrast* **lossy compression**.

lossless encoding. Same as lossy compression.

lossy compression. An image compression scheme where decompression yields an image that is not identical to the image that was compressed. *Contrast* **lossless compression**.

macroinstructions. The lowest level of user-programmable computer instructions.

matched filter. An operation employing an image that gives back high values when a mask is located on top of the object of interest and lower values elsewhere.

mathematical morphology. The study of shape using the mathematics of set theory.

memory caching. A technique in which frequently used segments of main memory are stored in a faster bank of memory that is local to the CPU (called a *cache*).

memory-mapped I/O. An input/output scheme where reading or writing involves executing a "load" or "store" instruction on a pseudomemory address mapped to the device. *Contrast* **direct memory access** and **programmed I/O**.

mesh processor. A processor configuration that is similar to the linear array processor except that each processor element also communicates data north and south.

microcode. *See* **microinstruction**.

microcontrollers. A type of von Neumann architecture where there is no decoding of macroinstructions.

microinstruction. A primitive instruction stored in CPU internal memory. Also called *microcode*.

microprogram. A collection of microinstructions corresponding to a macroinstruction.

MIMD. *See* **multiple instruction stream, multiple data stream**.

minimal representation. For a positive Boolean function, an equivalent representation where no product whose variable set does not contain the variable set of a distinct product can be deleted without changing the function.

minterm. In disjunctive normal form, a logical sum of products or conjunctions of Boolean variables is taken. These products are the minterms.

MISD. *See* **multiple instruction stream, single data stream**.

morphological gradient. The nonlinear analog to a linear gradient.

morphological pattern spectrum. The normalization of a granulometric size distribution.

Motion Picture Engineers' Expert Group (MPEG). An image compression technique used for motion pictures.

moving average. The average value of an image over the pixels in a window when it is centered at a certain pixel.

moving maximum. An image operation found by translating the image to a pixel and then taking the maximum of all values in the translate. *Contrast* **moving minimum**.

moving median. A type of binary image filter used to suppress salt-and-pepper noise and preserve edges.

moving minimum. An image operation found by translating the image to a pixel and then taking the minimum of all values in the translate. *Contrast* **moving maximum**.

MPEG. *See* **Motion Picture Engineers' Expert Group**.

multiconstraint-based motion detection. A gradient motion detection scheme where the optical flow estimation is transformed from an ill-posed to a well-posed problem using constraint equations.

multimedia computing. Computing that involves computer systems with high-resolution graphics, CD-ROM drives, mice, high-performance sound cards, and multitasking operating systems that support these devices.

multiple instruction stream, multiple data stream (MIMD). A computer characterized by a large number of processing elements, each capable of executing numerous instructions.

multiple instruction stream, single data stream (MISD). A computer that can process two or more instructions concurrently on a single datum.

multiprocessing operating system. An operating system where more than one processor is available to provide for simultaneity. *Contrast* **multitasking operating system**.

multitasking operating system. An operating system that provides sufficient functionality to allow multiple programs to run on a single processor so that the illusion of simultaneity is created. *Contrast* **multiprocessing operating system**.

natural image. The image as it comes directly from the camera.

non-interleaved data ordering. Data ordering in which processing is performed component by component from left-to-right and top-to-bottom.

opening. A key morphological filter involving the union of translates.

operating system. A collection of programs that controls the resources of the computer.

optical flow field. The changes in light intensity values in the image plane.

parallel thinning. A technique employing the hit-or-miss transform to restore noise-degraded images.

pipelining. A rudimentary form of instruction concurrency that is achieved through disjoint hardware to facilitate concurrent operations.

pixel. A single point or picture element of an image.

positive Boolean function. A Boolean function that can be represented as a logical sum of products in which no variables are complemented. Also called an *increasing Boolean function.*

preempt. A higher-priority task is said to preempt a lower-priority task if it interrupts the lower-priority task.

preemptive priority system. An operating system that uses preemption schemes instead of round-robin or first-come-first-serve scheduling.

Prewitt gradient masks. A set of two images that, when used in windowed convolution, provides an edge filter.

programmed I/O. An input/output scheme where special macroinstructions are used to transfer data to and from the CPU. *Contrast* **direct memory access** and **memory-mapped I/O**.

progressive DCT-based encoding. Image encoding in which the image is encoded in multiple scans in order to produce a quick, rough, decoded image when the transmission time is long.

progressive spectral selection algorithm. A selection algorithm in which DCT coefficients are grouped into several spectral bands.

progressive successive approximation algorithm. An approximation algorithm where all DCT coefficients are sent first with lower precision, and then refined in later scans.

quadtree compression. A lossless compression technique in which the image is divided recursively into four parts, stopping when each part is a constant value.

real-time system. A hardware and/or software system that must satisfy explicit bounded response-time constraints to avoid failure. *See* **hard**, **firm**, and **soft real-time system**.

receptive field. The part of the visual field of a neuron within which a stimulus can influence the response (i.e., the firing rate) of the neuron.

receptive field function. Describes the response of a neuron to a small spot of light as a function of position.

recursion. A programming language feature whereby a procedure can call itself.

reduced instruction set computer (RISC). A special class of SISD architectures where a limited number of macroinstruction types and addressing modes simplify the "decode" and "macroinstruction" execution process. *Contrast* **complex instruction set computer**.

regularization-based motion detection. A gradient motion detection approach that considers the optical flow estimation as an ill-posed problem according to Hadamard theory.

response store. In associative memory, the tag bits used to mark memory cells.

response time. The time between the presentation of a set of inputs and the appearance of all the associated outputs.

RISC. *See* **reduced instruction set computer**.

Roberts gradient. A morphological gradient calculated using a set of two images that, when used in windowed convolution, provides an edge filter.

run-length encoded. A lossless compression technique where the image is stored as a sequence of triples specifying a pixel at which the image is black, such that the pixel to the left is white for a specified run length.

scaled number. An optimization technique where the least significant bit (LSB) of an integer variable is assigned a real number scale factor.

secondary storage. Computer devices such as hard disks, floppy disks, tapes, and so forth, that are not part of the physical address space of the CPU.

segment. In pipelining, a disjoint processing circuit. Also called a *stage*.

sequency coefficients. The coefficients generated when multiplying an image by the Hadamard matrix.

sequential DCT-based encoding. Image encoding in which each image component is encoded in a single left-to-right, top-to-bottom scan.

SIMD. *See* **single instruction stream, multiple data stream**.

simple cells. Refers to the possibility of dividing the receptive fields of visual cells into separate excitory and inhibitory zones.

single instruction stream, multiple data stream (SIMD). A computer where each processing element is executing the same (and only) instruction but on different data.

single instruction stream, single data stream (SISD). A type of computer where the CPU processes a single instruction at a time and a single datum at a time.

SISD. *See* **single instruction stream, single data stream**.

smoothing filter. An operation applied to an image to suppress random additive pixel noise.

Sobel masks. A set of two images that, when used in windowed convolution, provides an edge filter.

soft real-time system. A real-time system where missing deadlines leads to performance degradation but not failure.

spatio-temporal motion detection. A motion detection technique for three-dimensional images where filters are applied to the volume image in space–time. *Contrast* **gradient** and **correspondence motion detection** methods.

stack filter. Positive Boolean function used as a filter in conjunction with threshold sets.

stage. *See* **segment**.

strong-neighbor mask. An image mask used in the moving median filter.

structuring element. Masking image used in erosion.

synchronous event. An event that occurs at predictable times such as the execution of a conditional branch instruction or a hardware trap.

synthetic image. A computational model of the natural image.

systolic processor. A computer consisting of a set of interconnected cells, each capable of performing a simple operation and synchronized by an external clock or "heartbeat."

templates. In a dataflow architecture, a way of organizing data into tokens. Also called an *activity packet*.

temporal determinism. In a deterministic system, when the response time for each set of outputs is known.

threshold method. A technique used in conjunction with the Hadamard matrix for selecting the compressed transform vector where those components with values above some threshold are kept. *Contrast* **zonal method**.

threshold set. A way of partitioning an image into subimages that stack on top of each other, with each being a subset of the one below it. *See also* **stack filter**.

time-loading. *See* **CPU utilization**.

time-overloaded system. A software system that has a 100% or more CPU utilization factor.

token. In dataflow architectures, data items employed to represent the dynamics of a dataflow system.

transputer. A fully self-sufficient, multiple instruction set, von Neumann processor designed to be connected to other transputers.

vector processor. *See* **linear array processor**.

velocity field. The three-dimensional vector attached to each image point that gives its current motion.

von Neumann architecture. A CPU that employs a serial fetch-decode-execute process.

von Neumann bottleneck. In a von Neumann architecture, the fact that instructions or data can never be concurrently exchanged between the main memory and the CPU.

watershed segmentation. A morphological gradient edge detection scheme.

wavefront array processor. Similar to a systolic processor except that there is no external clock.

weighted median. A type of moving median filter using integer weights a_1, $a_2, \ldots, a_m$. It is found by repeating a_i times the observation x_i, ordering the new set of $a_1 + a_2 + \cdots + a_m$ values, and then choosing the middle value as the output. *See also* **center weighted median**.

windowed convolution. A mathematical operation where a mask of numerical weights defined over some window is translated across a digital image pixel by pixel and, at each pixel, the arithmetic sum of products between the mask weights and the corresponding image pixels in the translated window is taken.

zonal method. A technique used in conjunction with the Hadamard matrix for selecting the compressed transform vector where one simply fixes the set of components to be kept. *Contrast* **threshold method**.

INDEX

Q

R

S

ABOUT THE EDITORS

Phil Laplante (Senior Member, IEEE) received the B.S., M.Eng., and Ph.D. degrees in computer science, electrical engineering, and computer science, respectively, from the Stevens Institute of Technology. He is currently the Dean of Engineering at the Burlington County College (BCC)/New Jersey Institute of Technology, Mount Laurel Technology and Engineering Center. Prior to this position, he was Chair of the Department of Mathematics and Computer Science at Fairleigh Dickinson University, a full-time consultant to several major corporations, and held various project management and engineering positions in the avionics industry.

Dr. Laplante's interests are in image processing, real-time systems, and real-time image processing, including virtual reality. He is a co-founding Editor-in-Chief of the journal *Real-Time Imaging* (along with Alex Stoyenko) and a member of the board of the journal *Multimedia Tools and Applications*. He has published fifty technical papers and eight books, including *Introduction to Real-Time Imaging* with Ed Dougherty (IEEE Press/SPIE Press) and *Real-Time Systems: An Engineer's Handbook* (IEEE Press/IEEE CS Press) and has been Guest Editor of *Real-Time Systems* and *Journal of Electronic Imaging*.

Dr. Laplante is a licensed Professional Engineer in the State of New Jersey, a member of IEEE, ACM, SPIE, and the IEEE Press Editorial Board.

Alex Stoyenko received a doctorate in computer science from the University of Toronto in 1987. Subsequently, he joined IBM's T. J. Watson Research Center as a Research Staff Member. Since Fall 1990, he has been on faculty with the Department of Computer and Information Science at the New Jersey Institute of Technology, where he founded and leads the Real-Time Computing Laboratory, and where he is currently an Associate Professor. His research interests are in real-time computing, distributed and parallel computing, engineering of complex computer systems, programming languages, compilers and tools, real-time imaging, biomedical computing, and software re-use and integration.

Dr. Stoyenko has published over seventy times in books, refereed journals, and conferences, including a co-authored book, *Constructing Predictable Real-Time Systems*. He is the founding Chair of the IEEE Computer Society Technical Segments Committee on Engineering of Complex Computer Systems, and of the new annual IEEE Conference on Engineering of Complex Computer Systems.

Dr. Stoyenko is the founding Co-Editor-in-Chief (with Phil Laplante) of the journal *Real-Time Imaging*. He is an Associate Editor of the journal *Control Engineering Practice* and has been Guest Editor of *Real-Time Systems* and *Journal of Electronic Imaging*.